STRUGGLE FOR THE SOUL
OF THE POSTWAR SOUTH

Struggle for the Soul of the Postwar South

White Evangelical Protestants and Operation Dixie

ELIZABETH FONES-WOLF
AND KEN FONES-WOLF

UNIVERSITY OF ILLINOIS PRESS
URBANA, CHICAGO, AND SPRINGFIELD

Manufactured in the United States of America
1 2 3 4 5 C P 5 4 3 2 1
∞ This book is printed on acid-free paper.

This book has been made possible through grants from the
West Virginia Humanities Council, a state affiliate of the National
Endowment for the Humanities, and from West Virginia University.
Any views, findings, or recommendations do not necessarily
represent those of the West Virginia Humanities Council or the
National Endowment for the Humanities.

Library of Congress Cataloging-in-Publication Data
Fones-Wolf, Ken.
Struggle for the soul of the postwar South : white evangelical
Protestants and Operation Dixie / Ken Fones-Wolf,
Elizabeth A. Fones-Wolf.
pages   cm. — (Working class in American history)
Includes bibliographical references and index.
ISBN 978-0-252-03903-4 (hardback) —
ISBN 978-0-252-08066-1 (paperback) —
ISBN 978-0-252-09700-3 (e-book)
1. Congress of Industrial Organizations (U.S.)—History. 2. Labor
unions—Organizing—Southern States—History. 3. Labor movement—
Religious aspects—Christianity. 4. Evangelicalism—Southern States—
History. 5. Christian conservatism—United States. 6. Social classes—
United States. I. Fones-Wolf, Elizabeth A., 1954– II. Title.
HD8055.C75F66   2015
331.880975'0904—dc23   2014030669

CONTENTS

PREFACE AND ACKNOWLEDGMENTS

For more than three decades we have been interested in the religious beliefs that animated a good deal of working-class life in America. As we rummaged through archival collections, newspapers, oral histories, memoirs, and other documents—often in the search for information about some other topic—we have been struck by how often matters of faith surfaced at the most unexpected times. Movements that strove to unite working people around issues of social justice have either had to incorporate the sacred into their programs or run the risk of having their nonbelief exposed, often to the detriment of worthy projects. In coauthored articles and in our separate works, we have written on some of the efforts that the trade-union movement made to attach a religious meaning to their undertakings, ranging from the Gilded Age to the 1950s. Still, we have always wanted to tackle jointly a moment in which faith appeared to be a central element in shaping how working people responded to a major union-organizing campaign. The CIO's Operation Dixie, which has not been the subject of a book-length study for a quarter century, seemed to us to be that moment.

Certainly, we knew of the importance of the sacred in southern society. One of the descriptors typically used for the South has been "Bible Belt." Historians, from Christine Heyrman in colonial times to Bertram Wyatt Brown in the nineteenth century to Charles Reagan Wilson in more modern times, have written about the southern spirit and identified religion as one of the pillars of southern culture, one that was instrumental in propping up the entire edifice.[1] For the vast majority of southerners, that religion was evangelical Protestantism. Ultimately, if the CIO was to be successful in bringing unions to southern working people in 1946, its organizers would have to understand their attraction to evangelicalism. What better place to investigate how religion intersected with the hopes, dreams, inclinations, and fears of working people considering whether or not to throw in their lot with a labor movement that sought to dramatically challenge southern society?

Equally important, the CIO's campaign had great ambitions. By the end of World War II, the CIO had established itself in many of the nation's core industries, and union density was climbing toward its highest level (about one-third of the workforce), which it would reach in the early 1950s. With greater success,

CIO leaders believed that they could also affect the nation's political climate, re-energizing New Deal liberalism. The weak link for organized labor was the South. The region continued to resist union-driven collective bargaining and the liberal Democratic politics that were intertwined with union growth. Consequently, not only was the CIO's Southern Organizing Campaign an ideal laboratory to examine the impact of religion, it was also a social movement that would have a significant impact on the sustainability of the New Deal system of labor relations. If organized labor failed there, the region would become a refuge for corporations that sought to escape the reach of collective bargaining and liberal politics. For us, the question loomed: What difference did evangelical Protestantism make in working people's feelings about not just union membership but also about the more expansive liberal state that national unions desired?

The CIO's Operation Dixie coincided with an upheaval in race relations and a debilitating "red scare" that complicated its chances for success among the white workers whom the campaign targeted. The choice to make white workers the focus was and continues to be a subject of controversy. Black theology in the main was less subject to fears about the Communist menace, more accepting of collective social action, and obviously more interested in overturning the racial status quo. Would not the CIO have enjoyed more success by playing to that strength? At the very least, would not Operation Dixie have left a more heroic legacy?[2] But that was not the way that CIO strategists understood their objectives. They felt that the CIO needed to achieve breakthroughs among the white workers who made up the bulk of the South's industrial workforce, especially in textiles, the industry that presented the greatest challenge to the spread of unionism in the region. Once achieved, CIO leaders reasoned, the organization of black workers would follow easily, and organized labor would realize its desired density. Given the CIO's understanding of what constituted success, we decided to focus on the religious culture of the white working class and its response to Operation Dixie. That meant grappling with how white evangelical Protestants felt not just about unions and liberalism but also how they reacted to Communism and black aspirations for equality. We are not satisfied with many depictions of white working people that emphasize only their race or class or gender. Instead, we have tried to give equal weight to their religious beliefs to see how those beliefs shaped their understanding of the threats and opportunities they faced.

To understand the faith of white workers has also pushed us to question the notion of a southern religion (by which many religious historians mean "white" southern Protestantism). If, in fact, many white southern churches were mired in a sort of cultural captivity that diminished their social conscience, it is not the case that they were stagnant.[3] A decade of economic depression and world war shattered any notion that there was a single southern religion that delivered a unified response. Consequently, we needed to explore how the southern religious landscape was changing and how both capital and labor hoped to take advantage of those changes. This becomes even more complicated when we consider popular religion, which exists alongside formal religious belief and practice. Popular religion reflects the fact that the sacred is not just the domain of institutions, theologians, and ministers, but is also about individuals interpreting their faith in practical terms for use and guidance in their daily living and to give meaning to their lives.[4] By examining the popular religiosity of the white working class, then, we hope to give a richer picture of how working people thought about the changes proposed for the postwar South. If the outcome for Operation Dixie appears to have been inevitable, employers, union officials, ministers, politicians, and the workers themselves perceived a contingency that gave real urgency to their actions. That is the struggle that was waged for the soul of the South.

We were also drawn to this project because of the labors of scholars and archivists who saved or created the rich sources that were essential to getting at more than just a surface understanding of the intersection of religion and this particular social movement. We knew from previous work of the existence of the voluminous Operation Dixie records at Duke University, as well as the very rich papers of Lucy Randolph Mason (Duke) and John Ramsay (Georgia State University). We were surprised at how many additional archival collections were available to shed light on business, labor, and religious organizations that determined the outcome of Operation Dixie. Most important, however, we benefited from the remarkable flourishing of oral history projects that captured the lives and outlooks of working people. This project could not have taken the shape it did without the huge collection at the Southern Oral History Program at the University of North Carolina (we owe a special debt of gratitude to Jacqueline Dowd Hall and the many fine historians who cut their teeth doing interviews for the SOHP) or numerous smaller collections at places like Samford University, Marshall University, Virginia Tech, Penn State University, Baylor University, Georgia State University, Radford College, and the multicollege Appalachian Oral History Project. The foresight that lured a generation of oral historians to gather these life stories is a gift to anyone interested in the culture of working people.

Thus, we begin our acknowledgements by noting that our first debts are to archivists and librarians who have helped us move expeditiously through cumbersome research materials. Since we have been remiss in writing down the names of all who have made our research trips fruitful, we will have to begin with a general shout out to the staffs of the following institutions: Auburn University Special Collections and Archives; Samford University Special Collections; Southern Labor Archives at Georgia State University; the United Methodist Archives and History Center, Drew University; Historical Collections and Labor Archives at Pennsylvania State University; Special Collections at Rutgers University; Southern Historical Collection and Southern Oral History Program at the University of North Carolina, Chapel Hill; Special Collections at Marshall University; David M. Rubenstein Rare Book and Manuscript Library, Duke University; Disciples of Christ Historical Society;

Southern Baptist Historical Library and Archives; Billy Graham Center, Wheaton College; Archives of Labor and Urban Affairs, Walter P. Reuther Library, Wayne State University; Presbyterian Historical Society; Robert F. Wagner Archives, New York University; State Historical Society of Wisconsin; Tennessee State Archives; Special Collections at Virginia Tech Libraries; Baylor University Institute for Oral History; and Berea College Special Collections and Archives. Staff members at these archives and special collections unfailingly were helpful, kind, and generous in meeting the demands of two very needy researchers.

As we have tracked down permissions and photos, or checked unclear references, the following individuals have gone above and beyond: Elizabeth Clemens (Reuther Library), Elaine Philpott (Disciples of Christ), Stephen Sloan (Baylor), Dominique Dery and Elizabeth Dunn (Duke), Jennifer Taylor (Samford), Jessie Wilkerson and Gwen Barlow (SOHP-UNC), Traci Drummond and Ellen Johnston (Georgia State), James Quigel (Penn State), Larry Hayer (Kannapolis History Associates), Rev. A. Mark Schudde (Concordia Lutheran Church), and Marc Brodsky and Aaron Purcell (Virginia Tech). We thank them for their personal help as well as the permissions we received from their institutions. Especially noteworthy were Wilt Browning and Marlene Burke, the son and daughter of the two remarkable millworkers we introduce at the beginning of chapter 6. Wilt not only gave us permission to quote from his wonderful book, but he also put us in touch with his sister, who searched her private photos and drove out in the snow to have copies made and sent to us, two complete strangers. Much thanks.

Long-time friends and colleagues in the field of labor and working-class studies have encouraged us along the way. Some commented on conference presentations and drafts of articles or just steered us from wrong-headed conclusions. We owe a great deal to their brilliance and generosity. They include, in no special order: Eric Arnesen, Leon Fink, Julie Greene, Donna Haverty-Stacke, Elizabeth Jameson, Joe McCartin, Nick Salvatore, Jim Green, Bob Korstad, Mike Honey, Jennifer Brooks, Ron Schatz, Jim Gregory, Jack Metgar, John Russo, Michelle Brattain, Roger Horowitz, and Phil Scranton. We enjoyed the hospitality and opportunity to present this research at the Hagley Seminar and the Labor and Working-Class Seminar at Hunter College. Thanks to Phil Scranton, Roger Horowitz, Donna Haverty-Stacke, and Eduardo Contreras for those opportunities. Two scholars who have been important to us and who talked to us about this project are no longer with us. Anyone who knew David Montgomery and Bob Zieger will see their enormous influence on our work. Two others deserve special mention. Danny Walkowitz has been a great friend and supporter of ours for way too long. It is hard to believe that it was thirty years between the time he guided us through one of our first publications for *Working-Class America* and one from this project for his and Donna Haverty-Stacke's *Rethinking U.S. Labor History*. That only begins to scratch the surface of his gifts to us. Then there is our good friend, Steve Rosswurm, who has talked to us so many times about religion and class that we sometimes think we know what he is going to say before he says it, but his advice and encouragement have made us better historians.

One of the wonderful things about taking on a research project is the chance to make new acquaintances and, hopefully, friends. We have been extremely fortunate not only to meet some great young scholars working in this area but also to share thoughts with some senior scholars who were charitable with their time and sometimes with their praise. In the first category, we feel that it has been a terrific boost to us to be able to participate on panels with the likes of Matt Sutton, David Evans, Darren Grem, Alison Collis Greene, John Hayes, Heath Carter, Matt Pehl, Chris Cantwell, Janet Giordano-Drake, Bethany Moreton, Jarod Roll, Erik Gellman, and the late Sarah Hammond (a tragic loss). We have learned so much from all of you. In the latter category, Ralph Luker, David Watt, Paul Harvey, Jim McCartin, and David Chappell have offered sage advice and encouragement. We hope that we can repay your kindness. Wayne Flynt, who did not know us from Adam, answered a desperate email request and agreed to read a draft of one of the first products to come from this project. Those who know Wayne will not be surprised at this; he is a most generous person. But to us at the time, because we were treading on ground that he had tilled so well for such a long time, his validation of what we were arguing was a tremendous shot in the arm. We hope that he knows how much his encouragement meant. Despite the counsel of all of these fine historians, we know that perhaps each of them will find things that we should have done better. We are the only ones responsible.

We appreciated working with editors who have included material from this research as we progressed. Our first effort, "Sanctifying the Southern Organizing Campaign: Protestant Activists in the CIO's Operation Dixie," was published in a special issue of *Labor: Studies in Working-Class History of the Americas*, vol. 6, no. 1 (Spring 2009), edited by Joe McCartin and Leon Fink. As mentioned earlier, we also published "No Common Creed: White Working-Class Protestants and the CIO's Operation Dixie" in *Rethinking U.S. Labor History: Essays on the Working-Class Experience, 1756–2009*, edited by Donna Haverty-Stacke and Daniel J. Walkowitz (New York: Continuum, 2010).

There is also the institutional support we have received. The American Council of Learned Societies awarded an individual fellowship to what was a coauthored project that has enabled us to finish this in a timely (at least for us) fashion. We have also benefited from fellowships awarded by the West Virginia Humanities Council. The Eberly College at West Virginia University and Dean Bob Jones have given us a great place to work and surrounded us with wonderful colleagues and students who have contributed to this project. At the end, the college also offered a nice subvention grant. We also greatly appreciate the ongoing support of Stuart and Joyce Robbins. WVU colleagues Ron Lewis, Matt Vester, Rev. Matthew Riegel, and Jane Donovan, and former students Joe Super, Hal Gorby, and Lou Martin have listened patiently and offered cheerful guidance as we muddled through our thinking about this topic. At the University of Illinois Press, Laurie Matheson has encouraged this project from its early stages and been a wonderful advocate. This is not the first time we have worked with her, and we hope it will not be the last. Laurie also recruited two (so far) anonymous readers, who pushed us to make our arguments sharper and to more fully develop the context. Perhaps one day we can thank them by name. We are appreciative of the efforts of our copyeditor, Julie Gay, who improved the manuscript in hundreds of ways, and the efforts of Roger Cunningham, Thomas Ringo, and others at the press who have worked on this project.

And then there is family. Our kids, Colin and Kasey, have always been a great source of pride and joy for us as we have watched them grow into adults. We apologize for any time that our work has gotten in the way of spending time with them and their partners. Luckily, our family continues to grow. In addition to Kay and John (their partners), we now have three marvelous grandchildren. Zoe, Zachary, and Hunter are wonderful diversions.

A NOTE ON RELIGIOUS TERMS

Some of the intricacies of southern religion were instrumental in shaping how particular groups of white southerners reacted to organized labor and the liberal political culture that buoyed the CIO. To help readers interested in this topic but unfamiliar with some of the terms that represent important differences within southern evangelical Protestantism, we include these brief descriptions of how we have used the terms in this book. These definitions are drawn from entries in *Encyclopedia of Religion in the South*, 2nd edition, edited by Samuel S. Hill and Charles H. Lippy (Macon, Ga.: Mercer University Press, 2005).

Dispensationalism: Dispensationalists believe that history is divided into seven epochs, or dispensations, and that mankind is living in the sixth epoch, which will soon end when Christ lifts up the saved in the Rapture before returning to Earth to lead the final battle against Satan. This belief relies heavily on apocalyptic Biblical prophecy in the books of Daniel and Revelation and became influential in Fundamentalist circles in the Depression-era South.

Fundamentalism: With origins in the late-nineteenth-century urban North, Fundamentalism was a self-imposed label aimed at defending traditional orthodox beliefs against newly emerging modernist theology and liberal trends in Protestant churches. Promulgated by such revivalists as Dwight L. Moody and Billy Sunday as well as the corporate-sponsored publication of a series of booklets called *The Fundamentals* between 1910 and 1915, Fundamentalism took on greater urgency in the South in the 1930s, when the region began to experience many of the social changes that had challenged northern Protestant churches. Following the founding of the National Association of Evangelicals during World War II, many Fundamentalists began adopting the label "Evangelical."

Hardshell (Primitive) Baptists: There are many smaller offshoots of Baptist faith arising from disputes in the nineteenth century. Hardshell, or Primitive, Baptists hold to a conservative belief in predestination and thus reject missionary societies and other "human inventions" that were not part of the original churches or "warranted from the word of God."

Holiness Churches: This church movement grew out of nineteenth-century Methodism's belief that a person reborn in Christianity should strive toward perfection and a "second blessing" of sanctification. Eventually, elements of the

Holiness movement began to reach beyond Methodism, especially in the Midwest and the South. When the Methodist Episcopal Church, South, tried to rein in Holiness advocates in the 1890s, many separated and formed more than twenty new religious groups. Among these were the Church of the Nazarene, the Pentecostal Holiness Church, and the two Church of God groups. After 1906, Pentecostalism further divided Holiness churches.

Pentecostalism: Pentecostalism grew out of the Holiness movement, but its advocates sought evidence of a more profound spiritual awakening than the second blessing of sanctification. Associated with speaking in tongues as a "sign gift" or physical evidence of the Holy Spirit's endowment, Pentecostalism spread rapidly following a series of revival meetings in Los Angeles in 1906. Among the most influential Pentecostal churches in the South were the Church of God (Cleveland, Tennessee), the Assemblies of God, and the African-American Church of God in Christ. Pentecostalism achieved a new level of acceptance in the 1940s, when the National Association of Evangelicals included Pentecostal churches.

Premillennial/Postmillennial: Millennialism derives from a belief that history will culminate in a thousand-year golden age (hence, millennialism) associated with the Second Coming of Christ. Premillennialists believe that the golden age will occur only after the Second Coming; postmillennialists believe that the Second Coming will follow immediately after the golden age. Where one stood on this issue took on increased importance in the twentieth-century South as Millennialism became entangled with Fundamentalist-Modernist debates and such movements as dispensationalism and the Social Gospel.

Rapture: An important term in dispensational premillennial eschatology, Rapture refers to the lifting up of believers to be with Christ in Heaven. In dispensational theology, the Rapture precedes a period known as the Great Tribulation, which then ushers in the Second Coming of Christ and millennial period of peace.

STRUGGLE FOR THE SOUL
OF THE POSTWAR SOUTH

INTRODUCTION

On a September day in the early 1950s, third grader Joe Bageant got off the school bus and trudged up the lane to his parents' home in Winchester, Virginia. Although the door was open, Joe found nobody home. He raced through each room in the house and then around the yard calling for family members and sobbing, a terrible dread building inside the young boy. Within about fifteen minutes his family returned home from visiting a neighbor's, not a quarter mile up the road, but young Joe did not calm down for hours. He dreamed about the incident off and on for years. Only later did he discover that other children with a similar family background experienced the same terror that Joe suffered that September day. The Bageants were fundamentalist Christians and dispensational premillennialists, believers that Christ's imminent return will precede the inauguration of the millennium and that He will lift the saved up to heaven and leave the rest to suffer God's terrible wrath in a period of tribulation. This was the fear that young Joe Bageant felt when he arrived at home and found his family gone, that they had been raptured up and that he would have to face the consequences alone. Some fifty years later, Bageant still recalled the episode and the permanent marks that "the grim fundamentalist architecture of the soul" left on him and other children reared in this Fundamentalist culture. "An apocalyptic starkness remains somewhere inside us," he confided.[1]

Bageant ultimately rejected the Fundamentalism of his working-class parents. But when he returned to Winchester in 2001, he discovered how much the ensuing fifty years had "clobbered" the white working class of his hometown, and he lamented the part played by religion. Although his father was a firm believer in the Rapture and his brother was a pastor at the independent Shenandoah Bible Baptist Church, Bageant could barely contain his dismay over the political ideas that he imagined emanated from their faith. Still, he loved his brother and struggled in his irreverent memoir to safeguard the trust of people who expected him not to "make fools of them." Bageant granted that some of the evangelical conservatism of Winchester's white working class came from their feeling that liberals disparaged working people and had abandoned them. Still, he had a hard time coming to grips with his family's belief that "the hand of Satan or demons afoot in the world" was behind everything from their personal anxieties to global conflicts.[2]

Bageant's dilemma is instructive for our purposes. For too long, historians, especially those studying the working class, made religion a prop, ignoring belief in the supernatural that is at the core of American popular religiosity. Scholars looked for how various groups used religion rather than to try to understand faith and the part it plays in the life of working people. Trained in "a materialist conception of historical change" that owes much to British Marxism, even the best American labor historians often elided or caricatured spiritual influences in their analyses. In many studies, religion served as an impediment to workers' understanding their class interests. Religion either divided workers of different faiths, served as a tool for the upwardly mobile, or provided a numbing fatalism (a "chiliasm of despair") that prevented working people from taking action against their exploiters.[3] In other studies, the stimulus provided by Herbert Gutman weighed heavily. He was drawn to the examples he uncovered of a Christian spirit infusing the rhetoric and writings of labor activists and offering a postmillennial justification for working-class solidarity.[4] Neither group of scholars tried to grapple systematically with the messiness of spiritual convictions and how those convictions interacted with lived experiences to shape the consciousness and actions of average working people.

As Bageant's example suggests, scholars have largely included southern white Protestant workers in the first category. Historians have been too easily contented with assumptions that southern evangelicalism spawned either intolerant or fatalistic outlooks that made any working-class social movement virtually impossible. For the mid-twentieth century, many scholars have relied heavily on analyzing radio preachers or such viciously racist, xenophobic, and antiliberal publications as *Militant Truth* or *The Gospel Trumpet*, newspapers that combined reactionary rhetoric with a staunch defense of traditional evangelical Protestantism.[5] Others have focused on the paternalistic textile mill villages and the ministers who were obligated to the company and to fostering a grateful, placid working class.[6] Both emphases assume a static Protestantism and an obedient, top-down religious culture, neither of which accurately describes the fiercely democratic and individualistic nature of southern popular religiosity. Nor can they account for all the evidence to the contrary—the Holiness miner/preachers who were devoted union activists, the mill villagers who defied the foreman and the local minister, the Pentecostal leaders who lifted the church ban and welcomed union membership, or the ministers gathered at the Southern Baptist Convention who voted to endorse the concept of collective bargaining. These anomalies, and many more, instruct us that we should give a closer look to the intersection of class sentiments and religious faith in the mid-twentieth century.

In this project, we build upon a growing literature that recognizes the power of the sacred. In the past decade, there has been a flood of exciting new work on the connections linking particular aspects of Christianity to the flourishing of modern capitalism and the rise of the New Right. Darren Dochuk, Bethany Moreton, Darren Grem, Kevin Kruse, and the late Sarah Hammond have unearthed the evangelical underpinnings of the free-enterprise ideology that spawned not only Billy Graham and Jerry Falwell but also Reaganism and the Walmartization of the economy.[7] However, while these historians have demonstrated how business-backed evangelicals seized the pulpits of key Protestant churches, their work leaves out the working people who ostensibly internalized Christian free enterprise and became the foot soldiers for the transformation of America's political economy. We need to know a great deal more about what in their understanding of evangelical Protestantism either bolstered or rejected a conservative, antistatist political economy and union membership.

There is a cohort of younger historians who are making progress in this direction. Joe Creech, Richard J. Callahan Jr., and Jarod H. Roll have each produced books exploring the religious worldviews of the poor and dispossessed and how those views took shape in politics, broadly defined. Each has benefited from the insights of religious scholars and anthropologists who have examined "how particular people, in particular places and times, live in, with, through, and against the religious idioms available to them in culture." Roll's work, in particular, exemplifies the possibilities of investigating the popular Christianity of working people. Experiencing the dramatic transformation of rural life in the bootheel of Missouri in the early twentieth century, black and white farmers, sharecroppers, and tenants gravitated to Pentecostal, Holiness, and independent churches, which fueled a range of contradictory political responses, from Garveyism and socialism to the Klan.[8] There is much more in the works from younger scholars who are dissatisfied with the tendency to separate the sacred from the secular, rather than treat them as intertwined.[9]

All this points to the inadequate understanding we have of the southern white working class in the decades bracketing World War II. Despite scholars' sympathetic treatment of black Christianity, the faith of poor whites claims few admirers.[10] Often, popular Christianity in the South is treated as a stagnant force in a region experiencing extraordinary social change. The Great Depression and war years witnessed extreme poverty and hardship, an exodus from rural agriculture, an expansion of cities and manufacturing jobs, a leap in union membership, and the incursion of the federal government into the social and political life of the South. Not surprisingly, southern churches experienced similar upheaval. Some denominations revitalized their social programs during the Depression and grew closer to northern counterparts; others turned inward, finding solace in traditional theologies and practices. Meanwhile, there was explosive growth in religious sects, institutions, radio programs, and itinerant revivalists. Southerners must have felt their sacred world was in just as much turmoil as their secular one.[11] And then, not a year removed from the war, the Congress of Industrial Organizations (CIO) followed one of the largest waves of strikes in American history by inaugurating a campaign to organize southern workers and bring the benefits of unionism to the South. The CIO asserted that its Southern Organizing Campaign would amount to "a spiritual crusade led by men with religion in their hearts."[12]

Historians have been slow to analyze how white, working-class southerners experienced this turbulence. How did faith influence attitudes about expanding government, labor conflict, and racial boundaries at this most critical moment? In some cases popular religion undoubtedly generated a fierce defense of the existing social order. The emphasis on local autonomy and independence, Biblical authority and inerrancy, premillennialism and holiness—these elements of working-class Christianity could be a powerful barrier against the CIO's message of class unity and a modernist, New Deal–style liberalism. But social and religious upheaval also created spaces where dissident voices clamored for change. Competing against conservative evangelicalism were the prophetic gospel teachings of radicals like Claude Williams and liberal clergy in the Fellowship of Southern Churchmen who had their own working-class followers. These voices had laid the groundwork for considerable optimism among veteran labor movement activists that the South was ready for change, secular and spiritual.

In short, there were multiple Protestant creeds in the South vying for the devotion of white, working-class adherents. Industrialists, hoping to tap new, cheap labor markets and relocate factories away from union strongholds, promoted a version of evangelical Protestantism that emphasized the benefits of individualism, free enterprise, loyalty to one's employer, and a suspicion of outsiders, be they government bureaucrats or union organizers. They traded on the Cold War fears of a dangerous drift toward a socialistic state that might limit personal freedoms, including freedom of religion. They also defended traditional hierarchies at a time of growing agitation against segregation and job discrimination. Employers found allies in the new National Association of Evangelicals and clergy influenced by premillennial eschatologies, and they contributed lavishly to amplify their voices in the media and in religious institutions.

On the other side, the CIO and its allies disseminated a version of Christianity that emphasized the brotherhood of mankind. They emphasized a postmillennial interpretation of Christ's Second Coming and a practical spirituality aimed at discovering the power of God within oneself and applying it in dealing with everyday realities. In their theology, Christ was not a weak and suffering figure; rather, he was a savior deeply interested in helping overcome the problems that kept people from fulfilled lives. The CIO's allies included the older and more modernist Federal Council of Churches of Christ in America, and it enlisted a cadre of northern, seminary-trained activists to counteract the proponents of free-enterprise Christians.

The stakes for both groups were enormous. Industrialists wanted to roll back the regulatory innovations of the New Deal and stem the tide of union opposition to their control of production. They feared that collective bargaining agreements mandating union membership and laws requiring fair employment practices would undermine their power over labor markets and their influence over politics. The CIO hoped to build upon wartime gains and complete the organization of workers in basic industry and thereby remove the incentive for relocating American industry away from areas of union strength. CIO leaders also understood that greater union density would enhance their political clout and protect the new system of labor relations ushered in during the New Deal. For both groups, the South was the key to furthering their goals.

In between were southern Protestant churches and clergy with their own ambitions. Experiencing a postwar resurgence of Christianity, denominations, independent church groups, and ministers felt that they had a unique opportunity to put evangelicalism at the center of American life. Christianity could help the South and the nation cope with the unsettled nature of postwar society and steer a steady course through the new threats to peace and security. But southern Protestant leaders had anxieties as well. The largest denominations worried about losing their distinctive southern character. Already the southern Methodists had merged with their northern coreligionists and had compromised on denominational structure. There was also a fierce competition between the major denominations and dynamic Pentecostal and independent Holiness churches. Which of these evangelical faiths would best serve the spiritual needs of uprooted people who found themselves "going among strangers"?[13] Southern Protestants found themselves increasingly pulled toward the National Association of Evangelicals, which revived conservative, Fundamentalist theology under a new name, evangelicalism. Consequently, religion was a potent but unpredictable force in the South at this critical moment in the contest over a postwar political economy.

This book's main contribution rests on making the sacred a major element in the story of the CIO's crusade for unionism and economic justice. To accomplish this, it is necessary to move the narrative beyond the easy targets of the quasi-religious, hate-filled newspapers, the Fundamentalist radio preachers, and even the prophetic radicals who tried to offer a gospel of class struggle. They are part of the story, but they cannot begin to represent the range of beliefs held by the denominations, fellowships, churches, ministers, and followers. Southern evangelical Protestantism was dynamic and constantly changing, forcing individuals constantly to measure church teachings against their daily experiences. We have attempted to explore the variety of creeds and Protestant faiths present in the South to complicate what all too often gets simplified under the phrase "southern religion."

At the same time, church publications and sermons did not set the boundaries for the faith of working people. They gravitated to particular churches that emphasized the spiritual equality of the preacher and the members, and they believed that they were perfectly capable of reading the Bible and coming to their own conclusions about its meaning for everyday life. Working people attached sacred value to their personal independence and self-reliance, but they coupled that with a strong sense of duty to live their lives in accordance with the Scriptures. They cherished being part of a community of believers, which might make them suspicious of outsiders or worldly items that threatened the harmony of the congregation and diverted attention from accepting and being thankful for God's grace. Most important, working-class Christians often saw the world as a contest between good and evil, and that God and Satan were ever present, intervened directly into their lives, and battled for their souls. This popular religiosity, we believe, provided the framework within which working people assessed unions, employers, politics, and conflict. It also provides us with a clearer picture of precisely what elements of their faith were helpful or pernicious to the CIO organizers who tried to appeal to them.

Of course, they evaluated the entreaties of employers and unions in a particular historical context that influenced their decisions. While the Depression and the New Deal made Christian working people more amenable to unions and liberalism, the war and postwar turmoil made them less so. The war diminished their belief that mankind might rise above its basically evil nature and improve the world before Christ's intervention. It also appeared to many that the war and its aftermath were moving the world closer to the end times, and that the salvation of souls, not societal reform, demanded greater urgency. The emerging Cold War and the specter of the Soviet Union only reinforced those notions. The fact that unions were allied with Leftists and a more powerful state made their appearance in southern communities seem dangerous.[14] Another result of the war was the impetus it gave to demands for black equal rights. For many white, working-class Christians, such demands threatened whatever privileges they had been able to squeeze from an unfeeling industrial capitalism. Finally, working people recalled the previous defeats they had experienced when they tried to unionize. This was particularly important in the textile industry, which was the primary target of the CIO's postwar campaign. Textile workers could weigh the horrible consequences of those defeats against their current material standards of living, which as a result of the war and federal regulations had never been better.[15] The sacred and the secular combined in a convincing postwar worldview that the CIO could not overcome.

The fault does not rest solely with southern workers, however. The CIO chose to concentrate on an industry and a strategy that omitted a sizeable evangelical Protestant population—African Americans—who could have brought a different theological emphasis to labor's crusade. Unlike white evangelicalism, which emphasized individual salvation, black evangelicalism placed far more emphasis on community solidarity and collective action. But by deploying such a large share of its resources on the predominantly white textile industry, the CIO made clear that it preferred to recruit white workers. Some CIO leaders even tried to downplay success among black workers because they were fearful that stories of black union growth would cause white workers to reject the CIO. For many historians of the CIO campaign, this was certainly an "opportunity lost."[16] The campaign compounded this problem by excluding alliances with organizations and individuals that had suspected ties to Communists, even though some had built strong records of activity among black workers. This weakened the voice of a prophetic Christianity by reducing the support of such allies as the Southern Conference for Human Welfare and Highlander Folk School. The Cold War exacted a toll on the liberal-Left coalition that had emerged during the New Deal.[17] We believe, however, that the religious faith of southern white workers helped dictate the path chosen by the CIO.

Equally destructive was the CIO's ignorance of southern white evangelicalism. The Southern Organizing Campaign established a Community Relations Department to work with southern ministers but put a man, John Gates Ramsay, in charge; Ramsay was steeped in northern, liberal Protestantism and knew very little about either southern race relations or southern evangelicalism. The CIO also hired a number of seminary-trained activists for staff positions, but they had attended northern seminaries and were committed to liberal Protestant theologies. Those people whom the CIO charged with religious work continually emphasized their stature in Protestant groups that were suspect in the minds of southern white Christians. Several of them also belittled Holiness and Pentecostal faiths, which were attracting the white working class.[18] Southern white Christians had bristled at this condescension before.

Ultimately, the failure of the CIO's Southern Organizing Campaign had long-term repercussions. Its defeat halted the expansion of organized labor and left a largely union-free region where American industry could expand and sap the vitality of union strength in the old rust belt. It also left the region's politics in the hands of conservatives who helped roll back many of the improvements the New Deal had made in the lives of working people. Southern congressmen's support for the anti-union Taft-Hartley Act in 1947 was only the beginning. CIO strategy also diverted crucial energy and financial support from liberal social-justice organizations, like Highlander and the Southern Conference for Human Welfare, which had been vocal advocates of organized labor and black civil rights. Those organizations were either weaker or no longer existed when the civil rights movement blossomed in the wake of the CIO's failure.

Might things have turned out differently? Inevitably, this leads to the question that historian Bryant Simon asserts all southern labor historians must ask: Why are there so few unions in the South? Many historians have speculated on this question, detailing the racial attitudes, the appeal of paternalistic practices, the individualism and suspicious nature of rural-born peoples, or the ability of southern elites and their police forces to repel unions through a mix of brutal repression, redbaiting, and paternalism. Others have focused on the poor organizing strategies and the bureaucratic conservatism of the unions, or the foreign character of a Yankee union invasion.[19] Simon attacked these elements of southern distinctiveness well. Drawing on his command of a plethora of case studies, he notes that many of these factors were not unique to the South. In the North some employers fought unions just as viciously, while others used the same paternalistic practices as their southern counterparts; and northern workers were just as racist and xenophobic, careful to protect the advantages of lighter skin pigmentation. Likewise, northern police and elites tapped into fears of centralized socialistic states, and unions there were no less bureaucratic or conservative. Still, the North had more than twice the union density of the sunbelt. In fact, Simon's argument fits well with a growing tendency to diminish southern differences, starting in the antebellum era and continuing to the present.[20]

We would like to weigh in on the other side. While Simon's article is stimulating, we believe that there are important differences that shaped a regional identity that doomed visions of a liberal, pro-union triumph in the postwar era.[21] To us, one of the key differences is religion. This takes shape not only as the ideology of Christian entrepreneurs and free-enterprise evangelicals who flourished in the South, but also in the ways evangelical Protestantism captured the hearts and minds of southern white working people and influenced their outlook on a range of issues. Years ago, a religious historian wrote about southern churches being mired in cultural captivity. In summing up this argument, one of the doyens of southern history, Samuel S. Hill Jr., noted the distinctive nature of a southern regional culture, expressed by "the lengths to which Southerners have gone in constructing regional myths" and consciously choosing an "identity by contrast, by dissociation from other cultures." Hill continued: "There is some kind of irony in the fact that a people live with such a hearty awareness of their larger secular context but have not assimilated a corresponding social awareness in their religious patterns of thought."[22] The evangelical Protestantism of southern white workers, then, intertwined with and provided a moral, legitimating impetus for that regional identity, which ultimately served the unity of the southern status quo in withstanding the challenges from the CIO and its liberal allies.[23] This was not easily achieved. The upheaval of the Depression caused many to question the region's culture, to infuse a contingency into the debate. But World War II, we argue, put in motion many changes that reinforced the South's resistance to labor and the modern liberal society it hoped to create.

Our book opens with two chapters on the state of the South beginning with the Depression. Chapter 1 explores the social and economic conditions that earned the region its label, "the problem South." Because we want to put religion at the center of our story, we use as our guide Alva W. Taylor, the Disciples of Christ minister, Vanderbilt School of Religion professor, and regular columnist on the

South for the major mainline-Protestant magazine of the day, *Christian Century*. Taylor is an excellent source to examine how the Depression and World War II appeared to an important element of southern Protestantism. Chapter 2 reverses the angle of vision and examines how southern religious institutions responded to economic collapse, social unrest, and a horrific world war. After experiencing a "religious depression" that decimated many southern churches, Protestantism recovered and was poised for a tremendous postwar surge.

In chapter 3 we examine the popular religiosity of the southern, white, working class, relying heavily on oral histories. How did the faith of white, Christian workers help them deal with the transformations occurring in the economy, society, and politics of the region? What changes did they make in their church membership? What practices and beliefs did they find comforting? Chapter 3 also investigates how work and place shaped their decisions about unions and politics during the Depression as well as how the values they held as sacred helped determine how they would respond to the appeals of employers and labor unions in the postwar South.

The next two chapters focus on the versions of evangelical Protestantism that appealed to employers and labor activists. Chapter 4 charts the emergence of a Christian free-enterprise ideology that meshed easily with the goals of corporate executives hoping to take advantage of the lower wages and conservative politics of the South. Christian entrepreneurs followed a variety of strategies to gain influence among the region's clergy and their congregations, but perhaps they had no better ally than the Cold War in spreading the free-enterprise ideology. Chapter 5 treats those on the other side who emphasized how the Bible spoke to labor. But while employers could present a united front on most issues, the CIO's Christian supporters were divided. Prophetic radicals, some of whom had close ties to the Communist party, were not welcome under labor's umbrella, despite the fact that they had devoted their lives to social and economic justice. Moreover, some of the key religious figures recruited by the CIO had a limited understanding of southern evangelical Protestantism.

The final two chapters take a closer look at the effect of the CIO's sacred messages in communities across the South. In chapter 6 the focus is on the clergy. If the goals of both free-enterprise Christianity and labor's gospel were to win the support of ministers, what factors determined how they would decide? What were the consequences of siding with the CIO when business had so much more in the way of resources and power? What were the sacred imperatives for the clergy's actions? Chapter 7 probes two issues that forced the CIO's religious cadre to make difficult decisions—racial justice and Communism. The Christian values that drove the Community Relations Department and the ordained ministers who served on the CIO staff pushed them ultimately to place racial justice above the immediate goals of the Southern Organizing Campaign, even when it meant that they had to defy CIO leadership. But on the issue of Communism, the CIO's religious activists shared the anti-Communism that permeated southern evangelical Protestantism. In some cases, their anti-Communism outweighed their commitment to racial justice.

In the end, the CIO's Southern Organizing Campaign failed for a number of reasons—employer intransigence, repression by local authorities, public opposition, racism, anti-Communism, CIO strategies, and the improving economic conditions of workers all contributed. Southern evangelical Protestantism also played a part, but not the one typically described in the historical scholarship. The larger lesson, we have come to conclude, is that social movements of any sort and at any time should begin by understanding the culture of the people that they hope will follow their lead. Understanding that only some sort of faith will generally move people to take chances, those social movements should strive to grasp the central elements of that faith.

CHAPTER 1

The Wages of the "Problem South"

Alice Grogan spent her early years on a farm in the South Carolina upcountry, the eldest girl in a family of five boys and three girls. She began helping her mother with household chores at age five, and as soon as she was old enough, she began helping pick her father's cash crops, cotton and corn. Among Alice's other chores were picking blackberries, minding her younger siblings, carrying water from the spring, helping fix dinner for the young men who helped thresh her father's wheat, and helping can fruit and vegetables and prepare virtually everything the growing family ate. When she was eleven, Alice contracted pellagra, a disease associated with poverty and a vitamin-deficient diet. It recurred several times before doctors finally cured her. For the Grogan family, the hard times of the Depression did not wait for the stock market crash. In the 1920s they found it difficult to make ends meet, even with the work of sons and daughters. As was the case for many other farm families, the jobs in the nearby textile mills looked inviting. Finally, in 1926, the Grogans made the move to Greenville, where Charlie Grogan and his oldest children found work at the Woodside Cotton Mill. Even Charlie's wife Lydia filled batteries in the weave shop in the hours around the noon break when the weavers lunched. Although Alice and her brothers found town living and wage work a respite from the long hours of hard work on the farm, Charlie Grogan merely made the best of the change. Like many southerners who grew up on the farm, he never liked leaving the life he had known.[1]

In some ways, the Grogans were fortunate to leave when they did, finding mill jobs relatively easily. Other country people made the difficult transition during less opportune times. At the outset of the Depression, Calvin and Lola Simmons were hardscrabble tenant farmers in Tennessee's Upper Cumberland region. Never able to get far enough ahead to acquire livestock, Calvin had to borrow a horse or mule to plow, which often meant that he had to plow in less than ideal conditions. Lola failed to make a sufficient garden for extra needs, and the couple was no more successful raising chickens or pigs, which Lola lamented "were two things it just wasn't no way for us to keep from dying." Eventually, the Simmonses left for Knoxville after Calvin had a fight with neighbors who accused his dog of killing their chickens. But middle aged and without skills, Calvin scrambled to make a living as a handyman, while Lola stretched his irregular income to meet rent, coal, and food for them and their son. They lived in a cold, damp, three-room apartment with a leaky roof and a "little water privy in the kitchen closet, but it don't flush right," Lola complained. Still, she noted, "being poor ain't easy nowhere, but it's a sight better in the city than on the farm."[2]

The Grogans and the Simmonses were part of a dramatic transformation of the South that began in the 1930s, one that demanded momentous adjustments for much of the white working classes. In significant numbers they left their rural places of birth, many for the North or West, many more for towns, mill villages, and cities in the South. They left the farms that they owned, rented, or sharecropped in favor of wage-earning jobs in factories, mines, shops, and ware-houses. They left the churches, schools, and kin networks, where they learned their values and their ways of understanding the world, for new homes where they had to adapt those values to new circumstances. They did this in a region with an economy ill suited for absorbing the masses of mobile people. The Great Depression began early in the rural South, and it flooded the labor markets of such low-wage regional industries as textiles, lumber, furniture, and tobacco, further depressing wages and leading to surplus production that only intensified price wars and put unhealthy industries on life support.[3]

By 1938, the administration of Franklin Roosevelt had identified what some called the "colonial economy" of the South as the nation's number one economic problem. In *The Report on Economic Conditions of the South*, key southern liberals, under the auspices of the administration's National Emergency Council, identi-fied the paradox of the South, a region "blessed by Nature with immense wealth" whose "people as a whole are the poorest in the country."[4] The report described the poverty of the region and highlighted the need to embark on a program of economic development to bring the South's economy into convergence with the nation's, but changes were already in the works. Between the issuing of the report and the end of World War II, the South made great strides forward, positioning the region for economic growth at a rate that would surpass that of the nation. These years raised hopes for some that progressive forces could break the shackles of traditionalism that many liberals believed rested at the core of southern poverty and underdevelopment. They also generated fears among others in the South that change would come at the expense of their regional identity and well-being. This should not surprise us; Vanderbilt University professor Edwin Mims noted that the parallel strains of provincialism and advancement had been engaged in this conflict "ever since Appomattox."[5]

To understand the powers at work as the Congress of Industrial Organizations launched its crusades to construct a new South, it is necessary to chart the changes that occurred starting with the Depression. By revealing both how much changed as well as how much remained to be accomplished, it is possible to see just how high were the stakes in that conflict between progress and reaction. Our guide through the late Depression and wartime South is another Vanderbilt professor and Disciples of Christ minister, Alva Wilmot Taylor. As professor of social ethics in Vanderbilt's School of Religion, Taylor was a strong proponent of the Social Gospel and thus a keen observer of both the sacred and the secular aspects of the South's transformation.

Correspondence from the New South's New Deal

Alva Wilmot Taylor was born in Anamosa, Iowa, in 1871 and moved with his family to western Iowa in a covered wagon at age three. After attending a one-room school in a rural area, he taught school in 1890 to earn the money to enter preparatory school at Drake University, graduating in 1896. He then completed two years of graduate work at the University of Chicago, studying with such luminaries as Albion Small, W. I. Thomas, and Lester F. Ward before spending a year under the tutelage of Graham Taylor, founder of the Chicago Commons Settlement House and editor of the leading Social Gospel magazine of the day, *Charities and the Commons*. During the first two decades of the twentieth century, Taylor ministered to a church in Cincinnati and then in Eureka, Illinois, punctuated by leaves to travel in Europe and Ireland, studying landlord and tenant conditions and earning a master's degree from Chicago in 1910. As his national reputation grew, the liberal Federal Council of Churches of Christ in America commissioned Taylor to write pamphlets on the 1919 steel strike and on the wage question. He also coauthored a book, *The Church and Industrial Reconstruction*, published by the Federal Council.[6]

In his denomination, the Disciples of Christ, Taylor was somewhat unusual as a forceful proponent of the Social Gospel. The Disciples, founded in the early nineteenth century, began as a protest against sectarianism and denominational exclusiveness. Disciples of Christ churches strove to restore Christian unity by returning to New Testament faith and practices and witnessing for Jesus as the Lord and Savior of the world. Taylor shared this faith but also combined it with the optimistic postmillennialism of Social Gospel advocates who believed that by blending science and religion they could reform society along Christian lines. In the Progressive Era, Taylor absorbed nearly all the currents of Social Gospel thinking, believing in the white man's burden to uplift all other peoples, in the importance of prohibition, in improving race relations, and especially in the need to reform industry to stop the exploitation of working people. In 1921, Taylor took a position at the Bible College of Missouri, where he taught courses on the social teaching of Jesus, the social work of Christian missions, and the social function of the work of the church. From 1921 to 1931 he served also as the Disciples' Secretary of the Board for Temperance and Social Welfare. In that position he fought against what he saw as the denomination's reactionary leadership and limited contact with working people. He confided to a friend that he was "a Disciple most of the time except Convention week." Nevertheless, he gained notoriety for the studies he directed on such topics as temperance, race relations, and labor-capital relations.[7]

In 1928 Taylor accepted a position as chair of Social Ethics in the School of Religion at Vanderbilt University. Although almost immediately labeled a "radical" both for the content of his courses and his encouragement of students to become involved in social problems, Taylor felt uncomfortable with the tag. In 1933, when Jerome Davis asked him to take on the editorship of the Religion and Labor Foundation's *Bulletin*, Taylor declined, claiming, "Frankly, my attitude [is] in contrast to that of your younger colleagues. I am progressive not radical, and I fear they would fret under the difference in expression." Taylor refrained from joining radical organizations despite his interest in social reform. "If we are to be 'ministers of reconciliation' and advocates of equity and justice, I belong," he insisted, but no matter how much he sympathized with the objectives of radicals, his vision of an ideal future was less secular and more sacred. "When science gives the technique and the Church gives the social passion," he wrote in 1931, "we will possess power to make the world over into the kingdom of God."[8]

Nevertheless, Taylor adopted causes and mentored students who linked his name to prophetic radicalism. Shortly after arriving at Vanderbilt, Taylor served as the chair of the Church Emergency Relief Committee, a left-leaning group of ministers who raised money and provisions for striking workers and their families. Committee members included the most-well-known prolabor clergy of the 1920s and 1930s—William B. Spofford, James Myers, Charles Webber, Jerome Davis, Worth Tippy, and Reinhold Niebuhr. In 1932 and 1933, appeals for assistance and condemnations of employer brutality in two of the most noteworthy and violent strikes of the time (in Harlan County, Kentucky, and Wilder, Tennessee) went out under his signature.[9] Among the students frequenting Taylor's classroom and accepting his mentoring were Howard Kester, Don West, Ward Rodgers, and Claude Williams, each of whom rose to prominence in labor and radical circles. Not only did they forge the intellectual tools of their prophetic Christianity in Taylor's classes, but they also developed the skills and passions necessary to maintain a life of social activism.[10]

Although Taylor frequently complained about the dogmatism of Socialists and Communists, he was uncompromising when it came to confronting injustice. In addition to coordinating fundraising to help strikers' families, Taylor participated in efforts to halt lynchings in Tennessee, to improve race relations in Nashville, and to support the Tennessee Valley Authority. By 1933 he was in trouble at conservative Vanderbilt, having run afoul of university officials as well as key donors and alumni. Most important among them was John Emmett Edgerton, a prominent industrialist, former President of the National Association of Manufacturers and founding member of the Southern States Industrial Council, a vociferously anti-Roosevelt and anti–New Deal association. Edgerton was a devout Methodist who led daily prayer meetings and hymn singing in his woolen mills; he also served as chair of the board of directors of Vanderbilt's School of Religion. As the Depression began to force cuts in Vanderbilt programs, Taylor's position, which had been part of an expansion project, came on the chopping block, a fact that he blamed on Edgerton and Vanderbilt's reactionary chancellor. In 1934 and 1935, his former students helped raise donations to pay Taylor's salary, but by 1936 their efforts were no longer enough. Vanderbilt announced that it was "transferring" Taylor to Fisk University, where he taught a couple of courses on Christian race relations, but this was merely an attempt to quiet student protests against Taylor's ouster.[11]

Over the next decade Taylor, then in his sixties, had to scramble to find positions and support his family. He worked for the Fellowship of Reconciliation, as manager of the Farm Security Association's Cumberland Homestead, and as an arbitrator for the War Labor Board. He also served, from the 1930s until his death in 1952, on the editorial boards of several religious magazines, including perhaps the most important mainline Protestant magazine of the day, *Christian Century*. Throughout the Depression and war years, Taylor wrote a regular column, "Correspondence from the New South," in which he observed the important social, economic, and political changes wrought by a growing federal government presence in the region. Although hardly a representative southerner, Taylor's

Alva Wilmot Taylor in Nashville, 1937. Courtesy of the Disciples of Christ Historical Society.

dispatches allow us to gain insights about how these changes appeared to an individual committed to applied Christianity.

When Taylor began reporting on the New Deal in the South, nowhere was the Depression's impact greater than in the rural, agricultural areas. Counties throughout the South struggled to meet the burdens of what were woefully inadequate relief efforts. Franklin County, North Carolina, for example, budgeted just $3,500 a year for 349 families on relief, and a county home provided food and shelter for only about thirty people. Meriwether County, Georgia, was in worse shape; it had 2,385 people on relief, 10.6 percent of its population. Leflore County, Mississippi, relief rolls topped 9,000 in January 1934, about one of every six in the county. Official surveys in Alabama listed 86,733 families on relief on September 1, 1933.[12] Federal agricultural policy, strongly influenced by southern planters and their representatives, sought to stabilize crop prices by subsidizing farmers to restrict production. Federal agriculture subsidies to plow up much of the cotton crop in fact raised cotton prices dramatically and provided a stimulus to regional purchasing power. South Carolina, for example, reported in December 1933 that its cotton crop was worth two-thirds more than the previous year's harvest; Tennessee increased its purchasing power by one-third. The southeastern division of the Chamber of Commerce described the improvements as "almost magic," noting that there had been no farm strikes in the South. Planting contracts for the 1934–35 growing season reduced cotton planting from 40 million to 25 million acres. For Taylor, however, there was "a dark side to this picture." No legal obligation required landowners to share benefits with tenants or croppers, resulting in thousands being "thrown back on wages, if any were offered, or upon relief."[13]

As early as 1934, one observer estimated that six hundred thousand families had been displaced by New Deal agricultural policies, which rewarded the large planters and encouraged them to evict tenants and sharecroppers. Many of these families had no choice but to turn to low-wage farm labor or leave rural areas altogether. Throughout the South, tenants began to organize to resist evictions and demand government assistance, while farm laborers mobilized to fight for higher wages. Alva Taylor received firsthand information on this rural social movement from his former students, Ward Rogers, Howard Kester, and Claude Williams, who were key activists in the struggle, working with the Southern Tenant Farmers Union and other agricultural workers' organizations. Taylor praised their protests and the changes they brought in agricultural policy, however limited they were. He also vilified the reactionary planters who met working-class mobilization with violence and repression. He reported in *Christian Century* about the "elements which have spread terror" by beating STFU organizers, shooting up the homes of black preachers, and attempting "to railroad Ward Rogers, a Christian minister, into the penitentiary" for organizing agricultural workers.[14]

Taylor worried about the spiritual as well as the economic consequences of the transformation of southern agriculture. As a strong proponent of rural community churches, he was not the least bit surprised at the ways sharecroppers, tenants, and farm laborers responded to the prophetic religious message carried into agricultural labor organizations by Rogers, Williams, Kester, and many others. One group of worried planters even "petitioned the churches 'not to make their tenants and croppers class conscious.'"[15] Taylor believed that a "southern awakening" was needed to deal with what *Raleigh News and Observer* editor decried as "the American ghetto of the economically damned . . . where a man is worth a lower wage than anywhere else in America." He reported with hope about the "extensive resettlement plan" proposed to help tenants and sharecroppers and the federal government's policy changes that aimed to give tenants a more equitable share of farm subsidies, but he recognized that reform was inadequate to meet the needs of the rural working class. Ultimately, he lamented that "profit is the only determinant" in agricultural labor relations "unless some civilizing or Christianizing factor in the personal life of the employer motivates a more humane policy."[16]

The displacement of such large numbers of the agricultural working class, what Gunnar Myrdal called an "American enclosure movement," had obvious ramifications for cities, towns, mill villages, and southern industries. Taylor wrote in September 1934, "The South has no greater problem than that of creating profitable employment for several million underprivileged people. There are several million tenants, mountain dwellers and wage earners who can never afford a decent American standard of living until their incomes are increased." Those rural folks, who, like the Grogans, sought refuge from the Depression in cities, discovered that they had negligible skills and few prospects in a saturated labor market. Moreover, two-thirds of the South's industrial jobs throughout the 1930s were in the low-wage industries of textiles, tobacco, food, paper, and lumber. Per capita income in the South actually fell relative to income in the North in the early years of the Depression.[17]

Many liberals, like Taylor, believed the problem was partly a political one. He pointed to the example of Georgia Governor Eugene Talmadge, who vetoed an appropriation bill passed by the state legislature to match funds donated by the chemical foundation to build a promising experimental pulp mill that could create jobs and a lucrative pulp and paper industry in the state. More persistently, Taylor pointed to the war of attrition that business groups waged against the Tennessee Valley Authority (TVA), which offered cheap electricity to consumers and possibly an incentive to industry looking for plant locations in the region.[18] In fact, wealthy landholders and their representatives, who hoped to maintain political and economic power in the region, had devised state policies hostile to industry. Georgia, for instance, restricted its cities and towns from offering subsidies to attract outside business, and the South was far ahead of the rest of the country by 1934 in imposing corporate income taxes. Political scientist V. O. Key bemoaned the fact that the southern political coalition committed to maintaining the low-wage labor market "included not just planters but lumber and sawmill operators, textile mill owners, and other employers."[19]

It was on issues such as these that Taylor generated opposition at Vanderbilt. The Southern States Industrial Council (SSIC) organized regional industrialists in an attempt to monopolize and control federal policy in the region. The council worked hard to keep a regional wage differential in the codes of fair competition developed by the National Recovery Administration to set wages and hours in the various industries. The council's president, John Edgerton, who also led the board of directors of Vanderbilt's School of Religion, was a determined foe of virtually all New Deal programs, but none more so than TVA. He believed that the program represented a form of socialism and state-sponsored social engineering, particularly when it began to sell inexpensive electricity to towns in competition with private utility companies, just the sort of activity that Taylor applauded.[20] In a desperately poor region, Taylor believed that TVA could be a model for southern development. In addition to providing electricity for many rural homes previously without, it created important by-products, including such new industries as high-grade phosphate fertilizer and a ceramic laboratory developing "a cheap process for turning the kaolin deposits of North Carolina into cheap and beautiful chinaware." TVA also earned both Taylor's praise and Edgerton's enmity by "illustrating a model method in labor organization and employer-employee relationships." The unionization of workers, trumpeted by TVA, was one of the SSIC's greatest fears, but a harbinger of a more Christian society to Taylor. For evidence, he pointed to the TVA company town of Norris, accused of being a "godless town" by TVA opponents. Norris, Taylor reported, has a community church with "a thriving fellowship embracing practically all the 1,100 dwellers in the village." Pastored by a Methodist minister, the church was open to anyone "upon a simple declaration of faith, all other questions being left to the individual conscience," a sentiment dear to Taylor's faith.[21]

Although TVA did not live up to Taylor's rosy predictions, Edgerton was troubled by TVA's willingness to engage in collective bargaining with its employees, which he felt was one of the worst outcomes of the National Industrial Recovery Act. A staunch opponent of unions, the SSIC president groaned about any southern employer who paid above standard wages and did not fight unions with all their might. That TVA workers had union contracts only added to his opposition to the program. In essence, Taylor and Edgerton were locked in a regional ideological battle over whether a continued low-wage strategy would revive the southern economy or whether the South's salvation would come from encouraging unions, attracting high-wage industries, and improving the purchasing power of southern workers.[22]

Both sides claimed victories during the height of the Depression. Conservative industrialists like Edgerton could boast that employers won regional wage differentials that kept southern wages at 71 percent of northern wages despite the efforts of the National Recovery Administration. They also gloried in the fact that they had defeated the general strike of workers in the largest industry in the region—textiles—and that unionization rates remained about half the national average, even as programs like Mississippi's Balance Agriculture with Industry recruited new industry to the South.[23] Taylor and fellow liberals pointed to victories of the United Mine Workers, overcoming vicious anti-union employers in the Appalachian Mountains, and the breakthroughs of unions in the steel mills, mines, and smelter works in the Birmingham district of Alabama in 1937. Garment workers and tobacco workers scored more modest successes. Liberals also saw hopeful signs in political outcomes. South Carolina voters elected former mill-hand Olin D. Johnston as governor in 1934 and 1936, while Alabama elected New Deal sympathizers Luther Patrick to U.S. Congress and Bibb Graves as governor. In Georgia, voters turned out Governor Eugene Talmadge, a major stumbling block to liberal reforms, in favor of E. D. Rivers, a New Deal advocate. A new generation of politicians, Lyndon Johnson of Texas, Lister Hill of Alabama, and Claude Pepper of Florida, tapped the poor people's admiration for Roosevelt and the New Deal and generated unease among the southern elites.[24]

The tensions contained in the debate over the economic transformation of the South burst through in 1938. In that dramatic year, Congress passed the Fair Labor Standards Act, which was a major assault on the low wages in southern industry, and the Roosevelt Administration issued *The Report on Economic Conditions of the South*, which called the South the nation's number-one economic problem. Both initiatives focused attention on the issue of underconsumption, which liberals viewed as one of the causes of the region's poor economic conditions. The *Report* also adopted the idea that the South floundered because it was a "colonial economy," a furnisher of raw materials without adding value to the products through human skills and technological input. To improve conditions, a massive federal effort was needed. The issuance of the *Report* coincided with the efforts of Roosevelt to unseat some conservative southern Democrats who stood as roadblocks to New Deal legislation. Following his landslide victory in 1936, Roosevelt miscalculated his ability to transform the South politically.[25] The final important event in the high tide of New Deal liberalism in the South was the November convention of the Southern Conference for Human Welfare in Birmingham, Alabama. Writer John Egerton, not to be confused with industrialist John E. Edgerton, called the huge, multiracial gathering of southern liberals, activists, and progressives "the revival in Birmingham" due to its prophetic Christian tone and enthusiasm. The revival challenged the traditional leadership of the South by planning to tackle economic, political, and racial questions, the latter of which had not been particularly high on the New Deal agenda. Chairman Frank Porter

Graham, the liberal president of the University of North Carolina, put the region on notice that "the black man is the primary test of American democracy and Christianity" and that the Southern Conference takes its stand "for the Sermon on the Mount, the American Bill of Rights, and American democracy."[26]

Alva Taylor, in the midst of scrambling to earn a living for his wife, disabled son, and two small daughters at age sixty-seven, nevertheless absorbed the enthusiasm of 1938. Although he recognized that Roosevelt's efforts to purge conservative southern Democrats had failed, he believed that "after all the ballyhoo" was over, the South would prove to be "about as solidly New Deal" as it was Democratic. He pointed to the fact that polls showed that southerners were "two to one for liberal policies, overwhelmingly for Roosevelt, [and] 60 per cent for the wages and hours bill." Taylor praised the Southern Conference for Human Welfare (SCHW) and the progress made by clergy on such issues as antilynching, ending the poll tax, and supporting unionism.[27] Still, Taylor prepared for a long struggle. He warned of continuing antilabor violence and violations of civil liberties in Tupelo, Mississippi, Gadsden, Alabama, and Dallas, Texas. In Little Rock, Arkansas, he noted, the Southern Tenant Farmers Union could not find a place to meet, and "anti-union gangsters" terrorized labor organizers in Vicksburg, Mississippi.[28]

Taylor also devoted increased attention to the concerns of African Americans. He was hopeful when reporting that the American Federation of Labor banned discrimination in its affiliates at an "all-south convention held in Atlanta," and he applauded that the race segregation issue was "the major immediate repercussion from the great Conference on Human Welfare" held in Birmingham. But he also reported that within weeks of the Birmingham meeting, a mob of five hundred Georgians "kept up a reign of terror," targeting black homes and schools, demanding that they be allowed to lynch a black youth accused of killing a white WPA worker; in Louisiana an armed mob held police at bay while they shot and burned a black man accused of murdering a white woman and her escort. Despite signs of positive change, Taylor mourned the resurgence of Ku Klux Klan activity in Atlanta and in Greenville, South Carolina.[29]

No one person can capture the essence of the events, policies, and individual choices that were transforming the South. Moreover, Taylor noted the ambiguous legacy of the Depression and New Deal. For each omen of progressive change, readers of his observations could point to signs that the forces of traditionalism and reaction were digging in, preparing to wage a war against liberalism. This dualism even carried over to the president and his wife, Eleanor Roosevelt. Oral histories overwhelmingly demonstrate the affection that most white workers felt for Franklin Roosevelt. They perceived that he was a president who showed compassion for the plight of the common man (in their view the word *common* meant *white*) and pursued policies aimed at ameliorating the hard times of the Depression. But as early as the 1936 election, Howard University political scientist Ralph Bunche commented on the growing disaffection of white southerners toward Mrs. Roosevelt, whom they viewed as too concerned about blacks and racial change. This disaffection only grew following her participation in the Southern Conference for Human Welfare, which many southerners viewed as a leftist group.[30] Certainly, there was a long history of white southerners characterizing any movement attacking Jim Crow as a radical plot, and it seemed during the 1930s that there was plenty of evidence for such a view, ranging from the celebrated Angelo Herndon and Scottsboro cases to internal squabbles within the Southern Tenant Farmers Union. When the SCHW met again in Chattanooga in 1940, Taylor did his best to uncouple that group from charges of Communist domination through such subtitles in his coverage as "young radicals on good behavior," "no radicalism in evidence," and "constructive forces mobilized." It seems unlikely that he convinced many who were certain that the organization harbored outside radicals.[31]

Moreover, despite the goals of federal programs, liberals found little solace in the economic condition of the South. Farm populations continued to decline at a rapid rate, and traditional low-wage industries dominated regional manufacturing, which had virtually stagnated in job growth between 1929 and 1939. Outmigration slowed during the 1930s only because the employment outlook in the North was so bleak. Meanwhile, southern manufacturers claimed that slow job growth in the South was the result of such federal policies as the Fair Labor Standards Act, which raised southern wages, and the National Labor Relations (Wagner) Act, which tried to protect workers' right to join unions. North Carolina Senator Josiah Bailey told the spring 1938 meeting of the Southern States Industrial Council that "the only thing to do in America is to reverse every policy that has tended to put a handicap on business and to put into effect every policy that will encourage American men to go to work and American investors to put their money in enterprise." Bailey singled out the Wagner Act, which he believed had destroyed order and discouraged investment. "You can't expect me to put my money in an enterprise as long as the government is so conducted that lawless men can sit down in that business and not work themselves and not let me work and not let others work." The proper solution, according to Bailey, was to follow the example of the Asheville, North Carolina, mayor who told labor organizers being harassed by a crowd that he would protect them until train time; if they stayed longer, they were on their own.[32]

As Bailey made clear, the economic and political leadership of the South felt itself under siege. Race and class relations in the region seemed destined for major changes, and the walls behind which southern elites sustained their traditional control and separate labor markets were already beginning to crumble. The poll tax, antilynching legislation, wages and hours laws, and government sanctions for labor organizing all threatened to upend the South's regional culture and identity. Even northern capital came in for criticism. Southern States Industrial Council president E. J. McMillan of the Standard Knitting Mills in Knoxville charged that northern employers poisoned the labor-relations atmosphere of the South, leading to "some of our worst unionism troubles." McMillan warned, "We don't want that kind of capital. We don't want that kind of people down here in the South. They don't belong to us. They are not our kind."[33]

Still, there were some businessmen who recognized opportunities in the New Deal. Illinois-based heavy-equipment manufacturer R. G. LeTourneau was as conservative and antistatist as any native southern employer. A devout Fundamentalist who spent millions of dollars in support of evangelical efforts, LeTourneau saw in the South a fertile ground for his business and religious activities. In 1938, in the midst of the ideological battle over the economic future of the South, LeTourneau selected Toccoa Falls, Georgia, for his new branch facility. He found the region's resistance to unions appealing, but he welcomed the presence of the New Deal's National Youth Administration, from which he obtained labor to build an airport for his plant, and TVA, from which he received cheap electricity. Southerners, in turn, decided that LeTourneau was an acceptable sort of northern capitalist. At the revival consecrating LeTourneau's new plant in 1939, Georgia governor Eurith D. Rivers promised, "He's not going to find Communists and sit-down strikes in the south!"[34] World War II would test Rivers's promise.

War on Two Fronts in the South

If Alva Taylor helped us gain perspective on the inconclusive social turmoil generated by the Depression and New Deal in the South, the concerns of another religious figure, Rev. George D. Heaton, can help alert us about the anxieties facing the South during World War II. Heaton was born in 1908 in Parkersburg, West Virginia, but grew up in Louisville. After graduating from Denison University in 1929, he enrolled in the Southern Baptist Theological Seminary in Louisville, graduating in 1931. He did additional postgraduate work at the College of the Bible in Lexington and received his Doctor of Divinity degree from Georgetown College in Kentucky. Throughout the 1930s, Heaton ministered at Southern Baptist churches in Kentucky and Virginia before building a large congregation at Myers Park Baptist Church in Charlotte, North Carolina. Heaton was no ordinary Southern Baptist. One of Heaton's church members in Kentucky—a future minister himself—remembered him as "the best pulpit orator that I've ever heard." Heaton's "approach, insight, commitments, style, and doctrine . . . were quite foreign to anything the young man had ever heard before," and "the first minister [he had] known for whom faith was not a complete drag or burden upon one's life." Heaton was thus something of an iconoclast in the Southern Baptist Church.[35]

Disturbed by growing labor conflict in the 1930s, however, Heaton began offering training classes for foremen and managers on how to increase productivity, win worker loyalty, and create a new industrial order by cultivating Christian leadership.[36] In 1939, he made his first appearance at the Blue Ridge Conference on Southern Industrial Relations. Thereafter, he began serving as the minister to the Southern Industrial Relations Conference, where he nurtured contacts with southern employers and began consulting on industrial relations. The topics of his popular addresses at Blue Ridge testify to the challenges posed by the wartime transformation of the South's economy, society, and politics. In the war years, Heaton spoke on "Creative Living in a Disintegrating Society," "Crisis in Industry," and "The Challenge to Modern Management." As early as 1944, Heaton dared "to suggest that one of the greatest contributions to American Industry in the years to come will be the throwing overboard of the fetish of collective bargaining," which he thought was fundamentally divisive and un-Christian.[37]

Heaton had his fingers on the pulse of an important segment of southern society, but the upheaval he captured in the titles of his Blue Ridge Conference speeches shook the outlooks of all strata of southern society. Perhaps no wartime change affected the South as much as the movement of people. Military service opened up the outside world for many southerners. For some ex-servicemen the experience of war was transformative. They returned with new attitudes about the rights of working people and a desire to change the South. Even the larger numbers of white veterans whose basic beliefs were not shattered came back with new expectations about community involvement, good government, and how to create brighter economic futures.[38] Moreover, those who stayed behind did not stay at home. Men and women began leaving the countryside before the war began. Between 1940 and 1945, a total of 1.6 million people left Dixie, while three times that many migrated within the region. For the first time, blacks living in urban areas outnumbered those in the countryside. It is no wonder that historian Pete Daniel describes the postwar southern experience as "going among strangers."[39]

Agricultural areas dealt with the losing end of these population movements. Texas planters alone lost one hundred thousand agricultural workers in 1942, following losses of thirty-four thousand the previous year. African Americans especially took advantage of new opportunities provided by war industries, leading one Mississippi cotton cooperative general manager to assert: "Our Negroes have moved away. I don't think they will come back unless forced by necessity." After years of effectively preventing the recruitment of their farm labor, planters were powerless to prevent the flight, which was in some cases compounded by the fact that defense industries had the power to expropriate rural farmland for new plant complexes. The powerful southern lobby in Congress had to use all of its muscle to maintain control over agricultural policy for their constituents, eventually winning federal support prices on basic commodities and deferrals from the draft for farm laborers. But the changes were irreversible; southern planters used the wartime migration to shift permanently to machinery and reduce its labor demand.[40]

At the other end, the war years dissolved the stagnation that had limited the expansion of southern industrial employment during the Depression. Southern manufacturing added eight hundred thousand new industrial jobs between 1940 and 1945, setting the stage for a postwar economic transformation. By 1950, the share of the southern labor force in agriculture dropped from nearly 35 percent to less than 24 percent.[41] Significantly, blacks gained industrial work at a disproportionate rate; by 1944, at least 1.25 million African Americans were doing industrial work, two and one-half times the number of black industrial workers in 1940. Many of these industrial jobs were in the South. The twin efforts of private recruiters and the federal War Manpower Commission decimated the tightly controlled agricultural labor force, much to the dismay of planters and powerful southern politicians.[42]

Federal defense contracts did what New Deal programs never could: they added to the industrial base, creating boomtowns and adding not only to existing southern industries but spurring a more diversified profile. Southern manufacturing employment rose from 1.66 million before the war to 2.84 million in November 1943. Higher-wage jobs in the manufacture of ordnance, ships, transportation equipment, and chemicals made up a larger share of the southern economy, while textiles, lumber, and food industries saw their share decline. In many respects, the war years triggered what some historians have called the "second wave" of southern industrialization. Examples include such places as Marietta, Georgia, which began building airplanes, and the expansion of the petrochemical industry along the Gulf Coast of Texas.[43]

These new or revitalized southern plants demanded new housing construction and welfare services, which in turn meant increased state and federal planning, something that many southern politicians stymied. By the middle of the war, the conditions in many Gulf Coast shipbuilding towns, like Mobile, Alabama, and Pascagoula, Mississippi, shocked reporters who wrote of the "rows of tents, trailers, and shacks inhabited by migrant families from the hinterland." Similarly, new ordnance plants from Radford, Virginia, to Texarkana, Texas, severely tested the ability and willingness of southern communities to tackle the infrastructure needs that accompanied such sudden growth.[44] Somewhat ironically, at the same time as booming towns built makeshift housing for new workers, the textile industry was beginning to dismantle its mill village system and sell the company-owned housing that had given mill owners a particular type of control over its workforce.[45]

Businessmen worried that defense mobilization, as it had in World War I, might create special ties between workers and government. The construction boom and new job opportunities that followed defense plant locations strained relations between low-wage rural industries and rural workers. Meanwhile, rapidly industrializing areas of the South had some difficulty in taking advantage of the South's reputation as a region of surplus labor supply because it needed more highly skilled workers, many of whom migrated to the South from other regions. The resulting dislocations put pressure on the federally affiliated State

Employment Services, the Farm Security Administration, and eventually the War Manpower Commission to assume mounting responsibilities for managing employment and services for the South's mobile labor force. This created a dilemma for southern politicians already unhappy with the Roosevelt administration for its expansion of authority. Even more agitated were the members of the Southern States Industrial Council (SSIC), whose board of directors proclaimed that "as a result of these Federal policies, the future of the free enterprise system itself is now gravely jeopardized," and "Southern industry's most urgent duty to itself, the South, and the nation is to resist—with every resource at its command—the existing trend towards some form of state socialism." This proclamation came just a day after the Pearl Harbor attack.[46]

America's entry into the war afforded the federal government even wider latitude on issues of vital importance to southern elites. The SSIC protested against the forty-hour workweek, government-guaranteed union maintenance provisions, union racketeering, and the government's role in manpower utilization. Between 1939 and 1942, competition was so fierce for labor as a result of a 50 percent increase in manufacturing employment that wages had climbed by 40 percent, in most cases surpassing the forty-cent-per-hour minimum wage even before the Fair Labor Standards Act target date. To pour salt on the wounds of southern employers anxious to maintain nonunion, low-wage advantages, the National War Labor Board used Frank Porter Graham, president of the Southern Conference for Human Welfare and member of the group that prepared the controversial *Report on the Economic Conditions of the South*, to serve as the primary liaison between Washington and the Labor Board's southern regional panels.[47]

In a time of labor shortage and with a War Labor Board sympathetic to facilitating unions' inroads against the low wages of the South, the American Federation of Labor and the Congress of Industrial Organizations made significant wartime gains in such diverse settings as Birmingham, Alabama, and Fort Worth, Texas. Building upon small achievements in the late New Deal era, meatpackers finally scored major victories in the large Armour and Swift plants in Fort Worth, but only after the National Defense Mediation Board compelled Armour to surrender and sign a national agreement with the Packinghouse Workers Organizing Committee (CIO). Similarly, in Alabama and Tennessee, steelworkers and ore miners, benefiting from the 1937 agreement that U.S. Steel signed with the Steel Workers Organizing Committee (CIO), won a December 1942 National Labor Relations Board election that finally gave the local unions at Tennessee Coal and Iron (a U.S. Steel subsidiary) plants exclusive bargaining power. Neither victory came without a fight that included attempts by the companies to divide workers along racial lines and efforts to mobilize public opinion and rival unions against the CIO.[48]

Unions established strong representation in the steel, pulp and paper, rubber, petroleum, and telecommunications industries during the war. Industrial union membership in the South nearly tripled from 1939 to 1953, much of which occurred during the war. In tobacco, for instance, the Tobacco Workers International Union, affiliated with the American Federation of Labor, added to gains begun during the New Deal, particularly once the U.S. Supreme Court validated the legality of the Wagner Act. During the war years, the CIO's United Cannery, Agricultural, Packing, and Allied Workers, a forerunner of the Food, Tobacco, and Allied Workers and a pioneer of industrial union organizing in the South, astounded observers by building a strong interracial union in Winston-Salem, North Carolina, and bringing the powerful R. J. Reynolds Company to the bargaining table. Together, the two unions represented nearly 90 percent of the workers producing cigarettes, chewing and smoking tobacco, and snuff.[49]

While Rev. Heaton wanted to dismiss collective bargaining as a "fetish" to the Southern Industrial Relations conference in 1944, workers clearly did not share his enmity. In a number of cities throughout the region, unions overcame the most intransigent employers and every weapon they had at their disposal to vote for unions and negotiate contracts. In Gadsden, Alabama, for instance, city leaders had counted on a strong probusiness climate not only to retain the town's iron furnaces and railroad shops but also to recruit new factories, such as the Dwight Manufacturing Company (textiles), the Gulf States Steel Company, and finally, a plant of the Goodyear Tire and Rubber Company. In 1937, *The Nation* magazine called Gadsden one of the "toughest" antilabor cities in the country. Despite using every bit of the anti-union toolkit, from anticommunist rhetoric to racial divisions to paternalistic religion, Gadsden employers could not forestall unionism. In 1943, locals of the United Steelworkers of America, the Textile Workers Union of America, and the United Rubber Workers organized the three largest employers and turned Gadsden into a model union city that the CIO used as an example of what organized labor could do for virtually all aspects of what makes life good in a community.[50] Memphis workers enjoyed a similar turnaround for labor during World War II. In a city led by one of the most ruthless antilabor political bosses, Edward H. Crump, no union organizer was safe from violence during the Depression. CIO organizer Lucy Randolph Mason, descendant of a prominent Virginia family dating from the American Revolution, wrote that in Memphis, business and political leaders used the Ku Klux Klan and the local media to create "a hysterical campaign" against union activists. By 1945, however, the Memphis CIO represented 32,500 workers at 117 different plants in the city. Unions there looked toward the postwar economic reconstruction with considerable optimism.[51]

The Memphis story, however, also points to an Achilles' heel in labor's wartime program—that is, that race in large part determined the benefits to be gained by workers in the chaotic wartime mobilization. Discrimination against African Americans in regional war production led to a massive outmigration of blacks. Net migration losses of blacks from the South tripled during the 1940s. The larger numbers who remained fought for access to jobs and job training opportunities that would enable blacks to move out of the low-wage occupations to which the Jim Crow South had relegated them. As had been the case for many New Deal programs, most federal administrators worried about antagonizing southerners and disrupting production by implementing measures that would give African Americans the same chances given to whites. Individuals who directed the most relevant agencies, the War Manpower Commission and the War Production Board, were military procurement agency representatives, local industrialists, and leaders chosen from labor organizations. Their concerns focused primarily on the war effort, and they rejected any suggestions that they use wartime exigencies to promote liberal social reforms. Historian Charles Chamberlain notes that conservatives on the WMC's southern regional boards were often "the greatest source of resistance" to fair employment efforts.[52]

Protest from national racial organizations and the threat of A. Philip Randolph's March on Washington movement forced President Roosevelt to issue an executive order to create the Fair Employment Practices Committee, which provided a tool for workers and civil rights activists to mobilize for fair employment, but with mixed results. If this was a "seedtime for the modern Civil Rights Movement," it was a slowly developing one, especially in the South. Indeed, even the left-leaning Southern Conference for Human Welfare sublimated civil rights for an emphasis on winning the war and promoting the unionization of workers. The Southern Conference did not oppose AFL or CIO practices that segregated union meetings and kept discriminatory job classification systems and racial wage differentials in place.[53]

Organized labor, particularly the national CIO, proclaimed loudly for fair employment practices, but the record on the ground demonstrated that southern locals and their members were more interested in winning contracts than changing Jim Crow practices or the attitudes of their white membership. Although the most famous hate strike of white unionists against the upgrading of black workers occurred in Detroit in 1943, the South experienced riots in Mobile, Alabama, and Beaumont, Texas, when the FEPC tried to force shipbuilding companies to upgrade black workers. In Mobile, white shipbuilders assaulted and injured some fifty blacks; in Beaumont, rioting whites not only targeted shipyard workers but also destroyed parts of the city's black ghetto.[54] In Danville, Virginia, white cotton-mill workers walked out for nearly two weeks in June 1944 when the Dan River Mills tried to place black women in the formerly all-white spinning department. Textile Workers Union of America regional director Boyd Payton tried to solve the case by asking the company to set up a separate mill department staffed entirely by blacks, but the company claimed that was impractical. Payton then agreed to the dismissal of the black spinners, causing the local chapter of the National Association for the Advancement of Colored People (NAACP) to become involved. Eventually, the CIO sent George L. Weaver, director of the organization's Committee to Abolish Racial Discrimination, to investigate and make recommendations, which ultimately led to the merger of separate black and white union locals in Danville and the end of the discriminatory policy. Meanwhile, the unions affiliated with the AFL moved at an even more glacial pace, led by the notoriously racist International Brotherhood of Boilermakers, which controlled access to 1.5 million jobs and resisted any semblance of racial equality in its unions.[55]

In all too few of the cases involving white resistance to fair employment practices did blacks achieve successful outcomes. By the end of the war, business groups like the Southern States Industrial Council felt fairly confident in their ability to prevent the federal government from making the FEPC a permanent fixture through legislation. The council announced that the "outlook is that Southern filibuster will succeed and this bill [the FEPC] will be put aside for the time being." Employers counted on the idea, nurtured during episodes of resistance to fair employment practices during the war, that race would continue to be a major stumbling block for any new campaign to spread unionism in the South. They could also use the specter of changing race relations to specifically target new efforts by the CIO.[56]

Unions had nonetheless already achieved significant growth in the South, masking the barriers to future growth. When Duke University labor economist Frank T. de Vyver surveyed southern unions in 1948, he noted remarkable gains over the previous decade. Starting from a base of between 450,000 to 500,000 in 1938, union expansion in the South had exceeded the national growth rate. Six unions each had more than 40,000 members in the region and fifteen had more than 15,000, up from only seven a decade earlier. The United Brotherhood of Carpenters and Joiners, the CIO-affiliated Textile Workers, and the United Mine Workers each had close to 90,000 southern members. Moreover, de Vyver's numbers did not include several important unions (the Teamsters and both longshoremen unions) in his survey. Still, it was also true that southern unions had made little headway among the vast majority of textile workers (especially in the huge mill complexes like Kannapolis, North Carolina) or the equally vast timber and food-processing industries. Together, these three industrial sectors accounted for more than four of every nine southern manufacturing jobs. Furthermore, the durability of many of the union agreements negotiated under wartime conditions were untested.[57]

Equally undetermined was the political impact of the enormous changes caused by the war. Liberals believed they saw signs that the bulwarks of the old political order were crumbling. Twice, the U.S. House of Representatives passed legislation eliminating the poll tax, only to be stymied by a southern filibuster in the U.S. Senate, and the U.S. Supreme Court ruled the Democratic white primary unconstitutional in *Smith v. Allwright* (1944). Moreover, despite the SSIC's confidence, a fight loomed over a permanent Fair Employment Practices

Aerial view of the booming textile mill town of Kannapolis, North Carolina, in the 1940s. Courtesy of the Kannapolis History Associates.

bill. Liberals were also hopeful that returning servicemen and war industries workers who had experienced more of the world would demand that the South become more progressive in their politics and their vision for the economy. Two veterans from Mississippi, Frank Smith and Claude Ramsay, found that the war had changed their outlooks on a number of issues, including race relations and southern politics. Smith went on to serve in Congress as a rare progressive from the Delta, while Ramsay rose to leadership of his local union at International Paper Company and eventually to the presidency of the Mississippi AFL-CIO. Black and white veterans in Georgia likewise returned from the war insisting upon racial, economic, and political reform, including repeal of the state's poll tax and an adjustment of its county-unit election system that favored conservative rural counties. The possibilities appeared limitless.[58]

Those possibilities, however, unified conservative southern politicians. During the war years, southern Democrats increasingly voted with the Republicans; by 1944 they were closer ideologically to the GOP than to their own party. Although the southern bloc did not have enough clout to nominate a candidate other than Roosevelt for president, they did succeed in ousting Henry A. Wallace as Roosevelt's running mate. Equally important, the South was gaining power within the Democratic Party's Congressional delegation. Southerners controlled key committee posts as a result of their seniority, and they made up a growing percentage of Democrats in Congress, widening their veto power over social policy. Conservative reaction filtered down to the state level as well, evidenced by the ability of anti-union coalitions to win referenda on new right-to-work laws in 1944. In Arkansas and Florida, voters chose to eliminate closed-shop union agreements—laws that proved to be forerunners of the federal Taft-Hartley Act of 1947.[59]

Clearly, the South's transformation during the Depression and World War II set the stage for a decade of political turmoil. Conservatives and liberals alike anticipated vigorous contests in the immediate future. Observers expected that the outcome of the region's political, racial, and social instability might rest in the hands of the region's working class, particularly if southern workers joined unions promoting a progressive agenda. The question for many: How did workers interpret the part played by unions in providing a solution to the upheaval stirred by a decade of change? CIO organizer Lucy Mason told workers that unions promised "strength to help and lift yourselves and those you love, strength to help make this city . . . a better place in which to live, strength to help make our nation safe for human liberty and progress and security." E. J. McMillan, president of the SSIC, had a different message. To him, unions permitted "labor bosses to put the individual worker under a system of enforced servitude."[60]

Whether workers believed Mason or McMillan often depended on their own experiences over the preceding decade. In the Carolina Piedmont region, for example, where textile, furniture, and timber companies had battered unions and carefully managed government interference, working people seemed indifferent to unions. CIO organizer Scott Hoyman recalled the impact of the failed 1934 strike on textile workers: "Oh God. They remembered it in the organized plants, but they really remember it in the unorganized plants." These workers were also grappling with the decline of the mill village, uncertainty about whether they would face a racially integrated shop floor, new intensified work regimens, challenges from more politically assertive blacks, and communities drastically reshaped by wartime migrations, military installations, and government regulations.[61] What had unions done for them, and how might they deal with these issues?

In Birmingham, Alabama, however, where unions had far more success, ore miner Jesse Grace remembered that "when they got the union in, see, that brought the wages and hours, shorter hours and things." The union even gave them "a chance to eat lunch." There, organized labor produced also nonmaterial benefits; in 1944 the AFL and the CIO cooperated with the NAACP on a voter registration drive, buoyed by the security and confidence that union contracts provided. International Ladies Garment Workers Union activist Maida Springer believed that working-class gains enabled "a virtual revolution in Negro leadership." For white workers there, these developments, and the role of labor in them, elicited both positive and negative feelings, a condition that increased racial tensions in the Birmingham labor movement even as their bargaining position improved.[62]

Ministers like Alva Taylor and George Heaton wondered what toll the Depression and war had taken on the South's spiritual makeup. Heaton worried about a new industrial relations system that to him appeared to be built on conflict and opposition. In 1947, he told the Blue Ridge Conference on Human Relations in Industry, "You cannot build good human relationships upon animosity, upon belligerency, upon the spirit of enmity between groups. I think the most unfortunate thing that has happened to us in the South in recent years has been that men have been taught to hate each other."[63] For Taylor, labor's struggle for "a living wage and the right to bargain" was "the greatest effort in human history to emancipate man from poverty" and create "the good society, i.e., the Kingdom of God." He was certain that only with the "ethics of Biblical religion" could society achieve that goal. "Jesus prophesied," Taylor wrote, "that if the church was built upon the solid rock of His teachings, the gates of hell could not prevail against it." These "social ideals" of Christianity could remake the South, he believed, but as yet "they have not percolated down to the rank and file in the pew."[64]

As is evident from the visions of Heaton and Taylor, religion, like the economy, politics, and labor relations of the South, was a contested terrain during the Depression and World War II. Hard times, uprooted families and communities, new ways of making a living, the anxieties and dreams of fresh possibilities, and the horrors of combat and inhumanity forced many to reevaluate their basic beliefs. In the South this posed a challenge for the evangelical Protestant denominations that were the bedrock of the religious culture there. In such a world turned upside down, the churches could hardly remain stagnant. The ways they responded helped shape the reactions of southerners to the changes all had witnessed.

CHAPTER 2

Unrest in Zion

Southern Churches in Depression and War

The Depression shaped forever Anne Queen's outlook on life. After losing her father when she was nine, Anne, her mother, and two sisters moved in with her grandfather in the hills of western North Carolina, where they managed to make ends meet through the 1920s. Although neither her grandfather nor her mother had much formal education, they were both avid readers, and they insisted that the girls finish high school even though they could not afford to send them to college. In 1930, Anne Queen graduated and began work as a paper cutter at Champion Paper and Fibre Company. The company was "very much a family institution," Queen remembered, but that did not mean the working conditions were attractive; Queen worked nine-hour days for fourteen cents an hour. Like many workers, she fondly recalled the day she learned that the National Recovery Act had passed and that she would soon earn forty cents per hour and work a maximum of forty hours per week: "This is why I am a New Deal Democrat and it is why I admired the Roosevelts." These experiences shaped more than her politics. She grew up in the fist Spring Hill Baptist Church, "baptized in a pond." In her twenties, however, Queen began to feel that "the church had no social message." In 1940, she finally got the chance to go to college at Berea in Kentucky. Founded in 1855 as the first interracial and coeducational institution in the South, Berea still pursued its mission to educate underprivileged Appalachians and promote inclusion. While there, Anne Queen's religious views opened. She read books by the Social Gospel Baptist Walter Rauschenbusch and was introduced to Christian activists like Howard Kester and the prophetic radicals in the Fellowship of Southern Churchmen. Her world was never the same.[1]

Mary Thompson experienced a different sort of upheaval in her spiritual outlook. She grew up in a strict, Hardshell Baptist (that is, conservative and Calvinistic) family that forbade dancing, smoking, and drinking, and made the church the center of their social life. She lived a childhood like many other mill children—homemade clothes, tending the garden or milking the family cow before school, and minding her younger siblings. School in the mill villages reinforced the religious culture she learned from her mother; teachers led prayer and devotion before school began and used Bible stories to teach "what's right and wrong." At fifteen, Thompson was married, but by eighteen she was divorced with a child. As soon as she weaned her daughter she went to work at the Poe mill in Greenville, hiring an African American woman to watch the child during the day for two dollars a week. Thompson quickly advanced to pattern maker, taking jobs at a variety of mills in the Carolinas and Virginia during the Depression years, often leaving her daughter with her mother and seeing her only on weekends. Like Anne Queen, Mary Thompson had positive memories of Franklin Roosevelt and the changes in working conditions his administration ushered in, even though at the time she thought that working only eight hours for what amounted to ten hours' pay "was the dumbest thing I ever heard tell of." Eventually, Mary settled in a mill village near Charlotte, North Carolina, in 1939, where she met her second husband, Carl Thompson, also a child of strict Baptist millworkers.[2]

Carl and Mary Thompson experienced many of the same things that led Anne Queen to the Social Gospel and a long association with liberal, prophetic, Protestant organizations. But the Thompsons never left the Fundamentalist, Bible-believing churches of their upbringing. Mary believed that "the Lord is all we are," and, as she said, "If I do things wrong, I know that I can always come back to Him." For Carl, his religious conversion experience was etched into his memory. He remembered going to a church revival and for two nights refusing to "give an account of my sins and be saved." On the third night he heard the calling: "I just went right on up there and fell down on my knees right in front of the church, and I started praying." He then stood and wiped the tears from his eyes and said: "Thank the Lord. I am saved. All my sins has been forgiven, and I've let Christ come into my heart tonight. I'm a different creature than what I was whenever I come in here." Although they remained Baptists, the Thompsons lent aid to a religious upheaval in their mill village, helping support Holiness tent revivals and the Pentecostal Holiness Church that drew increasing numbers of millworkers to a new expression of working-class spirituality. They never left their church, but they enjoyed the Pentecostal meetings: "They would shout and all. They had wonderful singing, and it done me good to go," Mary recounted.[3]

The Thompsons and Anne Queen represent different points on a spectrum of how religious people responded to the hard times of the Great Depression and World War II. As we saw in the previous chapter, dramatic changes swept the South in the 1930s and 1940s and shattered much of what was familiar to southerners. In the movement from country to town and from farm to factory, Dixie's "forgotten people" looked for answers to the chaos in the sacred realm. In some cases that meant finding solace in "traditional morality and the maintenance of a corresponding social order," according to political scientist John C. Green. For "many deeply religious" southern whites, he argues, "opposing sin and supporting Jim Crow were unconsciously bound together," a view which wrestled fiercely against change.[4] But at the same time, southern evangelicalism could inspire improbable discontinuities in politics. Consider, for instance, the ways that the rural-Georgia-born evangelical Don West moved from conservative theology to radical activism and poetry, or how Alabama fundamentalist preacher Fred E. Maxey blended his premillennial dispensationalist beliefs with an ardent defense of the rights of black and white working people in a regular column, "Pulpit in Print," for a local radical newspaper. Clearly, southern spirituality could take on many meanings in the tumult of Depression and world war.[5]

Religious attachments, however, were not static, and social change transformed southern Protestantism in important ways. During the 1930s church membership declined throughout the South as congregations, ministers, and church fellowships struggled with the hard times and the ensuing migrations. Those declines were not uniform; some Protestant churches responded to the material and psychological needs of its members better than others. Meanwhile, within and across denominations and church groups, debates raged about modernity, threats from an expanding government, and signs of the end times. Across the board, however, the experiences of hundreds of thousands of southern white Protestants like Anne Queen and Carl and Mary Thompson forced the region's sacred institutions to reevaluate what they offered to the region's working people. Then, during World War II, southern Protestantism turned again, buoyed by growing church membership and an increased public attention to faith. The war demonstrated for many the inability of humans to build God's kingdom on Earth; for others it signified the imminence of the second coming and the magnitude of individual salvation. To understand why religion played such an important role in the diverse hopes harbored by business, the working class, and the labor movement for a postwar South, it is necessary to survey the tremors that shook the religious landscape during the 1930s and early 1940s.

The Religious Depression in the South

Southern religion in the 1930s was overwhelmingly evangelical Protestant. The three principal denominations—Baptists, Methodists, and Presbyterians—accounted for more than three-fourths of all church members in the South. These included about five of every six in North Carolina, six of every seven in Alabama, and roughly nine-tenths of Georgians who attended church. Only Louisiana and parts of Texas were exceptions in the former Confederacy. Among southern whites, the numerical dominance of the Baptists, Methodists, and Presbyterians was not quite as high, but it was only marginally less than was the case for blacks. While these and the various other churches that could be counted as evangelical had many differences, evangelical religion was one of the pillars of southern identity and culture.[6]

What characteristics did evangelicals share? According to Samuel S. Hill Jr., one of the most distinguished historians of southern religion, there were four basic points of agreement. Evangelicals believed that the Bible is the sole reference point of belief and practice; that direct and dynamic access to the Lord is open to all; that morality is defined in individualistic and personal terms; and that worship is informal. These general traits made white southern churches appear to be old-fashioned and unchanging, a picture of continuity. Followers emphasized the centrality of individual conversion, the significance of God's grace, the importance of upholding strict standards of personal morality, and the necessity of bearing witness. They also placed a high value on their local religious community of neighbors and kin, drawing upon the "old metaphor of a church family."[7] The somewhat contradictory beliefs in the direct and dynamic access to the Lord and the importance of community perhaps accounts for the tendency toward schismatic behavior and the flourishing of new religious fellowships. But the voluntary nature of religious affiliation gave surprising power to one's community of "saints."

The social and demographic upheaval of the Depression provided a severe test of these traditional values, particularly since it followed a decade when Fundamentalist-Modernist divisions had already challenged evangelical Protestantism. In the wake of high-profile displays of controversy like the Scopes trial, influential clergyman Reinhold Niebuhr believed that the forces of religion suffered "a psychology of defeat, of which both fundamentalism and modernism are symptoms." By the early 1930s, religious observers were already writing of an American religious depression. By most measurements (foreign missions, church attendance, rural church life, and so on), mainstream Protestantism's loss of vitality actually began before the economic collapse but then plummeted even more with the hard times of the 1930s.[8] Although flawed, the U.S. Census Bureau's survey of religious bodies provides evidence for these assertions, particularly in the South. The number of churches in the South Atlantic states declined by nearly one-fifth between 1926 and 1936; in Georgia, about one in ten; in South Carolina, more than one of every four. In the eight South Central states, the decline was even greater, more than 23 percent; Texas, Arkansas, Tennessee, and Kentucky each lost more than one-quarter of their churches. The migrations of southerners out of the region and to more urban locations within the South took a terrible toll on rural churches, and this was only partly offset by growth in town and city churches. For the decade, church membership in Virginia dropped by 13.6 percent, in South Carolina by 18.8 percent, and in Kentucky by 13.4 percent. Throughout the former Confederacy, only Texas, Louisiana, and Florida did not experience a decline. Even accounting for underreporting in 1936, there was evidence of a religious depression.[9]

The hard times of the Depression were harder on some churches than others. Race was one factor. In the decade before 1936, the churches of the white Southern Baptist Convention lost 820,000 (or 23.5 percent) to fall below the number of members the convention had in 1916. Meanwhile, black Baptist churches gained more than 500,000 (18.3 percent). The white Methodist Episcopal Church, South, lost 420,000 members (17.1 percent), while black Methodists increased their numbers, but not at the same rate as the Baptists. Despite these somewhat better statistics, a crisis mentality emerged in black churches, which, like the black population, were more likely to be rural.[10] Denomination mattered as well; the Churches of Christ lost more than 85,000, and the Disciples of Christ lost about 75,000 southern members. Others experienced greater stability; Baptist fellowships, the Free Will Baptists, and the Primitive Baptists lost relatively far fewer members, and the white southern Presbyterian Church in the United States lost only 2,000 members out of a total of 450,000. Certain types of churches showed significant gains; Pentecostal and Holiness churches—the Church of God and the Church of the Nazarene—doubled their memberships. Some of these newer churches owed much to African-American Christianity and harbored interracial congregations, even in the South.[11]

The religious depression reshuffled the spiritual makeup of the South. Some of this reshuffling had begun earlier, complicating the idea that religion helped sustain a united and "solid South." The first quarter of the twentieth century witnessed scores of new churches protesting dominance by the southern mainstream denominations. With names like Assemblies of God, Pentecostal Holiness, Churches of God, Pillar of Fire, and many others, they captured the sacred energies of the poor, and these churches were the fastest growing churches in the region. Emerging first from the Holiness movement that developed within the Methodist churches as a reaction against the influence of modernism, these new churches rejected liberal, intellectual, and socially oriented religion to focus on the saving grace of the Lord. They adopted such doctrines as faith healing; puritanical dress codes; bans on gambling, liquor, dancing, and movies; and the premillennial second coming of Christ. For them, there were no boundaries separating the invisible world from the visible one; Satan was not only palpably real but also everywhere present. Charismatic churches were part of a religious subculture that emphasized "the old-time religion," especially for the region's poor. A second infusion of charismatic religious activity came from the influence of Pentecostalism, which led to additional splits within these churches over such theological and doctrinal issues as speaking in tongues, sanctification, and Trinitarianism. The South provided an ideal mix of factors for Pentecostalism to sink deep roots and transform both the white and black spiritual landscape.[12]

These charismatic churches gave the South a sectarian religious character that interjected social class more firmly into the sacred realm. Holiness and Pentecostal churches altered both the geography and the class composition of sacred institutions. The Assemblies of God spread through Missouri, Arkansas, Oklahoma, and Texas; the Pentecostal Holiness Church in Georgia and Oklahoma; and the Church of God in Tennessee, the Carolinas, and Georgia. The connection to social class was also evident. Consider the Church of God, for instance. This church doubled its membership between 1926 and 1936; 78 percent of Church of God members in Kentucky and 80 percent in West Virginia were in the coalfields. Granny Hager, the daughter and wife of coal miners in Harlan and Leslie Counties, Kentucky, recalled the transformation of religion in the coalfields: "The Baptist Church was [the biggest] to start with, but eventually the Holiness took over and they just about run all the Baptist Churches out." Clergyman and author Liston Pope found a similar makeover in the mill villages of North Carolina. These new churches spoke to a poor people's religion that preferred a plain style and association with marginal whites rather than the affluent. This poor, white religion was less bound by the conventions of southern mainstream churches with regard to race and gender, which at times could sow the seeds of protest and social justice activism. But at other times congregants in these churches transformed their poverty into a blessing because it saved them from worldly concerns that would have turned them from God.[13]

Charismatic churches were not the only ones that turned to old-time religion in the face of social change. Restorationist denominations, such as the Disciples of Christ, the Church of Christ, and various Baptist splinter groups, also clung to a more primitive Christianity that aimed to restore the form and structure of the original church. Many of these churches rejected hierarchies and insisted on the autonomy of individual congregations, some led by lay preachers without formal training. They often could be dogmatic, anti-intellectual, and intolerant. In the southern Appalachian region, only one-third of ministers had completed high school; only one in five had any seminary training; and more than half had other occupations. Luther Addington, who grew up in Wise, Virginia, spoke of his memories of the constant splintering of churches in his youth due to arguments over predestination or supporting missionary work, but that his Old Regular Baptist church also took care of "misdemeanors in the community" by exiling sinners. Moreover, these old-time churches encouraged a style of worship that the popular culture associates with southern "holy rollers"—it typically involved preaching, praying, and often ecstatic "testifying." These churches followed rituals like foot washing, and their services involved spontaneity and emotion.[14]

Hard times brought to the surface a popular folk religion in the mainline southern denominations as well. Churches in the Southern Baptist Convention (SBC), for example, struggled to deal with impoverished congregations, especially in rural parts of the South. Baptist polity had always allowed individual congregations a great deal of autonomy. In the 1920s, surveys discovered that seven-eighths of Southern Baptist churches were rural congregations, containing over two-thirds of SBC members. These congregations had little to do with denominational structure; only one of every eight sent a representative to the annual convention meeting, and only one of seven sent delegates to state conventions. Furthermore, three-fourths of the rural ministers had no seminary training; their churches often met just once a month.[15] Such autonomy from denominational authority (which was relatively weak anyway) gave Southern Baptists a great deal of latitude on doctrinal issues and worship practices.

Hocutt Memorial Baptist Church, 1930s. Courtesy of the Southern Historical Collections, University of North Carolina at Chapel Hill.

The depths of despair that came with the Depression elicited quite varied responses from Baptist preachers. The letters written by Alabama Baptist ministers describing the Depression in response to an inquiry from the Roosevelt administration show both material and spiritual effects. One rural tenant farmer and part-time preacher near Dothan believed that the hard times were a sign that the world would soon end, but another was more hopeful that the Democratic Party had "rescued the people." Still another struggling rural minister expressed disappointment with politics: "The poor or landless man, wage earners and sharecroppers in the rural districts are nothing but slaves for the big land holders. The big landlords like the 'New Deal' because they collect big cash rentals from the government and refuse to divide it with their tenants. They also work poor men on their farms for wages that are ridiculously low." Equally devastating assessments came from urban Alabama Baptist preachers. One worried that his congregations were confused, demoralized, suspicious of their neighbors, and without hope in government or God. Another, who ministered to a Birmingham congregation, pleaded with the federal government to help his starving families: "Like Lazarus at the rich man's gate this Depression has laid the poor at Uncle Sam's gate."[16]

As the Depression sliced the numbers of Baptist congregations and members, it also triggered spasms of change. Critiques followed contradictory paths. On one side, flamboyant fundamentalist J. Frank Norris kept up a steady barrage of criticism of the SBC for financial mismanagement, of the threats that convention authority posed to the independence of local congregations, and of the willingness of the SBC to work cooperatively with other denominations, positions he frequently outlined in shrill tones in his newspaper, *The Fundamentalist*. At the other end of the spectrum Baptist clergymen troubled by the nation's economic collapse, men like L. L. Gwaltney, editor of the *Alabama Baptist*, and Acker C. Miller, head of the Texas Baptist Social Service Commission, drew upon Social Gospel ideas. In 1938, the Southern Baptists' annual meeting endorsed legislation prohibiting child labor and passed a resolution recognizing "the right of labor to organize and to engage in collective bargaining to the end that labor may have a fair and living wage."[17]

Neither of these developments garnered large followings among Southern Baptists, since most ministers struggled to keep their congregations together and members were untouched by denominational debates. However, even during a time of economic crisis, congregations found time to debate theology, fight over biblical interpretations, and fire pastors who strayed too far from the beliefs of the aggressive individuals who dominated local churches. Sara Lowrey recalled an incident when more than fourteen hundred infuriated Fundamentalists marched to the Baptist-affiliated Baylor University to take issue with the teachings of her father, William Tyndale Lowrey, and several of his colleagues. The mob even put a rope around the throat of one particularly heretical student. In Jonesboro, Arkansas, the mayor telegraphed Governor Harvey Parnell, asking him to declare martial law when fistfights broke out between two warring factions of the First Baptist Church, caused by preachings of an end-of-the-world Fundamentalist, Joe Jeffers. The church in Anniston, Alabama, likewise slowly turned its back on its minister, Charles R. Bell Jr., after he criticized the SBC's social service commission for offering the use of tobacco as a major problem in its 1937 report when "all around us was a nation weakened by poverty, ridden by segregation," and drifting toward world war. Although some Baptist preachers spoke out against economic and even racial injustices during the Depression, other ministers and their congregations saw theological liberalism as heresy.[18]

Fundamentalism, far from being destroyed by the famous Scopes trial condemning the teaching of evolution in Tennessee, resurfaced as a more salient factor in the 1930s. Fundamentalists retrenched in a growing number of Bible colleges and institutes, Fundamentalist seminaries, radio programs, and itinerant revivalists. The most urgency behind Fundamentalism in the 1920s and early 1930s was in the North, where modernism, Catholicism, and secularism posed the greatest threats to mainline Protestantism. However, as social and economic changes that came with the Depression unsettled the South and the specifically southern denominations, Fundamentalism began to spread more rapidly there.

During the 1930s, Fundamentalism's center of gravity migrated decisively from the North to the South.[19] The shift began in the 1920s with itinerant revivals through the South headlined by preachers like George Guille, William Bell Riley, and Joe Jeffers. Their efforts led to a host of interdenominational institutions in the region, such as the Dallas Bible Institute, the Toccoa Falls (Georgia) Institute, the Southeastern Bible Institute, and Columbia (South Carolina) Bible College, aimed at training a new generation of Fundamentalist ministers for southern churches. They discovered a region where the cultural values worked hand in hand with a conservative understanding of Christianity.[20]

While Fundamentalism's impact on the Southern Baptists was minimal in the 1930s, it carried far more weight in the southern Presbyterian Church in the United States, where products of the interdenominational Fundamentalist schools formed a major faction. Fundamentalist-trained ministers like William P. Jones, a graduate of Dallas Theological Seminary in 1936 and minister of the large Westminster Presbyterian Church in Greensboro, North Carolina, thwarted the authority of southern Presbyterians by refusing to use denominational Sunday school literature, diverting money from Presbyterian missions to independent missionaries, and sending Westminster's children to non-Presbyterian summer youth camps. Ultimately, a special commission of the denomination recommended Jones's removal from Westminster, but Jones responded by splitting the congregation and starting an independent church. During the 1930s, the Presbyterians went from a denomination in which moderate church leaders fought off efforts of Fundamentalists to infiltrate the church to a denomination in which mobilized theological conservatives successfully blocked any attempts to liberalize church doctrine or traditions.[21]

What made Fundamentalism so much more explosive within southern churches in the 1930s was the infusion of dispensationalism. The product of nineteenth-century former Anglican priest John Nelson Darby, who subsequently founded the pietistic group called the Plymouth Brethren, dispensationalists believed that history could be divided into ages (dispensations) and that God dealt differently with humans in each age. The most important outgrowth of dispensationalism was that it viewed the present dispensation as the last before the imminent and premillennial return of Jesus. As a result, it was critical for true believers to separate themselves from nonbelievers in anticipation of the Rapture, which could come at any time. The Rapture would save believers and leave behind the nonbelievers who would face the judgment and the wrath of God. For the growing number of those who came to believe in dispensational premillennialism in the 1930s, the Depression and other world developments were signs of the end times and that Jesus's return was looming.[22]

For some premillennialists, President Roosevelt's New Deal appeared to be linked to other signs forecasting their anticipation of the coming global apocalypse. Interpreting a series of international crises through the filters of biblical prophesy, many influential Fundamentalists believed that the rise of Mussolini in Italy, with his plans to rebuild Rome, and Hitler's anti-Semitism in Germany, which was interpreted as part of God's plan to drive Jews to Palestine, were both preconditions for Christ's imminent return. To premillennial Fundamentalists, Roosevelt's New Deal also fit into this vision of impending doom. The president's charisma, his consolidation of power, his willingness to expand the power of the state, and his internationalism all were evidence of the growing power of the Antichrist in the minds of radio preachers like Charles Fuller of the nationally broadcast *Old-Fashioned Revival Hour* and itinerant revivalists such as William Bell Riley; as well, such matters were fodder for a range of prophetic Fundamentalist publications, including *Prophecy Monthly*, *Sword of the Lord*, and J. Frank Norris's *Fundamentalist*.[23]

Prophets of the coming end times, although fortified by newspapers, radio programs, and popular tent gatherings, confronted followers of folk religion who welcomed assistance from the New Deal. It is impossible to listen to the oral histories of working-class whites in a variety of settings and not come away impressed with the admiration that many deeply religious people had for President Roosevelt. Henry Wade, who sang in the choir at the Baptist church, was a young worker at Crown Mills in Dalton, Georgia, during the Depression. He recalled the passage of the Fair Labor Standards Act giving him an eight-hour workday as the "greatest day in my life" and the "reason I've always been a Democrat." Martin Lowe, who gravitated from the very strict Primitive Baptists of his Tennessee childhood to an equally strict Holiness Pentecostal Assembly of God congregation in South Carolina, also abandoned the Republican party of his upbringing for the New Deal. Lowe "voted for Roosevelt every time he run for President," because the president helped working people during the most dire times. Similarly, Ila Hendrix, wife of an Alabama coal miner and a devout member of the Nazarene Church, was always a Democrat because of Roosevelt's New Deal.[24] Perhaps the most interesting testimony was from Martha Atha from Beckley, West Virginia. Atha was the sixth of fourteen children, born in 1921. Her father was a carpenter and lay minister in a Pentecostal church in the coalfields, and despite struggling with a large family during the Depression, "did not believe in taking welfare," she said: "The Lord had promised to provide for him and his family." If ever there was an individual who should have been religiously predisposed to rejecting the New Deal, it was Martha Atha. But she had positive memories of Roosevelt and the programs he implemented, crediting them for helping things "get better."[25]

One wonders how working people who felt positive about their experiences with New Deal programs reconciled those feelings with the messages that they heard from popular radio preachers like J. Harold Smith, who railed against both alcohol and New Deal liberal reforms during his broadcasts from Greenville, South Carolina. Some undoubtedly focused their animosity on the president's wife, Eleanor, and blamed her for what they saw as unwelcome federal intrusions into the "traditional ways" of the region. Many other southern working-class whites distinguished between the class-based economic assistance programs that they welcomed and those that aimed at black advancement.[26] But whatever contradictions white Protestants exhibited, Fundamentalism revitalized the energy in southern religion that was lacking in the early years of the Depression and sparked the renewed interest in old-time Protestantism. Indeed, the spread of Fundamentalist institutions and the growth rates of independent Fundamentalist churches, denominations, and fellowships in the South set the stage for the power of evangelicalism in the postwar years.[27]

In the Depression era, conservative evangelicalism was a growing force but not yet dominant. Many rejected the harsh forebodings and social conservatism of the Fundamentalists. During his seminary training in Louisville during the 1930s, Warren Tyree Carr, a future voice of liberalism in the Southern Baptist Convention, recalled, "It did appear to me that the students who loved to call themselves fundamentalists were mean." This experience helped shape his beliefs: "I don't mean to say that all fundamentalists are mean; I'm trying to say the ones I knew—and I said if what they believe makes them like that, then I don't know what I'm going to believe, but I'm not going to believe that." Many others in the southern denominations also fought against the inroads of Fundamentalism and worked with groups seeking to limit the spread of what they viewed as a polarizing theology. In fact, the Depression era witnessed the beginnings of liberal Protestantism's efforts to keep radio preachers like J. Harold Smith off the air. A variety of liberal groups, including the Federal Council of Churches, forced Smith to abandon Greenville, first for a small South Carolina radio station, and then ran him out of the state altogether.[28]

Moreover, one of the major southern denominations, the Methodist Episcopal Church, South, was actually moving toward unification with its more liberal northern counterpart. The southern Methodist Church had lost about one-sixth of its members between 1926 and 1936, many to Holiness and Pentecostal churches. The denomination responded to the tough economic climate by slashing budgets and the salaries of bishops and preachers. By 1938, the southern Methodist *Daily Christian Advocate* and other regional Methodist publications were critiquing capitalism in terms similar to those used by their northern brethren, some of whom were drifting toward socialism. Unification had been on the agenda of both northern and southern Methodists for decades, and the ecclesiastical, doctrinal, and theological differences had largely disappeared by the 1930s. The primary barrier to full unification was what to do with black Methodists; the southern churches rejected the idea that Negro delegates to the General Conference would be included on the same basis as white delegates. Ultimately, the United Methodists temporarily resolved the problem by adding a sixth jurisdictional conference—five were based on geography, the sixth would be made up of the Negro Annual Conference. While this did not force southern Methodists to deal equitably with their racial biases, they had strong women like Dorothy

Tilly and Jesse Daniel Ames, who fought against lynching and racial injustice. In addition, unification committed them to a broad Social Creed and to support the Methodist Federation for Social Action, led by such prolabor, left-leaning activists as Harry F. Ward and Charles Webber.[29]

The turn Methodists took hints at yet another side of Depression-era Protestantism, one that offered a radical, prophetic vision. No one individual better represents that side better than Alva W. Taylor, who served as our guide to the economic and social changes overtaking the South in the previous chapter. To Taylor, Jesus was "the real progenitor" of a democracy that would sweep away class and racial distinctions and pursue social justice. Taylor believed that if Jesus were alive during these hard times, he would be "at the head of these vast, marching columns of labor that are moving on to claim their part in the common heritage of the earth."[30] Even more important, Taylor attracted an incredible group of young activists while teaching in Vanderbilt's School of Religion. Claude Williams, Don West, and Howard Kester were the most well-known activists from among his students, and through them Taylor influenced others such as Myles Horton, Harry Koger, James Dombrowski, and H. L. Mitchell.[31]

These rebels joined numerous social justice struggles and built an array of radical institutions that spread a prophetic Christianity directly opposite the premillennial forebodings of the conservative evangelicals. Early in the Depression years, Taylor's students raised money and provided assistance to the efforts of coal miners in Widen, Tennessee, and Harlan County, Kentucky, to win collective bargaining rights. They also led a battle against landlords in the Mississippi Delta states on behalf of tenants and sharecroppers, both black and white. Don West was immersed in union organizing and in the Communist Party's defense of Angelo Herndon, a black organizer charged with violating an archaic Georgia insurrection statute.[32] Later in the Depression, the prophetic Christians touched by association with Taylor were instrumental in the Highlander Folk School, the Fellowship of Reconciliation, the Southern Tenant Farmers Union, and the Fellowship of Southern Churchmen, a group that united a wide range of southern religious liberals and radicals. Although Taylor did not share the radical temperament that led many of his students to uncompromising positions and a sectarian spirit of the sort that split Fundamentalists, he did share their perspective on social and economic imperatives. He approved of the statements issued by the founding meeting of what became the Fellowship of Southern Churchmen, expressing "the need of developing a radical political party of all races . . . with a program of socialization of natural resources, the principle means of production and distribution, including the nationalization of land, with the clear understanding that the farmer retains possession of the land he uses." Clearly, the Left in the South had a "prophetic front" firmly rooted in a postmillennial evangelical Protestantism.[33]

The radical prophets denied that it was "the will of God that five million children should starve." They also rejected the insistence of premillennial preachers that individual salvation was the only sacred concern. Activist Claude Williams countered: "Preachers have been trained to tell you the soul is the most important. If you starve to death, your soul will go flying to the pearly gates a hundred million light-years away. But Jesus didn't put it in that order. 'Give us this day our daily bread'—the body first." Jesus wanted to build the Kingdom of God on earth, Williams asserted, "an order of justice and brotherhood for everybody." For Williams, the unity of all working people, black and white, would be the instrument to usher in that new order. Similarly, Howard Kester's writings blended Bible verses and prayers with vivid descriptions of the horrible conditions that faced sharecroppers, agricultural tenants, and farmworkers. He praised their fortitude and their faith in a religion that told them that "all the hellish evils of King Cotton's Kingdom are not ordained of God."[34]

This prophetic radicalism found popular followings not only in the new cotton South but also in the coalfields of Appalachia, the ore mines and steel mills of Alabama, and even at times in the Piedmont textile mill villages. At times, working people provided their own postmillennial interpretations based on their day-to-day life experiences. Textile worker James Edmonds was a devout Christian who participated in the welfare committee work at Cone Mills near Greensboro, North Carolina. Although a valued employee, Edmonds spoke out against the injustices of mill practices on several occasions. Finally, in the 1930s, the "stretch out" practiced by textile companies, which greatly intensified workloads, encouraged Edmonds and others to seek the help of the United Textile Workers, which the company lampooned as the work of the devil and his imps, who had been driven from Heaven. At the next open meeting of the union, Edmonds responded:

> If the textile companies want to start the practice of settling disputes with labor by the Bible I was with them 100 percent. But I wasn't for taking a part of it, such as "Servants, obey your masters," a favorite text with preachers who stood in well with the company, to prove that a Christian oughtn't to protest when his bread was being taken out of his mouth. And as for the Devil and his union, I said, that "according to Scripture the Devil had attempted to break the union [in Heaven] and was kicked out" and that he was at work in the world today trying to break the union of peace and brotherly love.[35]

Witherspoon Dodge, an ordained Presbyterian clergyman who went to work for the CIO during the Depression, witnessed the same sacred spirit fill union meetings in Alabama, where workers from the local mills sang such religion-inspired songs as "We Shall Not Be Moved," with its powerful refrain rooted "in the Book of Psalms."[36]

This radical, prophetic spirit at times overcame the racial divisions that proved so damaging to social movements. In the mines and mills of the Birmingham district, in the coalfields of Appalachia, and on the cotton plantations of the Mississippi Delta, unions like the United Cannery, Agricultural, Packing, and Allied Workers, the United Mine Workers, and the Mine, Mill, and Smelter Workers propounded a religious faith that appealed to black and white workers alike. African American church groups, in fact, seemed better able to blend conservative, old-time religion and collective action than white churches, and they served to inspire some white religious radicals. But there was also a strong element of antiradicalism in southern religion, whether white or African American.[37]

There was perhaps no greater expression of the postmillennial Christian outlook than the founding meeting of the Southern Conference for Human Welfare in Birmingham, Alabama, in November 1938. The Conference billed its Sunday evening opening session as a "devotional service," and in the spirit of a Pentecostal revival the mixed-race crowd broke with standard southern segregationist practices. A local minister offered an opening prayer followed by stirring songs and an inspirational address. Finally, the crowd, which contained the leaders of southern progressivism from an array of organizations and social movements, stirred with anticipation for the main speaker of the evening, University of North Carolina president Frank Porter Graham, one of the South's most well-known liberals. Coming at a moment when the world feared the threats posed by totalitarian powers, Graham offered the optimism of Christianity and American democracy. "Repression is the way of frightened power; freedom is the enlightened way," he proclaimed. "We take our stand for the Sermon on Mount, the American Bill of Rights, and American democracy." Virginia Durr, one of the meeting's participants, said her experience there made her feel as if "we had crossed the river together and entered the Promised Land."[38]

War and Salvation

The coming of World War II posed new challenges and new opportunities for southern Protestantism. Military service took many southerners from their families and exposed them to danger as well as both the horrors and pleasures of a wider world. The expansion of military bases forced many communities to adapt to an influx of outsiders that included different ethnic and religious backgrounds. Migrations from rural agricultural regions to urban industrial areas began to accomplish what the New Deal had only begun. Meanwhile, broader federal involvement in southern industrial production meant better wages and working conditions and greater possibilities for unions and collective bargaining, but it also made employers more likely to intensify the pace of work and to apply rules more rigidly in workplaces that had been known for their flexibility. It is not surprising, then, that in the most religious region in the country, many southerners turned to churches to comprehend, find comfort, or express indignation at these changes.

In some respects, the nation's drift toward becoming a wartime state appeared to confirm the direst predictions of premillennialists. Worried that the war would provide the means for the Roosevelt administration to centralize power and authority and resemble a totalitarian state, Fundamentalists began to explore unifying efforts. Despite their rejection of ecumenicalism as exemplified the liberal Federal Council of Churches of Christ in America, several Fundamentalist organizations emerged during the war. On the far right, defrocked Presbyterian minister Carl McIntire created the American Council of Christian Churches, which called for strict separation from mainstream culture. Far more influential was the National Association of Evangelicals (NAE), which formed in St. Louis in 1942. Uniting the most well-known white Fundamentalists in the nation, the NAE became a conservative political lobby associating Roman Catholicism, modernism, secularism, and liberalism with apocalyptic consequences. These things, they believed, threatened the existence of democracy and the free enterprise system, making the era extremely dangerous for the survival of true Christianity.[39]

Because the NAE included formidable preachers, editors, and radio personalities claiming to represent more than one million Christians, it was easy to command the attention of the business community and politicians. It also grabbed the attention of mainstream Protestants who battled for the next decade to limit the radio access of the evangelicals. Beginning in the 1930s, in large part in reaction to the controversial messages of Father Charles Coughlin, the Federal Council of Churches began working with the Federal Communications Commission (FCC) and the National Association of Broadcasters (NAB) to influence the content of religious broadcasting. In 1939, the NAB developed a code that gave the Federal Council of Churches considerable sway over access to free radio time, much to the consternation of Fundamentalist radio preachers. During the war, the battle shifted to paid programming when evangelicals like Charles Fuller (*Old Fashioned Revival Hour*) demonstrated their willingness to buy radio time at market rates. The council complained about the "distorted and one-sided picture of current religious thinking because most of these programs follow the ultraconservative fundamentalist pattern" and began to oppose the relicensing of stations by the FCC if the stations violated the code.[40] Although this was a national struggle, it had particular resonance in the South, where such radio preachers as J. Harold Smith portrayed themselves as martyrs to the forces of modernism and state control, blaming the Federal Council when radio stations discontinued their religious programs.[41]

Religious leaders recognized the shot in the arm that the war provided to Fundamentalists and charismatic churches, who began calling themselves evangelicals. Reverends Harvey McArthur and Anton T. Boisen believed that mainline churches did themselves a real disservice by underestimating the power of evangelicals, and they argued that liberals should concede the "tremendous numerical and spiritual power of fundamentalism" that mushroomed during the Depression and war. Rev. Charles S. Braden wrote that mainstream churches had much to learn from the so-called "sects" or "cults" that could help revive Protestantism. To Braden, charismatic churches had a "definiteness of conviction concerning their faith," a willingness "to witness" that was often lacking in many churches, a lack of concern for how the general public viewed their "pursuit of the values they seek through religion," an appreciation of the valuable role that laymen can play, and "the strong sense of urgency under which they operate." Braden claimed. "What they have to preach greatly matters," he said, "and it matters *now*," which he viewed as an important factor in making these churches the fastest growing in American Protestantism.[42]

The business community viewed this conservative, procapitalist segment of Protestantism as an opportunity. Like the evangelicals, many industrialists were frustrated by the prolabor and progovernment biases of the Federal Council of Churches. Such groups as the Christian Business Men's Association made regular and sometimes substantial contributions to the National Religious Broadcasters, an arm of the National Association of Evangelicals, to make certain that conservative evangelicals competed effectively for airtime. Meanwhile, key laymen from the business community worked both within and outside mainstream Protestant organizations to strengthen the conservative evangelical message. The National Association of Manufacturers pressured churches to mute their prolabor positions; others bankrolled the American Council of Christian Laymen, which later published a pamphlet suggesting that the Federal Council's leaders were enmeshed in a spider's web of left-wing organizations. These business groups also set up conferences with ministers in various parts of the country to emphasize a free-enterprise agenda for postwar reconstruction. The message they relayed to evangelicals at a 1943 Jackson, Mississippi, conference was clear; clergy had a vital role in halting the "subversive forces that would destroy [the American] Way of Life and at the same time blow out Christianity and American Business."[43]

The modernist tendencies that had dominated mainline religion and the Federal Council during the Depression generated increased opposition in southern churches. Some of the more socially conservative southern Presbyterians, for example, questioned their cooperation with the Federal Council. The *Southern Presbyterian Journal* editorialized that the "meddling of the Council, in the name of the Church, in economic and social problems is a menace of the first magnitude." The Federal Council did not believe in the virgin birth, miracles, or divine inspiration according to the editors, and some even denied it was evangelical since it cooperated with Unitarians and Catholics and since there was "voluminous evidence of its Modernism." Charles Dickinson, an elder in the Malden, West Virginia, Presbyterian Church, asserted, "This war is bringing about a spiritual awakening and a golden opportunity for our Church to reap a rich harvest of souls, if we will stick to the historic faith . . . and avoid any alliance with those who question that faith, or may bring politics into our church courts." By the early postwar years, there was considerable sentiment among southern Presbyterians against membership in the Federal Council.[44]

Fundamentalists and conservatives made inroads into the Southern Baptist Convention as well. Although there were several liberal editors of state Baptist newspapers, men like James S. Farmer of the North Carolina *Biblical Recorder* and L. L. Gwaltney of the *Alabama Baptist*, evangelicalism and Fundamentalism gained ground at the expense of liberalism within the SBC during the war years. J. Frank Norris, the Fort Worth, Texas, independent Baptist minister with reputedly the largest single congregation in the country, maintained a steady drumbeat of criticism of his fellow Baptists for keeping Fundamentalism at arm's length. Meanwhile, historical events during those years—war, concentration camps, the atomic bomb, and the creation of the nation of Israel—encouraged many Baptists to believe the end times were imminent, much like the premillennial dispensationalists. This gave a critical boost to those who wished to reject cooperation with organized labor, liberal political groups, and state ecumenical bodies affiliated with the Federal Council of Churches. It also spurred Baptists to shrink from talk of building a "new world order" that would substitute "man's thinking for God's laws."[45]

Much of the impact of World War II on southern churches, then, was to inspire a turn toward more conservative theological and social thinking. Amid the unspeakable horrors of war, many white southern Protestants heard religious leaders tell them to take comfort in traditional southern culture, American democracy, and the capitalist free-enterprise system. Nowhere was that message more emphatic than in strident, Christian-proclaiming publications such as Rev. E. G. "Parson Jack" Johnston's *The Trumpet* and Sherman Patterson's *Militant Truth*. Johnston built a large following at his Roberts Memorial Baptist Tabernacle in Columbus, Georgia. The tabernacle opened in 1932 and was named in honor of Columbus Roberts, a prominent industrialist who had interests in Coca-Cola and who bankrolled the tabernacle. During the Depression, Johnston's *Trumpet* was a monthly religious magazine, but at the end of the war he began publishing bi-weekly and then weekly, and he changed the name of the paper to the *Columbus Tribune*. He also published special issues of *The Trumpet*, which denounced organized labor and the New Deal as subversive and Communist-dominated. *The Trumpet* banner carried the subhead "Orthodox—Fundamental—Pre-Millennial—Missionary," an effort to maintain the religious character of the original publication. Backed by local industrialists, issues of *The Trumpet* miraculously appeared at the homes of Georgia and Alabama textile operatives "free, without having subscribed or asked for it." "Parson Jack" took as his primary biblical text the admonition, "Be ye not unequally yoked together with unbelievers," and then set out to show that unions were un-Christian organizations, and he exhorted violence against them. In *The Trumpet* Johnston defended the racist Senator Theodore Bilbo ("a friend to the Negro race"), the Ku Klux Klan, and right-wing, pro-fascist organizations like the Columbians. He denounced labor and fair employment legislation proclaiming, "Let the New Deal die, like its founder, and thank God for it."[46]

Sherman Patterson's *Militant Truth* was equally strident in its content. Begun in Chattanooga, Tennessee, in 1939, Patterson's monthly publication battled the spread of labor unions, particularly the CIO, in the region. Like *The Trumpet*, it carried a masthead emphasizing its religious message: "Interpreting Current Events from a Fundamental Christian and Constitutional American Viewpoint," and it likewise appeared in the mailboxes of workers, especially when a union-organizing campaign was in progress. *Militant Truth* also routinely endorsed the passage from 2 Corinthians 6:14–18 concerning "the unequal yoke." It carried articles and speeches from ministers, interspersing attacks on the threat of "dictatorship" posed by the federal government, the "treason" practiced by unions, and the fallacies of anything that impeded free enterprise. By 1945, Patterson was expressing fears of the government's desire for postwar planning, in part because he began receiving advice and assistance from the Southern States Industrial Council, which was worried about such government initiatives as fair employment practices and wage and price controls continuing into the postwar period. Patterson offered two premillennial cautions to liberals who believed that Americans could create a better world: "The Total Depravity of man, and . . . the Terrible power of Sin and Satan." *Militant Truth* asserted, "Two ways stretch out before the world: Revival, or Judgment—'Repent, or Perish.'"[47]

Conservative evangelicalism in the South surged during the war in part due to the diminished white Christian Left. Howard Kester, a leading prophetic radical, grew increasingly frustrated with Communists and secular radicals and thus retreated from the Southern Tenant Farmers Union and the Committee on Economic and Racial Justice, moving from Nashville to the mountains of North Carolina. His declining social activism also sapped energies from the Fellowship of Southern Churchmen, which languished under his direction. Alva Taylor struggled to find work and then retired during the war years, limiting his activism. Claude Williams left the South to work as an industrial chaplain for the Presbyterian Church in Detroit. Although Williams continued to preach a radical gospel among southern migrants, his absence took a vital voice from the region. Franz Daniel, another seminary-trained activist, moderated his views during the war and broke with the radicals at Highlander, leveling charges against the Folk School that caused Highlander to have somewhat strained relations with the labor movement. Finally, the defection of the United Mine Workers from the CIO reduced the critical mass of activists with a left-leaning Christian perspective. They did not leave the labor movement, but their support for New Deal liberalism and interracial unionism garnered far less support in the American Federation of Labor and kept the miners at arm's length from other progressive unions.[48]

Some of this weakened Christian radicalism owed to growing doubts, particularly among white activists, about working with Communists. Daniel, Kester, and Taylor followed a path charted by Reinhold Niebuhr, the influential Union Theological Seminary professor who had a hand in shaping the thinking of a number of members of the southern Christian Left. The horrors of totalitarian regimes in Europe pushed Niebuhr away from his support of radical politics and prophetic

Christianity toward what he saw as a more realistic neo-orthodoxy. With the founding of *Christianity and Crisis* in 1941, Niebuhr announced his willingness to defend the world from totalitarianism (either Communism or Fascism) and from naïve Christian radicals who attempted to "establish a heaven on earth," which "turned out in the case of orthodox Marxism to be a communist hell."[49] Others sought solace and understanding in the spiritual world as well. Even the old Social Gospel optimist Alva Taylor felt the effect of the war's horrors. He wrote to a close friend that his experiences fighting poverty had left him "a good deal of a humanist, rather convinced that there is a mighty lot of superstition in a good deal of the preaching we hear, but that a life or a world without belief and faith in God is one without reason."[50]

Union Theological Seminary shaped another minister who played a major role in trying to sustain a Christian social vision in the Methodist Church during the war: Charles Webber. Born in 1892 near Ann Arbor, Michigan, Webber was the son of a flour miller. He attended the University of Michigan, the Boston University School of Theology, and Union Theological Seminary. During his time in college and seminary, he paid his bills by installing pavements in Ann Arbor, doing janitorial work for the Methodist Church, working for the YMCA, and serving as the co-headworker with his wife, the former Ardelle Perkins, of Jamaica Plain Neighborhood House in Boston. His first ministerial position was with the Holy Trinity Italian Evangelical Church in Denver, Colorado, where he also became president of the Denver Labor College. Between 1923 and 1935, he spent time as superintendent of the Coke Missions of the Methodist Church in western Pennsylvania, as president of the Lower East Side Community Council in New York, where he mediated strikes, and for nine years as the assistant director of field work for Union Theological Seminary. Webber took a sabbatical leave in the summer of 1935 to become an organizer for the Amalgamated Clothing Workers in Richmond, Virginia. When he returned, he took over as National Executive Secretary of the Methodist Federation for Social Service, a position he held when the northern and southern churches merged in 1939. Along with the venerable Harry F. Ward, Webber was one of the best-known social justice activists in the Methodist Church, having worked in the coalfields of Harlan County, Kentucky, among textile workers in Paterson, New Jersey, and in the clothing factories of Richmond.[51]

In 1942, Webber caused controversy in the Methodist Federation for Social Service when, although he was a staunch anti-Communist, he signed a statement of clergymen asking President Roosevelt to release Communist Party leader Earl Browder from jail. Webber also became increasingly frustrated with the Church's unwillingness to adequately fund the Federation's work. Finally, in December 1943, Webber resigned and took a position as national representative with the Amalgamated Clothing Workers, assigned to Knoxville, Tennessee. But he still had influential friends in the United Methodist Church. In May 1944, Bishop

Francis J. McConnell gave Webber an appointment as "Chaplain to Organized Labor" in recognition of more than twenty years' work with unions. The following year, the liberal Bishop G. Bromley Oxnam, who was also active in the Federal Council of Churches, renewed the appointment when Webber was reassigned to Virginia, even though Oxnam's region did not include Virginia.[52]

Webber's appointment demonstrated the uneasy accommodations that southern Methodists were making to unification. Dr. George S. Reamey, editor of the *Virginia Methodist Advocate*, appealed to Virginia and North Carolina Bishop W. W. Peele to revoke Webber's Methodist credentials. Particularly rankling to Reamey were his concerns about the labor movement's goals of abolishing the Virginia poll tax and supporting a permanent fair employment practices law. The editor believed that continuing a special ministerial assignment to someone who endorsed these goals would hurt the Methodists, not only in Virginia but also elsewhere in the South. The future proved Peele to be a perceptive judge of his members.[53]

Consequently, the war caused another shifting of the ground underneath white southern churches. Most had moved in a decisively more conservative direction with respect to social issues. If the Depression had warmed many southern Protestants to a more liberal state, progressive legislation, and institutions like unions that helped soften the blows of hard times, the war years had disillusioned large numbers of white Protestants against relying on the actions of inherently sinful men and women and an expanding government apparatus that might threaten freedom. It helped, of course, that their standard of living was on the rise. Where necessary, workers had formed unions and bargained collectively with their employers. But at countless other worksites, government actions guaranteed better wages and working conditions.[54]

One thing the southern white working class did not want was racial change. White southern workers had welcomed a politics of class through the Depression, but a politics of racial segregation made inroads amid the more cautious realism of the war years. Starting with the inability of white millhands in South Carolina to elect Olin Johnston, one of their own, to the Senate in 1938, through the triumph of Herman Talmadge in Georgia in 1946, the entrenched racism of regional politics seemed to demonstrate that white workers would not completely reject politics as usual in the South. Many determined to protect the improvements they had already made in their lives by denying opportunities to blacks promised by legislation to protect voting, access to public institutions, and equality of opportunity at the workplace. Southern Protestants even developed a "theology of segregation" that began to take shape during World War II among conservative evangelicals but that also captured followings in the mainstream southern denominations, even in the Southern Baptist Convention, which wrestled with its position on segregation.[55]

The response of southern white Protestantism to the war, however, left much room for interpretation. Memories lingered concerning the social justice impulses that the Depression had triggered among Protestants, and there was scattered evidence of a "new social climate" in the South. Among Holiness and Pentecostal churches, CIO organizer Lucy R. Mason found local ministers who were "very friendly to the unions and participation in church affairs by union leaders and members." In Alabama, Methodist layman William Mitch was helping to break down segregation in the state's labor movement. In Georgia, Baptist preacher Joseph Rabun returned from his service in the war with a new attitude about the poll tax and the all-white primary, which stifled black and poor white participation in attacking the status quo in southern politics.[56]

Thus, there were considerable barriers to overcome but also many resources upon which to draw when the Congress of Industrial Organizations planned its ambitious Southern Organizing Campaign at the war's end. Southern society had begun to make progress toward becoming an industrial economy and upending the old plantation mentality. Southern religion had also been transformed in the process. Although the same denominations continued to account for the majority of the region's churchgoers, their relative weights had shifted, and they now had to adapt to a national association of evangelicals, a resurgence of Fundamentalism, and the rapid growth of charismatic religious groups. Southern Protestantism had not only survived the religious depression that characterized the early 1930s, but it was on the cusp of a spectacular growth period. What that meant for labor and liberalism in 1946 was unclear.

CHAPTER 3

"If You Read Your Bible"

The Faith of Southern White Workers

Ralph Simmons grew up on a farm in Catawba County, North Carolina, an area that was soon to become a regional center for furniture making. His grandfather had emigrated from Holland and married into the German farming community that surrounded Concordia College in Conover. Ralph was one of seven children in the struggling family, so after sixth grade he left school and began working, first on the farm, but soon in public work. He graded roads and hauled lumber before catching on at a furniture company in his early twenties. When that company went bankrupt during the Depression, Simmons had already become proficient enough at building lathe heads, sharpening saws, and cutting wood that he caught on at Southern Furniture, a company making the transition from upholstering buggy seats to making upholstered home furnishings. He remained there until he retired with a partial disability in his sixties.

Throughout his life, Simmons was a member of the Lutheran Church—Missouri Synod, becoming a member of the Concordia Lutheran Church when he joined Southern Furniture in the 1930s. Although Lutherans were a distinct minority in the South, Missouri Synod Lutherans fit in well in the evangelical Protestant culture there. Like most southern churches, Concordia Lutheran Church espoused that salvation came by faith alone and only through God's grace, purchased by Jesus's suffering on the Cross. Similarly, Concordia asserted that the Bible is God's inerrant and infallible Word, in which He reveals His Law and His Gospel of salvation in Jesus Christ. To those who belonged to the Missouri Synod, it was the sole rule and norm for Christian doctrine. For Ralph Simmons, it was a simple and personal faith. His education and his slow speech made him reluctant to be a Sunday school teacher or church leader, but, he said, "I attended church as regular as I handily could," and he read his Bible every day. Later in life, he tried to interest his grandson in becoming a minister and read the Bible with him every morning, but he regretted this when the boy became a Mormon. Simmons worried that it might have been his fault, but it never shook his faith. He continued to discuss his faith and distribute religious literature to interested coworkers. "We're supposed to do it, you know, and look forward to it. We were intended to work and proclaim Christ," he believed.

Concordia Lutheran Church and the Bible provided Simmons with a guide for living. Although the local filling station was a popular gathering spot for men, he followed the advice of Concordia's preacher about not spending time there because they sold beer and used "rough words." For Simmons, "that's not the place to be. The Bible says we're not to 'set in the seat of the scornful.' And you take where it's something done that's not right, I'd call that scornful." Those beliefs guided his behavior at work as well: "[I am] supposed to use my time for the best of their [Southern Furniture's] advantage, regardless of how they treat me or anything, what they pay me, how much or how little." When his own work was slack, Simmons helped by sweeping the floor or running a lathe for an absent co-worker. This was not a strategy for advancement (he turned down an offer of promotion to foreman) but rather reflected his sense of duty to God and the company "to make an honest day." In many respects, Simmons believed that this example was also his way of proclaiming his faith.

Unions, to Simmons, were not part of God's plan. "I always tried to be satisfied, and I didn't pay no attention to what anyone else said," he explained. This was a part of his upbringing but also a belief that shaped his attitudes about collective action. "If you read your Bible, you'll see in there that you're supposed to be satisfied with your wages. It don't say how much or how little. John the Baptist spoke well of that, and also Christ did. And whenever we go beyond that, we go beyond our Supreme Being." As someone whose church and whose faith taught that the Bible was "God's inerrant and infallible Word," Simmons looked for some sanctifying evidence that unions were part of God's plan. "I don't believe that anyone can show me between the leaves of the Bible where it gives you a right to force anyone to pay you more money. I don't think you can," he claimed. "And I believe in doing the thing that's right. It don't make any difference what might happen to you here; it's what happens to you beyond the shore. That's it."

Listening to Ralph Simmons's interviews, it is tempting to imagine him as hard-boiled and fatalistic individual who had been forced to make it on his own and had little sympathy for those who had faced life's challenges with less success. He admitted that he always had a job, even during the Depression. He put aside extra money so that when hard times hit, he could manage until conditions improved. He even admitted that he was proficient enough at his job that he could turn down the offer of a foreman's position because he could make just about the same amount of money without the added responsibilities. And Simmons was quite satisfied with his independence at work. "See," he said, "every person's got a talent, and if they use it, they don't need too much outside help." He mainly wanted his supervisors to tell him what they needed: "Then," he said, "I looked forward to doing it the way I seen fit. I didn't want them to inform me how to do it. If I made a mistake, I could correct my own mistake quicker than I could the ones that would tell me."

But there was a kind and just side to Simmons. He was "well pleased" to see black and female workers receive fairer treatment and better opportunities in the postwar era. He admired the New Deal programs and President Roosevelt for the good they did during the Depression, and although he had worked all his life, Simmons did not object to welfare or food stamps. "We've got to have some way or another to take care of the people that's more disadvantaged in life than others," he asserted. He would also fight for what he thought was fair for himself, even if it meant defying the company. When he had a bad fall at work and broke his back due to what he thought was company negligence, he threatened legal action to make certain that the company accepted responsibility and helped him with compensation. Although awarded only a ten percent disability, Simmons did not express any bitterness about the settlement.

Scholars typically describe such working-class religiosity as fatalistic, the psychological compensation of the underprivileged for a life of unceasing toil. Ralph Simmons, however, would certainly not have described his life that way. His marriage lasted more than six decades, and he raised four children. He had steady work at a job he liked until retirement and was proud that job opportunities were better in the 1970s than they had been in the 1950s. His expectations were minimal: "I'd just take an interest in my work and look forward for the best," he said. And although he had a much less abundant material wealth than his employers, he was their equal at Concordia Lutheran Church. Simmons recalled that both he and his employers did "their part" in helping maintain the church, but he did not remember any of them holding a church office or having more say than he had over matters of faith. He also had respect for other churches. To him, "it didn't make no difference what church you belong to as long as they proclaimed Christ and Him crucified." Faith, for Simmons, was simple; "If you got a belief and look forward to the best, you've got a Supreme Being to lead you to where you should go."[1]

Ralph Simmons was like many workers in the mid-twentieth-century South. Shades of his sort of popular religiosity are evident in the scores of transcripts gathered in oral history collections that include the voices of working people in the region. Even people who did not regularly attend church felt the impact of popular religion in their music, folk art, adages, and moral instincts. Flashes of a sacred spirit were pervasive in twentieth-century southern culture, and that spirit helped shape the good and the bad of southern politics and identity.[2] But religion was not just the domain or property of preachers and religious organizations, it was also claimed by wage earners like Ralph Simmons. In and among the conservative evangelicalism of some Christians, the sermons and daily ministering of local preachers, and the prophetic radicalism of those who hoped that southern spirituality would result in support for unions and liberal politics, there was the popular religiosity of thousands of working people who read the Bible and came to their own conclusions about what was right.

Popular religiosity has been the subject of a great deal of debate in the scholarly literature. For us, the summary provided by religious historian Charles H. Lippy perhaps best captures the essence of what we have seen in the oral histories of southern white workers. To Lippy, popular religiosity exists alongside formal religious belief and practice, but it is also about "the ways in which individuals take religious belief, interpret it in practical terms, and put it to work to do something that will give order and meaning to their lives." He suggests that Americans have long operated within both sacred and secular realms, each with their own measure of power. For those without power in the material world, access to sacred power can nevertheless give someone "a sense of control, of being able to chart one's own destiny. That control becomes the key to experiencing happiness and to seeing life as endowed with meaning."[3] Access to sacred power will not lead everyone to the same conclusions. The mix of determining factors typically derives from localized conditions and individual psyches. The influence of the sacred on the politics of working people may follow patterns, but is rarely certain. Ralph Simmons felt a genuine sense of spiritual equality with his employers, which came from their relations in church and the independence he claimed for himself at the workplace, regardless of the pay he received. But others, like Anne Queen, whom we introduced at the beginning of chapter 2, took the strong religious faith and turned it toward a prophetic social activism.

This chapter explores the popular religiosity of the southern white working class from the 1930s to the 1950s. How did the search for the religious meaning of their lives affect how they reacted to the blandishments of new evangelicals or those of the prophetic religious activists on the Left? What did they take from their reading of the Bible, from the sermons they heard, and from those aspects of regional culture imbued with the sacred that led them to accept or reject a new liberal regime of union membership and state-sanctioned collective bargaining?

Interpreting God's Word for a Life of Toil

During the Great Depression most working people did not lose their faith even if church numbers declined. Some temporarily strayed from church membership as they relocated in the North or felt uncomfortable in the transition from a small, familiar country congregation to the more formal surroundings of an impersonal urban church. Others left the faith of their parents for what seemed like more dynamic churches that helped them to better cope with the turmoil they experienced in their everyday lives. Most clung to the religious traditions in which they had been raised, although those traditions were not quite the same.

Whatever the case, the southern white working class found religious fellowship in churches that maintained the core elements of southern evangelicalism.[4]

Listening to the voices of white working people at times can make denominational choices seem almost serendipitous. For some the choice of church was simply a matter of location. Growing up in Rock Hill, South Carolina, Eva Hopkins's family, like many others, did not have a car. On Sunday, "You went to the church that was closest to you." Ethel Faucette recalled that her mill village "didn't have but one" church, and "most everybody here on the hill went to this little church."[5] Mining and farm communities were similar. In Cumberland, Kentucky, Worley Johnson remembered that "there wasn't as many denominations as they are now." The only church in his mining village was "what they called non-denominational," but he noted that "[some] places they had what they call the Holiness Church." In Cleveland, Mississippi, Kathleen Knight's only choice was a Baptist church.[6]

Even workers who made choices often appeared to make them without reference to doctrine or theology. Eva Hopkins became a Baptist after attending Methodist churches in her youth. When asked why, she stated: "Well, I don't know; I went down there to visit, and I liked the preacher. I liked the sermons he preached better, and I enjoyed the Sunday school class and the teachers, the way they taught and all, more. I just really enjoyed it more, so that's where I went." Margaret Dorsett, raised in Docena, Alabama, recalled that the Baptists and Methodists alternated Sundays, and that most went no matter which denomination was holding services. Dorsett even noted that the Baptists did not follow the normal practice of a closed communion when they ran the services.[7] Flake and Nellie Mae Meyers switched from a Lutheran to a Methodist church because their children had friends there. Theology appeared to have little impact to the Meyerses: "Like we all say, the church is not going to save you; it's the way you live. One denomination's no better than the other," a refrain that appears in the interviews of many southern working-class whites.[8]

Some switched less because of doctrine and more because they wanted to attend churches where the expectations for Sunday clothes were more modest or where the congregations were either all of one class or less demeaning toward the poor. In Gaston County, North Carolina, Liston Pope attributed the growth of what he called "sects" to these factors. In Alabama, a Baptist women's missionary report noted the class divisions in one community where five churches and a mission each ministered to "mutually hostile socioeconomic classes."[9] Oral histories confirm this. Mrs. L. A. House, raised Methodist in an Alabama farm community, switched to a Baptist church when she moved to a mill village because she felt more comfortable in a congregation of laborers. Ethel Hilliard resented going to church with overly proud women who would come to church in silk and "rattle" as they walked, thinking they were better than anyone else. In the coalfields of Kentucky, miners often switched to Holiness and Pentecostal churches to worship

separately from the mine operators or the "uplift" missions of mainline denominations. Even in the paternalistic textile villages, some refused to worship at the
company-approved church.[10]

At times, the choice to join a working-class church was made for poorer whites.
In Harlan County, Kentucky, George Lyon reminisced about what must have
happened many times: "One time at my church some very poor kids came to
our Sunday school and they were clearly not welcome; the Sunday school teacher
didn't like having them there. That bothered me a lot and the next week, when
the kids didn't come back, I asked the teacher about it. She said, 'Well, it's really
for the best. They wouldn't have been happy here. They're more the Church of
God type.'"[11]

Increasingly, however, the church preferences of the South's white working class
reflected conscious decisions. As mill villages and industrial centers increased in
size, the options for working people exploded. At the same time, mills began the
process of selling off company-owned housing, and more and more blue-collar
families owned cars, freeing them from the homogeneous mill-village church.
While Depression-era reminiscences often reflect the lack of choice for places
to worship, postwar surveys and remembrances attribute church membership
to a more conscious decision-making process. George G. Suggs Jr., who grew up
in the cotton mill town of Bladenboro, North Carolina in the 1930s and 1940s,
noted how the war changed the town, generating jobs at nearby Fort Bragg or

This was the evangelical church at the end of the Browning family's street, which the
family attended from 1946 to 1948, when they bought a car and began attending the
Easley Church of God. Courtesy of Marlene (Browning) Burke.

the Wilmington shipyards as well as improving the wages of jobs in the textile mills. Suggs was also able to recreate an intricate social geography of religious affiliation surrounding the town. Interestingly, he noted that many families might drive past several churches, including one or more of the same denominational affiliation, to attend a particular place of worship.[12]

One of the places scholars have studied the social nature of working people's religious preferences most closely is Gaston County, North Carolina, a county made famous by Liston Pope's study of its 1929 textile strike. Pope noted the shift in church preferences in the aftermath of the strike and the hard times of the Depression. He found that twenty-one of the twenty-four churches established in the 1930s were outside the mainstream denominations, which had previously accounted for 88 percent of Gaston County's church members. Holiness and Pentecostal churches were the biggest gainers, especially among the millhands, although they remained minority churches. Over the subsequent two decades those churches continued to grow, but such changes paled in comparison to the shift within the major denominations. Between 1939 and 1959, Southern Baptist Convention churches grew by 224 percent, southern Presbyterian churches by 81 percent, but Methodist churches by only 29 percent, and they showed no growth after 1949. Clearly, the distinctly southern churches (the southern and northern Methodists unified in 1939) were increasingly attractive to Gastonians, who prized local autonomy and congregational choice. One working-class churchgoer believed that Methodist unification destroyed many southern congregations. Formerly, he claimed, "the power of choice was in the congregation and the local church. And in this new [Methodist] organization it comes down from the bishop to the district superintendent and then to the pastor."[13]

Evidence from other industrial centers points to a similar pattern of working-class religious change. Although the 1936 census figures are somewhat unreliable, when matched with the 1952 survey undertaken by the National Council of Churches they show significant changes in church preferences. In Calhoun County, Alabama, home to the manufacturing hub of Anniston, Southern Baptists outnumbered Methodists by less than three to two in 1936; by 1952, the ratio was more than three to one. In Floyd County, Georgia, one of the most industrialized counties in the state, Baptists accounted for about 54 percent of the three major denominations in 1936, but that number grew to more than 77 percent by 1952. In Pittsylvania County, Virginia, which contained the vast Danville Mills, Methodists outnumbered Baptists in 1936; by 1952, not only was Baptist the leading denomination, but there were three Baptists churchgoers in the county for every two Methodists. Some other industrial areas witnessed a dramatic growth in Holiness and Pentecostal churches. In Anderson County, South Carolina, for instance, Holiness and Pentecostal membership grew to 6.6 percent; in Greene County, Tennessee, to 5 percent.[14] These changes reflected a trend toward church affiliations that emphasized greater local autonomy, more traditional theologies, stronger reliance on Biblical authority and inerrancy, and more emotional, informal religious practices. Southern whites, in essence, became even more evangelical in the decade after World War II, and this evangelical culture was, at its core, less hospitable to national institutions and modernism.

Sociologist John Kenneth Morland's fieldwork in the South Carolina mill town of York, South Carolina, describes a parallel shift in the church membership of textile workers. The older interdenominational chapel, which had been alternately serviced by the downtown Baptist, Methodist, and Presbyterian ministers, lost ground to a separate Baptist church established in the 1930s. The Depression years also gave rise to a Church of God congregation, which began in a tent and subsequently moved to a garage, and provided a real challenge to the Baptists. In 1938, a third major mill-village congregation emerged from a revival, a Wesleyan Methodist church that catered to those who "desired the Holiness doctrine but felt that the Church of God was too undignified." There were a few more efforts to create new churches in the postwar era, including a snake-handling sect in 1948, and other millworkers avoided the mill churches altogether, either for one of the downtown churches or for a rural church. By the early 1950s, seven of every ten York mill-village families were church members, a majority in the diverse mill-village congregations; those with a more hierarchical structure lost ground, however.[15]

Working people expressed various reasons for their choices. Textile worker Martin Lowe was raised a Primitive Baptist, but when he moved to Greenville, South Carolina, he and his wife attended the Methodist church. After the war, however, they felt that churches were drifting away from "the straight and narrow, . . . just a-going for a big membership and a big dollar." The Lowes began attending the Assembly of God church, a "full gospel, friendship church," but it was "a Holiness church, too," Lowe stated, just as he remembered from his Primitive Baptist upbringing. Anna Mae Cook also preferred the strict morality of the Pentecostal congregation in favor of her earlier membership in a Methodist church because the Pentecostals were "very strict and according to the Bible." They taught you "to live holy, live free and separated from sin, sanctified and filled with the Holy Ghost." But Cook also preferred the emotion of her new faith. She felt that the members there were more "sanctified and filled with the Holy Ghost," and she enjoyed "evidence of speaking in tongue."[16] Hoy Deal, who worked in Piedmont lumber and glove factories, felt uncomfortable in the Lutheran Church because of its concentration on the catechism. He became a Baptist after listening to the local preacher whose sermons came straight from the Bible. Deal also regularly listened to radio preachers who featured people testifying to their faith: "That's one thing that any Christian is supposed to do when they get a chance, to witness to anybody about the Savior."[17]

Others sought a more responsive and morally strict faith, but without the extreme expressiveness typical of Pentecostals. Ila Dodson recoiled at the Church of God services where the "women would shout, you know, and their hair'd fall down, and I didn't know what was taking place." However, in the 1940s she chose a more subdued Holiness church because of its behavioral code. She believed that it was important to try and live a godly life. Alice Evitt was likewise "scared" by her mother's "shoutin'" at a Pentecostal revival, but she eventually joined a Methodist church that allowed emotional and participatory services where "we all stand up and read the Bible" and where the minister asked for spontaneous prayers from members of the congregation. She was aware of its unusual character; if anybody who had "been in another Methodist church come in here, they wouldn't believe it was a Methodist because [we] have all that. . . . It's like old-timey," she claimed.[18] Popular Christianity affected all denominational cultures, especially but not exclusively in congregations that were heavily working class in composition, confounding the distinctions that we might expect to find in southern religion.

The churches that working-class whites attended reflected personal choices about styles of worship and message. For example, in York, South Carolina, millhands who joined the working-class-oriented Baptist church made a decision against both the rural and the town (or middle-class) Baptist churches, and their congregation had little fellowship with the others. They were proud of their modest church structure and brick pastorium. Their services had become more subdued, although the minister did get emotional when delivering his sermon. The sermons typically emphasized the authority of Scripture and encouraged humility and dependence on the Lord. In the eyes of observer John Kenneth Morland, "the mill people themselves [at the Baptist church] appear to be characterized by attitudes of humility, lack of self-confidence, and nonaggressiveness." Members often attended Sunday school and either one or both of the regular Sunday services (morning and evening). The core leadership of the church attended a Wednesday evening prayer service; other groups gathered at various times during the week. The church held two revivals each year, but its membership did not grow.[19]

In contrast, the working people who attended the Church of God or the Wesleyan Methodist church tended to be the poorer millworkers, evidenced by their more modest buildings and their simpler dress, which even included overalls for children. But these churches were more aggressive in seeking new members and proud of giving a warm welcome to strangers. Sunday school classes competed to achieve the best attendance. The services had little routine or formal organization, characterized by more energy and emotion as well as spontaneous participation. The favorite church songs were more upbeat and jazzy, and the preachers tended to promote a celebratory atmosphere, which might include shouts of "Amen" or "Glory," along with handclapping and foot tapping. Prayers were open to the congregation, and anyone in attendance might participate, often more than one speaking at the same time. Although the trappings of the Holiness and Pentecostal churches were modest, the members were "strict tithers" who also gave additionally for special offerings.[20] Sermon topics added to the differences; they were more likely to focus on "the imminence of the Day of Judgment and the need for salvation." The Church of God especially emphasized that the Devil was becoming stronger in the world, and its evening services appeared to be a time when attendees might "receive the rapture" of sanctification, although many of those who went to the altar were backsliders who had already been "saved and sanctified numerous times previously."[21]

There were many commonalities in the beliefs promoted by working-class churches. George Suggs remembered that many followed an ascetic behavior, avoiding alcohol, tobacco, movies, dancing, and even Coca-Cola, whether or not they attended Southern Baptist Convention churches, independent Free Will Baptist churches, the Emanuel Holiness Church, or the Pentecostal Church of God. They found in church a "welcome sanctuary" from the stresses and demands of their lives. Some of this no doubt grew from the privations of the Depression or the strains brought by World War II, but a disregard for worldly things continued to be a part of their faith even as their material standard of living improved. Although workers in York or Bladenboro might choose different churches in terms of styles of worship, they shared much in terms of outlook. Most members of the distinctly working-class churches believed that "sin and evil lurked everywhere," and that Satan was "as much alive and at work as God." In fact, the world was "a battleground in which God and the Devil strived for each individual soul," both present as one went through the routines of each day. Avoiding the clutches of the Devil depended on living exemplary lives and adhering strictly to religious convictions.[22]

Churches helped keep believers from losing their way and falling prey to Satan. In the coalfields of western Virginia, churches held trials against members accused of "misconduct in the community," which might have involved drinking too much and "walking in an un-Christian like manner." For Sam Johnson, born in 1892 in the coalfields of eastern Kentucky, the worldly presence of the devil was real: "That old Satan's got plenty of power, he's going to get everyone he can." Johnson became "a bad man," he recalled. "I loved the world too much," he said, until he opened his heart to the Lord. Then, in August 1935, he began preaching at an Old Regular Baptist church and committed himself to the Lord.[23]

Strong church leaders could transform the morality of a community. A number of individuals who grew up in Burlington, North Carolina, in the mid-twentieth century remembered the influence of preacher George Washington Swinney, who won many converts to the church and cleaned up the reputation of the city formerly known as "little Chicago." Although uneducated, Swinney was a charismatic preacher and revival leader who managed to convince the city's textile workers to take personal responsibility for their neighborhoods and their behavior. One child of textile workers, Robert Eugene Latta, was so impressed by Swinney's example that he became a Baptist minister.[24]

Some of the churches in both York and Bladenboro had educated ministers, either full time or part time, while others produced homegrown preachers who doubled as millworkers. Both types of clergymen might minister to more than one congregation, alternating Sundays or times of Sunday services. Often, lay preachers debated about whether or not they should accept pay for their efforts. Regardless, the churches that attracted the white working class all shared some basic religious beliefs. The most important of these included a striking faith in the Bible "as the ultimate authority in all religious matters." Most members and many nonmembers accepted the notion that true religion was "living according to the Bible." Because many of the working-class churches "called" their ministers to preach, they insisted that they preach from the Scriptures. Hoy Deal, a Piedmont glove worker, best captured the sentiment expressed by many others: "I can tell pretty quick whether a man's a-preaching from the Bible or not. If he ain't a-preaching from the Bible, I don't want to hear him."[25]

Popular religious expressions were not limited to Sunday services. Even many who did not regularly attend church believed that they met the requirements for salvation because they routinely read the Bible and followed its teachings. Textile worker Edward Harrington's mother taught a very strict code of living by the Bible. "My mother," he recalled, "wished that she'd spent more time reading the Bible to her children. . . . Anything the Bible said, she believed it. Things were pointed out to us."[26] The Bible was a guide for everyday life and personal morality, warning of temptations, false prophets, and political intrigues—but always subject to the individual interpretations of each believer. Other basic beliefs imparted by all of the working-class churches included the conviction that salvation came only through God's grace and as a result of one's acceptance of Jesus as Lord and Savior, a pride in being different from the majority and rejecting materialism, and that God rewards or punishes people "in much the same manner as in the biblical accounts of the wrath of God."[27]

The music of evangelical Protestant churches likewise suffused the popular religiosity of working people beyond particular congregations. Ethel Hilliard learned numerous songs that emphasized her devotion to Christian faith. She could play them on the piano even though she had no musical training and could not read music. That musical ear served her well when the Holiness Church needed a piano player, and she changed church membership comfortably because of the feeling that the Holiness members brought to their singing. Others recalled that church singings were a vital part of their religious participation. Mary Gattis, who grew up in the textile town of Bynum, North Carolina, recalled regular gatherings in homes for prayer meetings and hymn singing. She loved the "old timey hymns: *The Old Rugged Cross, Sweet Our Prayer, Jesus Saves.*"[28] Martha Atha, who grew up in a West Virginia Pentecostal church, remembered her preacher-carpenter father as "an extremely good banjo picker" who won a statewide contest. But later in life he "didn't play worldly music, he played [only] Christian music." George Suggs recalled, "The informal singing of hymns at White Oak Church and the memories associated with them are among the greatest contribution of the church to my spiritual development as a youth." No matter what Protestant church Suggs attended after leaving his parent's church—whether Methodist, Nazarene, Church of God, or Presbyterian—he was always familiar with most of the music. To Suggs, "the knowledge of the theology found in these hymns, musically expressed, is one of the major links that bind Protestant denominations together."[29]

Sacred musical influences reached far beyond the churches, however, and became pervasive in the South, influencing popular musicians not normally associated with Christianity. In Alabama, country-music legend Hank Williams first learned music from his church-organist mother. During World War II Williams worked in the Mobile, Alabama, shipyards but also began blending religious and secular musical strands, including the blues, for gigs in honky-tonks. Although his fame degenerated into a life of alcohol and drugs, his music resonated for southern white working people raised on "open Bibles, small country churches, and resounding sermons and hymns," according to historian Wayne Flynt. Williams's songs blended sin, sex, and salvation for a postwar generation experiencing the uncertainty of a newly urban and industrial society. But these were people who "attributed what happened in their lives to the inscrutable will of God." The country music that was capturing the South in the postwar years owed a great deal to gospel groups and religiously inspired songwriters.[30]

Some working-class churches followed meaningful rituals that more mainstream churches were abandoning. Lawrence Baldridge, who eventually left the Old Regular Baptist churches of his youth for training in a Southern Baptist seminary, recalled the bans on women wearing makeup, the spontaneity and informality of the services, and the belief in miracles that characterized his religious upbringing. But he remembered also their "religious expressions in which they were totally uninhibited in terms of their expression of their faith in God and their love for their fellow man. It was quite emotional."[31] Other churches believed in faith healing, speaking in tongues, spontaneously shouting, and drawing upon a holistic medicine for the physical body that derived from Fundamentalist beliefs. In northern Alabama, one of the most renowned herb doctors was Tommie Bass, who summarized his cures with the following:

> "I feel there's only two ways to go—the good way and the bad way. And I go by the Bible. I take the whole book, not just a little bit because you got to go all the way to the end to find out what happens.
>
> The good Lord tells me in the Bible that he made us out of the dust out there. A lot of people don't think that. . . . I hadn't found too many that didn't, but some of them does, I understand.
>
> Anyway, we're made out of that earth out there and we've got to go back out there and get some of it to nurse this body. Each [plant] has something that we use in our body."[32]

Equally important were biblical practices like foot washing. Martha Atha, who grew up in southern West Virginia and converted from the Primitive Baptist church of her youth to a Pentecostal church, spoke of the experience of washing the feet of other church members. Although she participated in the ritual only once, washing the feet of a "little southern lady" who still had her dialect, she knew that she "would never forget her or the experience of kneeling on the floor and washing her feet. I found that one can not harbor any egotistical or unclean feelings while washing another's feet." Similarly, George Suggs, who offered John 13:4–17 as the biblical reference for the practice, remembered it as a "truly humbling experience" that emphasized the basic equality of both lord and servant.[33]

Although many working-class churches emphasized "the rewards of [the] life to come for the faithful," they were not necessarily fatalistic. Belief in faith healing, uninhibited expressions of one's faith and love for one's fellow humans, absorption of the theology found in sacred music, rejection of the world's standards for measuring success, willingly engaging in the humbling experience of symbolically "washing the disciples' feet"—these demonstrations of the importance of the sacred in their lives revealed that they looked forward to the here and the hereafter with optimism and confidence. Many had experienced disappointment in their lives, but their faith enabled them to overcome their frustrations and be thankful for what they had. For one rural-born white, church was a place "where you meet God, where for a little while you find Him and keep Him, where He tells you that it's all right, and it's going to be all right, and that no matter what, you'll come out on His side."[34]

The church was also a sacred realm in which working people could achieve the status, influence, and equality denied them in everyday life. George Suggs's father, George Sr., was a textile worker at the Old Mill in Bladenboro, yet he was also the treasurer of the White Oak Church, where he exercised his authority to refuse payment of unauthorized expenditures or to pay agreed-upon wages for construction work on the church even when the minister told him to pay less. One of the other church leaders was a supervisor at the Old Mill who expected his secular authority to carry over to church affairs, but not with George Suggs Sr. When the supervisor denied Suggs a plum job and demoted him to a sweeper position, Suggs quit rather than accept the change. Still, at church, he continued to wield power equal to both the minister and the Old Mill supervisor. Moreover, he eventually got his earthly reward when the company brought him back to a comparable position in the New Mill, outside the authority of the supervisor. Another textile worker, Edward Harrington, spoke of a final equality with his employer: "He's just a man, just like I am. He's dead now. Of course, he didn't carry nothing with him either. He had all that money and he didn't carry it with him."[35]

At times, the sense of spiritual equality provoked in workers a stubborn defense of their social class. James Pharis defied the secular authority of the company in his North Carolina mill village. He remembered coworkers saying, "If you didn't belong to the Hocutt Memorial Baptist Church over here, you didn't get along too well in the Plaid Mill." But Pharis would not be intimidated. When the preacher of the Hocutt Baptist Church asked him about church membership, he replied that he was "of the Christian faith." When the preacher tried to convince him that it would be to his benefit to join, Pharis replied: "Now listen, Preacher. If you want to talk church with me, you talking on the wrong line. I don't join nothing because my boss is a member if I don't want to join. If I go to the Baptist Church or join the Baptist Church, it's going to be because I want to join the church and not because my boss is a member."[36] In intriguing ways, the personal access to God that southern white workers found in their religion encouraged them to assert a personal authority that would not bow to either employers or unions. However, as the future would make clear, they could more easily avoid unions than employers.

In some cases, ministers and church leaders felt uncomfortable with the changes spurred by popular religious expressions that grew amid the Depression. Francis Curnutte, a seminary-trained Methodist minister who grew up in the Mingo County coalfields of West Virginia, scorned the popular Protestantism of his region. "There was very little reason, understanding, there was very little use of the Scriptures," he recalled. "A few of them might have been interested in religion and their souls," but for others, it appeared to him to be a chance for boys to meet girls, for selling whiskey, or "a frolic for everybody in the area." On the other hand, Mingo County Baptist minister Raymond J. Adkins remembered the local popular religious culture with much greater empathy. Although he also mentioned the moonshine that might accompany religious gatherings, he admired the Freewill and Old Regular Baptist preachers: "They preached in their own style to their own people. And, ah, many of them did a terrific job [and] became famous in that area as preachers."[37]

Many observers, both then and today, dismiss the turn to popular religious beliefs during hard times as escapist, fatalistic, and otherworldly. Such convictions, they might argue, diverted the poor from attending to the tasks of improving the conditions of their lives.[38] However, believers were hardly out of touch with reality. Belief in God's grace, the hope of salvation, and even the worldly presence of Satan "all had real and precise psychological and social functions," according to historian Wayne Flynt. Their practices and faith were reassuring in difficult times; they allowed the emotional release of "resentments and fears" and brought "calm as well as excitement."[39] Textile worker Louise Jones's faith was critical to her surviving hard times: "God helped us through. He's been with us all the time. I give God credit for being what I am and having the life I've had, and helping me all of my life." Mozelle Riddle, the daughter and wife of millworkers, echoed Jones: "If I hadn't had the faith in God, I'd a-never got by. I feel like if I hadn't, I wouldn't be here today. Cause he's really stood by me in hard times and rough times."[40]

The religious activities and beliefs of working people fulfilled a variety of needs during a time of turmoil and change. Sociologist John Kenneth Morland, a keen observer of the sacred world of millworkers, identified a number of reasons why religion continued to be important in working-class life. First was its role in helping people adjust their own mortality. Recognizing the struggle between God and Satan for every soul, many working people believed deeply that by adhering to precepts laid out in the Bible and Jesus's teachings they could expect that "death will be a great victory," despite the knowledge that mankind by its very nature makes everyone a sinner. God's grace and belief in Jesus as savior nevertheless opened a path to salvation. In many respects the promise of life in the hereafter is compensation for the travails of life in the present. This strikes some as fatalism, but it also reflects a belief that Christians are merely passing through a world of sin and that the trials of the present are a test of one's faith. Particularly for working people attracted to Holiness and Pentecostal churches, this belief became a repudiation of the world, which they equated with something evil.[41]

Meanwhile, according to Morland, religion gave working people both a community to hold in high esteem and a strong sense of their own individual worth. As was evident in the reminiscences of Ralph Simmons, which began this chapter, workers believed "that every person, no matter what his ability or accomplishment, is of infinite value and concern to God and to Jesus." The Church of God in York, South Carolina, demonstrated this weekly when it sent its bus to all the neighboring villages so that anyone who wanted to attend would have transportation. Unfortunately, Morland never comments about whether the bus driver drove through black neighborhoods or opened the bus doors for African Americans. Finally, churches provided opportunities for self-expression and positions of authority. These might occur during the actual religious services—testimonies, prayers, singing, approaching the altar—or in some leadership capacity in church governance.[42] In all these ways, religion met real needs in the minds of working people. We would be astonished if it did not also shape attitudes about how believers should interact with the political and economic groups they encountered.

We Got the Lord, Too, on Our Side

The popular religious beliefs of the southern white working class were more than individual and community coping mechanisms for a life of toil. Popular religiosity inevitably confronted instances of danger, privation, and brutality that made many working people feel in the grip of un-Christian and inhumane injustices. Under some circumstances, Christian workers felt compelled to take action rather than seek the means to cope. During the Depression in Harlan County, Kentucky, many Pentecostal miners felt that their faith gave religious sanction to union activities. Lay preachers, like Findlay Donaldson, who made his living as a miner, could assert: "A man who won't support his children [by supporting the union] is worse than an Infidel, and there is no place for that man but Hell." Social activist Myles Horton tried but never quite understood the paradox of popular religion. He noted that unpaid preachers would "preach on Sunday, this fundamentalist religion, then go out on the picket line all week." Meanwhile, "preachers in the cities were talking liberal theology, liberalism, all the modern . . . interpretations of religion, yet they would side" with the coal operators.[43] Similarly, sharecroppers and tenants joined the Southern Tenant Farmers Union in Arkansas and Missouri in part because organizers like Claude Williams and Howard Kester brought a prophetic Christianity to rural struggles. Williams interpreted the Bible as a "continuous record of revolutionary struggle."[44] These individuals plumbed the radical implications of faith. Southern whites could take a variety of messages from emotional but theologically conservative folk religion in the 1930s and 1940s.

One reason prophetic ministers like Donaldson, Kester, and Williams succeeded was their appreciation of the possibilities of popular Christianity in local contexts. Alva Taylor praised their acceptance of the newer sects. Writing to Williams, Taylor asserted, "The mountain preachers have agreed with you regarding the sincerity of their Pentecostal preaching brethren. Now if we could induce the more highly educated men in our mountains to adopt your method rather than one of criticism and denunciation, we would get somewhere."[45] Through the radical People's Institute of Applied Religion, which Williams created in 1940 to recruit "leaders from the people to preach and practice the Gospel of the Kingdom of God on earth," he trained effective labor organizers—people like Harry Koger of the United Cannery, Agricultural, Packing, and Allied Workers. Williams taught Koger not only to embrace the spirituality of southern workers but also to link it to "a God who wants them to get their bellies full of food" and "a Jesus who, much to their surprise, is actually interested in them having a more abundant life here on Earth and not merely 'pie in the sky' after they get up to that gold-paved city."[46] Of course, this was more effective in the Depression than it would be in more prosperous times.

Southern Protestantism during the 1930s was remarkable for its heterogeneity and for the variety of ways that it had helped people cope with privations. Religious beliefs helped southern whites interpret the day-to-day experiences that they had with labor organizations. It was often through the sacred that they made sense of their worldly achievements and disappointments. To return to the coalfields for a moment, many interviewees remembered the struggle to win collective bargaining rights there as a Pentecost, despite the harsh and often bloody conflict that was required. In an occupational setting where death was ever present and struck with suddenness, a collective mentality grew among miners and their families, emphasizing the need to band together. There is no better example of this than the reaction of miners to an explosion or cave-in. Every available miner will throw caution to the wind to reenter the mine to rescue any survivors or to retrieve the dead for a proper burial. Warren Lilly, who grew up in the mining region of western Virginia, believed that miners "tend to have a deeper faith than a lot of people," because "when you go into the mines in the morning, you don't know whether you are going to come out in the evening or whether you will be carried out." This omnipresent dread fueled both a powerful emotional religion (and the spread of Pentecostalism in the central Appalachian coalfields) as well as a fierce determination to build the union, not just for material gains but also for the safety and security of miners and their families. More than one Depression-era miner linked the two in much the same way Delbert Jones did: "I think they got the principle of the union from Christianity. And, to be honest with you, I think just as much of my union as I do religion. Because if it wasn't for the union, we wouldn't get treated, get medication . . . 'Course, we got the Lord, too, on our side. And it's a blessing to have both."[47]

The often-violent reaction of coal operators to union organizing only served to sanctify the meaning of union victories. Granny Hager, whose father and husband were miners, was a devout member of the Holiness Church in Leslie County, Kentucky, but was also a regular on the picket line despite getting "slapped around pretty bad" by mine guards. In her mind, the union's success was evidence of her faith. Debbie Spicer recalled the efforts to intimidate UMW organizer and Church of God minister B. H. Moses in Harlan County, Kentucky, efforts that included an attempt to dynamite the Clospint Church of God. Spicer attributed the survival of Rev. Moses and the UMW to divine intervention. "You can't destroy a child of God as long as the Lord's got something for him to do," Spicer testified. "They didn't do nothing with Daniel, they put him in the lions' den but the lions wouldn't eat him, they just laid down." Likewise, the dynamite "didn't blow brother Moses up. Didn't even singe the hair on [his] head. Brother Moses was a real man of God, he's a real preacher."[48]

At the same time, the popular religious beliefs that appeared to protect the miners' leaders against unrighteous persecution from the coal operators could betray radical union organizations. In the Kentucky coalfields in the 1930s the principal union was the Communist-led National Miners Union. For a time, that was not a problem for Pentecostal miner-preachers like Finley Donaldson. But when the union sent Donaldson and other Kentucky miners to Chicago for training, they learned that the charges of atheistic Communism that union opponents had used contained more than a grain of truth. Upon their return, these miners turned against the National Miners Union and published a pamphlet in which Donaldson's statement read: "The teachings of the Communist party would destroy our religious beliefs, our government and our homes. In teachings they demand their members to teach their children that there is no God; no Jesus; no Hereafter; no resurrection of the dead." Donaldson warned his "fellow workers and citizens" that in Chicago he attended a demonstration and heard the Party "denounce our government and our flag and our religion."[49]

In the iron-ore and coalmining company towns around Birmingham, Alabama, eventual union triumphs also reinforced notions of the righteousness of collective action. Frank Bonds grew up in the company town of Docena, Alabama. He recalled that union organizers put a lot of pressure on miners to join during the late 1930s, but also that "the miners themselves were ready to be organized due to safety conditions, wages, that sort of thing." The union thus contributed to a strong sense of community among Docenans: "They were very hardworking. They were very patriotic. They were very, I wouldn't say over-religious, but had a very strong faith." Christine Cochran, the wife of a Docena miner and a devout Baptist, believed that one of the major benefits of the union was that the company-town sheriff could no longer terrorize the people who lived in Docena. Eula McGill, whose "very religious" father carried a union card in notoriously anti-union Gadsden, Alabama, took to heart his reasoning. He said: "If a person lives in this world without trying to make it a better place to live in, [then] he's not living, he's just taking up space." Jack Durden, a Baptist who helped organize the United Steel Workers of America local in the Birmingham suburb of Fairfield, felt the union improved conditions and made the workers "proud to work for the company." Even disputes over work rules did not create permanent rancor, according to Durden: "I think U.S. Steel intended to live up to the contract," but disputes meant "you had to file a grievance because different people put different interpretations on things. Just like you would on the Bible."[50]

In the Birmingham area, however, entrenched attitudes about race complicated the religious sentiments that workers attached to their experiences with unions. Evangelist Hiram Hutto recalled that the white community in Docena put on blackface minstrel shows for entertainment throughout the 1930s. Others remembered that black and white youths often engaged in scuffles over community space. Coal- and ore-mining towns typically provided segregated and inferior facilities to African Americans and encouraged racial animosities that were difficult for the unions to overcome.[51] Some black miners and steelworkers felt that the unions in the Birmingham district, with the notable exception of the Mine, Mill, and Smelter Workers (Mine, Mill)—a union with a large black membership and radical leaders—did little to advance blacks once they won collective bargaining. Black worker support for Mine, Mill raised another divisive issue in the Birmingham district—fears about Communism, particularly for deeply religious people.[52] Although it would not reach its peak until after World War II, the overlapping suspicions arising from race and politics meant that the religious interpretation of unionism in Alabama was far from clear.

Dalton, Georgia, offers another variation on the ways people filtered everyday experience through their religious beliefs. Crown Cotton Mills in Dalton was one of a small number of textile firms in which the workers successfully unionized during the 1934 general strike. But instead of solidifying a community, unionization actually split the workers into two mutually hostile groups. Crown Mills intensified the workload and rigidly enforced work rules put in place by the collective-bargaining agreement. The more casual atmosphere of the mill disappeared, and the workers—all poor, white, and overwhelmingly Protestant—chose sides based on values, which quickly became entangled with their personal religion. For instance, Henry Wade, who played on the Crown baseball team and sang in the choir at Crown View Baptist Church, believed strongly in the union and the improvements that came with New Deal labor laws. He walked the picket line when the union struck against the stretch-out in 1939 and took a job in Chattanooga when the action dragged on for six months. He returned when the company reopened, but only for two shifts. The new workload "was more than we could do," he recalled, and Wade took a job in the burgeoning non-unionized carpet industry. Earl Hardin played for the same company baseball team, and he sang at the Mt. Rachel Baptist Church where his father was the choir leader. For Hardin, however, his most vivid recollections of the 1939 strike included the harassment he received for crossing the picket line, and he remained militantly anti-union in the strike's wake.[53]

People on both sides used religious beliefs to understand the divisions even though they attended the same Baptist churches. Thelma Parker, who went to Crown Baptist, remembered that some pro-union workers left the church because of the hostilities: "You couldn't go to church and not speak to people," she claimed. Sibyl Queen associated the strikers with fallen Christians. She spoke of one woman who went to church, but "every time they'd have a meeting, she'd have to get saved again." When the woman yelled at Queen for crossing the picket line, Queen responded, "Get your hand down. There'll be a [revival] meeting in town next fall and you'll be wanting to shout."[54] Most remarkable was the response of John Cronic, a devout Baptist millworker, who parodied the turmoil of the strike by using the Twenty-Third Psalm:

> The CIO is my enemy. I am always in want.
> It makes me to lie down in hog wallows, it leads me beside the still factory.
> It troubles my soul. It leads me in the paths of destruction for its own sake.
> It makes me walk in the valley of starvation, and I fear all evil for it has with
>   it.
> Their rods and brickbats trouble me; they prepare an empty table for me in
>   the presence of my friends.
> They anoint me with embarrassment; my cup runs empty, and surely
>   starvation will follow me all the days of my life and I will dwell in the
>   poorhouse forever.[55]

Union supporters likewise related the strike's outcome to issues of religious conscience and morality. John Bramblett, for one, generally "felt better about a person that did belong to the union." He noted, "I, myself, am a Baptist by choice, I also always have been. If I felt right doing it, I sort of felt like it was right," but he also acknowledged that "the next feller has a different way of thinking," and he was entitled to that as well. In many respects, Bramblett's attitudes captured the independence of thought emphasized by Baptist teaching. Such ideas could bolster strong bonds among a community of likeminded people, but they also undermined some of the compulsory features of unionism, such as the closed shop and the very essence of collective bargaining, which took away a worker's right to make an individual bargain.[56] This would become increasingly important in the postwar era, as the passage of the Taft-Hartley Act enabled states to outlaw the closed shop and make union membership completely voluntary.

For large numbers of workers in the Piedmont textile factories, their Depression-era experiences with unions elicited a more consistent reaction. The largely unsuccessful general strike of 1934 and failed union campaigns during the remainder of the decade had an enervating effect on workers. Most feared the animosity and divisiveness that might ruin their community or force them to leave. Alice Evitt joined the union during the 1934 strike because "everybody else did out here," but she refused to participate in the strike because, as she said, "I don't believe in trouble. If I can't do somethin' for somebody, I sure don't want to do nobody no harm." Geddes Dodson also heard stories about the consequences of losing a job and being blackballed from his brother-in-law. Although Dodson "joined a union one time," he realized "I was wrong, and so I just fell out and turn agin them whenever I seen what was coming up to me."[57]

These regional capsules cannot begin to capture the complexity of the South during this period or even the variations of thinking within each of these examples. Popular religion, after all, exists alongside formal religious belief and practice, but it also relies on the ways individuals interpret and use those beliefs to give order and meaning to their lives. There were people in the coalfields whose sacred values rejected unions and defied the union influence that emerged there. Some Piedmont millworkers overcame fear, intimidation, and defeat to believe strongly in the union. In Dalton, Georgia, textile unionism rebounded from the devastating defeat of 1939 and reemerged during World War II. The religious ideas that workers developed about unions were not the result of some inherent fatalism or optimism, and nor were they the inevitable product of sermons, doctrines, and ecclesiastical policies. Instead, people blended messages they heard in churches, revivals, and midweek prayer meetings with the things they experienced in the mines, mills, and communities where they lived the rest of their lives. Moreover, those messages and those experiences were constantly changing, particularly after World War II.

I Don't Know if You Can Modernize God

While there was much continuity in working-class religious patterns on both sides of the war, there were also some important differences. Increasingly, workers made their choices about where to worship in a new economic and social climate. If the religion of working people during the Depression was a "religion for the blues," postwar workers went to church better off materially than they had ever been. The large numbers of coal and ore miners in Tennessee and Alabama saw their wages soar as a result of union contracts. The industry depression that would slash jobs and weekly paychecks was still in the future. Complementing coal and ore mining were the well-paying jobs in the bustling iron and steel industry. White employment in Alabama's iron and steel mills shot up from 21,428 in 1940 to 33,578 in 1960. The postwar decade also continued to expand opportunities for workers to move into defense-related jobs around southern military bases and establishments like the Oak Ridge National Laboratory in Tennessee, the Savannah River Plant in South Carolina, and the Redstone Arsenal in Huntsville, Alabama. Textile workers in eastern North Carolina could exert greater pressure on wages as a result of expanded shipbuilding in Wilmington or work at the military base, Fort Bragg.[58]

The South continued to attract more than its share of low-wage jobs, particularly in textiles, apparel, paper, lumber, and woodworking, but workers in those industries experienced improvements in wages and working conditions even as they remained well behind their northern counterparts. Southern wages rose from between 50 percent to 60 percent of their northern counterparts during the 1930s to between 70 percent and 80 percent by 1950. Most important to many whites still making the transition from farming and rural life to modern urban living, the decade after the war saw the South gain jobs at a faster rate than did the nation as a whole. Political leaders and industrialists understood this well; one of the most effective tools that they could use against unions was the charge that organized labor was only interested in organizing southern workers to protect northern workers and prevent factories from relocating in the region. Southern elites emphasized that if working people would only resist the lures of union organizers, jobs would flow into the South. Moreover, with the guarantees of the Fair Labor Standards Act, many millhands thought long and hard about the question "What do we need a union for?"[59]

At the same time, the feeling of being more prosperous came with a price. The rural worlds of most southerners were disappearing amid a massive reshuffling of people and upheaval in their communities. More than one-half of the counties in the South actually lost population during the decade following the war, taking a terrible toll on families and small towns, even as southern cities grew at rates above the national average. Adjustment to modern, urban environments occurred during growing tensions and fears that came with the Cold War. Music that appealed to the southern working class suggests a changed outlook. During the late 1940s and early 1950s, the religiously inspired country songs that attracted large country music followings increasingly reflected interest in Christ's Second Coming and the Rapture or in restoring the centrality of religion to domestic life that had dissipated because of consumerism and modern values. Mac Odell, for instance, wrote a number of hit songs that predicted the imminent end of the world, such as *Battle of Armageddon* and *This World Can't Stand Long*. Meanwhile, musical acts like the Bailes Brothers called to mind how modern living often came at the expense of traditional rural Christian values in songs such as *When Heaven Comes Down* or *Dust on the Bible*.[60]

Worshipping, often in a distinctly working-class congregation, helped people make sense of their changing circumstances. The values and lessons churchgoers absorbed through rituals, sermons, sacred music, and religious fellowship did not dictate how they would react, but these experiences did reinforce instincts and perceptions about the instability that worshippers felt all around them. The recollections of working people offer glimpses into how their faith influenced their feelings about the labor movement as it sought remake southern society in the postwar era. What were the religious values that workers drew upon to cope with the transformation of their lives? Oral histories emphasize the pride white workers took in being self-reliant as far as possible, a value reinforced by the local autonomy and the respect for individual expressions of faith encouraged by evangelical churches, which prized a degree of personal independence but coupled that with a feeling of duty that arose from what they felt were sacred obligations as spelled out in Scripture. Working people of faith balanced their independence and insistence on a personal relationship with their God with deep-seated connections to their congregations, or what they saw as voluntary communities of believers. If these seem contradictory, most were able to harmonize the individual and communal aspects of their faith as a result of the sectarian character of southern evangelicalism, which left people free to seek out or form churches that matched their beliefs. Once created, these communities emphasized building harmony and avoiding the sorts of conflict that would pit one child of God against another. The attraction of these communities of believers had a flip side—the suspicion of outsiders and those who were not part of the fellowship, which not only targeted nonbelievers but also blacks who shared similar evangelical beliefs.

Many reminiscences also reveal that faith helped working people accept their lot in life. This suggests a degree of fatalism, but it was often expressed with hope and thankfulness for the gifts they had received, the most vital of which was their faith in God and His grace. Thankfulness was easier for many working people because their religion also shunned materialism and worldly things, a sign that they were spiritual beings. Finally, many workers spoke of their belief that their conversion experience compelled them to lead a new life, one that more closely adhered to all of the other things their faith valued. These faith-based values affected how working people viewed the CIO organizers who arrived in town.

One of the most frequently mentioned values in the oral histories with workers, particularly Carolina Piedmont millhands, was the importance of freedom and independence. There is a certain irony here; the mills had a reputation among labor-union people as being among the most oppressive environments. But many felt as did Eula Durham, a textile worker in Bynum, North Carolina, who rejected the appeals of labor organizations because, as she said, "I didn't want to give up my freedom for a union." She claimed to have told CIO organizers, "I can go outdoors when I get ready and come in when I please and I ain't paying that union nothing." Similarly, Mabel Summers, who worked in a hosiery factory, spurned unions for similar reasons: "I wanted to be my own person. If I wanted to quit, all right. If I wanted to go somewhere else to work, I wanted to, and I didn't want no man over me to tell me that I could not work." Clearly, they did not understand textile-union goals, and many were swayed by the scare tactics used by employers who argued that a union would destroy flexibility in the workplace. But they often equated the freedom to make choices with the autonomy they expected in their churches, and they used the informality of the workplace to help their fellow workers in what they believed was a truly Christian fashion. Durham fondly recalled the early days in the factory when, if someone fell behind in work, everyone pitched in to help catch up; "It was just like a big family down there," Durham claimed.[61]

Others related the provisions of a union contract to a loss of independence. Murphy Yomen Sigmon, who spent most of her working life in a Hickory, North Carolina, cotton mill, acknowledged that unions had been useful in pushing wages up, but she preferred to work in a nonunion mill. "The union has got laws, too, to go by, and if I'm working with the plant, I just don't feel like I can satisfy both" the company and the union. S. L. Hardy, who began working at the Avondale Mills in Graniteville, Alabama, in 1939, believed the company helped workers become leaders in the church and the community. Organized labor, in contrast, denied individualism. "The way I understand it," Hardy asserted, if "the unions set up something, and if you work, you have to accept it. And it's just not that way." Des Ellis, who worked for the Crown Mills in Dalton, Georgia, stated it simply, saying that most workers "just didn't want the union telling them what they had to do," especially now that the wolf was no longer at the door.[62]

Throughout the South, the churches that were most successful in attracting working people were those that emphasized local autonomy and respect for personal convictions. Robert Latta, who grew up in preacher George Swinney's Baptist Church in the 1930s and 1940s and became a minister himself, accounted for the success of the Southern Baptist Convention's growth among workers in the postwar years: "Baptist churches are supposed to be a democracy, you know, one of the last bastions of democracy we have, and they just feel like they've [Baptist people] got a right to complain." He added, "One of the things that Baptists have always held dear, that although the minister occupies a place of prominence . . . he is really no different from them. No more important. God may speak to them just as much as He may speak to the minister," and "the person in the pew has just as much authority as anybody else to cast his vote as to which way he wants to go."[63] This was also true of the Holiness, Pentecostal, Wesleyan Methodist, and smaller independent churches that expanded in the postwar South. Consider the implications of this personalistic religious culture against what many working people understood about the CIO and the collective-bargaining process.

Workers also had a fierce sense of self-reliance nourished by their faith. Josephine Glenn, a devout Baptist millhand, blanched when union organizers told her that if she did not join the union, she might be out of a job. She replied, "I never have looked for one, [when] I didn't find it [a job]. It might not be what I wanted or where I wanted, but you can always find one till you can do better." She rejected the union in large part because, she said, "You'd have to come up to their standards. And we worked just about like we wanted to, as long as we stayed at work." Union people, she felt, were "just restless." Many were "drunks and drifters," she said. "If they wasn't out drunk, they was quit and gone."[64] Some others felt that unions would dictate work stoppages that would undermine their self-reliance. Flake Meyers, a furniture worker and a Methodist who liked to visit a variety of churches around his home in the Carolina Piedmont, worried, "If you'd bring a union in there they'd come in and tell you what to do, like when we'd go out on strike." To Meyers, "where you had a good job that was paying you pretty good, why [would you] get a union in there to tell you what to do?" Most of the workers who wanted a union, he asserted, "were all the time cracking about something. They wasn't satisfied about their job. Just drifters, mostly."[65] For people like Glenn and Meyers, who valued their churches and stable communities, unions threatened what was most important to them—steady work.

Mary and Carl Thompson bought a house when the company decided to sell its mill village homes in 1939. Later, the Thompsons came to know some of their bosses personally, not only through work but also through church, but the company never tried "to dictate to the churches at all." Every decision "was voted through the church." Mary Thompson's faith made her satisfied with her lot and thankful to God. "I think the Lord is all we are, in my life," she asserted. He helped her through illnesses and heart trouble, and he consistently provided for her and Carl. The Thompsons' faith made them content with working hard: "It's just in the Bible that people is supposed to make their living by the sweat of their brow," she insisted. Walter Scott Workman, a furniture worker, opposed unions because he felt they ceased to be what they were supposed to be, "a bargaining unit." Instead, he believed that "the employees start hiding behind it," rather than do their duty.[66]

These sentiments came through over and over in the interviews with working-class whites. Ina Lee Wrenn, who married a loom fixer in Glencoe, North Carolina, claimed that the union was not successful because people were "pretty satisfied." Wrenn, who loved Glen Hope Baptist Church, had no complaints: "I knew before I went to work what I was supposed to make. If I hadn't been satisfied, I wouldn't [have] started." She candidly assessed her life: "We make a living, own our own home, got two children in college, if we owe anybody a penny I don't know it. What more can a poor man ask for?"[67] Similarly, Lora and Edward Wright were content with "the way we were working." The Wrights attended the Baptist church and even taught Sunday school. They read the Bible every night and always tried "to put Christ first" in their lives. The Wrights also had family prayers, believing that "that's the way to keep your married life in harmony." Whenever they faced troubles, they read the "Ninety-First Psalm," which was "a good Psalm to teach you how to put your faith and trust in the Lord for safekeeping."[68]

For many white, working-class Christians, work was a sacred duty. In Dalton, Georgia, the millhands at the Crown Cotton Mill Company often agonized about their responsibilities when employees chose to challenge the company. Sybil Queen, who was baptized in the Crown Mill Lake at age eight, believed that "if you went ahead and did a good job, you would [always] have a job," but that the "union didn't want to do the right thing." She claimed that "there was plenty of bad work once they got the union. That was what closed the mill." When strikes occurred, she crossed the picket lines without shame: "There's plenty of people on this picket line that should be working," she told the union, pointing out a man who owed fifty dollars for milk and groceries. Steelworker Edward H. Ratcliff agreed with the notion that "either you work or you don't eat." For him, an ex-Marine who appreciated the strong Baptist faith he found in eastern Kentucky, "this goes back to Biblical days and that's what is written. That's the way it's supposed to be."[69]

The commitment to hard work and being grateful for God's gifts meshed with a religious belief that Christians should put no stock in worldly possessions. Leonard Curtis Wilson, a loom fixer at Roanoke Rapids, North Carolina, did not "think it fair to God and our country for the unions to insist on raising the prices of everything that is made or growed by escalating the price of labor and making the promise of more and more money each year." His faith taught him otherwise: "I do believe it is against God's will for the unions to preach more and more money, for 1 Timothy 6:10 tells us that the love of money is the root of all evil." Thomas Snipes, a Methodist and a machine fixer in the Burlington Mills, made a virtue of his antimaterialism: "I never accumulated a whole heap, and never particularly wanted a whole heap. Just to make a decent honest living; that's about all there is in the world anyhow."[70] Of course, making a decent living was easier in the postwar South.

Working people emphasized their access to a spiritual equality. Ethel Hilliard criticized a woman who seemed too proud: "That's not Christianity, that's not the right kind of heart to have." Rhoda Napier, who gravitated from the Old Regular Baptist church of her youth to a Holiness church in the coalfields of eastern Kentucky, claimed that "God loves the poor person just as good as he does the rich one. In my belief," she said, "a poor person, a real poor person, has a better chance [of salvation] than the rich people. Do you know why? They pray more and things. Rich people living so high, they don't think of God, they don't give him a thought." Christine Cochran, an Alabama Baptist, preferred the simplicity of small, older churches. "I think that the church was more meaningfully for God when we were in the old church," she claimed. "The spiritual past was much more meaningful in those days. I don't know if you can modernize God or not."[71] In a world where community, politics, race relations, and even family faced modernization, Cochran felt safer believing that God remained traditional.

The personal relationships of the church community at times continued paternalistic patterns. Although many chose to worship in class-segregated churches, congregations might include overseers and management people as equals. Louise Rigsbee Jones singled out one overseer, Edgar Moore, who taught Sunday school in her church. Fred Fox, who worked at Conover Knitting in Conover, North Carolina, remembered the owner as a good employer who offered bonuses and insurance ahead of other companies and as a good church member who "did a lot for the church, too," including donating land. But Fox did not resent the owner. Instead he praised him for living up to the ideals posted on a plaque over the factory door: "Life's Material Resources Are Entrusted to Many by God for the Benefit of All."[72]

Others appreciated the potential assistance gained by worshipping with the boss. Everett Padgett "was not a number on the payroll" to the local mill owner who attended his Baptist church. Religious fellowship enabled him to borrow money from the owner for his wife's emergency operation. Likewise, Johnnie Jones, a Methodist millhand, preferred paternalism over the CIO "because you got anything you wanted. If you needed fifty dollars [to help build a house] you could go right there [to the employer] and get in. A union wasn't going to let you have it."[73] Some Christian working people repaid employers with loyalty. Virgil Prewett, who worked in an Alabama hosiery mill following World War II, asserted that the owners "were individuals who felt pretty strongly about the people that worked for them" and also "gave something to the church." As a result, those "hard-working, honest Protestant people" would not even think about trying to form a union, according to Prewett.[74]

As conditions improved in the workplaces throughout the South due to government regulations and wartime conditions, workers valued informal community harmony over the divisiveness that unions seemed to bring. Willie Mae Defore believed that the combination of the work at Crown Mill and the services at Crown View Baptist Church created a community in Dalton, Georgia, where "everybody was like kinfolks." But when a strike occurred, it divided families, including her own. Her sister crossed the picket line, which made Willie Mae feel "hurt," even though she tried not to show it.[75] Several others recalled how strikes resulted in workers leaving a particular church. Mack Fetrell Duncan, a loom fixer at the Poe Mills in Burlington, North Carolina, recalled the impact on his Baptist church. Although his minister worked with both strikers and nonstrikers during a strike in 1946, Duncan said that "a lot of people that were coming to the Baptist Church and pretty faithful, that joined the union, after that they left the church. You didn't see them in church after that." Such events took a toll on the factory as well as the church. George Shue, a millhand and a devoted Baptist, believed that unions sapped feelings that helped create a community. Previously, Shue insisted, "people lived more happy." They "didn't have nothing," but if "somebody'd get sick, they'd [neighbors and other millhands] come down to see about it and help 'em." When the union came, he believed, it forced people to get approval for everything, and there was "no satisfaction in a mill like that. That's just like you're under a gun."[76]

In a postwar atmosphere where religious voices increasingly warned of the coming end times and the need to separate from nonbelievers, the divisiveness that inevitably emerged when unions arrived repelled some religious workers. Ethel Faucette feared union organizers who, she said, "came in from somewhere else, and I don't know who they was." George Elmore "didn't want to see that outside crowd come in there and taking dues" from the workers, because they "basically didn't give a damn about the good will of the people."[77] Lucille Hall, a worker at Crown Cotton Mills in Dalton, Georgia, resented that the union would "send outsiders in here to tell you how bad you were treated. You'd know better." Musker Semple Moore disliked that the union was run by people whose names you had difficulty pronouncing: "All the high knockers were some kind of foreigners," he stated.[78]

Ethel and George Faucette, Baptist millworkers at Glencoe Mill from the 1910s to the 1950s. Courtesy of the Southern Historical Collections, University of North Carolina at Chapel Hill.

Religious conversion experiences in the Cold War era seemed to gain in importance for some who felt it was their new duty to shun worldly issues. Sam Johnson, a miner in the coalfields of eastern Kentucky "loved the world too much" in his early life. He drank liquor, "picked the banjer," and was hindered by the Devil before being saved. "When God forgives ye, you're no longer the keeper of yourself," he noted. In his changed life, Johnson no longer paid attention to elections and stopped voting. "Too much evil around the voting place," he claimed. "God tells me to shun all kinds of evil and to keep myself unspotted from the world." Kasper Smith, who joined the Church of God in the 1940s, felt remorse for his participation in the 1934 strike. His religious conversion convinced him that unions and strikes were contrary to God's will. "I couldn't do that now," Smith reminisced about his earlier union activities. "See, I joined the union before I joined the church. I haven't joined no other organizations *since*."[79]

Changing Christian values did not keep all workers out of unions. Annie Perkins, a Bynum, North Carolina, textile worker, credited unions for protecting job fairness, particularly seniority rights. Senior workers who were qualified should have the first opportunity to move up to a higher-paying job, she asserted. John Bramblett rose to become president of the union at the Crown Cotton Mills after World War II in part because he always stood up "for the underdog." J. W. Crow likewise felt that Crown workers turned to the union for a "little bit of security." In Dalton, Georgia, many had their "entire life wrapped up in the mill, and it was terrifying to think that they would be fired from the job or laid off." If the union could offer some security, many workers would join, Crow claimed.[80] Loyd Winn, a tobacco worker who was active in a Holiness church in Durham, North Carolina, joined the union and became the local chaplain because the foremen were "unfair at times." Frank Bonds, who worked as a coal miner for a time in Docena, Alabama, believed that "one of the major reasons for unions . . . was for safety." In his experience, workers were attracted to the possibility that collective bargaining agreements could improve safety conditions even more than wages. Ernest Carico, a miner in southwestern Virginia, was equally devoted to the improvements brought by the United Mine Workers and the Old Regular Baptist church.[81]

Even when workers interpreted religious messages to support unions, however, they did not lose sight of the Christian values that turned other workers away from organized labor. Recall the attitude of John Bramblett, the union president at Crown Mills, who nevertheless respected the right to anti-union feelings shared some of his co-workers. Ernest Carico praised the United Mine Workers but felt "that they strike when they shouldn't," often doing harm to the local community. Loyd Winn, a former union chaplain, complained that "the union has fixed it so that so many people don't even earn their money."[82] James Pharis, who was a local union officer for the United Textile Workers, asserted that he "ain't joined no organization against the company" even though he supported collective bargaining. He insisted that he was "fair for the union and . . . fair for the company." When the union sent "radical speakers" to the union hall, Pharis protested: "Wait a minute. You're on the wrong track here. You ain't going to make no hit with the people here." Clifford Simmons, the brother of Ralph Simmons, whose story opened this chapter, was more favorable toward unions than his sibling. They grew up in the Lutheran church and both worked for Southern Furniture. But Clifford joined the union, even though he objected to strikes and anti-company attitudes. He probably would have agreed with Claude Thomas, a Pentecostal and a union member who asserted that workers "regardless of how embittered they may be toward the very company that's put bread on their table . . . it doesn't change the fact that they should be grateful for having made a living."[83]

As mentioned in chapter 2, there was an interesting contradiction in the attitudes of many religiously inclined working-class whites toward politics. Much in the postwar evangelical culture railed against a powerful national state, but those who lived through the Depression and benefited from the National Industrial Recovery Act and the Fair Labor Standards Act often defied the warnings of apocalyptic preachers and remained dedicated to President Franklin Roosevelt's New Deal. Hoy Deal, the devout Southern Baptist who listened to premillennialist radio preachers and the literal truth of every word of the Bible, also had pictures of John F. Kennedy and Martin Luther King Jr. on the walls of his home in the 1970s. "I'm a Democrat in my voting," he proudly stated, ignoring the discord between his evangelical beliefs and admiration for a Catholic president and a black civil rights leader. Eula Durham, who did not want to lose her freedom to a union, remembered that virtually all the millhands in North Carolina had fond memories of Roosevelt and the New Deal. "They loved him to death. Well, everybody everywhere I've ever heard say anything about him [loved him]." Ila Hendrix and Martha Atha attended Holiness and Pentecostal churches and likely encountered the antistatist warnings of the Nazarenes and the Church of God. Nevertheless, both were Democrats as a result of the Roosevelt administration.[84]

Religious devotion was a much less consistent force on racial attitudes of white workers. Although many of the churches that catered to poor whites, such as the Holiness and Pentecostal churches, had interracial traditions, by midcentury most white working people worshipped in segregated churches. Whether or not one agrees that southern white churches were in cultural captivity, the mainstream religious culture encouraged Jim Crow.[85] For every Hoy Deal whose wall had a picture of Martin Luther King Jr. or a Ralph Simmons who appreciated that black workers had a fairer shot at job equality, others developed a theology of segregation. They scoured the Bible for justification of Jim Crow, using Old and New Testament passages and narratives constructed by ministers and laypeople to sanctify segregation. The governor of Mississippi told ministers that his "knowledge of the Scriptures is extensive and nowhere can he find where the Bible advocates mixing the Races."[86]

White, working-class Christians allowed their own fears and anxieties about work to reinforce racist patterns. Baptist textile worker Josephine Glenn, for instance, complained about a deteriorating sense of responsibility that jeopardized the mills: "They have so many blacks, so to speak, and they will never carry their end of the load." Furniture upholsterer Eunice Austin, raised as a Methodist, recalled that women in the department were unhappy when the company first hired black women because they worried about what effect sharing the water fountain and the bathroom with blacks might have on their respectability.[87] For others, racist attitudes justified white advantages in the workplace. Mary Robertson, who helped organize in the racially mixed tobacco industry, recalled the unapologetic rationalizing that she found typical of many whites: "That was just the way God had created the world, that white people made cigarettes and the black people made chewing tobacco." Ironically, for people who felt it was a sacred duty to work hard, some nevertheless associated hard work with race. Jefferson Robinette, who worked in the Piedmont textile and furniture factories, still claimed to be in good shape in his seventies: "Oh, I get out here and work like a nigger all day long," he bragged.[88]

Ideas about gender relations did not always conform to what we normally think of as traditional Christian precepts either. Some workers believed that their evangelical Protestantism dictated a strictly patriarchal household. When Eunice Austin married, she left the Methodist church of her upbringing for her husband's Lutheran church because "he didn't think a man should go with the wife; he thought the wife should go with the man." Austin decided that she "wasn't going to be that contrary about it," so she changed churches and became chairperson of the altar committee. Pauline Griffith waited until she became pregnant before leaving her Baptist church for her husband's Methodist faith. She stated, "Because I don't believe in a man and wife being separated in their Christian living, I went with him and I worked in that church just as much as I ever worked in the Baptist." Emma Whitesell waited even longer than Griffith. She attended the Reformed church until her third child was born before going to the Methodist church that her husband's family attended, even though she still preferred her own.[89]

In many cases, however, women were more assertive in the spiritual life of the family. Geddes Dodson remembered his mother as the guiding religious force in the family. "She set and read the Bible and rocked the cradle with her toe. . . . She'd set and read her Bible to us children and tell us how to do." Bill Morris returned to southern West Virginia after experiencing "the wild side" during his service in the military. When he met his future wife, she and her mother were active in the Milton Baptist Church, so Bill started attending and had a conversion experience. Eventually he taught a Sunday school class and became a devoted Christian. Beatrice Adkins, whose first husband was an alcoholic, decided that her second marriage would benefit from religion. She and her new husband began reading the Bible together with a friend and they were both "saved" at their kitchen table.

The following Sunday they found a Baptist church to attend and became lifelong members.[90]

For a few women, spiritual equality within the family even led to a defiance of husbands on social issues. Tessie and George Dyer were textile workers in Charlotte, North Carolina. George was raised as a Hardshell Baptist but later joined a Missionary Baptist church. In his younger years, George left the South and worked on a railroad in Virginia and New York, where he joined the union and enjoyed the benefits that union membership provided. However, George was a union moderate. He appreciated what unions achieved, but believed that the employer needed to make a profit and wanted "nobody to tell them how to run their business." Eventually George returned to the South and moved to Charlotte, where he had to adapt. He married Tessie, who converted him to the Methodist church. Tessie admitted, "He says he is still Baptist, but he's joined the Methodists." While George and Tessie worshipped at the same church, their ideas about unions could not have been more different. George bristled at working in a nonunion environment, which he resented for "taking advantage of people. They can do it because they can." Tessie, on the other hand, always crossed union picket lines. "I was supposed to go to work, and I was going," she professed, and George assented. She argued with strikers and defied their slurs even though her husband was a union sympathizer. They nevertheless enjoyed a marriage of more than four decades.[91]

George and Tessie Dyer each interpreted their faith in ways that defied normal expectations, showing just how difficult it is to easily categorize the social attitudes of white, working-class Protestants. They are excellent examples, however, of how individuals took their religious beliefs, interpreted them in practical terms, and put them to work to do something that gave order and meaning to their lives. Neither had much real power on a day-to-day basis, but both felt a sense of control over their destiny and saw their lives as endowed with meaning. Yet one praised unions for holding employers accountable while the other disregarded the taunts of strikers and went to work.

The years around World War II heightened divisions within southern evangelical Protestantism. While historians like to speak of *a southern evangelical Protestantism* (by which they imply "white" evangelical Protestantism), social class fractured that notion. Christian workers and their bosses generally did not eat or socialize together and did not intermarry. Music, clothing, homes, language, terms of ridicule, and the wielding of power separated evangelical Protestants based on class.[92] We would be astounded if class did not also shape the passions, rituals, and practices of the sacred. There is no simple formula for understanding the ways that class sorted religious experience. Some workers worshipped with their employers, others in homogenous churches; some were Pentecostals, others were Lutherans; some were shouters, others were subdued. Similarly, their faith empowered them to give their own practical applications of the messages that religion imparted. But increasingly during these years, the combination of the changing circumstances of their lives and the religious values that they absorbed led a majority of southern white workers to cast a suspicious gaze on the promises that union organizers made. World War II was something of a watershed in that regard, as the postwar decade challenged the racial order, raised the specter of Communism, and reminded Christians of the horrors that could result from powerful states. Employers, as we will see in the next chapter, did their best to fuel those suspicions.

CHAPTER 4

Constructing a Region
of Christian Free Enterprise

In March 1942, Roger Norman Conger left his successful sales career to work with his father-in-law, William S. Hammond, to expand the market for the Hammond Laundry-Cleaning Machinery Company, headquartered in Waco, Texas. Waco was a small city in central Texas, famous only for a horrific lynching in 1921 until World War II transformed it, first by reviving the demand for cotton products and later by making it a center for military establishments and defense industries. Almost overnight, the previously stagnating city sprang to life; Waco became the armed forces' leading manufacturer of cots, tents, mattresses, and barracks bags. The Waco Army Air Field opened in 1942 to train pilots, followed by the building of the Bluebonnet Ordnance Plant. By 1943, Waco was home to nine defense plants. Roger Conger saw his opportunity. The Hammond Company converted to "war production," winning a contract to produce the laundry machinery for Henry Kaiser's shipbuilding operations in addition to government contracts for military-base laundry equipment. The company soon outgrew its production facility but benefited from the end of the war and the availability of a building erected by the North American Aircraft Company in Waco to manufacture airplane wings. Within a span of three years, the Hammond Company had tripled its manufacturing space and become one of the major laundry-machine making companies in the country.[1]

The Hammond story ran counter to the experiences of many local employers. Population skyrocketed, surging from 55,000 in 1940 to 84,000 by 1950, placing a terrible strain on wages and housing. In 1943, a War Manpower Commission study found only four vacant apartments in the area as soaring rents pinched the pockets of Waco workers. When the war ended, numerous major industrial concerns, starting with the Owens-Illinois Glass Company, sought to take advantage of the abandoned war production factories, the excellent transportation network, and the plentiful supply of labor that existed in the region. General Tire and Rubber soon followed, opening its plant with "a patriotic display and pageant and all sorts of commotion" encouraged by the Chamber of Commerce and local boosters. Newspaper editor Harry Mayo Provence remembered the hopes but also the anxieties generated by the arrival of large modern companies, some with unionized workforces: "There was a good deal of heartburn about it among the garment people and some others who [employed] mill workers—who weren't used to paying that sort of money." The changes also frightened the strong religious community in Waco (home to the Southern Baptists' Baylor University), which mobilized to pass a countywide prohibition law in 1944.[2]

Even Roger Conger worried about the toll that industrial development took on Waco and the Hammond Laundry-Cleaning Machinery Company. Before long, union organizers made their first efforts to gain representation rights for Hammond workers, to Conger's dismay. "We had always been a close-knit, family-knit sort of an organization," he recalled, even opening every Monday morning with a "devotional" meeting with employees in the assembly room on company time. "We gave the men an opportunity to either voice, if they felt sufficiently confident, a favorite scripture of theirs . . . or invite their minister or their Sunday school teacher to come down to their place of business and give a brief devotional" before work began. But as the workforce grew, Hammond hired workers who had been union members in other places, and they began to agitate for collective bargaining among the workers. Eventually, the employees voted to be represented by the Machinists Union, and "one of the first things the union did" after winning "was to eliminate the Monday morning [devotional] assembly," claiming that it was a "paternal" attitude that was no longer appropriate. William Hammond wanted to close the factory immediately, but Conger, after consulting with the company's lawyers, convinced Hammond that they could negotiate so slowly that the union would be forced to strike, at which time they could either replace the workers or "get a contract that we could live with."[3]

The struggle at the Hammond Laundry-Cleaning Machine Company to win the hearts and minds of the South's working class was repeated in thousands of workplaces as World War II came to an end. Waco turned out to be one of the hundreds of southern towns and cities that felt the first effects of the restructuring of American industry that followed the war. The story of the Hammond Company in Waco is particularly instructive, however, because it points to the role of religion in the competition between employers and unions for the loyalty of the workers. Religion, especially evangelical Protestantism, was a crucial part of the fabric of the informal employer-employee relations that existed in southern workplaces. After the war, many companies encouraged religious observances to reestablish the bonds that they believed they shared with their workers. These bonds included acknowledgement of the tremendous costs of maintaining democracy in an unstable world as well as the hopes for postwar prosperity. Numerous employers even utilized the model of military chaplains to experiment with programs that would bring ministers into the factory to counsel workers coping with the new circumstances remaking postwar America.[4]

This chapter will explore the articulation of a Christian free enterprise vision for the South at the end of the war. For evangelical businessmen, the region seemed a new promised land for growth and investment with a hard-working, low-wage labor force. The South was also a bulwark against the further spread of liberal, New Deal politics. For white Protestant evangelicals, Christian free enterprise could protect the region against the threats that modernism and state-centered bureaucracies posed to the southern way of life.

The Lure of the South

World War II left the South poised for dramatic postwar economic growth. Southern manufacturing had added thousands of new industrial jobs and attracted huge investments in technology, plants, and infrastructure.[5] These changes meshed with, and became an encouragement for, the industrial restructuring of the United States. Restructuring included a range of strategic moves that corporations used to revive sagging profits or, as was the case in the postwar era, regain control over production costs that the expansion of organized labor had eroded. Among the strategies employed by factory managers were revitalized programs of welfare capitalism aimed worker loyalty, public-relations campaigns on behalf of free-enterprise capitalism, and legislative lobbying designed to restrict union clout. Perhaps none of these strategies was as important as plant relocation, which was designed to tilt control over production in management's direction. This produced a spectacular transformation of the South.[6]

Companies claimed that they made decisions about where to locate new factories in the postwar years on the basis of a number of factors, only one of which was labor costs. For example, in 1949 the National Planning Association conducted a study, "Why Industry Moves South." Surveying eighty-eight industries, the study discovered that few executives could "justify a large investment based only on such an uncertain matter as a North-South wage differential." Most companies had a variety of reasons, ranging from tax inducements, materials availability, and markets, to cheap energy, land, and freight costs. But the relocation of American industry to the South seemed unstoppable. *Nation's Business* magazine heralded this trend as "America's 3rd Migration." Milder climates, increased leisure time, and agricultural prosperity added to the inducements attracting industry and people to the Sunbelt. From 1939 to 1954, the South and Southwest exceeded the national averages in nonfarm employment increases while the old manufacturing region in the Northeast fell well below those averages.[7]

Of course, the primary impetus for northern employers to pursue plant relocation at the end of World War II was the pitched contest between organized labor and large manufacturing concerns. During the war, union membership had grown from under 8 million to 12.5 million. Moreover, CIO membership grew at a much faster rate than that of the more conservative AFL.[8] In the fall and winter of 1945 and into 1946, a wave of CIO strikes swept through the nation's core industries as workers sought substantial wage increases to bring buying power into line with wartime inflationary prices. Equally frightening to the business community was the CIO's effort to get the federal government to play a broader role in smoothing the shift from a wartime economy to a peacetime one, including continuing wage and price controls. Starting in November 1945 and running through March 1946, 180,000 autoworkers, 200,000 electrical workers, 150,000 packinghouse workers, and 500,000 steelworkers walked picket lines, contributing to the greatest number of man-days lost to strikes in American history. When the dust settled, the CIO claimed that its unions had won wage gains of between 15 percent and 20 percent for more than 1.7 million workers. The strikes also announced that unions would be fixtures in American society for the foreseeable future.[9] As much as any other factor, this show of power by organized labor provided the critical context within which manufacturers began to explore the shift from the Rust Belt to the Sunbelt.

There were important distinguishing characteristics to the South's manufacturing growth. Despite some diversification during the war, the region remained wedded to industries from the first industrial revolution (textiles, clothing, woodworking), not the second. The apparel industry is an excellent example. In 1937, fewer than one of every ten apparel industry employees worked in the South. By 1947, the ratio was nearly one of every seven; in 1954 it was inching toward one of every five. During those years, apparel workers increased their share of the southern labor market from 5.3 percent to 8.3 percent. When combined with textiles, these two low-wage industries totaled almost one-third of all southern workers. Moreover, the textile industry had long proved to be difficult to organize for both the AFL and the CIO, regardless of region. Meanwhile, the high-wage industries that had appeared in the South during the war—transportation equipment and metals products—lost much of their labor market share in the first decade after the war, in contrast to what occurred in Waco.[10] Even when high-wage industries, such as electrical manufacturing, opened plants in the South, it was often to add low-wage factories making components. Radio and sewing-machine companies, such as Magnavox and Singer, moved cabinet-making operations to places like Greeneville, Tennessee, and Poinsett, South Carolina, in the 1940s, but not their primary products. Regardless of what manufacturers said publicly to groups like the National Planning Association, low-cost labor was the single most important factor determining plant location. One study conducted in Tennessee claimed that wages were critical to two-thirds of the firms opening plants there, and favorable labor-management relations (the lack of unions) ranked third. These factors set in motion a vicious cycle: the more dependent the South became on attracting low-wage industries to compensate for the decline in agricultural employment, the harder its leaders worked to ensure that wages remained low.[11]

To make certain that low-wage industries would find the South attractive, employers attacked measures they believed would improve the leverage of workers in labor markets. For example, many corporate leaders feared that fair employment practices legislation would raise the wages of black workers and diminish the power of employers to threaten to replace white workers who demanded wage increases. Consequently, in April 1945 the Southern States Industrial Council's Nashville and Washington offices made "defeat of the Fair Employment Practices Act the major objective for the months to come." Nine months later, the council congratulated its lobbyists, noting that the "outlook is that Southern filibuster will succeed and this [Fair Employment] bill will be put aside for the time being."[12] Other issues that occupied the council's work included wage and hour laws and unemployment compensation, but by far the most vital political target of southern employers was the closed shop demanded by unions. During the war, the National War Labor Board had encouraged collective bargaining and granted unions "maintenance of membership" awards that forced employers to accept unions as the bargaining representatives of their workforces—essentially a union shop agreement. Despite making gains (organized labor won the guarantee in sixty-seven of seventy cases heard by the Atlanta regional board), employers began to ignore the Board's orders as the war progressed. In Texas and Georgia, noncompliance with board orders by many firms became almost "epidemic," leading to widespread and uncontrollable strikes in the summer of 1944 and early months of 1945.[13]

Southern industrialists made it clear that contesting the union shop and collective bargaining was at the top of their legislative agenda. In Arkansas, the state legislature passed an "antilabor violence" measure in 1943, spurred to action by farm groups and a shady organization called the Christian Americans. This organization was a right-wing group headquartered in Houston, Texas, funded by generous gifts from corporate executives like John Henry Kirby, a Texas oil millionaire. A year later, the Christian Americans directed the campaign for a right-to-work amendment to the Arkansas constitution, the first such law in the land. This Arkansas law, which outlawed the closed shop, passed in spite of opposition in the older Populist strongholds in the northwestern part of the state and disapproval from future governors Sidney S. McMath and Orval Faubus.[14] The other state to ban the closed shop in its state constitution was Florida, where State Attorney General J. Tom Watson led the campaign with assistance from the Christian Americans. Watson sued to revoke the Tampa Shipbuilding Corporation's charter because its union shop agreement violated public policy, but the Florida Supreme Court overruled his actions. When the state passed a right-to-work amendment to its constitution, the labor federations advised their affiliates to appeal to the Department of Labor if a company refused to bargain a closed-shop agreement. Other southern states—Texas, Mississippi, Alabama—passed "antiviolence in strikes" laws to try and limit labor militancy, and several states passed laws requiring unions or union organizers to register and obtain identification cards, file financial statements, and limit initiation fees. However, many of these laws did not survive constitutional challenges in state courts. The Christian Americans also faced growing scrutiny; when the organization proposed a right-to-work amendment in Texas in 1945, the legislature instead voted 111 to 14 to investigate the organization's lobbying tactics. The negative publicity that resulted temporarily stemmed the right-to-work efforts in Texas, Georgia, and Tennessee.[15]

Employers hoping to diminish the threats of unions found allies who had their own reasons for fearing the changes that new factories might bring to the region. Local merchants and shopkeepers worried that industrialization would weaken the South's system of racial control. High-paying manufacturing jobs that offered a measure of independence to ex-servicemen, both black and white, might be lethal to Jim Crow if those servicemen also came back with new ideas about race relations. Already, newspapers reported on confrontations involving returning black servicemen in places like Columbia, Tennessee, where in January 1946 a minor dispute in a radio repair shop escalated into an armed conflict between blacks, a white mob, and local authorities. Four policemen died in the shooting before state patrolmen arrived to quell the unrest. Equally disturbing for much of the middle class in Columbia, the attorney who arrived to defend the blacks arrested by the state authorities was Maurice Weaver, an attorney for the CIO, a member of the Southern Conference for Human Welfare, and an advocate for social change. To many middle-class southerners in the 1940s, black demands for equality appeared to be bound up with the presence of the CIO.[16]

Southern planters joined the antilabor efforts of industrialists. In the Mississippi Delta, many planters believed that industry was necessary to provide new jobs for people displaced by the mechanization of cotton production, but they recognized that enticing northern factories often brought unions that were key components of the liberal coalition in the Democratic Party. Liberal Democrats supported antilynching legislation, abolition of the poll tax, and the establishment of a permanent Fair Employment Practices Committee among other issues that might undercut older political leadership. Consequently, Delta planters were the backbone of both segregation and right-to-work legislation. If they could successfully tap and combine fears of external threats to free-enterprise capitalism *and* white supremacy, they could create an industrial prosperity that would help them maintain political and social control. This they did, attracting factories with assistance from the state's Balancing Agriculture with Industry program. Jobs in places like Greenville Mills, a runaway carpet mill from Yonkers, New York, quickly became the most desirable in the region. Not only did employers hire grateful workers at wages far below what they paid in the North, but transplanted employers also followed the South's racial order by segregating black workers in the worst jobs and hiring whites to supervise them.[17]

Most ominous for many southerners was the apparent link between the growth of the CIO's unions and America's greatest postwar enemy, the Soviet Union.

For large numbers of Fundamentalists, who increasingly referred to themselves as evangelicals, the emergence of totalitarian states in the 1930s was a sign that the end times were near. Even the more modest state authority of President Roosevelt's New Deal government was suspect in their eyes. World War II had eliminated some of the powerful states—Germany and Italy—that were a threat to the American way of life, but the Soviet Union remained. To premillennialists, the Soviet regime, with its rejection of God and religion, became the embodiment of the Antichrist. Other evangelicals assigned the Soviet Union a different role in the coming Armageddon, but in either scenario, the reputed sympathy of unionists for Communism put them on the wrong side of the struggle for America's future. Even the most influential evangelist of the day, Rev. Billy Graham, included regular warnings of Communism as "a religion that is inspired, directed, and motivated by the Devil himself who has declared war against Almighty God." Labor's socialistic beliefs were thus a menace; for Graham, paradise was a place where there were "no union dues, no labor leaders, no snakes, no disease."[18]

Christian Free Enterprise

The rapid spread of evangelicalism in the South was a vital force attracting the attention of manufacturers looking to locate or relocate factories. Many companies began to realize that churches in their home communities in the North were unreliable partners. During the long and bitter strike in 1945–46, for example, General Electric Corporation "suddenly learned that many groups in the local communities distrusted its aims and objectives." This was true of clergymen who, to GE's amazement, "joined the picket lines in protest against our actions."[19] In response, companies explored rural locations in the postwar years looking for stability and more harmonious labor-management relations. In particular, they looked for towns that "possessed racial and religious homogeneity" and where the workers were "independent" in their thinking "but at the same time susceptible to supervision," according to the *Harvard Business Review*.[20] During the postwar decade, company executives found such potential factory sites in the South. There, chambers of commerce advertised the benefits for factories locating in a "distinctly religious city" where the "labor is of native Anglo-Saxon stock—loyal and efficient."[21]

Southern industrial boosters and their supporters had plans to cement the bonds of evangelicalism and free-enterprise capitalism. The recently created National Association of Evangelicals (NAE) provided a useful vehicle. Although ostensibly a clearinghouse dedicated to spreading a conservative evangelicalism, the NAE was also an unabashed proponent of the American free-enterprise system. The association's newspaper, *United Evangelical Action*, not only attacked the modernist tendencies that undermined the evangelical mission of Protestantism, but it also brought to light what NAE leader Harold Ockenga believed was the "terrible octopus of liberalism" that insinuated government into every aspect of people's lives. For proof, *United Evangelical Action* pointed to the "modernist regimentation" supported by the federal government during World War II, which included rules imposed on "the conduct of religious services in government housing projects adjacent to plants engaged in the manufacture of war materials."[22] If the government could regulate business, evangelicals reasoned, it could also regulate religion.

Christian free enterprise was the antidote to modernism and liberalism. To cultivate the support of friendly businessmen, the NAE's office in Washington, D.C., kept close tabs on legislation and public policies inimical to business and employed an official liaison with the National Association of Manufacturers. Like the Southern States Industrial Council, the NAE bitterly opposed extending the Fair Employment Practices Committee (FEPC) or any sort of legislation that constrained the evangelical entrepreneurs who gravitated to the association. Of the FEPC, the association claimed "it is class legislation" that would "encourage rule by minorities," create social friction, "imperil the freedom and integrity of many Protestant organizations," and "give political bureaucracy another instrument of terrorism."[23] In return, key businessmen were the backbone of the NAE's fundraising, marketing, and recruiting, giving them an important say in the association's political agenda. Christian capitalists wanted help in reducing racial and industrial strife, which they believed strengthened the "forces of apostasy"—"Communism, Roman Catholicism and Secularism." They also welcomed NAE opposition to the spread of liberal, New Deal–type government regulation that received the endorsement of mainstream denominations represented by the Federal Council of Churches.[24]

Although the NAE was the brainchild of two New Englanders, its program resonated for many evangelical entrepreneurs in the South. Especially in the postwar Southwest, where the oil industry was prominent, the NAE found some of its most fertile ground. The link between oilmen and conservative theology was not new; in the early twentieth century, oil entrepreneur Lyman Stewart funded the Bible Institute of Los Angeles as well as the publication of the twelve volumes of *The Fundamentals* between 1910 and 1915, which were the foundational documents of the Fundamentalist movement. In the postwar era, the NAE once again found that oilmen welcomed the seemingly complementary aspects of evangelical theology and a free-enterprise approach to oil development. Oilmen Sid Richardson, Clint Murchison, "Tex" Thornton, H. L. Hunt, and J. Howard Pew plowed the huge profits from oil into a range of conservative seminaries, Bible colleges, churches, evangelistic ministries, and Christian schools in the Sunbelt. Several popular evangelists (Oral Roberts and Charles Fuller, for example) moved in the opposite direction, investing their earnings in the oil industry. Charles Fuller became so wealthy from his Providential Oil Company that in 1947 he used the profits to establish Fuller Theological Seminary, which included Harold Ockenga and Billy Graham on its board.[25]

The oilmen's desire for freedom from government interference suited a religious culture in the region that also emphasized autonomy and independent choice. Evangelicalism in the Southwest grew fastest among Baptists, Pentecostals, and Church of Christ adherents who rejected ecclesiastical or denominational dictates on worship practices, creeds, and beliefs. Centralizing and collectivist tendencies in either government or religion threatened individual initiative and local control, whether at church or in the workplace, and seemed at odds with the nation's heritage. At stake, according to the *United Evangelical Action*, was not only religious liberty but also the beliefs that "the 'profit motive' and 'private ownership' are sinful and that the individualism which has made America great" were outdated. The NAE even developed a long list of "Scriptural proof for the free enterprise system," in which it gave biblical chapter-and-verse justifications for the American form of Christian capitalism.[26]

In the textile mills of the Southeast, the probusiness message of evangelicalism took a somewhat different shape. Many textile firms tapped into a viciously racist and anti-Semitic fearmongering of the self-professed Christian newspapers, "Parson Jack" Johnston's *The Trumpet* and Sherman Patterson's *Militant Truth*. In Georgia and Alabama, for example, such major textile firms as the Bibb Manufacturing Company, the Swift Manufacturing Company, and Avondale Mills led groups of employers that printed full-page advertisements in Parson Jack's *The Trumpet*, claiming to support "full employment and improvements in every way possible," and then mailing the newspaper to every employee, free of charge. Spread among the columns of *The Trumpet* were Johnston's railings against Jews, Catholics, and blacks; the misinformed racial theories of the Methodist Church; and the opponents of Fundamentalism within the Southern Baptist Convention. His greatest enemy was the CIO. When journalist Stetson Kennedy surreptitiously subscribed to Johnston's "Christian Crusaders League," the acknowledgement letter attested to Johnston's hatred of the CIO: "We are doing a little of everything to combat their efforts." He wanted to prove that unions were "un-Christian" and not worthy of evangelical support. So long as unionists remained connected with men like Jacob Potofsky (the Jewish president of the Amalgamated Clothing Workers), Johnston claimed, "they could not expect a Christian organization . . . to open her doors and invite them to 'come in and sup with us.'"[27]

Sherman Patterson's *Militant Truth* equally exploited the anxieties of Bible-believing Christians. In 1944 and 1945, Patterson wooed the approval of the Southern States Industrial Council, which "was very much impressed with the earnestness and sincerity" of Patterson and wanted "to lend advice and assistance to the publisher in every way possible, including the contribution of articles which would enable the readers of the publication to get the right

Flyer emphasizing the "outsider" character of the CIO's Operation Dixie leaders, 1940s, in the Stetson Kennedy Papers. Courtesy of the Southern Labor Archives, Georgia State University, Atlanta.

views on the industrial problems confronting the employees of today." The "right views" included sentiments expressed in a Special Labor Edition of *Militant Truth*, which carried a front-page cartoon titled "Land of the Free?" This cartoon featured "Labor's Ball and Chain," which pictured the leg of an American worker shackled to a ball labeled "Agitators, Organizers, Communist Propagandists, Gangsters, Racketeers, Threats, Violence, Terrorism" in front of closed factories. Page 2 featured a column on "Christians and Labor Unions" in which Patterson exposed the un-American lineages and Catholic or Jewish faiths of CIO leaders. Patterson then elaborated on biblical verses against being "yoked with unbelievers" (2 Cor. 6:14), on honoring one's employers with loyalty, and on avoiding strife (1 Tim. 6). As to labor's claim to religious sanction, Patterson charged, "Even as the devil himself quotes Scripture, so do the satanic hordes of socialism, communism, modernism and materialism stop at nothing in their efforts of deception, to undermine and destroy all that God-fearing, home-loving patriotic Americans hold dear."[28]

The *Militant Truth* and *The Trumpet* brands of probusiness Christianity that blended with a fierce resistance to unionism on the part of low-wage employers has long been the staple of those who believe that religion was an uncomplicated tool manipulated by business. Certainly, there were some professed Christians,

Collage of the masthead and two cartoons from *Militant Truth* in the 1940s and 1950s. Courtesy of the Southern Labor Archives, Georgia State University, Atlanta.

like Parson Jack Johnston and Sherman Patterson, who probably put their hopes of reaping more earthly rewards from their defense of free enterprise above their religious principles.[29] But that ignores the full scope of Protestant evangelicals' worries about the tumultuous postwar world. Living through a devastating war that uncovered an almost unfathomable capacity for human brutality dimmed the hopes of many Christians that mankind could chart a path to a better world without the aid of God. The end of the war triggered a revitalization of spirituality in America, symbolized by the fact that Bible sales more than doubled between 1947 and 1952, that religious books typically led the bestseller lists, and that religious rallies drew tens of thousands of worshippers.[30]

For conservative evangelicals, however, the postwar religious awakening was a time for battle. Struggles with modernism, liberalism, and more extreme collectivist systems that began during the Depression now assumed a greater importance. Perhaps no institution captured the anxieties of the evangelicals more than the

Federal Council of Churches, with its endorsement of the Social Creed of the Churches. The founding of the National Association of Evangelicals offered an institutional counterweight. When seeking to expand membership in 1945 and 1946, the NAE emphasized: "At last there is a growing bond of unity among Bible-loving churches which adhere to the fundamentals of our once-delivered faith. At last evangelicals have a united voice in the nation apart from the misguided voice of modernism." Previously there had been no alternative to the Federal Council, which had been "the only authoritative spokesman of Protestantism in America. But being strongly liberal and seeking to further the ends of modern-ism and liberalism, the Federal Council could not properly speak for millions of Bible-believing Christians."[31]

This choice between two visions of Protestantism's future, as well as fears of unions, motivated Sherman Patterson in the pages of *Militant Truth*. In Febru-ary 1945, Patterson ran a front-page story, "When Satan Joined the Church," just below an article about "fifth columnists" as America's greatest menace. In this article, Patterson noted that when Satan failed to destroy the apostolic church, he switched tactics and joined the church to introduce "all manner of heresies" and bring about "discord and divisions." The devil, he continued, "doesn't object to religion—as long as our religion rejects the blood of the Lord Jesus." The greatest threat was those who have religion without Christ. "The anti-Christian influences of modernistic infidelity have penetrated deeply into our church organizations of today," he warned. In a later issue, Patterson offered a table laying out the dif-ferences between the Christian's Creed and the Modernist's Creed. Important for Patterson's brand of Christianity were the inspiration of the Bible; the absolute authority of Scripture; the deity and virgin birth of Christ; the sacrificial death, resurrection, ascension, and intercessory work of Christ; belief in a literal Heaven and Hell; and that eternal life depends on "Faith in Jesus Christ as Saviour." Mod-ernists in the Federal Council, which harbored fifth columnists and "reds," did not believe these things. Nor did modernists believe that all men were sinners, that the Bible was an "infallible guide," or that Jesus was coming back to reign on earth.[32] Thus, for many evangelicals, supporting free-enterprise capitalism and recognizing the dire threats facing religion were intertwined.

The blending of concerns for religious freedom and free enterprise in the postwar era reached a fever pitch in the conflict over religious radio broadcast-ing. The Federal Communications Commission and the National Association of Broadcasters had first attempted to limit controversial religious broadcasting before the war by denying sustaining (or free) airtime to programs that attacked other faiths or proselytized intolerance. But this did not stop some on the religious right who either purchased time on the networks or turned to independent sta-tions, sometimes even buying their own. Then, during the war, those religious broadcasters still eligible for sustaining time, upset by both the content of evan-gelical programs and the constant solicitation of funds, attempted to change the broadcasters' code to prevent programs from buying time and asking for money, a policy that appeared to target evangelicals. While unsuccessful in completely banning evangelical programs, the major networks did confine them to the hours before noon on Sundays.[33] As the war ended, the Federal Council of Churches consolidated its radio department with the in-house radio departments of constituent churches to form the Protestant Radio Conference, which then proceeded to form a Joint Religious Radio Committee that included representatives of the Roman Catholic and Jewish faiths. The NAE and other evangelical publications immediately sensed danger. The *Brethren Missionary Herald* warned against the Federal Council's designs on a radio monopoly, and *The Church Press* of Birmingham, Alabama, asserted that the council posed a danger to free speech through its effort to enforce "regimentation of [radio] broadcast."[34]

One of the most dramatic conflicts occurred over the broadcasts of J. Harold Smith, a former millworker and folksy, Fundamentalist radio evangelist. In early 1946, Knoxville, Tennessee, station WNOX notified Smith that it would no longer allow him to buy radio time for his popular *Radio Bible Hour* due to new station policies. Smith already had a controversial career. In 1939, the Textile Workers Organizing Committee produced evidence against Smith for his role in an unfair-labor-practices case in the Spartanburg region of South Carolina. Just a year later, the local Spartanburg radio station decided to stop selling airtime to Smith, to which Smith responded with charges that the Federal Council of Churches, deemed a "red" organization by the Dies Committee, was behind the cancellation.[35] Smith moved to Knoxville, where he purchased time on WNOX until 1946. When the station cancelled the show, Smith demonstrated how popular he was by organizing a protest parade on April 14 attended by between fifteen thousand and twenty-five thousand people. Led by Knoxville police, more than two thousand ex-servicemen, and a large truck with sound equipment and musicians, the parade marched past the front of WNOX, where they stopped and prayed for fifteen minutes. They then proceeded to the offices of the *News-Sentinel*, which owned WNOX, where Rev. T. W. Hill, pastor of the Bible Baptist Church, led more prayers. Just three weeks later, another mass meeting of more than ten thousand people, including one man who came because "his poor hillbilly mother of 17 children" could not attend, gathered to hear Rev. Harvey H. Springer of Colorado and Rev. Carl McIntire of New Jersey defend Smith against the vendetta of liberals and the Federal Council of Churches. Thousands of Smith's largely working-class listeners wrote to the Federal Communications Commission, demanding that Smith be put back on the air. The evangelist described the affair in a pamphlet, *Termites in the Temple*, in which he charged that the Federal Council was in league with the Soviet Union. Smith claimed that his fight was not just about his case; he fought on principle for our "Precious Privileges," freedom of speech and religion. "These two gone," he lamented, "we become slaves."[36]

Smith's case captures the tangled fates of liberalism, labor, and religion in the postwar South. Although unionism did not become an issue in Knoxville, the Textile Workers had played a role in Smith's earlier plights, and many evangelicals believed that the Federal Council and labor unions were united in an ominous expansion of national organizations backed by the federal government that threatened local control and individual freedom. That Smith could mobilize thousands of followers for protest demonstrations that dwarfed most of the actions orchestrated by organized labor alerts us to the problems unions confronted in winning the hearts and minds of the southern white working class.

To make certain that the antimodernist, free-enterprise message would flourish in the postwar South, evangelicals secured business funding for a number of Bible schools and Christian colleges. Entrepreneurs such as Jesse H. Jones, Robert G. LeTourneau, and J. Howard Pew raised funds for the growth of John Brown University, Harding College, Bob Jones University, and the LeTourneau Technical Institute, all of which educated young southerners in the finer points of Christian free enterprise. Meanwhile, the Southern States Industrial Council printed a steady stream of pamphlets for schools and communities warning of the dangers of central planning and "government by bureaucratic direction." These pamphlets also touted the special patriotism and Christianity of the people of the South. One, a sermon preached by Dr. Walter R. Courtney at Nashville's First Presbyterian Church, warned that the danger to America today is not big business but rather "Big Government backed by Big Labor." He reminded people that "the key to individual salvation is obedience to the will of God as we know Him in Jesus Christ and the Holy Writ. . . . The key to social salvation is also to be found in the same person and the same place," not in organized movements with "high-sounding phrases and titles, indicating interest in human welfare."[37]

Evangelicals and businessmen coupled their educational efforts with a Youth for Christ movement, which provided the vehicle for southerner Billy Graham's ascendancy. Although its origins predated World War II, Youth for Christ soared after 1943 as savvy promoters, with substantial backing from businessmen, and rode the wave of patriotic and religious awakenings that swept the nation. Giant youth rallies featured speakers who adopted the personal styles and charisma of popular entertainers and updated gospel music that drew upon contemporary dance-band swing. By 1945, promoters estimated several hundred rallies occurred weekly, with attendance running to more than three hundred thousand. The National Association of Evangelicals successfully built a network of more than thirty Christian Business Men's Committees throughout the country, including executives from such major corporations as Sears, to bankroll Youth for Christ activities. Thus, these rallies had a conservative evangelical message. Concern for the moral decline of America (rising rates of alcoholism, divorce, and juvenile delinquency) acquired new importance if the nation was stave off the threat of the Soviet-style state socialism and keep the world free. Popular Youth for Christ speaker Torrey Johnson warned: "We are headed either for a definite turning to God or the greatest calamity ever to strike the human race."[38]

Another promising development for evangelical employers was the effort to expand the industrial chaplain movement, which had begun during the war. The idea for bringing chaplains into the factories originated with mainstream ministers in the North who wanted to help migrating war-industries workers adjust to unfamiliar environments. One of the first industrial chaplains was Claude Williams, the radical minister who had worked with the Southern Tenant Farmers Union. The Detroit Presbytery hired Williams because of his knowledge of rural southerners, but he ultimately ran afoul of the Presbyterians due to his politics. The Federal Council of Churches, inspired by efforts in Great Britain as well as military chaplains, began to sponsor industrial chaplains, although the council's efforts typically tried to gain cooperation from labor, business, and a full range of religious groups, including Jews and Catholics.[39]

Christian industrialist Robert G. LeTourneau offered a more inviting model for evangelicals. LeTourneau, a manufacturer of heavy earth-moving equipment, attributed his success in industry to his "business partnership with God." In 1932, he vowed to give 90 percent of his profits and much of his time to the cause of religion, and he contributed millions of dollars each year to religious institutions, published religious tracts, sponsored revivals, and ran religious camps for children. On Saturdays and Sundays, LeTourneau flew in his own plane to attend religious meetings or to preach, averaging six engagements each weekend. As his company grew, LeTourneau dedicated each new plant to the Lord with a series of revival meetings featuring music, preachers, and barbecue for thousands of guests. Banners adorned worksites with slogans reminding workers: "Believe in the Lord Jesus Christ and thou shalt be saved."[40] During the 1930s, LeTourneau had invited evangelical ministers to shop meetings at his plants, but he expanded this practice in wartime, hiring full-time chaplains to give him both a more direct access to the spiritual lives of his employees *and* improvements in employee morale and productivity. At first, liberals praised the plan. The March 1945 issue of the Methodist journal *Zion's Herald* applauded LeTourneau's innovative "down-to-earth plan that puts religion into everyday living of mankind." Three months later, however, the Methodists reversed when the U.S. Supreme Court ruled that LeTourneau's company was guilty of unfair labor practices for intimidating workers attempting to organize a union. *Zion's Herald* scolded LeTourneau: "'Winning men to Jesus' must never be a guise for social injustices," and denying workers their democratic right to join unions was "not in harmony with Christian social ethics."[41]

With the end of the war, different visions for industrial chaplain programs became another point of contention between evangelicals and the Federal Council. In 1946, liberals in the Federal Council of Churches held a series of meetings, culminating in a conference in New York City that discussed the future of industrial chaplaincy. They attempted to define the goals and duties of the position and the relationship of the chaplains with management and organized labor. One of their basic assumptions was that chaplains would work in a unionized environment. The churchmen suggested that industrial chaplains should be specially trained ministers who would engage in both personal counseling (pastoral work) and evangelical outreach. They further recommended that the chaplains operate under interdenominational sponsorship and obtain financial support equally from unions, employers, and churches. While all the groups would have a voice in shaping the program, industrial chaplains should "clearly represent the church" and "avoid identification with either labor or management" to maintain their legitimacy. The FCC conference did not envision the industrial minister becoming directly involved in adjudicating industrial disputes. The liberal Protestant model of industrial chaplaincy emphasized the complete independence of the minister.[42]

The Federal Council critiqued the industrial chaplaincy model promoted by the National Association of Evangelicals, which favored LeTourneau's model wherein chaplains worked exclusively for management and represented Fundamentalist religious beliefs.[43] In fact, the NAE's National Commission on Industrial Chaplaincies, formed in 1944, had close ties to the business community. Eight of the eleven members of the commission were officers of manufacturing firms, and there were no representatives of organized labor. The NAE emphasized that industrial chaplains should serve the interests of the church and business simultaneously, and they set up programs to recruit and provide ministers with special training for factory work—one at Wheaton College, an evangelical institution, and one funded completely by LeTourneau himself. Irwin W. M. McLean of Detroit, secretary of the NAE commission, reported that the "system of industrial chaplaincies which we are promoting in the plants of America will prove a major means of winning thousands to Christ and the church and will greatly reduce industrial unrest."[44]

The chaplaincy at D-X Sun Ray Oil Company (later Mid-Continent Petroleum Corporation) of Tulsa, Oklahoma, exemplified what the NAE had in mind. Its chaplain, Charlie Martin, initially joined the company in 1925 as an operator. During World War II, Martin became an ordained Assembly of God minister and took leave from the company to organize a group of Christian Service Centers for military personnel in Tulsa. There he came in contact with businessmen who were promoting the idea of a chaplain service for industry. Enthusiastic about the concept, Martin completed the training program at Wheaton College and convinced the company to hire him to minister to the firm's one thousand employees. Martin conducted weekly noontime Bible study classes during which workers played music and participated in prayers and Bible readings. He also spoke to workers on "how to be victorious in their Christian life on the job and amidst the trials encountered in a routine day."[45] Sun Ray found Martin's counseling work to be an ally in production. His counseling helped "keep human machinery producing at top efficiency by assisting employees with their personal as well as company problems." Martin resolved conflict between workers and supervisors and helped employees change "bad work habits" because he was alert to "the unconscious motives" that led employees to become "careless or dilatory with their work." He also called on sick workers, helped retirees with benefits, and awarded service pins to long-time employees.[46]

Eventually, the NAE's vision for industrial chaplains attracted a following as the Federal Council's version withered. By 1954, *Nation's Business* estimated that forty companies had hired clergy to provide for the spiritual and emotional needs of their workers; among the more prominent were R. J. Reynolds, Fieldcrest Mills, Texas Aluminum Company, Swift & Company, and Lone Star Steel. A range of industries employed chaplains, including heavy equipment, steel, oil, textiles, and tobacco. Most significant, the movement had a strongly southern focus, reflecting the growing strength of evangelicalism in the region. The companies that made the largest financial commitment for full-time chaplains were located in the South and with one exception—Lone Star Steel—were non-union.[47]

Perhaps the individual who best captures the essence of ministers in service of anti-union employers is George D. Heaton, introduced in chapter 1. Recall that Heaton was no ordinary anti-union southern minister and no ordinary Southern Baptist. He served simultaneously on major state and national commissions of the Baptists and the liberal, ecumenical Federal Council of Churches at a time when Southern Baptists despised modernist theological tendencies. Although a Southern Baptist, he followed a liberal creed. However, Heaton's connections to the Southern Industrial Relations Conference and his industrial relations consulting business turned increasingly lucrative after World War II, and his practices changed. Among his high-profile clients were J. P. Stevens, Burlington Mills, Alcoa, Thomasville Furniture, Bibb Manufacturing, and Champion Paper.[48] While Heaton publicly professed indifference about whether or not workers joined unions, his actions contradicted this. In 1944 Heaton asserted that collective bargaining was fundamentally divisive. He offered instead a vision of blending Christianity with human relations in "the cause of developing a new and superior relationship of human beings in industry." Heaton claimed he did "not want to be labeled a 'crusader against unions'" but would "like to be labeled a 'crusader for good human relationships.'"[49] In many respects, Heaton's theology of class emphasized social harmony, a throwback to turn-of-the-century Social Gospel advocates who acknowledged social differentiation and potential conflicts between labor and capital but nevertheless emphasized that mutual goals, interests, and dependencies ultimately outweighed the bases for conflict.[50] Christianity's role at the workplace, in Heaton's mind, was to model good human relationships.

Shaping good human relationships for Heaton increasingly meant operating without unions. While recognizing that churches endorsed labor's right to organize, he asserted that they "have not said that to exercise this right is a religious obligation or the proper thing to do." One of Heaton's most gratified clients was

Bibb Manufacturing Company of Macon, Georgia. Bibb president C. C. Hartwig, a devout Presbyterian, felt so strongly about Heaton's ability to effectively counsel supervisors on building "family" feelings in a non-union environment, he scheduled regional meetings and conferences for executives and clergy on "the place of religion in business" featuring Heaton. In return, Heaton encouraged Hartwig: "Let's see if we can't sweep the South by the indoctrination of preachers in a way that the C.I.O. has been taking the stage. We can whip them at their game, and do a better job of it because we have something really to sell."[51] T. N. Barbour, vice-president of American Furniture Company in Martinsville, Virginia, praised Heaton's ability to offset a "union disturbance" and restore productivity and "the morale of our plants." He added, "If there is a man in the country who is capable of coping with a situation such as this, it in our opinion is Dr. George Heaton of Charlotte."[52]

Across a broad front, employers and the primary voice of evangelicalism—the NAE—seemed ready to protect the South for Christian free enterprise. They reached everyone from young people in schools and at rallies to the elderly who listened to the *Radio Bible Hour* with devotion. They preached their conservative message to politicians, to veterans, and—perhaps most important for the business community—to workers. They warned that the interference of national organizations and the federal government not only damaged the factories that provided local communities with employment but also threatened their freedom to worship as they chose. For these advocates of evangelically inspired capitalism, it was a slippery slope from legislation endorsing fair employment practices or the union shop to the regimentation of a Godless totalitarian state like the Soviet Union. It was difficult for some to disentangle racial integration, labor unrest, Communism, and religious freedom, especially in an unsettled postwar America. The fears emphasized by the NAE resonated for many in southern churches who saw disturbing trends in their denominations. They, too, believed that they were in a momentous struggle to defend the "historic doctrines" and "essentials of the faith."[53]

Southern Churches in Conflict

Southerners who worried that national organizations and modernist trends heralded an attack on their traditional faith had to look no further than the unified Methodist Church. The southern and northern branches of Methodists had united in 1939, finally overcoming the resistance of the Methodist Episcopal Church, South to including blacks. In turn, the northern Methodists compromised by including blacks as a separate regional group and by relenting on their desire for a strongly centralized church. Unification, however, lived up to the fears of some in the South that the "modernism in the North" would come to dominate. Perhaps the most vital influence for spreading the liberal, social-justice orientation of northern Methodism was the Methodist Federation for Social Service. For years, the Federation reflected the energy of Harry F. Ward, one of the preeminent Protestant social-justice advocates in the nation. Through its monthly publication, *Social Questions Bulletin*, the federation touted its support of organized labor and racial justice while criticizing the existing system of capitalism as "unchristian, unethical, and anti-social because it is largely based on the profit-motive which is a direct appeal to selfishness."[54]

Concerns for social and economic justice were not totally foreign to southern Methodists, and they sustained pockets of liberalism. For some time, the Woman's Missionary Council of the southern Methodists had fought against Jim Crow and lynching; as well, several southern Methodist newspapers, such as the *Wesleyan Christian Advocate* of Macon, Georgia, and the *Alabama Christian Advocate*, were strong opponents of the Klan, the white primary, and racial violence. In 1946 the Macon weekly even voted in favor of federal intervention in lynching cases after the brutal murder of four blacks in Monroe, Georgia.[55] Both newspapers also supported organized labor. The *Alabama Christian Advocate* pointed with pride to two of its ministers who served in the labor movement, Rev. Nelson H. Cruikshank, who was a social insurance analyst for the American Federation of Labor, and Rev. Charles C. Webber, the recently elected president of the Virginia CIO. The *Wesleyan Christian Advocate* even editorialized that capitalism was a greater danger to the peoples of the world than "any of those theories of Government which so greatly excites fear in the mind of the average American." In his 1945 tour of the region, Methodist Federation for Social Service secretary Jack R. McMichael claimed to see a "new social climate in the South," one that supported voting rights for blacks and cooperation among the races, with Methodist laypeople like William Mitch of the United Mine Workers playing a leading role. In October 1946 the Methodist Federation for Social Service formed an "Advisory Committee for Cooperation with Organized Labor in the South." Included were some of the most liberal men and women in the South—Jessie Daniel Ames, Rev. Dan C. Whitsett, Dorothy Tilly, and Harry Denman.[56]

Not all Methodists welcomed these changes, some of which they attributed to unification. Doris Dennison of the General Board of Education warned, "If any move is made so that persons in the South feel that the committee is the offshoot of a Northern organization, you will be defeated in the beginning." She advised, "There is a deep, heated resentment to leadership on social issues that do not originate within the area being served." Almost as if to fulfill Dennison's prophecy, in May 1946 the First Methodist Church of Lawrenceburg, Tennessee, formed a committee to protest CIO research director Kermit Eby's suggestion that Methodists should join with the CIO to fight injustice. The committee blanched at Eby's assertion that "the church has failed throughout these centuries in its endeavor to instill the teachings of Christ into the fabric of society and that a recently founded political organization has discovered the answer to the spiritual problems" of America.[57] Furthermore, the steady barrage of forebodings and dire predictions circulating in the South caused some Methodists to begin to second-guess their support of social action. For example, the *Wesleyan Christian Advocate*, which had sought federal intervention in 1946, ran an article just two years later that asserted: "If our Jim Crow laws should be abolished and segregation eliminated, the culture of the South would be destroyed; the morals of our people would degenerate beyond description." Its columns on labor came under the control of John L. Travis, who cautioned against "elements in this country who with marvelous cunning try in every possible way to stir up discord and strife among our people." Travis's favorite whipping boy was United Mine Workers President John L. Lewis, whom he blamed for much of what was wrong in the country.[58]

Perhaps the most heated reconsideration among Methodists arose when the bishop of a northern conference, G. Bromley Oxnam, reappointed Charles C. Webber as a "minister to labor." Dr. George S. Reamey, editor of the *Methodist Advocate* published in Richmond, Virginia, demanded that Oxnam withdraw the appointment or that Webber surrender his credentials as a Methodist minister if he continued to hold office as president of the Virginia CIO and director of its Political Action Committee. Reamey and other ministers in the Southeastern Conference found Webber's activities "exceedingly embarrassing" to Methodists in Virginia. They especially objected to his political work against the reelection of Virginia Senator Harry F. Byrd. Enough voices insisted that the Methodist bishops take up the issue that they put this on the agenda of one of their meetings. In the summer of 1947 Oxnam finally withdrew Webber's appointment as "minister to labor."[59] Other churches picked up on the conflict within and the increasing number of accusations against the radicalism that appeared to flourish in the Methodist Church. Many were probably also aware that, despite a period of rapid growth in church membership, the Methodists grew at a considerably slower rate in the South.[60]

The denomination that felt it had the most to fear from what was happening to Methodism was the Presbyterian Church in the United States. Like the Methodists, the two major Presbyterian churches had been contemplating unification but met more steadfast conservative opposition from the southern branch. Leading the opposition was L. Nelson Bell, a former Presbyterian medical missionary who founded the *Southern Presbyterian Journal* in 1942 to give a voice to those clinging to a Fundamentalist theology. Bell believed that liberalism and advocacy of social justice confused generosity with the Gospel and did not uphold the "integrity of Scripture." Contributors to the *Southern Presbyterian Journal* feared absorption by the northern church and fought against unions, racial integration, and political and economic liberalism, which the journal associated with participation in the Federal Council of Churches.[61]

Articles and editorials from conservative evangelicals lambasted the Federal Council for its theological and political activism. Rev. Robert L. Vining noted that the council was a "foe of capitalism" and too soft on Communism, but also that "it sails under the old flag of evangelical Christianity, but in it are all the modernists and skeptics of the churches, and they are in control," even willing to cooperate with Unitarians and Catholics. An editorial asserted: "We do not believe that a theological outlook which makes 'electives' of the infallibility of the Bible, the virgin birth, the miracles, the bodily resurrection and the blood atonement, can beget a true effective Christian leadership."[62] Participation in the Federal Council would force southern Presbyterians to support a permanent Fair Employment Practices Committee, socialized medicine, socialized insurance, full employment, a socially controlled economy, the distribution of wealth through taxation, and a nonsegregated church and society. Rev. J. E. Flow, among many others, wrote: "If we have to choose between segregation of the races and race riots, we prefer segregation of the races, or even 'Jim Crowism.'"[63]

Because the CIO was far more progressive on a range of social and political issues than the AFL, it was a particular target of southern Presbyterians who opposed church unification and participation in the Federal Council. In 1942, students participating in the Inter-seminary Movement in Tennessee complained of the address made by James Myers, a northern Presbyterian minister and the Federal Council's industrial secretary, which one person described as "an un-adulterated CIO organizer parading in the guise of a Presbyterian minister."[64] Even supporters of the liberalism within the southern Presbyterian Church at times regretted the Federal Council's prolabor speakers. Aubrey N. Brown, the editor of the liberal *Presbyterian Outlook* published in Richmond, Virginia, wrote to the Federal Council in 1947 that Cameron P. Hall, a minister in the northern Presbyterian Church, addressed several CIO meetings in North Carolina which "has caused a good bit of concern among business men." The visit provided ammunition to building opposition to church unification. The debate peaked that year, when a number of prominent Presbyterian laypeople in such places as Rock Hill, South Carolina, Dallas, Texas, and Bastrop, Louisiana, wrote to Samuel Mc-Crea Cavert, the Federal Council's general secretary, asking about the council's position on such matters as labor's right to strike. Often, these letters mixed questions about the Federal Council's union supporters with questions about its beliefs on the virgin birth and "that old-fashioned substitutionary doctrine of Atonement."[65]

For Presbyterians in the early postwar South, feelings about the CIO were intertwined with anxieties about federal government intervention into regional racial beliefs, political self-determination, and freedom of religion. This had significant implications. At the 1946 General Assembly of the Presbyterian Church in the United States, several presbyteries made overtures to the assembly requesting they "cease contributing to the support of the Federal Council" because "many of our churches are forced to support an extra-denominational agency against their conscience." In 1947, those overtures increased to "an unprecedented number of presbyteries" who protested "the alleged improper acts of the Federal Council." Although the 1948 General Assembly voted to retain membership in the Federal Council, they passed a resolution in 1950 disassociating southern Presbyterians from the council's social and economic statements. Meanwhile, the General Assembly meetings put into abeyance discussion of a merger with the northern Presbyterians.[66] Church opponents of modernism also constantly played on the fears that the Federal Council was in league with the CIO in promoting racial equality, social unrest, and state control of the economy, all themes that alarmed southern Presbyterians. One liberal clergyman, Henry W. Sweets, lamented, "I have been greatly distressed to see the attitude" of members of the National Association of Evangelicals who "make a great display when they pose as martyrs." He warned that such displays were "sapping the very life of the church" and painting liberals and the CIO as outside aggressors.[67]

Southern Baptists composed the largest and most important religious group in the South. Moreover, they were growing at a rate well above the regional average or that of their principal regional rival, the Methodists. While the Southern Baptist Convention had adopted a resolution supporting the rights of workers to engage in collective bargaining during the Depression, the Convention had a belief system that caused many Baptists to question support for unions, particularly in the context of a growing fear of Communism and the widespread strikes that plagued American society at the end of the war. As a convention, Southern Baptists tried to straddle the fence. In 1947, the convention noted: "As we face the imminent possibility of industrial conflict in our area," Southern Baptists "do not believe that the church can take sides in the struggle." "To do so," they said, "would be to negate the greater mission of the church. The Kingdom of God cannot be coerced into the narrow confines of labor unions [or] industrial management."[68]

Southern Baptist beliefs reinforced that position. They believed in the authority and sufficiency of the Scriptures; that salvation came only through the grace of God by faith in Jesus Christ; that each church is an independent, self-governing body; that each believer has direct access to God's word; and that church and state must be separate. To many Southern Baptists, developments in postwar America posed a serious threat to those beliefs, particularly with regard to the spread of a modern industrial society. To a church that fiercely defended the autonomy of the church and the individual, modern industry appeared to be pushing individuals into groups that forced them to conform, a denial of an individual's free agency. Baptists responded that neither labor nor management should be able to dictate opinions or behavior, which made union-shop provisions, strikes, and even collective-bargaining agreements suspect.[69] As the previous chapter noted, many working-class Baptists worried that union contracts would abolish the informality of the workplace, lead to heavier workloads, and ruin the harmony of their religious communities.

Baptists thus found the CIO's expectations that southern churches should support labor to be at odds with their theology. When the CIO Organizing Committee began distributing copies of its pamphlet, "The Church and the CIO Must Cooperate," it inflamed many Southern Baptists. The *Religious Herald* of Richmond, Virginia, fiercely objected to its lack of understanding of the history and aims of the Baptists. It disputed the CIO's claim that the church should "ally itself with an organization which proposes to advance the interests of a particular group." The aim of the church, the *Herald* editorialized, "is to spread the Gospel of Christ among all men, and not merely" a single group, no matter how large. Second, the editorial objected to the statement that the CIO would bring "a more abundant life" to all men, pointing out that the organization represented only a fraction of the population. Finally, the *Herald* objected most strongly to the use of the word "must" in the pamphlet's title: "The Church is not required to co-operate with any group of men to promote their own particular ends. The only imperative for the Christian Church is to preach the Gospel of Christ to men everywhere."[70]

Southern Baptists' passionate belief in the separation of church and state also had implications for unions and liberals. Many Baptists were so adamant in demanding separation that they opposed prayer or religious instruction in schools, and this belief made them particularly suspicious of Catholicism, even to the point of resenting the appointment of Myron C. Taylor as the president's ambassador to the Vatican. But such principles also made Southern Baptists reluctant to support legislation aimed at equality and almost completely apathetic on social and economic discrimination. Of course, most Baptist leaders were extremely worried that the growth of the liberal state portended a dangerous drift toward centralization of state power, which they asserted "is opposed to free speech, free press, freedom of religion, free enterprise (which includes medicine), free assembly [and] free pulpit." Under the guise of liberalism, one Baptist declared, reformers "have brought to near full socialistic growth many innocent looking schemes."[71] Thus, labor was unlikely to win support from many Southern Baptist leaders on laws pertaining to minimum wage and fair employment practices or even elimination of the poll tax.

Finally, the Southern Baptist Convention was steadfast in its opposition to ecumenism and in joining with interdenominational groups. In 1948, E. P. Alldredge began a campaign to force any Southern Baptists who participated in the Federal Council of Churches to leave either the Council or the Baptist Church. During this time, the well-known independent Baptist and leading Fundamentalist J. Frank Norris tried to gain Alldredge's cooperation in embarrassing the convention by showing that "the proof is indisputable" that Southern Baptist seminaries have "gone over to modernism." Norris enlisted the assistance of "Parson Jack" Johnston, editor of *The Trumpet*, to put pressure on the Baptists, but Alldredge refused to join the group. Still, the controversy showed just how much Fundamentalist and anti-ecumenical sentiment existed within the Southern Baptists and just how threatening they felt the Federal Council of Churches to be.[72] The turmoil of the postwar years together with Southern Baptist beliefs, then, built a difficult wall for labor and liberals to scale.

The fast-growing Pentecostal and Holiness churches posed an interesting challenge to advocates of Christian free enterprise. Some groups, such as the Church of God (Cleveland, Tennessee) had early stigmatized unions with the "Mark of the Beast" from Revelation 13:11–18, and only slowly did they lift restrictions against its members from belonging to unions. However, Pentecostal churches also flourished among the working class, and they resented the worldliness of the businessmen who preyed on ordinary folk. In many respects, Pentecostalism represented a conservative counterweight to the modernist materialism of the middle and upper classes.[73] By the end of the World War II many Holiness and Pentecostal churches had made peace with the members' participation in unions so long as they understood that there were limits on their actions, such as not participating in strikes. In 1946, CIO organizer Lucy Mason sensed a change in the attitudes of Pentecostal ministers, remarking on "the adaptability of the new small sects, such as the Assembly of God, Church of God, Pentecostal Holiness, etc., in meeting the increase of unionism among the people they serve." She even found local Pentecostal churches to be "very friendly to the unions and participation in church affairs by union leaders and members."[74]

There were, however, too many aspects of Pentecostal and Holiness churches' theology that viewed national unions as anathema to Christian life. They cultivated an estrangement from American society and politics that discouraged joining groups concerned with improving society. To the extent they engaged on social issues, there were likely to be questions of personal morality such as alcohol, movies, or dancing. The Church of the Nazarene, a Holiness group, asserted that "it is the church's business" to fight the liquor traffic, but the church counseled that the "great battle between industrialists and labor" demanded that Nazarenes pray for and promote a "wide-spread spiritual revival," not strikes and bitterness.[75] Pentecostals also tended to resent large institutions and impersonal aggregations, including the United Nations, the Roman Catholic Church, and the United States government, which they felt was racing toward socialism. Like other southern Protestants, many Pentecostals despised the Federal Council of Churches and liberals who "want an ideal government without God and without Christ." The *Pentecostal Evangel* warned that "there will be false Christs, and we shall doubtless see many false Antichrists."[76]

Particularly troublesome for labor unions was the dispensational premillennialism of most Pentecostal and Holiness advocates. Members of the Church of the Nazarene, Assembly of God, and Church of God congregations believed, especially in light of World War II, that all who looked at the world with a clear eye could see that it was headed toward its imminent demise. For them, Satan was palpably real and everywhere present. Some believed that the labor strife that emerged at the end of the war was a sign of the end times, and that would usher in the Rapture. *The Pentecostal Evangel*, for example, pointed to the General Motors strike in the winter of 1945–46 in apocalyptic terms: "The Bible speaks of such conditions existing in the last days. Read the fifth chapter of James. The rich men are pictured weeping because of the treasure they had heaped together for the last days, while the laborers are pictured crying out against the fraud which has kept back fair wages." Similarly, when the *Herald of Holiness* looked to assign blame, it noted: "The industrialists involved may have been as blameworthy as labor, but labor called the strike." That labor was increasingly associated with Catholic leaders like Philip Murray only added to the dispensational tendency to see unions as part of a worldwide confederacy against Christ.[77] Such statements from Pentecostal voices gave the proponents of Christian free enterprise an enormous advantage among the fastest growing churches in the South.

Conclusion

This is by no means complete coverage of predominantly white Protestant denominations and churches in the region and their beliefs about industrialization, labor, and modern liberalism that were vying for ascendancy in the postwar South. There were the Restorationist churches—Church of Christ, Disciples of Christ, Christian Churches—and a wide variety of smaller Baptist, Presbyterian, Methodist, and Holiness groups, in addition to the Episcopalians, Unitarians, Adventists, and Congregationalists. In Louisiana and parts of Texas, moreover, the Roman Catholic Church was preeminent. However, the Southern Baptists, Presbyterian Church of the United States (South), southern Methodists, and Pentecostals included the vast majority of southerners, and they together composed a "southern church" that shared an evangelical mindset.[78] These churches also shaped the broad parameters of religious thinking on what path the South should follow in its social and economic development. Had they challenged southern norms, it is likely that those norms would have cracked. At the same time, these churches thrived in the culture in which they existed. They were mutually reinforcing.

Southern evangelical spokesmen, by and large, worried about the drift toward state and bureaucratic control that threatened religious liberty far more than they worried about economic or social inequality. The churches listened to the foreboding forecasts of Christian-entrepreneur-financed publications, radio broadcasts, and rallies, and they feared that organized labor and modernist Protestant organizations like the Federal Council of Churches would undermine the racial order, freedom of opportunity, separation of church and state, and regional industrial development. Many looked for signs in the labor turmoil that the end times were near and believed that they should redouble their efforts to save souls, not a broken economic order. Moreover, the evangelical defense of a distinctly southern religion complemented a regional suspicion of anything arising from northern organizations or the federal government.

As much as these evangelical voices molded the discourse of southern religion, there were alternative prophetic perspectives that surfaced among such groups as the Fellowship of Southern Churchmen and among individuals as well, ranging from a liberal anticommunist like Liston Pope to the radical Claude Williams. Fairly quickly, labor organizers recognized that if they were going to have any success in the South, unions would need to win friends in the churches. In 1946, when the CIO began its Southern Organizing Campaign, it had more religious goodwill than most union leaders realized, but those sources of support were fragile, constantly under siege from the surging evangelicalism in the region.

CHAPTER 5

The Bible Speaks to Labor

In 1945, a young Congregationalist minister, David S. Burgess, took over as head of the labor commission of the Fellowship of Southern Churchmen. The son of missionaries to China, Burgess had already completed a number of home missionary assignments by the time he went to work for the fellowship. He graduated from Oberlin College in 1939, served as an assistant to California's U.S. Congressman H. Jerry Voorhis for a year, and then alternated time at the Union Theological Seminary with service as a minister to migrant farm workers. After being ordained into the Congregational Church in 1944, the denomination's Home Missions Board appointed Burgess as minister to the Southern Tenant Farmers Union (STFU) in Missouri and Arkansas. While there, the young minister worked with black and white sharecroppers in an unsuccessful effort to revive the STFU and on a more successful campaign to save the Farm Security Administration's Delmo Homes Project from being sold to private interests who would likely evict the more than five hundred tenant families from their homes.[1]

When Burgess accepted leadership of the Fellowship of Southern Churchmen's labor commission, he hoped to revitalize Christian support for labor unions. He worked with Alva W. Taylor to host the fellowship's first labor–church conference in Nashville and prepared a special issue of the fellowship's journal, *Prophetic Religion*, on "what churches and unions have in common, and the theological basis for stronger cooperation."[2] But from the beginning Burgess ran into roadblocks. His work with the Southern Tenant Farmers Union exposed him to the political disputes and red-baiting that afflicted the efforts to build unions in the agricultural South. He chafed at the charges and countercharges hurled by Communists, Socialists, and liberals that limited the actions of such groups as the Southern Conference for Human Welfare and the American Youth Congress. Burgess found that even compiling a list of whom to invite to the fellowship's conference was far more politically sensitive and controversial than he had imagined. Moreover, his insistence that the conference, held at Fisk University, be interracial opened him to criticism from some of the clergy he hoped to attract. Still, Burgess left the conference feeling optimistic about the potential of labor, claiming, "The CIO is doing far more for racial understanding and economic equality than the church or any other institution. More power to your efforts!"[3]

Burgess and the fellowship are reminders that the attempts of businessmen to project the virtues of Christian free enterprise did not go unchallenged. The churches growing most rapidly in the South may have been unlikely to support unions, but denominational sources hide a level of support that existed among individual clergy and among some local congregations. While the war years had damaged the prospects of labor's winning widespread support from Protestant ministers, there were also signs that all was not hopeless. The Fellowship of Southern Churchmen began its most active period, building a membership of social-justice-oriented clergy throughout the South. In 1946, a small group of Southern Baptist clergy began a new journal, *Christian Frontiers*, which declared in a banner headline, "Welcome Labor Unions!" That summer, the citizens of Danville, Virginia, rallied behind a local minister and the local of the Textile Workers Union of America to create a Citizens' Committee to fight for economic justice and defy charges that they were led by outsiders "with Communistic leanings."[4] There were also allies in the Southern Conference for Human Welfare, at Highlander Folk School, and in the industrial department of the YWCA who sought to fuse Protestantism's social message to the organization of southern workers. These pointed to a reservoir of prophetic Christianity upon which the CIO could draw when it mobilized for its crusade to organize Dixie. Perhaps most important, the CIO had a cadre of men and women with ties to Protestant churches whom it could send to build favorable community relations. This chapter will explore the religious resources that the CIO utilized to offer an alternative to Christian free enterprise and bring collective bargaining to the South.

Bonds of Fellowship

In 1934 a group of young church people met at Monteagle, Tennessee, to examine what they might do to put "the resources of their faith to work for God and man" at a time when "the entire fabric of our national life lay prostrate before the onslaught of the Great Depression." They formed the Conference of Younger Churchmen of the South, soon to be renamed the Fellowship of Southern Churchmen. Included in the group were Howard Kester, T. B. "Scotty" Cowan, Franz Daniel, James Weldon Johnson, Gene Smathers, James Dombrowski, and Charles Webber, among other men and women who carried a Christian message into struggles for social justice. Members organized the unemployed in Louisiana and tenant farmers and agricultural laborers in Missouri and Arkansas, created a model cooperative farm on the Cumberland Plateau, and helped sharecroppers regain hope at the Delta and Providence Cooperative Farms in Mississippi. They paid a price for their convictions; some lost churches or church members, some lost teaching jobs, and others lost control of the organizations they had helped create.[5]

Struggles of the 1930s and World War II significantly diminished the energies of the Fellowship of Southern Churchmen. One of the key reasons was the leadership of Howard "Buck" Kester. A founding member of the fellowship, Kester took over as its general secretary in 1936 at a time of turmoil in his own life. He was already serving as the field secretary of the Committee on Economic and Racial Justice when he had dived into work with the Southern Tenant Farmers Union. In the mid-1930s Kester drew upon his deep religious faith to power his social consciousness. He used the examples of Jesus and the Old Testament prophets to inspire his mission as a prophetic radical working against "the oppressors of the poor, the weak and the disinherited."[6] But within just a few years, Kester, a devoted Socialist, had grown weary of battling Communists working among agricultural laborers and sharecroppers. The CIO's union in agriculture, the United Cannery, Agricultural, Packing, and Allied Workers of America (UCAPAWA), expelled Kester from a meeting involving negotiations with the Southern Tenant Farmers Union. In turn, the STFU retaliated by expelling the prophetic activist most closely associated with the Left-led UCAPAWA, Claude Williams.[7]

Kester carried his anticommunism into the Fellowship of Southern Churchmen. Throughout the late 1930s, Kester refused to work with Communists or any organization that included Communists, including the Southern Conference for Human Welfare. At the same time, he drifted toward a deeper religiosity.[8] By 1940, not only had he forced Communist fellow travelers out of the fellowship, but he had also lost many members who were disgusted by the intensely spiritual perspective with which he approached every problem. The housecleaning came at a time when Kester's energy was flagging, a casualty of years of courageously defying arrests and threats on his life at the hands of planters and southern sheriffs. During the war years, Kester worked full time as the executive secretary of a greatly diminished Fellowship of Southern Churchmen. In 1945, he wrote to David Burgess, explaining his changed outlook: "I had lost faith in the promise of politics, unionism and the organized church. The kind of health [the South] needs will come not through politics or economic organization. There has to be an ethical orientation, a moral confrontation based on the teachings of Jesus and the principles of democracy."[9]

In 1944, Kester turned the reins of the fellowship over to Nelle Morton, an East Tennessee–born Presbyterian. The daughter of a schoolteacher, Morton attended a small Presbyterian college in North Carolina and then left for seminary training in New York City. After working with Plymouth Congregational Church in New York and offering seminars for ministers at Union Theological Seminary in the 1930s, Morton returned to the South as youth director for the Presbyterian church in Richmond. During her time there she confronted southern Presbyterians on race issues by organizing interracial youth camps and conferences, a practice she took into the Fellowship of Southern Churchmen. The fellowship's conferences were typically interracial weekend affairs held in secluded rural places. On one occasion the campers had to hide in a cornfield to elude a group that threatened to harm them. In 1947 Morton participated in an early "freedom ride" that challenged the South's segregated public transportation. Eventually, the black and white passengers had to take refuge from a mob in Rev. Charles Jones's Presbyterian church in Chapel Hill, North Carolina.[10]

Morton's leadership of the Fellowship of Southern Churchmen from 1944 until 1949 marked its most dynamic period, although its emphasis began to subtly shift from class and economic justice to racial equality. Still, Morton believed that building unions was necessary to changing the South's social climate. She later recalled, "This was the time when people like [oilman H. L.] Hunt in Texas was giving big sums of money through industry to set up the offshoot evangelist tent meetings in areas where labor was organized, to preach anti-Semitic, anti-labor, anti-race gospel." From her youth in Kingsport, Tennessee, Morton knew that companies like Eastman Kodak indoctrinated communities through churches and public schools when they built factories in the South, even though their employees struggled to make do. By 1945, Morton had increased the fellowship's membership to more than 120 church leaders throughout the South.[11]

Taking the lead in the fellowship's work with organized labor was David Burgess. In 1945, Burgess was living in the Delmo Homes Project, and he worried that America's social climate was turning against economic justice. As early as April 1942, he wrote of the changed atmosphere already taking hold at Union Theological Seminary. "Gone are the days of Harry Ward and the radical social gospel based on an essential optimism," he claimed; "Today Union is filled with plodding and tough-minded seminarians engrossed in the incrises of theology. They are, in the main, stayed [sic] and conservative." Burgess blamed much of the change on the new realism of Reinhold Niebuhr, who had been so influential to many Christian social activists. The war transformed Niebuhr into a skeptic, and he infused a pessimism rooted in the basic sinfulness of man and the omnipresence of evil into the atmosphere at Union. To Burgess, Niebuhr's teachings only reinforced the middle-class complacency of the average seminarian and offered "new support for his inherited social conservatism."[12]

Burgess sought refuge by ministering to migrant farmworkers in New Jersey and Florida for the Congregationalists' Home Missions Council. These interludes stoked his enthusiasm for religious work with a social justice emphasis, but it also sparked his antipathy toward conservative evangelicalism. More than fifty years later, Burgess vividly recalled his attendance at a Church of God service in Florida and his dismay at the preacher's "depiction of the proper life as a series of self-denials" for a flock that appeared to be "reaching out from sheer desperation." In his final report on his Florida work, Burgess wrote in a condescending tone: "I tried to make my sermons as practical as possible . . . instead of using the usual negative method of the liberal in tearing down their 'outworn' beliefs, I tried to be more constructive by re-interpreting their religious words such as sin and salvation." Burgess emphasized that the prophets were interested in things of this world, and that Christ was not "a weak and bleeding savior on the cross who had little or no relations with the everyday problems of life," as He was portrayed in much of southern religion. Although Burgess did not approve of Holiness and Pentecostal sects, he did admire their insight that a "vital religion . . . is not a set of wordy dogmas but a deep emotion and conviction of the heart." Anyone who wanted to reach the "dispossessed" of the South would do well to recognize this. In 1944, Burgess returned to Union to finish his thesis, "Holiness Sects of the Contemporary South."[13] He and his wife then gladly accepted an appointment from the Home Missions Council to work with the STFU in Missouri and Arkansas in 1944. There, Burgess entered the maelstrom left by the bitter battle between the STFU and UCAPAWA. He heard firsthand the STFU side from Kester and Harry Leland (H. L.) Mitchell, and the CIO side from Claude Williams, whom he had known for several years, and from Reverend Sam Howie. Burgess believed that the STFU leaders were "suffering from a communist-phobia," but that UCAPAWA was a "northern-dominated" union that was making mistakes that weakened its appeal among southern agricultural workers.[14]

This was the context in which Burgess took over the labor commission of the Fellowship of Southern Churchmen and began planning a conference on "Church and Labor Cooperation in the South." The conference brought together labor people and progressive ministers and introduced him to a number of union leaders, including Paul Christopher of the Tennessee CIO, William Henderson of the Arkansas CIO, Frank Prohl of the Teamsters, and John Ramsay of the Steelworkers and the CIO. Over two days of meetings in Nashville, prolabor clergymen such as Alva Taylor, Scotty Cowan, A. L. DeJarnette, and Father J. C. L. Elliott discussed the "wide gap between what is known as the social and individual gospel." Pointing to ministers' friendship with employers, to the agricultural economy, the one-party political system, poverty, the wave of Fundamentalism, and to the "general lack of faith and hope in possibilities for individuals and groups to change," the conference listed some of the well-worn explanations for labor's inability to make headway in the region. Participants spoke of the South at a crossroads, which must choose between "the storm of post-war reaction" and "the light of some liberal tomorrow" with apparently little awareness that they betrayed the smug attitude of "enlightened" Christianity with which many southerners were quite familiar.[15]

Enlivened by the conference, Burgess threw himself into the campaign to save the Delmo Homes Project. This federal resettlement project had rescued evicted sharecroppers and tenants during the Depression, but in 1945 it faced sale to private landowners. Burgess formed the Citizens Committee to Save the Delmo Homes and recruited the St. Louis–based Episcopal bishop William Scarlett to head it. Scarlett's connections with wealthy benefactors helped raise the needed funds, but not before Burgess confronted his own prejudices against the religious culture of rural southerners. In March 1946 Burgess complained that "a holiness revivalist tried to take over the project with that don't drink, don't smoke, but roll-on-the-floor stuff," which alienated at least one important family from the Citizens Committee. Burgess noted, "Above all, the Gospel needs to be preached in this part of the country," betraying his own animosity toward the conservative evangelicalism spreading in the rural South. But Burgess had reservations about an ultra-radical theology: "I do not want to cheapen religion by using it as a secondary instrument to promote unionism, as Claude Williams and several other C[ommunist] P[arty] evangelists do."[16]

In 1946, Burgess questioned his career path. He felt like a failure in Delmo and disliked ministerial duties. He confessed to his father, "I have very little fundamental interest in Sunday school, in boys work, in the usual church responsibilities such as calling, preaching, etc." What he did like was working with labor. He was disillusioned with people like Williams because of what he saw as the Communists' inclination "to break up or take over every progressive movement this country has had in recent years," so he began to build closer ties with the CIO, particularly through the Fellowship of Southern Churchmen.[17] In the fellowship, Burgess communicated with union people like Kermit Eby, a Church of the Brethren minister who headed the CIO's Education and Research Department; Brownie Lee Jones, director of the Southern School for Workers; Willard Uphaus, director of the National Religion and Labor Foundation; and John Ramsay, who was in charge of church relations for the Steelworkers. For the fellowship, Burgess produced a pamphlet that described "an imaginary labor conflict in a typical Southern mill town." Published in 1946 and circulated throughout the South, *Trade Unions and Preachers* told its story through the perspectives of "a middle-aged minister, a young liberal minister, a labor leader, a millhand, and a mill manager," with the purpose of educating "church and labor leaders about the avowed aims of their respective institutions."[18] Burgess began to seek a career with the labor movement, aware that both the AFL and the CIO had plans for postwar organizing campaigns in the South.

In August 1946 Burgess and Scotty Cowan sent a letter with a summary of denominational statements about labor to ministers throughout the South. The cover letter acknowledged that churches had too often failed "to champion the cause of justice and to redeem men and women from exploitation and insecurity" despite the fact that southern churches "have upheld the right of labor to organize and bargain collectively." Now churches have a new opportunity, Burgess and Cowan explained: "Many Christians have seen in the labor movement an extension of democracy, and a way of life in which individuals have opportunity to achieve the dignity and self respect worthy of the children of God. Our Christian religion is rooted in the Bible message of God, speaking through the prophets for freedom and justice, and His revelation in Christ who came preaching the Gospel of the Kingdom of God on earth." They warned, contrary to the message that ministers were hearing from business-influenced evangelicals, that "if

David S. Burgess giving a speech before the Georgia CIO State Council in the early 1950s. Courtesy of the Archives of Labor and Urban Affairs, Reuther Library, Wayne State University, Detroit, Michigan.

democracy and religious freedom are to survive, we must count on a strong and idealistic labor movement."[19]

One of the CIO leaders drawn to the work of Burgess and the fellowship was labor organizer Franz Daniel, who was soon to become the South Carolina Director of the CIO's Southern Organizing Campaign. Daniel was born in Osceola, in the Ozarks region of Missouri in 1904, one of eight children. He first became interested in the labor movement in 1927 during his senior year at the University of Wisconsin. He then attended Union Theological Seminary in New York for three years at the peak of Harry Ward's influence there.[20] Impatient to effect social change, Daniel never graduated from Union and thus was never ordained, but the effect of the experience on him was lasting. Among his classmates were James A. Dombrowski, future head of the Southern Conference for Human Welfare, and Myles Horton, one of the founders of the Highlander Folk School. In 1930 Daniel went to work for the Socialist Party in Philadelphia. As party organizer in the area, he spent most of his time with trade unions. During those years he received several beatings from members of the Communist Party, toward which he developed a lifelong antagonism. In 1933 Daniel went to work for the Amalgamated Clothing Workers of America. A year later the Amalgamated sent him to organize the shops opening in the South, and in 1937 the organization assigned him to the Textile Workers Organizing Committee's southern campaign.[21]

During the 1930s, Daniel was also associated with the Highlander Folk School, where he and his wife Zilla (Elizabeth Hawes Daniel, also a union organizer) taught. Highlander reunited Daniel with his old seminary friends, Dombrowski and Horton, forming a link to another strong pole of southern prophetic religion. Unfortunately, this link did not last. As early as 1935 Daniel berated Dombrowski for his willingness to work with Communists. By 1939 Daniel was becoming openly critical of Highlander policies, reflecting his long suspicion of the Communist "game" of "coming into a labor situation from the outside and attempting to give leadership to the poor dear workers, who are too dumb to know what is good for them." Although he repeatedly avowed that Highlander was not Communist dominated, he began counseling leaders in the Amalgamated Clothing Workers to stop contributing to or using the school. In 1941, Daniel formally severed ties with Highlander after Dombrowski hired suspected Communists for work at Highlander and for the Southern Conference for Human Welfare. A year later the board voted to ask the Daniels to not return to Highlander, accusing him of misrepresenting facts in his criticism of the school and its programs.[22]

Daniel's reputation as a troubleshooter for the Amalgamated kept him active in the early years of World War II. He helped administer a new Amalgamated local of twenty-five thousand New York City laundry workers and then took charge of a difficult situation rebuilding labor-management relations for clothing workers in New Orleans. In between, the Amalgamated detailed him to help the United Auto Workers on the West Coast. His problem-solving reputation nearly turned into tragedy in 1943, when the Amalgamated sent him to prevent District 50 of the United Mine Workers from raiding the membership of an Amalgamated local union in LaFollette, Tennessee. On March 22 a half-dozen men representing District 50 entered the Amalgamated office, cut the telephone wires, and brutally beat Daniel and the local union business agent with blackjacks and gun butts. As the assailants fled the scene, one fired a shot at Daniel, which fortunately lodged in his wallet and did not penetrate his body. Nevertheless, the beating left him in a "nervous state" and forced him to take time off from troubleshooting and return to Philadelphia.[23]

Daniel gained a great deal from his religious training even though he never finished seminary. One article in his later life talked about his speeches still carrying a "revivalist's zeal," which is a bit odd given that Daniel was by then a Unitarian. His message, "with its idealistic moral overtones," clearly harkened to his earlier desire "to become a preacher of the 'social gospel.'" His efforts in New Orleans earned the praise of a Catholic priest, Father J. A. Drolet. After Daniel's beating, Drolet compared it to those suffered by St. Paul. He wrote to Daniel, "Your work is at least implicitly, and I like to think explicitly in your own heart, for the love and sake of Christ in His brothers, and therefore you have the right

Franz Daniel, circa 1950.
Courtesy of the Southern
Labor Archives, Georgia
State University, Atlanta.

to 'glory' in your 'stripes' too."[24] When Daniel resumed labor organizing in the South at the end of World War II, he established a relationship with the Fellowship of Southern Churchmen and sought out young organizers with a religious passion for building unions, men like Scott Hoyman, the son of missionaries, and Joe Pedigo, who grew up in a religious union family in the mountains of Virginia and became one of the South's better labor organizers.[25] Not surprisingly, Daniel also saw the "revivalist's zeal" in Burgess, whom Daniel hired in late 1946 for the CIO's Operation Dixie, but not before another tragedy struck. In 1946, Daniel's severely asthmatic son choked to death sitting in a doctor's waiting room. This helped cement a bond between Daniels and Burgess, whose own daughter nearly died in a household accident around the same time, but it also undoubtedly contributed to a drinking problem and melancholy that afflicted Daniels for the rest of his life.[26]

The Fellowship of Southern Churchmen brought together many Christians with a prophetic outlook to work on issues of social justice. By 1947, the group's journal, *Prophetic Religion*, reached fifteen hundred southern religious activists. Members addressed a number of gatherings, ranging from Baptist and Methodist Youth Fellowship meetings to ministerial association conferences to labor union institutes. Southern cities such as Atlanta, Richmond, Nashville, Memphis, and

Raleigh had regular Fellowship of Southern Churchmen dinners, and the group also sponsored work camps for students in Atlanta, Columbia, and Phoebus, Virginia. An increasing share of fellowship activity targeted civil rights issues and sought to protect interracial unity practiced in its camps and in communities such as minister Clarence Jordan's Koinonia Farm, but Alva Taylor and Burgess regularly reported on the doings of the fellowship's Labor Commission.[27]

Dixie's Radical Prophets and Dissenters

As its revitalization demonstrated, the Fellowship of Southern Churchmen operated within a changed climate for liberal Christians. Fears regarding Communism's influence in labor and civil rights activity drove a wedge between prophetic Protestants and reinforced the message of Christian free enterprise advocates. Progressive groups like the Southern Conference for Human Welfare and the Highlander Folk School felt the effects of the cold shoulders of Daniel, Kester, and others in the fellowship who, in turn, influenced the labor movement's determination to distance its organizing from radicalism. At the same time, Christian activists advocating racial justice confronted an increasingly hostile environment in the South. During World War II the nation had transformed race relations at many workplaces through its need for constant production, fueling the expectations of blacks through its propaganda for democracy. But many whites rejected change and turned to terror. Lynchings, riots that targeted black people and property, and the resurgence of white supremacist organizations testified to the disquiet in the region. The rise of Mississippi congressman John Rankin to the leadership of the House Un-American Activities Committee in 1945 gave opponents of civil rights a powerful ally in their efforts to link Communism, liberalism, and struggles for social and economic justice.[28]

There were also dissenters to this trend, men like South Carolina–born D. Witherspoon Dodge. Son of a southern Presbyterian minister, Dodge followed in the same path, attending Davidson College and the Union Theological Seminary in Richmond. Ordained in the Presbyterian Church of the United States, he took his first job in Anderson, South Carolina. In 1917, at the age thirty, Dodge faced heresy charges brought by the Piedmont Presbytery for "denying the sacred doctrines of predestination to Hell, and everlasting punishment, as taught in the Holy Bible." Although excommunicated, much of Dodge's congregation in Anderson followed him, first to an independent church and eventually into the Congregational Church. In the 1920s, Dodge moved to Atlanta and held positions in the Atlanta Theological Seminary, Central Congregational Church, and Ogelthorpe University, where he grew increasingly uncomfortable with the South's social order. In 1930, he organized the Radio Church at Atlanta and began broadcasting a Christian social gospel, which outraged Fundamentalists and led to the station's decision to drop the program in 1935. Dodge came to a turning point; he felt that there was no place within mainstream churches for his "radical religion," which emphasized "the righteous and loving will of God, not as a pious sentiment but as a powerful spiritual and social dynamic." Instead of returning to a church, he "chose the challenges of the labor movement."[29]

During the last years of the Depression, Dodge was on the staff of the Textile Workers Organizing Committee in its southern campaign. In August 1938, the union sent Dodge to Fitzgerald, Georgia, where company goons had already attacked and chased off several union organizers. There, a dozen men grabbed him from the porch of a local hotel, blindfolded him, and threw him in the back of a pickup truck. The men beat Dodge and left him by the road that led out of town. Dodge convinced the FBI to investigate, and federal authorities obtained indictments against the mill owner, his foreman, and some of their workers as part of a felonious conspiracy. In a trial that lasted ten days, a Georgia jury took only forty-two minutes to render a "not guilty" verdict.[30] Dodge nevertheless continued with the Textile Workers Organizing Committee, taking tough assignments throughout the South. He was both inspired by the ballads of the union movement that adapted religious and folk music and fearful of the constant police presence at union gatherings, a "reminder of the current state of union freedom." During World War II, Dodge took a position with the War Production Board, which led to his 1944 appointment as the southern regional director of the President's Committee on Fair Employment Practices (FEPC).[31]

As a CIO-man-turned-government-official, Dodge drew the wrath of southern conservatives like Representative Rankin of HUAC. The FEPC was the bane of industrialists who preached free-enterprise ideas. Operating out of Atlanta, Dodge and the FEPC became convenient targets for everyone from the racist demagogue and Georgia governor-elect Eugene Talmadge, to moderate newspaper editor Ralph McGill, to conservative white unionists in the AFL's Boilermakers Union. The vitriolic and typically anonymous letters Dodge received in his office saddened him, in part because he realized that most southern whites did not really know black people. Dodge recommended that the best place to "begin a voyage of discovery" would be in the black church. In Atlanta, he recommended Rev. William Holmes Borders's Wheat Street Baptist Church, "one of God's finest churches" where members "have no objection to worshipping the one God along with their white brothers and sisters."[32] Few took his advice.

The emerging anticommunist hysteria resulted in a different trajectory for some of the prophetic religious activists who had long been associated with Highlander Folk School. James Dombrowski, for example, found himself cut off from labor-union allies despite his best efforts. Dombrowski had one of the more interesting paths to his career as a Christian radical. Born in Florida in 1897 but raised principally in New Jersey, Dombrowski served as a mechanic in the Army Air Corps during World War I before entering Emory University and then moving on to Union Theological Seminary in New York. Under the influence of Harry

Ward, Dombrowski worked with the textile workers' uprising in North Carolina and Tennessee in 1929 and was arrested as a leftist conspirator in the shooting of the Gastonia police chief. Authorities ultimately dropped the charges against Dombrowski, but his reputation as a radical continued. Later in 1929 he joined Harry Ward for an extended trip to the Soviet Union. In the Depression years, he was one of the circle of supporters who established Highlander, but by 1941 Dombrowski was at odds with Highlander's support of the Textile Workers Organizing Committee. Dombrowski felt that the union's policy of excluding black workers from the organizing drive was wrongheaded. He also began to question Highlander's supportive relationship with the New Deal. As a result, Dombrowski left Highlander to become the director of the Southern Conference for Human Welfare.[33]

During World War II, Dombrowski and the Southern Conference turned their attention to race issues, but his acceptance of Communists and fellow travelers caused divisions within the organization. Although the Southern Conference still had friends in the Roosevelt administration and in labor unions, southern senators began to turn up the heat on Dombrowski. Senators James Eastland and Theodore Bilbo, in particular, waged campaigns to label Dombrowski and the organization a Communist front, particularly when the Southern Conference took up the defense of the African Americans herded into jail following mob violence in Columbia, Tennessee, in February 1946.[34] Dombrowski's office and home received threatening phone calls. Even many southern liberals distanced themselves from the Southern Conference, and the organization teetered on the verge of collapse. The conference's publication, *The Southern Patriot*, desperately tried to retain support from labor unions, particularly their financial contributions. *The Southern Patriot* ran articles discussing the pseudoreligious attack on the CIO by Sherman Patterson's *Militant Truth*, as well as Patterson's ties to the Southern States Industrial Council. It also laid out southerners' "stake in labor's organizing drive," claiming that everyone should recognize that "an organized South is a prosperous South."[35] But funds from unions dried up. When the CIO announced its plan to begin a major campaign to bring unions to the South in April 1946, the campaign's director, Van A. Bittner, promised: "We will tolerate no interference from organizations outside the CIO. No crowd, whether Communist, Socialist, or anybody else, will be permitted to 'mix up' in the campaign and that goes for the Southern Conference for Human Welfare and any other organization living off the CIO." The implications were clear; Dombrowski and the Southern Conference were out. Later that year, the board voted to dispense with Dombrowski's services, and assigned him to the Southern Conference Education Fund.[36]

Conservative congressmen and federal authorities also hounded Donald Lee West. Born in the upland region of north Georgia in 1906, West drifted through several colleges before coming under the tutelage of Alva Taylor at Vanderbilt.

In the early Depression years, he worked with the coal miners in Wilder, Tennessee, and the Communist Party in Birmingham and Atlanta. With Myles Horton, West began Highlander Folk School, although he was too radical to stay long. He returned to Communist Party work in the South before moving through a succession of positions in educational and religious institutions, all the while developing a reputation as a poet of the class struggle who preached a "class-conscious Jesus." Near the end of World War II, West won a Rosenwald Fund fellowship for a year of study at Columbia University, where he finished and arranged for the publication of his fifth and perhaps best-known book of poetry, *Clods of Southern Earth*. But in 1946 West was back in Georgia, teaching at Oglethorpe University and raising the ire of *Atlanta Constitution* editor Ralph McGill as well as that of the House Un-American Activities Committee for his work on race and economic justice issues. West received death threats and was even sued for libel, putting a great strain on his meager financial resources. Increasingly, he became a polarizing figure for a range of liberal and labor groups, temporarily retreating to the family farm near Douglasville, Georgia.[37]

Before being driven into exile, West renewed his acquaintance with another radical prophet, Claude Williams. Born in rural western Tennessee in 1895, Williams grew up in a divided household. From his father he absorbed the racism of southern Redemptionists; from his mother, a duty to be on the side of the poor; from both, a rebellious Cumberland Presbyterian heritage. Following service in World War I, Williams attended Bethel College, a Cumberland Presbyterian institution, to prepare to become a minister. During the 1920s Williams wavered between an attraction to Billy Sunday's Fundamentalism and Harry Emerson Fosdick's modernist theology, foreshadowing the incredible lack of orthodoxy in his religious beliefs. Then, in 1929, Williams moved with his young family to Nashville and became one of Alva Taylor's disciples. He quickly formed fast friendships with West and Kester.[38] In the early 1930s, Williams worked with coal miners while serving as a Presbyterian minister in Arkansas. He also participated in Commonwealth College, a small, socialist school close to his church, and began reading Marxist literature. He eventually tangled with the district leadership of the United Mine Workers when he encouraged a democratic rebellion against unresponsive leaders. His church, dismayed over his activities, tried to have him excommunicated.[39]

For the next decade, Williams moved through work with black and white sharecroppers and tenants in the Southern Tenant Farmers Union and UCAPAWA. He also began the New Era School of Social Action and Prophetic Religion, an idea that evolved into the People's Institute of Applied Religion during World War II. He tutored black ministers, such as E. B. McKinney and Owen Whitfield, as well as young white disciples like Ward Rodgers and Harry Koger. His work with Bible Belt southerners attracted enough attention that during the war the Detroit Presbytery of the northern Presbyterian Church recruited him to minister to the thousands of southern migrants who came to work in the defense plants. While in Detroit, Williams and his People's Institute made some powerful enemies, including the reactionary clergymen, J. Frank Norris and Gerald L. K. Smith. Opponents retaliated with charges that Williams was a Communist, unifying a diverse coalition against the People's Institute.[40]

In 1945 Williams returned to the South and reestablished the People's Institute in Birmingham, eager to assist the CIO's planned campaign. Harry Koger and William DeBerry, both of whom used Williams's applied-religion techniques in their organizing for UCAPAWA, called on Williams for assistance, but most kept their distance. Ironically, Williams may have been one of the more effective ministers at reaching some workers drawn to new religious sects. Alva Taylor touted Williams's ability to work well with rural preachers because he understood "the sincerity of their Pentecostal preaching brethren."[41] Williams carried with him a revival tent and charts using scripture to preach "a Biblical orientation which will enable the fundamentalist, the progressive, the shop preacher and the share-cropper preacher to PROCLAIM." In 1943 Koger used Williams's charts among the union seamen, longshoremen, and textile and food workers in New Orleans, and then brought them to bear in UCAPAWA organizing drives in Arkansas and North Carolina. Koger admitted to "a mighty thrill when I see the faces of those poor people who, for the first time in many cases, hear about a God who wants them to get their bellies full of food instead of going hungry, and about a Jesus, who, much to their surprise, is actually interested in them having a more abundant life here on Earth and not merely 'pie in the sky' after [they die]."[42]

The promise of Williams's applied religion, some believed, was that it could incorporate a wide range of theologies and appeal to both black and white Holiness and Pentecostal followers, just the sorts of people many labor organizers found difficult to reach. Certainly, his work with both white and black ministers in places as different as rural Arkansas and Detroit suggested as much. It was one of the reasons he and Don West began cooperating after the war; West had the same rural South roots and similar inclination in his religion.[43] Others, however, saw Williams's applied religion as little more than a crass attempt to fuse Marxism and a very selective reading of Scripture. Highlander's Myles Horton was critical of Williams's "business of teaching people to join the C.I.O. by his charts" and for "wanting to have revival meetings to make people religious and then after they got saved, then you give it [the CIO] to them." Horton saw religion "as something in its own right," not "as a tool for this kind of thing."[44] David Burgess, who initially admired Williams, was even more emphatic. Burgess thought, "[the] Institute of Applied Religion is . . . a racket because Claude Williams prostitutes the Christian religion to his immediate purposes, and because he lacks any concept of love, forgiveness or the life here-after in his preachments."[45] Some reacted to Williams's willingness to slander opponents. Liston Pope recoiled at Williams's assertion that any minister who questions the value of his program must be a fascist. He also objected to a statement used repeatedly by Williams: "I am a fellow traveler with the Man who went to the Cross." Pope admitted the statement was "clever, but so ambiguous as to be fundamentally dishonest." Nelle Morton believed that Williams's flair for dramatic statements was inflammatory and unproductive.[46]

The institution that united some of the most prophetic voices supporting labor and social justice was the Highlander Folk School. Myles Horton, the long-time leader of Highlander, could trace his career, like so many of the others, through Union Theological Seminary in New York. Born in western Tennessee in 1905, Horton was the child of teachers and sharecroppers. Like Williams, he attended a Cumberland Presbyterian undergraduate institution in Tennessee. After college, he worked for the Presbyterian Church organizing Bible schools in the mountains of Tennessee and as the state secretary of the YMCA. In 1929 he attended Union Theological Seminary for just one year, deciding that although he had a deep appreciation for religion, he "didn't want to work in the Church." What he did take away from Union, however, were ideas about a "synthesis between actual religious values, moral values—right and wrong—and the economic situation, the way society was run, the way people were exploited."[47] After leaving Union, Horton worked for a year in Chicago and then traveled to Denmark to learn about its folk schools. Upon return, he sought support for establishing a folk school in the United States. Sherwood Eddy, the national secretary of the YMCA, contributed $100, and Reinhold Niebuhr wrote a fundraising letter for Horton. Traveling in the South, Horton met Don West, who was drawn to the idea. They had the good fortune to meet a well-to-do elderly woman, Lillian Wyckoff Johnson, who used her home near Monteagle, Tennessee, for community education. Ready for retirement, Johnson gambled on Horton and West, in part because they had letters of support from a number of clergymen. She turned over her property to them and Highlander Folk School was born.[48]

Horton never went back to religious work and actually refused to become a member of the Fellowship of Southern Churchmen. Later in life, he explained his decision: the churches, he said, "were against us when we were for labor, they were against us when we were for integration, they were against us when we were against war." Still, Highlander applied the moral vision Horton had learned at Union to a program to "multiply leadership for radical change."[49] In 1945, however, Highlander was equally noteworthy for the number of southern prophets who had left the school. Kester, Daniel, Dombrowski, and West had all broken with the school. Horton hoped his few allies in the labor movement would help rebuild the school's relationship with the CIO. In particular, Horton was close to Paul Christopher of the Tennessee CIO. Christopher, the child of textile millworkers in South Carolina, had risen rapidly as a union leader with the Textile Workers Organizing Committee, directing the flying squadrons that achieved a modicum of success in East Tennessee in the late 1930s. At age thirty in 1940, Christopher became the state CIO director. But the charges made by

Franz Daniel that Highlander was under the direction of "Communist stooges" carried into the postwar period. The desire of CIO leaders to avoid any taint of radicalism made some of the CIO's regional directors unwilling to use Highlander for training. The emphasis on racially integrated gatherings and activities at the school also dismayed some union officials. Although Christopher and other CIO leaders continued to serve on the Highlander board, red-baiting and race-baiting limited the school's ability to serve as a training center for labor at a critical time.[50]

As is evident from the snapshots of Dodge, Dombrowski, West, Williams, and Horton, as well as the many close associates they had at the time, the rising volume of anticommunist and prosegregationist racket at the end of the war walled off some of the most prophetic, prolabor Christians from others who followed their religious beliefs into the labor movement. Unlike the proponents of conservative evangelicalism, who seemed to be able to overcome their differences and defend an ideal of Christian free enterprise, the Left was wracked with animus and accusations of betrayal. The sacred landscape of the South was indeed a battleground, but the armies were far from evenly matched.

The CIO's Christian Ambassadors in the South

One of the more remarkable persons navigating the obstacles of southern religion and labor activism was Lucy Randolph Mason. The daughter and granddaughter of Episcopal clergymen with roots running through the most prominent families of Virginia—the Masons, the Randolphs, and the Lees—"Miss Lucy," as she was known, had an unusual background for one of the CIO's main troubleshooters. Born in a family home near Alexandria, Virginia, in 1882, Mason spent most of her youth in a fairly liberal circle in Richmond. From her parents she absorbed "a strong sense of social responsibility." "It was part of their religious conviction," she recalled. Her mother ran a Bible class in the Virginia State Penitentiary and exposed abuses there. Mason wrote, "Mother and Father practiced what Jesus said when he described the final test that made men fit to inherit the Kingdom of God, . . . they served God as they cared for His children."[51] She carried those ideas with her always.

The Mason family lacked the money to send Lucy to college, so she took a stenography course and worked in one of the city's most respected law firms. Through her twenties she devoted time to helping working women at the YWCA and pushing for woman suffrage while caring for her nearly blind father. During World War I, American Federation of Labor president Samuel Gompers appointed her Virginia Chairman of the Committee on Women in Industry for the National Advisory Committee on Labor. After her father died in 1923, Mason took a position as industrial secretary of the Richmond YWCA, focusing on the issues facing working women and beginning work with labor unions in the city. Her growing reputation led to her appointment as director of the National Consumers League in 1932, replacing the recently deceased Florence Kelley. Yet although she moved to New York City, the South was never far from her concerns. When testifying at hearings establishing National Recovery Act codes for wages and hours, Mason's knowledge of the South impressed not only commissioners but also a number of union officials. In 1937, she met CIO and United Mine Workers leader John L. Lewis, who was so struck by Mason that he hired her as public-relations specialist for the CIO in the South.[52]

Operating from Atlanta, Mason spent the next fifteen years as roving ambassador for the CIO. She felt that among her most important duties was combatting "religious fanatics," the mill village preachers and freelance evangelists who received assistance from business interests wherever "the Textile Workers Union was organizing." One of the first things Mason did upon arrival in Atlanta was to send out five hundred letters to southern ministers, enclosing the Labor Day message of the Federal Council of Churches, unaware that many southern churches despised the modernist Federal Council. In her memoirs, Mason boasted that she won her first convert to the cause of labor, Arthur James Barton, by mentioning her connections to General Robert E. Lee and the Confederacy. She took great pride when Barton supported the Southern Baptists' endorsement of collective bargaining in 1938.[53]

Mason's work for the CIO took her into harrowing situations. Throughout the South, CIO organizers faced harassment, intimidation, and violence, not just from company thugs but also from local law enforcement. The CIO often sent Mason, in part due to her gender and age and in part due to her prominent family connections, into situations where violations of civil liberties were most extreme. Mason's correspondence during her CIO years are filled with urgent entreaties to city and state attorneys, federal authorities, congressmen, and even President Franklin D. Roosevelt and his wife Eleanor, with whom Mason had developed a friendship. On countless occasions, Mason convinced authorities to intercede to stop kidnappings, mob actions, beatings, arrests, and other forms of intimidation directed at union organizers and workers brazen enough to join the CIO. Her memoir of her time with the CIO recounts frightening episodes in Tupelo, Mississippi; Huntsville, Alabama; Tifton and Tallapoosa, Georgia; and Gaffney and Lumberport, South Carolina. She spent her first years principally with the Textile Workers Organizing Committee, but she soon assisted the woodworkers, copper miners, steelworkers, clothing workers, and virtually any other group attached to the CIO. Although she considered herself a daughter of the South, Mason had only been working for the CIO a short time when she wrote to Molly Dewson, a friend and close associate of Eleanor Roosevelt, saying that "the South is Fascist—its domination of the Negro has made it easy to repeat the pattern for organized labor."[54]

Mason was typically more temperate in her public statements, but her understanding of Christianity ruffled feathers in the South. In a correspondence debate with Rev. F. M. McConnell, editor of the *Baptist Standard* of Dallas, Texas, Mason agreed that "the teachings of Jesus, if applied to human society, would solve both economic and labor problems." But, she continued, these teachings have not been applied, and "in this very complex industrial and economic society personal goodness is not enough" to ensure fairness.[55] In 1943 she became embroiled in controversy when she spoke to classes as part of "Religious Emphasis Week" at Vanderbilt University. In one class, a student hostile to her message about the interweaving of political and economic democracy monopolized the discussion period and the exchange became heated. In another, a student accused the CIO of stirring up blacks, getting "them out of their place," and encouraging them to "make unreasonable demands," which included refusing to cook or do housework and taking white people's jobs. Mason tried to defuse the tension by asking if the student supported the teachings of Jesus and their application to life. When he answered affirmatively, she then asked if he thought "the Golden Rule, 'Do unto others as you would they should do unto you,' should be taken seriously by Christians." But the antagonistic exchange was fodder for Nashville newspapers, which called her a radical "labor monger."[56]

Despite a keen awareness of the difficulties labor faced in the South, Mason saw bright spots. During the war, she witnessed the startling change of fortunes of CIO unions in Memphis, Tennessee, where just a few years earlier city police, with the blessing of city boss Edward H. Crump, had thwarted union drives and chased supportive clergy from the city. In 1943 Mason addressed the Tennessee Synod of the southern Presbyterian Church and helped convince the members to adopt a resolution supporting collective bargaining. Mason was also able to get statements of support for collective bargaining from nearly all of the mainstream denominations, and she was optimistic about friendlier relations with Holiness and Pentecostal churches, even though she failed for years to get a public endorsement from the main officers of any of the Pentecostal churches. In 1946 Mason wrote to Rev. Cameron Hall of the Federal Council of Churches that she "frequently finds local [Pentecostal] churches very friendly to the unions and participation in church affairs by union leaders and members."[57]

By the end of the war, Mason could count a growing number of religiously minded individuals who believed the South was ready for change on issues regarding race and class. Among many other such friends was Stewart Meacham, an ordained Presbyterian who ministered to a church in Alabama before he received permission from the Presbytery to join the southern staff of the National Labor Relations Board. Another religious friend was Rev. William H. Marmion, a Texan who attended the Virginia Theological Seminary and ministered churches in Birmingham, Alabama, during the Depression. Between 1946 and 1950, Marmion led a local Religion and Labor Fellowship and opened the fellowship gatherings to black union leaders and ministers.[58] One of Mason's longest-lasting friendships with a prolabor, pro–civil rights minister was with Rev. Samuel E. Howie,

Lucy Mason addressing an early morning union meeting of textile workers in Buffalo Springs, South Carolina, 1940s. Courtesy of David M. Rubenstein Rare Book and Manuscript Library, Duke University, Durham, North Carolina.

a Presbyterian minister in Memphis. Because Mason spent a good deal of time in Memphis, she appreciated the work Howie did for black and white workers during the war. She sent Howie a letter of appreciation, noting, "I have long thought and said as much . . . that the place to begin to change adverse public opinion about labor unions is through the churches." A few years later, when Howie's support for labor and liberalism in Memphis threatened his church, Mason reminded the city's CIO leaders that Howie had opened his church to unions and that "labor should surely support him" against his enemies.[59]

Mason relished her CIO work and the men with whom she formed strong bonds, but she also developed allies with a number of strong Christian women committed to social justice in the South. Her early position in the Richmond YWCA introduced her to Brownie Lee Jones, a native southwesterner who served the Richmond YWCA as industrial secretary. Mason recalled Jones as "unusually effective in opening people's minds to progressive ideas." Born in 1897, Jones grew up in Arkansas but learned of impressive female reformers like Jane Addams from her father. However, both her parents died at a young age, and she and a brother went to live with a lively, energetic grandfather and a stern Methodist grandmother. Jones attended a women's college in Oklahoma, where she became active in the YWCA and in teaching Sunday school. After college she obtained clerical work in Denver, where she attended the Labor College and developed interest in the plight of working women. The Denver YWCA recruited her to be their industrial secretary, a position that she later filled in Flint, Michigan, and Richmond.[60]

Jones left Richmond for California in the 1930s and 1940s, and worked with the state welfare department, the National Youth Organization, and the Office of Price Administration during World War II. Then, in 1944, the Southern School for Workers asked Jones to head up its new initiative in Richmond.[61] Jones jumped at the chance to return to Richmond, which, she admitted, was not "a completely southern city" in her mind. For the next six years, until the school closed in 1950, Jones was one of a liberal circle in Richmond who brought blacks into contact with labor-movement progressives. The school conducted classes on issues of importance to workers, and it also offered a great deal of political education, holding literacy classes and anti-poll-tax programs to help workers, particularly blacks, register to vote. As a result, Jones and the Southern School were the subject of rumors, particularly among the Steelworkers Union, that it was too close to the Communist Party, but Mason rallied to Jones's defense and put a stop to the rumors.[62]

During the 1940s, Jones and Mason kept in touch regularly. They both worked with other women in labor and social movements, women like Ruth Gettinger, a young Baptist hired by the CIO to work in its Community Relations Department during the 1940s; Nelle Morton of the Fellowship of Southern Churchmen; and Zilphia Horton, who was a fixture at the Highlander Folk School. And, of course, each had a large female support network from their years in the YWCA and other organizations, which provided them with valuable access to prominent women.[63] But although both Jones and Mason developed close personal friendships with women, their professional lives largely revolved around men in the labor movement, some of whom they admired greatly. Both women singled out Paul Christopher as a key supporter who would buck conservative tendencies in the labor movement. They also admired Boyd Payton of the Textile Workers. Jones remembered, "[Payton,] more than any one person in the South that I know, was concerned about what was happening to women workers and about their children," something atypical in the male-dominated culture of southern labor. Interestingly, Jones and Mason ignored whatever gender-related slights they may have received from CIO leaders in the South. Jones admitted later that perhaps she faced discrimination, but said, "I didn't feel it." She did confess that Mason often used her image as a proper southern woman to sway men to her point of view, but Jones never "thought about being a woman," she said. "And I don't know if I thought about my friends being women."[64]

One man both Mason and Jones identified as special was Charles Webber. The former field director of the Methodist Federation for Social Service who created such uproar when the church named him "minister to labor" in Virginia in 1945, Webber became a prominent labor activist in Virginia. In 1946, Webber combined his staff position for the Amalgamated Clothing Workers with his election as president of the Virginia CIO. Although Mason remembered Webber as a patient, methodical organizer who "worked among the people in an educational way," Webber also gained a reputation for taking on tough organizing jobs and working at breaking down racial barriers. Webber perplexed many Methodists when he took control of the state CIO's Political Action Committee and turned it against Senator Harry F. Byrd, a supporter of the poll tax and an opponent of "the major progressive social welfare bills." He further upset the status quo when he went to Smithfield, Virginia, to prevent the P. D. Gwaltney Company from intimidating black workers from voting in a representation election sanctioned by the National Labor Relations Board. Virginia Conference bishop W. W. Peele and George Reamey, editor of the *Virginia Methodist Advocate*, sought sanctions against Webber, demanding that he "either surrender [his] credentials as a Methodist minister or confine [his] work to the spiritual activities as a labor chaplain" and resign as head of the Virginia CIO.[65] He refused to do either.

Webber actually found much in his devotion to Methodism to reinforce his labor career. He pointed to John Wesley's recognition of "the necessity of field preaching as a means of reaching the toiling masses," and that at election times he urged "members of his Societies" to "vote for the candidate of nobler character who would support humanitarian and Christian principles." Webber noted that the history of the labor movement in Britain had strong connections to Methodism, and that "three of the six 'Tolpuddle Martyrs' of the early English Trade Union movement were Methodist local preachers."[66] When the Methodist Bishops Council asked Webber to defend his appointment in 1947, Webber replied, "I am fully persuaded that when I, as a 'Chaplain to Organized Labor,' bring to unorganized Negro and white workers the moral sanction of the Methodist Church of their efforts to organize, and when I aid them, through collective bargaining, to end Jim Crowism, and to secure a more equitable amount of the products of agriculture and industry, I prevent another world-wide calamity that may bring destruction upon us all."[67] Although the bishops of the Methodist Church decided that Webber could not be reappointed as chaplain to labor, Webber nevertheless defied Bishop Peele's request that he leave Virginia, asserting that Peele was too worried about the moderate reputation of the church.[68]

Webber's beliefs earned him Peele's rancor. For Webber, working with labor was "a unique opportunity to aid the Crusade for Christ movement which has for its goal the establishment of the kingdom or commonwealth of God and man upon the earth." He reached back to the postmillennial traditions of Methodism. By helping win collective-bargaining rights for workers and encouraging the election of "socially minded legislators," unions were teaching working people "to rely on ballots, not bullets, for the solution of their religious—social—economic and political problems; and these activities further the Crusade for Christ." Far from hurting the reputation of the church, Webber asserted that his appointment as chaplain to labor allowed him to be "a living demonstration that the Methodist Church not only believes in, but also practices its Social Creed at the point where it hurts—namely, at the risk of loss of financial support from its anti-union members."[69]

The controversy surrounding Webber's appointment that began in early 1946 was a signal of what the CIO might expect in the South as it prepared to launch its ambitious Southern Organizing Campaign. While Mason applauded the Methodist bishop G. Bromley Oxnam for defending the appointment of Webber, evangelical groups sided with Bishop Peele. Ultraconservative Methodist minister Robert Shuler of Los Angeles spoke for many when he decried the "political" nature of the appointment, which was "really made to further the cause of radicalism in church and state." He added: "It is very doubtful if the CIO is becoming more Christian."[70] In retrospect, however, what should have been one of the most important revelations for the CIO was lost. The mainstream and evangelical churches that were most likely to rush to Webber's defense were the African American churches. The bishop of the Negro Methodist Churches, Alexander P. Shaw, was not embarrassed by the connection to the CIO because these unions were trying to end "Jim Crow discrimination, and are fighting for the abolition of the Poll Tax and for the adoption of a permanent Fair Employment Practices Commission." Shaw echoed Bishop Oxnam: "I see more religion in ending Jim Crow than in preaching abstractions about brotherhood." Shaw applauded the CIO leaders who "are a genuine religious force in the Southland."[71]

The American Federation of Labor did not have a similar cadre of progressive Christian activists. The AFL individual most consistently praised by liberal religious organizations was William Mitch of Alabama, who was closely associated with the Alabama CIO until the United Mine Workers disaffiliated as a result of John L. Lewis's petulance. Mitch was a devout Methodist who carried his unionism and his religious faith in the same bag. Still, many southern religious and political leaders had made accommodation to the AFL because they concentrated on skilled tradesmen and did not challenge the region's politics or racial norms. Many employers preferred to sign contracts with AFL unions rather than risk a CIO organizing victory. Representative of the AFL in the South was its regional director, George L. Googe, a middle-aged Southern Baptist and member of the conservative Printing Pressmen's Union, a combination that did little to break down racial barriers in many unions. Other unions, however, recognized that court and government rulings meant they could not permanently exclude black workers. As a result, some of the unions in the construction, transportation, and food industries, which had large southern workforces, opened membership to blacks, which the AFL claimed totaled more than four hundred thousand in the region. By the war's end, the AFL was a much larger force in the South than the

CIO. The CIO had between 250,000 and 400,000 members, while AFL unions had roughly three times that number.[72]

The CIO's Southern Crusade

As World War II ended, the leadership of the CIO recognized what the advocates of Christian free enterprise also understood, that the workers of the South represented a critical untapped resource. Whichever group could win the loyalties of southern workers would gain an enormous advantage in the contest over whether or not the nation would resume its march in the direction of liberalism or reverse the direction the nation had taken under Roosevelt's New Deal. In 1945 CIO leaders in Washington, D.C., could survey the South with some optimism. After all, CIO membership in key southern industries showed positive signs. Major gains in the oil, steel, rubber, automobile, meatpacking, and pulp and paper industries promised a bright future.[73] However, these sectors also faced a daunting task, made more difficult by the memories of earlier failures, particularly in the textile industry. In mills across the South, textile operatives remembered the disastrous 1934 general strike in the industry as well as the largely unsuccessful organizing drive of the Textile Workers Organizing Committee, which in 1939 became the Textile Workers Union of America. These failures pointed to just how much might be at stake. By the end of the war, the southern share of the industry had gained significantly at the expense of northern mills, which had 250,000 fewer textile jobs. The garment and woodworking industries were following the same alarming pattern, making union leaders nervous about maintaining union density where it was strong unless they could transform the South.[74]

Equally urgent for the CIO was the hope of changing the political environment of the South. Labor's leaders understood that government intervention into labor relations had helped the CIO grow, first with the National Labor Relations Act and then with wartime regulations. They also knew that the recalcitrance of southern Democrats had prevented even more sweeping changes. Throughout the war years, southern congressmen wailed about labor's efforts to mobilize black and poor white voters for the expansion of New Deal programs. By the end of the war, southern Democratic congressmen helped kill measures that would strengthen the federal government's role in the workers' compensation and make the Fair Employment Practices Committee a permanent fixture. Moreover, elections in 1938 and 1942 had made the southern congressional delegation even more conservative.[75]

State-level politics was equally important. As previously noted, Arkansas and Florida led the way in right-to-work laws in 1944, and other states passed antiviolence measures in strike laws and acts inhibiting the freedom of union organizers. As Lucy Mason and CIO organizers knew all too well, state and local officials had routinely participated in efforts to intimidate black and white workers from participating in elections of all sorts, whether for union representation or political representation. But in 1944 the grip of the old politics, which relied on racial and class domination by conservative Democrats, also showed signs of wear. In Georgia the moderate Ellis Arnall defeated the Talmadge regime; in Alabama, blacks mobilized to demand political rights in the wake of the Supreme Court decision (*Smith v. Allwright*) that outlawed the white primary; in South Carolina, a Progressive Democratic Party rose to challenge the state's all-white delegation at the party's national convention. The southern political scene at mid-decade had a schizophrenic quality. The CIO's Political Action Committee, if successful, might tip the balance. North Carolina conservative senator Josiah Bailey, for one, was worried: "[The CIO-PAC] will seek to purge us and every other self respecting and honest man who runs for office."[76]

The CIO, then, had good reasons to embark on an ambitious southern crusade. In the thick of an epic battle for collective-bargaining gains in the winter of 1945–46, a CIO committee began exploring the prospects for a postwar organizing campaign in the South. The two things were linked; in their minds it would be impossible to sustain the achievements already accomplished in the North if the economic and political environment in the South remained hostile to unions and liberalism. Although improvements for black workers factored into their calculations, such gains were clearly secondary to protecting unions and New Deal political programs. In early 1946 the plan began taking shape. The committee, consisting of David J. McDonald of the Steelworkers, James Carey of the Electrical Workers, George Addes of the Autoworkers, Allan S. Haywood, and two TWUA representatives, recommended the appointment of Van Bittner as director and George Baldanzi as assistant director. Bittner was a veteran of more than three decades in the labor movement, having begun his career with the United Mine Workers and later the United Steelworkers; Baldanzi was a thirty-nine-year-old vice president of the TWUA who had directed the startling union victory at the huge Dan River Mills in Danville. The CIO Executive Board approved of the plan, which called for the affiliated unions to contribute one million dollars and hire two hundred organizers to "organize everything in sight."[77]

The CIO designed its Southern Organizing Campaign (SOC) to be a highly centralized affair, controlled out of offices in Atlanta. The headquarters there would make all the decisions involving the assignment of organizers, the submission of petitions for NLRB elections, and the awarding of jurisdiction over workers organized. The campaign also insisted that all its state directors resign from any CIO Political Action Committee to make certain that they concentrated solely on organizing workers. While Bittner served largely as the conduit from the CIO Executive Board to the campaign's headquarters, Baldanzi directed the campaign, targeted first and foremost at the textile industry. Among the state directors Baldanzi chose were Franz Daniel (South Carolina) and Paul Christopher (Tennessee), both of whom had ties to the prophetic religious culture in the region. Others included Carey Haigler (Alabama), Ernest Pugh (Virginia), William Smith (North Carolina), and Charles Gillman (Georgia), all men with experience but none terribly dynamic. To deflect charges that the labor movement was "un-American" and made up of "outsiders," refrains familiar to most unionists who had worked in the South, Baldanzi tried to hire southerners and World War II veterans whenever possible. In May 1946 Bittner brazenly bragged to the *Gastonia Daily Gazette*: "Employers and their stooges will have an awful time convincing the people that these boys are here to destroy the government."[78] Of course, that also meant that the CIO hired many unseasoned organizers. Joe Pedigo, a veteran organizer by the time the campaign began, recalled the impact of Baldanzi's policy: "So what did we do? Hire a bunch of people, just hire everybody right and left and find and hire kids that don't know nothing and have no background and have no knowledge." To get the two hundred organizers in the field, the SOC at times unknowingly hired company spies, Pedigo claimed.[79]

At the same time that the CIO was hurriedly getting its staff in the field, Bittner and Baldanzi were trying to insulate the campaign from other charges they felt could make them vulnerable, particularly any connection to Communism. This was difficult to do. On the one hand, conservative industrialists and many evangelicals claimed that any agitation on behalf of labor, civil rights, and social issues was proof that Communists were involved. On the other hand, the AFL's southern director, George Googe, who was starting an AFL organizing drive, famously asserted that "neither reactionary employers nor Communists in the CIO can stop the campaign of the American Federation of Labor to enroll 1,000,000 unorganized Southern workers in the next twelve months."[80] Although historians have criticized Bittner for his public statement rejecting assistance from Socialists, Communists, and groups like the Southern Conference for Human Welfare, he was certainly between a rock and a hard place. The problem was that the more Communism was mentioned by and in conjunction with unions, the more that association stuck in the minds of southerners. Any of the prophetic Christians who had worked for labor and social justice in the South over the previous decade could have told Bittner that no matter what he said publicly, the press and business interests would call it Communism.

The friends of labor in progressive and liberal organizations were dismayed if not surprised by Bittner's bluntness. Alva Taylor wrote to Claude Williams that Bittner could not stop outsiders from giving help even if he wished, but he underestimated the damage that the CIO was causing the southern prophets on the left. The CIO leader in Alabama, Carey Haigler, blocked the use of Highlander Folk School for training and refused to raise funds for the school. Williams and Don West, hoping to assist the CIO in its drive, found themselves excluded and redbaited. Clark Foreman of the Southern Conference for Human Welfare saw its sources of union support diminish as the CIO funneled everything into its Southern Organizing Campaign, quickly dubbed by the press as "Operation Dixie." In fact, it was a Southern Conference employee, Osceola McKaine, who triggered Bittner's comments. McKaine, although supportive of the CIO, wrote to CIO vice president Allan Haywood that he hoped the CIO would use organizers who would exhibit better "racial attitudes and approaches." Haywood was not happy with the criticism; shortly after, Bittner's press conference specifically mentioned not needing help from the Southern Conference. The carefully constructed alliance of religious activists and labor was crumbling under the sting of Bittner's comments.[81]

Lucy Mason and Paul Christopher tried to keep the alliance alive within the CIO. They interceded with Haigler, and Christopher kept open the lines of communication with Claude Williams and Harry Koger. Even Franz Daniel, who remained suspicious of the Southern Conference and Highlander, expected that these valuable resources could still contribute to Operation Dixie. Daniel told David Burgess that Bittner's "statement about not wanting the help of communists, socialists and the Southern Conference, etc. was merely 'for the record.'"[82] But the CIO had damaged relationships and hurt organizations that were desirous of lending support to Operation Dixie. Particularly among prophetic southerners who hoped that the CIO's crusade would be as important for changing the racial climate as it was the labor scene, early information about Operation Dixie was disconcerting. "The CIO," Burgess learned, "will start in the all-white industries first such as textiles. In fact about 70% of the funds will go into the textile organizational drive." Foreman lamented that "the leaders of 'Operation Dixie' resorted to opportunism in the hope of making the CIO respectable in the South."[83]

If the CIO expected Bittner's opportunistic statement to make its southern crusade respectable, it learned quickly that would not be the case. In June 1946 Operation Dixie launched its drive in the Piedmont textile villages so tightly controlled by paternalistic employers. Operating on a model adapted from the heyday of CIO growth in the sit-down era, the Southern Organizing Campaign believed that if they targeted the largest corporations in an industry and won with a rush of activity, they could then more easily spread the momentum of organization to the rest of the industry. Operation Dixie thus began by assigning ten of its twenty-five North Carolina organizers to the huge Cannon Mills complex in Kannapolis, North Carolina. But rather than swarm the twenty-four thousand millworkers in the large, unincorporated city, they found an environment suffused with the stern but loving paternal figure of Charles Cannon. Millworkers combined an odd mixture of familial loyalty with fear that they would fall out of Cannon's favor (and thus the warm embrace of company benevolence), which could easily turn to banishment from jobs and community. At the same time, the organizers discovered that Cannon Mills workers were not isolated from the outside world. They had automobiles and radios, and they read more than the organizers expected, but these workers also seemed content with their situations:

"The desire to improve present material conditions is almost non-existent," a CIO report claimed, a sign of just how difficult organizing would be.[84]

In so many such villages throughout the South, employer paternalism and the emotions it evoked rested upon a religious culture. Mill owners cultivated a family feeling designed to replicate the communities of believers that workers found in evangelical Protestant churches. Paternalism also allowed for individual interaction with superiors and for personal recognition, which likewise was ingrained in the culture of evangelicalism. Because Van Bittner distanced the campaign from so much of the Protestant Left in the South, Operation Dixie was unprepared at first to meet the challenge that religion presented to organizers. Although Lucy Mason remembered Bittner as a sincere Christian, others attest to how uninformed he was about southern Protestantism. Jerome Cooper, an attorney for the steelworkers assigned to the Southern Organizing Campaign, "never knew him [Bittner] to attend church," although, he said, "I suppose that as a union official he did." Bittner once told Cooper, "I've read and I believe in the Good Book, and I know it says, 'if your enemy smites you on one cheek, you should turn the other cheek,' but I haven't read anywhere in the Bible where it says you've got to make a damn whirligig out of yourself." The one religious book that Bittner found comforting was Rabbi Joshua Liebman's *Peace of Mind*.[85] As a result, Operation Dixie began without knowing much about the region's religious culture. Meanwhile, they faced not only the quasi-Christian hate sheets like *Militant Truth*, but they also encountered the solid, honest, mill-village preachers who hoped to maintain community and congregational harmony.

Within the first two months, CIO leaders realized that they needed a new approach to the South's churches. Organizers' reports flooded into the campaign's headquarters detailing the local clergy's fierce opposition to unions in a number of settings. In July, the CIO Executive Board decided to establish a Community Relations Department for the campaign, which would report to Allan Swim, the CIO's national public-relations director. One of the main objectives of the department was to make contacts with ministers and community leaders and try to blunt their criticism of the union campaign. There was no person better able to contribute to that job than Lucy Mason, with her southern manners, her family background, and her religious faith. The CIO's Southern Organizing Campaign also assigned a young, southern Baptist woman, Ruth Gettinger, to the work.[86]

Over the course of the campaign, Mason and Gettinger visited hundreds of towns and cities where the CIO was launching campaigns. Once in town, they spent days calling on ministers, newspaper editors, merchants, police chiefs, city attorneys, and anyone else they believed who might be open-minded about the organizing drives. By 1946, Mason had been engaged in this sort of work for a decade; what was different was that Operation Dixie's leadership, particularly Van Bittner, dispatched her and Gettinger in advance of a drive rather than in reaction to community and religious opposition. Mason was still a troubleshooter who called government attention to violations of civil rights and liberties, but she also got the lay of the land and tried to soften the ground for teams of CIO organizers who followed.[87]

Mason and Gettinger routinely sought out friendly clergy. Mason's report of a visit to Thomasville, Georgia, in early 1947 was fairly typical. She started with the local Episcopal minister because that was her own church background. She found an "intelligent young" minister who had been in Thomasville for nine years. The congregation included several of the principal local employers, men who were active in the church. Mason then met with Rev. T. F. Callaway of the First Baptist Church, "one of the town's leading men." In a brief conversation, Callaway appeared to be "intelligent, open minded, sincere and takes for granted that workers should organize in unions." First Baptist also included a number of employers, including a meatpacking plant executive who was a deacon. Thomasville's Methodist minister was young, Mason noted: "[He] knows little or nothing about unions and seemed to be nervous talking to the organizer and me." The Church of God minister "seemed very ignorant," and she judged him to "have little influence with the people." A second Methodist minister was "rather aloof from the community," Mason reported, but the Presbyterian minister "has a very good reputation." Mason made similar snap judgments about city officials, based on brief meetings. The city attorney kept the city council from passing an ordinance to license organizers, but the mayor was "very unfriendly to the CIO," in part because the CIO was trying to organize his employees at the Powell Produce Company.[88] In general, Mason and Gettinger praised ministers and officials who greeted them warmly, but they often disparaged those who were reluctant to work with them.

To head the Community Relations Department, the CIO assigned John Gates Ramsay. Ramsay was an atypical labor leader. Born in Howe, Oklahoma, in 1902, Ramsay was the son of a mining engineer and mine operator who had actively fought the United Mine Workers. During World War I, the Ramsay family moved to Bethlehem, Pennsylvania, when the Bethlehem Steel Company recruited the elder Ramsay to rebuild a coke works, but then the company demoted him after the war ended. John Ramsay, already a devout Presbyterian as a result of a youthful conversion through the Christian Endeavor movement, seemed headed for a life of inspiring young people to serve Christ, but his father's demotion and his large number of brothers and sisters derailed those plans. He left high school to help contribute to the family income, trying sales work before going to work in Bethlehem's steel mills. Ramsay was far from discouraged, however. During the 1920s he married the daughter of Moravian missionaries, started a Boy Scout troop for working-class youths, and continued his work with the Christian Endeavor movement.[89]

During the Depression, Ramsay assumed leadership positions in the local Presbyterian church, which thrust him into the middle of a struggle between the young minister, Paul Cotton, and Eugene Grace, president of Bethlehem Steel, who worshipped there. When hard times hit, Cotton began helping the local Unemployed Citizens League and encouraging workers to form unions. Ramsay followed his lead, joining and becoming vice president of the lodge of the Amalgamated Association of Iron and Steel Workers. Grace used his influence to oust Cotton from the local church and turned to intimidating Ramsay—including threatening to fire Ramsay's father and asking him to withdraw from membership in the church. Ramsay, however, held firm and eventually became local president of Steel Workers Organizing Committee Local 1409, which succeeded in bringing Bethlehem Steel to the bargaining table in 1939. Central to Ramsay's rise to leadership were his integrity and fearlessness, which he attributed to his religious convictions, even though Protestants were in the minority in Local 1409. He was also able to call on the support of prominent religious leaders, including Rev. James Myers, a fellow Presbyterian, who headed the Industrial Department of the Federal Council of Churches.[90]

As events unfolded in Bethlehem, Ramsay's principled leadership of Local 1409 attracted the attention of the Oxford Group, a religious movement that infused Christian ideals into everyday life. Headed by the controversial Lutheran evangelist Rev. Frank Buchman, the Oxford Group was dedicated to the recruitment and activism of laypeople to build a new world order for Christ. In 1938, as Europe appeared headed toward a military crisis, Buchman renamed his movement Moral Re-Armament, emphasizing the need for nations to "re-arm morally." Moral Re-Armament hoped to solve not only the international crisis but also conflicts of every variety through Christly reconciliation. Obviously, Ramsay's stature in the Presbyterian Church and in organized labor made him a valued recruit for Moral Re-Armament, which not only brought him into the organization but also sent him as a labor representative to address a meeting in Switzerland. Buchman and Moral Re-Armament became controversial both for their anti-Communism and for their attempt to reach out to Nazi leaders, believing that they could be influenced by Christ's moral values. Despite the flirtation with Nazism, Moral Re-Armament worked hard to establish a base among labor unionists and provided training for promising Christian local and national union officials. Ramsay, in turn, felt he could help shape the group in a different way. At one of the first big meetings of Moral Re-Armament in the United States, Buchman asked Ramsay to address the audience. Flustered, Ramsay told Buchman that he needed to talk to the Lord before doing so. When his time came, Ramsay began: "I've had a talk with the Lord and he told me not to talk about personal sin and personal salvation; everybody's talking about that. He wants me to talk to you about the social sins." Ramsay then proceeded to denounce the sweatshop sin and to encourage the audience to buy union-label products. In addition to Ramsay, John Riffe of the Steelworkers, later to be director of Operation Dixie, was a prominent labor-union member of Moral Re-Armament.[91]

Ramsay's success in organizing Bethlehem brought him to the attention of the United Steelworkers of America. In 1941, Steelworkers president Philip Murray put Ramsay on staff to help organize the Bethlehem plant in Lackawanna, New York. His primary role was to build community and religious support for the union, and again he called on James Myers and organized luncheons where Catholic, Protestant, and Jewish clergy ate with leaders of the local unions in Lackawanna. As the Steelworkers racked up victories in steel factories during the war, Murray sent Ramsay to the important steel centers of Johnstown, Pennsylvania; Sparrows Point, Maryland; and Ashland, Kentucky. Murray, a deeply religious Catholic, developed enormous confidence in Ramsay who, in turn, transformed his idea of informal lunch meetings that began in Lackawanna into a series of Religion and Labor Fellowships that he spread wherever he went. For Ramsay, the fellowships became almost more important than the organizing campaigns; they were "something to last." He believed that he "was organizing for a basic principle above organizing," one that meant that "labor could be heard and it also could hear." Murray agreed, and he made that his staff assignment.[92]

When the CIO's drive confronted hostility from clergy, Murray felt he knew just the person to change the situation. With the Steelworkers paying his salary, Bittner brought Ramsay to Atlanta but warned, "You're up against something different here in the South. You're up against the Ku Klux Klan." One of the CIO organizers told Ramsay that southern churches were even less hospitable to unions than other civic and fraternal organizations. He claimed, "When I go into my church and tell them I'm in the CIO, I don't have a friend that will be open with me."[93] Ramsay believed that he had the experience to break through to southern ministers. He had successfully maneuvered in a difficult religious situation when he organized at ARMCO Steel in Ashland, Kentucky. His efforts to build a Labor and Religion Fellowship met harsh resistance from employers, who went so far as to drive a sympathetic minister and the secretary of the YMCA out of town. They also tried to make Ramsay's wife feel uncomfortable in the local Presbyterian church, but Ramsay was eventually able to work effectively in Ashland among "a very devout, religious southern group of people." Reminiscing about Ashland thirty years later, however, Ramsay betrayed some of his misgivings about the influence of southern religion on ministers and working people: "If he's in [a working-class church], he's probably fundamentalist and stays out of everything. If he's in the boss's church, then he's in the other" side's circle. "It's hard to find men who are in a balanced situation."[94] Ramsay had very little contact with the prophetic religious activists of the southern Left.

Lucy Mason, for one, worried about how little experience Ramsay had with southern workers and southern churches. In July 1946, as the Fellowship of Southern Churchmen planned a conference to "awaken rural ministers of the South

John G. Ramsay at his desk in Atlanta during the CIO's Operation Dixie. Note the picture of Philip Murray (center of three) on the wall above his desk. Courtesy of the Southern Labor Archives, Georgia State University, Atlanta.

to the need of applying Biblical teachings to social justice," David Burgess and Nelle Morton wanted someone from the CIO to lead discussions on religion and labor. Morton contacted Mason, who could not attend because of previous commitments but who candidly replied, "If John Ramsay is there, you will have a much better person than I for the religion and labor discussions. The thing you may lack is someone familiar with the southern labor situation, about which I am concerned." She admired Ramsay but noted that he was just making his first forays into the South. She advised instead that Paul Christopher might make a better contributor if he were able to attend. The conference, however, included Ramsay and also Broadus Mitchell of the International Ladies Garment Workers Union, both of whom tried to dispel the notion that unions were "outside groups entering the South without invitation." Ramsay noted that the CIO was receiving many invitations for organization from veterans, "who have seen something different away from home . . . and will not put up with poor working conditions and low wages at home."[95]

Mason later came to rely heavily on John Ramsay and called him "God's Good Man" in her reminiscences of a life in the labor movement. She first met Ramsay at a conference on the role of churches in a just and durable peace in January 1945.

She remembered him at this meeting as "a tall, good-looking man with a light upon his face." They developed a close friendship working on labor and attending conferences sponsored by the Federal Council of Churches as representatives of their respective denominations. Mason believed that Ramsay's name had appeared in more religious publications "than that of any other labor layman." Most of these publications attested to the spirit of cooperation and mutual understanding that Ramsay promoted in the relationships developed between churches and labor. From his earlier association with Moral Re-Armament he carried over his opposition to Communism and the notion that "the church has a job to do to educate both labor and management as to its social vision." But he also asserted that his work in the CIO was "trying to make men feel like men." Working people were "not out for paternalism." Instead, it was "every man's right to earn enough so that he can give—in all the little ways that are so important to the dignity of the human spirit."[96]

Ramsay also wrote frequently for religious publications, such as *Christian Century, Michigan Christian Advocate, Christian Endeavor,* various Presbyterian magazines, and the United Methodist Church's *Motive.* Liston Pope included a chapter from Ramsay on the reconciliation of religion and labor for his book, *Labor's Relation to Church and Community,* published in 1947. Ramsay typically emphasized his work for labor as a Christian vocation, and that he hoped to "bring about a closer relationship between working people and their churches." Although he was not a deep theological thinker, Ramsay also believed that religion was critical to finding a solution to labor strife; not that it would end conflict, as Frank Buchman had hoped to effect with Moral Re-Armament, but that it could be resolved peacefully and democratically. For people striving to win fair wages and working conditions, "Does religion have an answer?" he asked rhetorically. "I believe it does," he answered, "and my coworkers and I will continue through the help and the love and patience of Jesus Christ to carry on a peaceful strike" despite what comes, he wrote. He asked of the church only that it "sustain its members as we meet the challenge," remembering the commandments that you must "love the Lord your God with your whole heart" and that "you must love your neighbor as yourself."[97]

Ramsay's religion, however, was not the religion of the South. He was ecumenical in the broadest sense; his Labor and Religion Fellowships sought to be all inclusive, reaching out to Protestants, Catholics, and Jews. His boss, Philip Murray, was a devout Catholic. In one of their meetings, Ramsay told Murray: "I'm glad to see you're a man of prayer. I know you're a Christian Catholic and I am a Christian Presbyterian. I want to stop being a Christian Presbyterian and be a Presbyterian Christian."[98] Such an inclusive interpretation of Christianity was out of step with the vast majority of Protestants in the South, where sectarianism seemed to grow out of the soil. Similarly, Ramsay was a member of a more hierarchical religious culture with a much stronger emphasis on social responsibilities. While he had effectively utilized his prominence in the Federal Council of Churches to bring ministers into conversations with labor people in the North, this simply did not work in the South, where many ministers reviled the Federal Council. Shortly after arriving in the South, Ramsay received a letter from Tennessee CIO director Paul Christopher, who was troubled over a run-in with "an intolerant preacher" who had denounced social Christianity and ecumenical liberal Protestant organizations. Ramsay wrote to Christopher not to worry because "his rantings on the Federal Council will be a boost to us when he [subsequently] rants about the CIO."[99] To Ramsay, who had operated in the North, a minister attacking the Federal Council would certainly suffer a loss of credibility. But in the South, such a declaration typically met with enthusiasm. Thus, despite having very impressive religious credentials and connections, those associations did not serve him well with most southern Protestant ministers.

A Time of Hope and Fateful Decisions

In the first months of 1946 the CIO had many issues to consider as it pondered its future. The strike wave that ran through the nation signaled a new commitment on the part of corporations to roll back the gains that labor had made over the past decade. At the same time, the war-induced industrial development of the South was attracting the attention of employers and union leaders alike, who alternately viewed this development as promise or as peril. There were also signs that southern African Americans, industrial workers, and war veterans expected to be able to return home to new economic opportunities and political participation at the same time that the forces of southern reaction were mounting campaigns to maintain the low wages and racial order of the region. This was an explosive mix and, so it is not surprising that the first year following the end of the war witnessed episodes of racial violence, class conflict, and political upheaval that made the future of the South unpredictable. For white southerners comfortable in the old society, many felt (as one historian notes) "There goes my everything."[100]

One thing was certain: the religious beliefs of southerners would greatly affect the outcome. The creation of the Community Relations Department of the CIO was in many respects a reaction to the earlier recognition by companies that a popular religiosity flourished in the South and that free-enterprise evangelicals were shaping the personal worlds of political meaning that many southern Protestants attached to their beliefs, which included the notion that "the world of everyday life is a realm of power, an arena where supernatural forces of good and evil are operative," according to religious historian Charles H. Lippy. If they made the correct choices and sided with the forces of good, they could participate in the triumph over evil—perhaps not in the present but surely in the future. For the working-class adherents of popular Christianity, the ability to gain power in this sacred realm at times offset their lack of control in the secular one. To them, the eventual triumph of good will more than compensate for the hardships they endured.[101]

Unfortunately for the CIO, the organization felt that it had to keep the religious activists who best understood the popular religiosity of the South at arm's length. Those prophetic radicals professed political ideas that made them too risky to include in Operation Dixie. At the same time, it is questionable whether Claude Williams, Don West, Ward Rodgers, and others could have held together local unions and withstood the attacks that came with a growing anti-Communist hysteria. Even on those occasions when prophetic radicals cultivated followings through their appreciation of and comfort with the spirituality of the poor, once opponents exposed their association with Communist political beliefs, their support evaporated, especially among religiously inclined workers.[102] The CIO also did not make good use of others who shared much of the southern religious culture, especially many African American ministers for whom traditionalist theology was no barrier to collective social action. Among the most notable ministers from black churches were E. B. McKinney and Owen Whitfield, who worked with sharecroppers and tenant farmers, William Holmes Borders of Atlanta, James McDaniel of Memphis, and AME bishop B. G. Shaw of Birmingham. But the CIO's decision to devote so many of its resources to textiles and to try to organize white workers first in order to avoid race-baiting closed off the possibility of maximizing the influence of black churches.

The CIO did have a reservoir of white Protestant support from which to draw. The Fellowship of Southern Churchmen offered its assistance. Nelle Morton, David Burgess, and many other fellowship members were eager to work for change in the South that would include unions. Similarly, there were young women who came to industrial work through the YWCA. Brownie Lee Jones was perhaps the most noteworthy, but others, like Helen Matthews Lewis, gravitated to CIO unions armed with a spiritually inspired sense of social action. There were also the large numbers of southern clergymen willing to give the CIO a fair hearing in part because they found it so difficult to disappoint Lucy Randolph Mason. It is equally important not to overlook some key CIO leaders who were role models for blending strong union commitments with deeply religious values. Paul Christopher, William Mitch, William Crawford, John Ramsay, and others worked hard to sanctify their social activism. Finally, there was a corps of seminary-trained CIO activists who chose the cause of labor as their sacred mission. Franz Daniel, Witherspoon Dodge, and Charles Webber hoped that their religious credentials could offset the growing influence of Christian free-enterprise ideas among southern clergymen and their congregations. The CIO campaign underway in the summer of 1946 was, indeed, a struggle for the soul of the postwar South.

CHAPTER 6

Ministering in Communities of Struggle

Having grown up as the child of "lintheads" in Easley, South Carolina, Wilt Browning recalled the tense months in the late 1940s when his father and mother, a loom fixer and a spinner at the Easley Mill, talked quietly over meals about the arrival of union organizers and "the pressure they felt to resist" their enticements. It was still a time when the majority of local disputes, even ones as minor as young men hitting a baseball onto another man's porch, might be settled by the superintendent of the cotton mill. The arrival of the union was thus a considerable challenge to mill management. Browning, however, remembered it as a "boom time" for local evangelical churches, which received new pews for the sanctuaries, new pianos, or fresh coats of tar or gravel for the parking lot. On a Sunday shortly before a looming union representation election, the mill superintendent attended the services at the Easley Church of God, even though it was not his church, to accept the gratitude of the congregation on behalf of the mill owners who lived elsewhere. The sermon that day at Browning's church began with the Book of Revelation, chapter 14, dealing with worshipping the beast and receiving his mark. The preacher concluded by reading the verses 19 and 20 of Revelation 19:

> And I saw the beast, and the kings of the earth, and their armies, gathered together to make war against Him who sat on the horse and against His army.
>
> And the beast was taken, and with him the false prophet that wrought miracles before him, with which he deceived them that had received the mark of the beast, and them that worshipped his image. These both were cast alive into the lake of fire burning with brimstone.

With those words, the preacher closed the Bible with a thump and claimed that the "mark of the beast would most certainly be conferred first upon union members, people who through greed sought more than their fair share from their employers."[1]

Browning's preacher resembles the iconic clergyman who appears in many histories of the southern working class. Happy with the largesse of the company,

Picture of the workers in the Easley Mill where millhands voted against the union. Wilt Browning's mother is behind and to the left of the woman who is behind and to the left of the man seated at the table. Courtesy of Marlene Burke.

mill-village ministers delivered sermons that counseled millworkers to be content with their wages and living standards and to avoid the temptations of union organizers who promised them earthly rewards that guided them away from a life of serving Christ. Whether in mainline denominations or in Pentecostal churches like the one Browning attended, the message of evangelical Protestantism condemned unions, particularly those godless, communistic groups attached to the CIO. Those preachers who frightened workers by claiming that the CIO was the "Mark of the Beast," and that it stood for "Christ Is Out, Communism Is On," are the ones that most historians of southern labor choose to feature.[2] Some of this is inevitable; CIO activists themselves overstated the power that union-hating ministers wielded. David Burgess prepared the brief for the CIO's complaints when he testified to Congress in 1950. He then repackaged those charges in everything he subsequently wrote about the CIO's Southern Organizing Campaign.[3] Burgess and those who followed in his wake made a compelling case, one that helps explain away the failures of the CIO to win the hearts and minds of southern workers, but it is not the entire story. The span of ministers' attitudes and the factors that shaped their responses were far more complicated.

As the previous two chapters demonstrated, the post–World War II years comprised a time of interreligious wars over the economic future of the country.

The Depression had energized prophetic, collectivist voices within the religious community. Organizations ranging from the Federal Council of Churches to the Southern Baptist Convention appeared to suggest that God leaned in favor of government intervention in the economy and on the side of collective bargaining. In sharp contrast, the horrors of war and the frightening specter of totalitarian states, whether fascist or communist, convinced others that collectivist solutions and state power were misguided and dangerous. They implied conflict, privations, and a loss of freedom, which ultimately evolved into tyranny and threatened personal religious choice.

During the years after the war ended, the Left lost important allies in the sacred and the secular worlds. The most famous dissenter in the former was Reinhold Niebuhr, who had been an inspirational mentor to many of the prophetic radicals active in the South. A key turncoat among the latter was the prominent journalist John T. Flynn, who in 1949 published *The Road Ahead*. In it Flynn wrote that the Federal Council of Churches, "by all odds the most powerful apparatus in existence for propaganda among the Christian laity of America," was a "front organization" for a socialist revolution that would lead to "slavery to government" in the United States.[4] The relationship of religion to the capitalist free-enterprise system was experiencing a seismic shift. Nowhere were the tremors more perilous than in the South, where labor organizers hoped to capitalize on a dramatic economic transformation.

For hundreds of southern preachers, a choice had to be made when the CIO arrived. Some, like Wilt Browning's preacher, had no difficulty. Most, however, struggled with their consciences and religious values, used their own life experiences, read their denominational newspapers, took the pulse of their congregations, and weighed the relative merits of arguments they heard from factory and union representatives. They also thought about the consequences their pronouncements might have on their communities, their flocks, their families, and themselves, but they did not contemplate what was morally right in a neutral environment. One side had an enormous advantage in resources that they could, and would, bring to bear on southern ministers. The decisions ministers made and the influence they had cannot be reduced to a formula. To understand the role that the sacred plays in social movements, it is important that we examine how ministers understood their responsibility and conveyed that to their congregations.

Presenting the CIO's Gospel

In the summer of 1946, the CIO's Community Relations Department set out to counter the influence of anti-union preachers. During the early weeks of the Southern Organizing Campaign, *Militant Truth* and *The Trumpet* had mysteriously appeared in the mailboxes of millhands wherever CIO organizers operated. In communities across the South, employers complemented the newspaper propaganda by holding face-to-face meetings with preachers, lavishing gifts on their churches, and blaring anti-union scare tactics over friendly radio stations. One CIO organizer vividly recalled the experience of arriving to begin a union drive. "The company would not only make radio announcements, they'd get a preacher on Sunday: 'We have a labor organizer in town who is nothing but an agitator and will tell nothing but lies to get you to join and sign a union card and have an election!' The company would put it out in leaflets! And then the preacher would take that leaflet and read it at the pulpit."[5] When combined with the Book of Revelation warnings about the "mark of the beast" that were etched into Wilt Browning's memories, it is possible to imagine the fear that such a broadcast might incite.

In fact, the CIO first appeared in Browning's hometown in September 1946. Lucy Mason and Fred Wingard of the CIO Organizing Committee staff were in Easley, South Carolina, at the time investigating reports from local union members that a Baptist preacher had been advising people not to join the union. The report targeted Robert S. Wheeler, who received a list of union members from the company and invited all of them to a meeting at his church. There, Wheeler "attacked the union as a Godless and subversive organization" and told those in attendance that "church people had to choose between God and the unions. He said that those who did not leave the union would be expelled from the church." Mason and Wingard also talked with a young Methodist minister, Virgil Mitchell, "who vigorously denounced the CIO as an evil institution, and one that should be avoided by all Christians." Finally, Mason learned that at Glenwood Baptist Church in Easley, the anti-CIO statements of preachers in the community led a number of church members to refuse to teach or be connected with the Sunday School because the superintendent was a union member. Church members asserted that "no CIO member can go to heaven."[6] Clearly, Browning's minister followed a strong tradition.

The Fellowship of Southern Churchmen discovered a similarly widespread "uninformed and reactionary criticism" among the region's clergy. In August 1946, the fellowship's Commission on Labor sent a circular to twenty thousand southern clergy, which included pronouncements from various denominations in support of labor and collective bargaining. The circular, signed by Burgess and Scotty Cowan, asked ministers to set up meetings with representatives of union-organizing campaigns to explain labor's aims and discover how they might help. Burgess and Cowan advised special services with invitations to unions, distributing denominational pronouncements and encouraging youths to discuss labor problems. Timing was critical, they argued: "If democracy and religious freedom are to survive, we must count on a strong and idealistic labor movement."[7] What Cowan and Burgess discovered was daunting. Responses to the circular argued that the church "should not pontificate on any labor or political question"; that Christians should "come out from the world" and avoid unions or any organizations "in which some members are as yet unsaved"; that unions bring agitation and instill confusion, preventing "man from living at peace with his neighbors"; and that many believed union leaders were "un-Christian."[8] One Presbyterian minister wrote that he was "strictly opposed to all efforts of any man or group of men to use the church of Jesus Christ in questions of this nature." "Our duty," he said, "is to win men to Christ. Our work is spiritual, not political." A Methodist pastor replied, "We know what [labor's] aims are, and until you get some Christian Leaders they will not receive an invitation" to his services.[9] Some replies were more specific about their opposition. An anonymous reply claimed: "I think the South was doing pretty well for itself until Northern Labor interests (Communists) took a hand about 1929. Since then I have seen no peace here. Count me out!" Another unsigned letter accused Burgess and Cowan of being "ministers—or so called ministers [who] have so far fallen away from their sacred vows to preach the word as to sell out to such a band of racketeers as the C.I.O." He compared labor to the notorious gangster Al Capone and claimed to know organizers who were "drinkers and woman hoppers."[10]

Most worrisome for Burgess and Cowan and for the CIO's Community Relations Department were responses like the one from Congregationalist minister Roy D. Coulter. He complained that "union leaders can threaten the families of working men with violent bodily harm unless they join the union, they can close the doors of small business establishments by mass picketing or boycotts, they can engage in extortion or blackmail with impunity, they can throw rocks through windows or deprive men of their livelihoods, they can beat up and kill men who want to work when they are on strike, they can do everything or anything wicked they please so long as the sacred name of union labor is invoked." Gaston Boyle, a Virginia Presbyterian minister, echoed Coulter. He pointed to the rail and mine strikes that had recently brought hardship to the nation, and he asked why Burgess and Cowan were not concerned about the need to "'redeem men and women from exploitation and insecurity' that are imposed upon us all by unprincipled leaders of labor." Boyle refused to support unions "until labor shows some sign of appreciating the immense power that has been placed in its hands."[11]

The CIO complained most about the extremist anti-union preachers because they were the ones chosen for special meetings with company officials or airtime on anti-CIO broadcasts, but the CIO's religious activists gave the greatest attention to moderate and liberal clergy who they hoped would temper anti-union messages. As head of the Community Relations Department, John Ramsay turned to a method he had used effectively for the United Steelworkers: religion and labor fellowships. Upon arrival in Atlanta, Ramsay established the first of these local fellowships with the help of Lucy Mason and the leader of the Steelworkers in the city, William H. Crawford. Ramsay and Crawford recruited Dean H. B. Trimble of the Candler School of Theology to chair monthly "interfaith, interunion, and interracial" meetings aimed at "building bridges between religion and labor on which each can cross to the other." The Atlanta group met for dinners or lunches on a monthly basis. Its constitution listed lofty purposes, including to "define the social teachings of our religious faith and apply them to our economic and industrial life"; to "deepen the sense of religious commitment and vocation among all who work" regardless of race, creed, color, or national origin; and to "help the forces of religion and labor to discover and apply the techniques of social action that will achieve the ideals of our democratic faith." Members also pledged to "defend the trade union movement when attacked by the forces that would destroy it" and "to resist totalitarianism whether expressed in fascistic, communistic, or monopoly capitalistic forms."[12]

Over the next six years, Ramsay spread the idea through the South. Four Texas cities had Religion and Labor Fellowships (Dallas, San Antonio, Fort Worth, and Waco), as did five in Virginia (Richmond, Lynchburg, Roanoke, Radford, and Staunton). Louisiana, South Carolina, North Carolina, Mississippi, Tennessee, and Alabama each had two, and Arkansas, Kentucky and Oklahoma each had one. Texas CIO activists found the fellowships so effective in bringing about "better relationships between various segments of organized labor, between races, and between labor and the church," that the state CIO convention set up a committee to foster the fellowships in every community.[13] One of the important functions of these fellowship meetings was to call attention to the fact that labor leaders considered themselves to be good Christians. Key religious leaders in the cities that hosted them attested to the value of considering labor's goals. Meetings sometimes received coverage from local newspapers, such as when sixty-five people attended the December 1949 Atlanta meeting and had a photograph taken for the media. Clippings from newspapers in Texas, North Carolina, Georgia, and South Carolina reveal that the programs and meals shared by ministers and labor people managed to break through the unflattering picture usually reserved for CIO coverage in the press. Although they invited union officials from the AFL, the CIO was clearly the force behind the fellowship meetings; AFL people often shunned them because they challenged racial customs and even some local laws.[14]

The Religion and Labor Fellowships became an entree for the Community Relations staff to a number of religious organizations and speaking engagements. When John V. Riffe of the United Steelworkers took over as director of the Southern Organizing Campaign following the death of Van Bittner, he gave added weight to the religious activities of the staff. In 1950, Riffe, a born-again Christian, reported that Lucy Mason had recently attended the founding conference of the National Council of Churches of Christ in America and became the Episcopal Church's delegate to the Church and Economic Life Conference, and that Ruth Gettinger was serving on the Human Relations Committee of the North Carolina Council of Churches. Riffe also noted that John Ramsay's religious connections included serving on the Executive Committee of the Department of United Church Men of the National Council of Churches, on the Committee on Evangelism of the Presbyterian Church U.S.A, and as co-chairman of the National Religion and Labor Foundation.[15] In 1950, Texas CIO officer, Mabel Kuykendall, arranged to have Ramsay speak to the Southwestern Baptist Theological Seminary, the YMCA-YWCA Student Conference, the Wesley Foundation at the University of Texas, the Austin Presbyterian Theological Seminary, the Wesley Foundation at Southwestern University, and the Ministerial Association of Austin.[16] Full calendars were not unusual; Ramsay and Mason took nearly every opportunity to try and convince Christians to support the CIO.

The Community Relations Department had a more difficult time combatting the enormous advantages that employers and conservative religious voices had in access to radio. While radio stations in the South routinely broadcast employer messages and many of the conservative evangelicals for whom liberalism and organized labor were cursed, the CIO often found it difficult to get its views on the air. At the outset of the Southern Organizing Campaign, Ruth Gettinger confronted a station manager in Gastonia, North Carolina, who refused airtime to the CIO. In Kannapolis, the effort to organize the huge Cannon Mills complex confronted a similar reluctance from station managers, even though they had signed a contract to provide airtime for the Textile Workers Union. Local union members there joked that radio station WGTL's motto was "Hear no unionism, speak no unionism, see no unions." Shortly thereafter, WGTL cancelled its contract with the CIO.[17]

Radio stations at times turned to broadcasting codes to justify rejecting CIO programs, claiming that they were political and controversial. When David Burgess negotiated for a series of broadcasts to complement the CIO organizing drive in Rock Hill, South Carolina, the station insisted that he "practically castrate the radio script by taking out all references to the boss." Subsequent broadcasts involved similar haggling over the content of the programs. In Anderson, South Carolina, the local radio station rebuffed the CIO during 1949 when it sought airtime, filling its programming instead "with the most vicious anti-union propaganda imaginable." Lucy Mason discovered that the Anderson Citizens Committee had visited the radio station and the local newspaper to convince them to deny the CIO "paid or free newspaper space and radio time to tell its story." When Mason met with local media representatives to investigate, Robert Meeks, the secretary of the Anderson Chamber of Commerce and leader of the Citizens Committee, attended. Meeks told Mason that "the business men of Anderson" would "fight this [CIO] menace," and that they would do "whatever it might take to keep them out." Only after innumerable formal complaints to the Federal Communications Commission did the station give airtime to the CIO, but not until 1951, when Operation Dixie was on the downswing.[18]

Although access restrictions dampened the high hopes the campaign had for radio's ability to "penetrate the iron curtain of reaction" in the South, the Community Relations Department spent a great deal of effort countering conservative evangelicals' religious anti-unionism. Initially, when the CIO bought airtime it focused on rebutting the charges leveled by *Militant Truth*, claiming, "Ministers who have seen [this paper] despise it and consider that it does religion harm for such a paper to pretend to represent Christian teachings." Instead, the CIO offered pamphlets created by the CIO and the Textile Workers Union that included statements from denominational and ecumenical sources championing unions. In a 1947 Columbus, Georgia, broadcast, Ramsay asserted that the "Christian Church and the Labor Union have common social vision and objectives. Both have contributed to the attainment of a better and more just social and economic life." He warned against preachers who "bear false witness" and "publications that masquerade under the name of 'Christian' but . . . do not represent the expressed convictions of the great body of American Church men and women."[19]

The religious content of the CIO's radio programs hoped to educate ministers. In 1949, Lucy Mason told a Chattanooga radio audience that Christianity instructed men to love and help one another, and that the men and women who formed the CIO "have applied this Christian doctrine by working together" to improve people's lives, taking "interest in *all* that makes life better for all people." CIO "union folk" give generously to community services, serve as directors of local welfare organizations, and cooperate "with the Church" for the benefit of others. Labor's meetings and conferences, Mason continued, set aside time "for a service of worship" and, like the church, "recognize the dignity of all human life and the supreme value of every human being." She quoted southern clergy to support her points. H. B. Trimble of the Candler Theological Seminary in Atlanta or Lee C. Sheppard of the Pullen Memorial Baptist Church in Raleigh, Mason realized, were likely to have more sway with southern ministers than the Federal Council of Churches.[20] Ramsay learned that lesson far more slowly. He continued to boast of his standing in the Federal Council and of friendships with the New York Methodist bishop G. Bromley Oxnam and Catholic bishop Robert E. Lucey of San Antonio. But Ramsay did learn to quote Scripture to counter the conservative evangelicals. Favorite verses for Ramsay were Psalms 133:1—"Behold, how good and pleasant it is for brethren to dwell together in unity"—and Galatians 6:2—"Bear ye one another's burdens, and so fulfill the law of Christ."[21]

Mason and Ramsay sought to ease the fears of southern ministers by emphasizing the broad social goals of the CIO. In Oklahoma, Mason told her radio audience that while once "the objectives of organized labor had to do largely with wages, hours and working conditions," union leaders in 1948 were also "giving intelligent thought to international peace, full employment, social justice, political integrity, and industrial democracy." Indeed, "to achieve a more democratic and secure society," she said, "industry must cooperate with labor." Thus, unions were not selfish and materialistic as some critics claimed; rather, they drew upon God's wisdom in "building into the cooperative commonwealth those spiritual values which alone can make it endure." By 1949, CIO radio broadcasts added another element aimed at calming southern ministers: they featured Ramsay claiming that the religious beliefs of CIO leaders made them a bulwark against fascism and communism. Solid unions guided by devout Christian beliefs were essential in combatting the threat that extreme ideologies posed to American democracy and religious freedom.[22]

The Community Relations Department, together with such religiously oriented labor people as David Burgess, Paul Christopher, Franz Daniel, and Charles Webber, did most of their work on the ground in communities across the South. Mason and Ruth Gettinger, in particular, met hundreds of southern preachers in manufacturing communities where the CIO hoped to gain a toehold. In Kannapolis, North Carolina, where the Southern Organizing Campaign hoped to lay claim to a major early triumph, Gettinger looked for hopeful signs. A Baptist herself, she targeted six Baptist ministers in the sprawling textile center. Three seemed likely to be helpful; each had either been a textile worker or had family in the mills. Of course, that could pose a different problem. One of the three stated that even if sympathetic, "he could not preach labor unions from the pulpit." It was not clear if he took that position on theological grounds or for practical reasons, fearing there might be repercussions for family members if he took a strong union stance. Two of the other three promised to study the issues and consider attending a gathering that might bring together ministers and CIO people. Only one of the six was decidedly hostile. He asked pointed questions about whether the CIO "tolerated communists" in its unions and "how we would handle the Negro situation," two issues that anti-union propaganda consistently emphasized. The minister professed that "every sincere religious person would uphold anything that benefited the working man," but he did not believe that either unions or racial egalitarianism benefited the people he considered worthwhile.[23]

Mason kept a detailed card index of the places she visited in her work for the CIO with names of ministers who might be helpful or harmful to organizing drives. Reading the numerous memoranda she provided to the Campaign's organizing staff, historians might expect a more positive role for the sacred in Operation Dixie. In Cuthbert, Georgia, for instance, she visited a Methodist, a Presbyterian, and a Baptist minister. The Methodist minister was a student and friend of Liston Pope's, who wrote the study of religion in the Gastonia strike of 1929. He had met Mason in 1938 and had attended several conferences where she spoke. He also hosted union meetings at his church, at which attendance spiked. At the other end was the Baptist preacher, an "elderly, nice, conservative" man who was president of the Rotary Club and had "little idea of unions." The Presbyterian minister was young but was "said to be a good man."[24] In Morristown, Tennessee, the situation seemed even brighter. The three Methodist ministers "furnished [a] most outstanding leadership and energy in putting religion into action." One of the three Baptist ministers carried a union card, and one was neutral. Even the Church of God preacher was not overtly anti-union. Only the Presbyterian minister turned out to be a "great disappointment" and saw "no reason" for a meeting to introduce Ramsay to local ministers.[25]

Most towns lacked the same promising mix of ministers. In Pell City, Alabama, on the outskirts of Anniston where the Textile Workers had won a major victory at the Dwight Mills in 1943, Mason might have expected a friendlier reception from local preachers. Instead, the town's Methodist congregation consisted mostly of mill-management people. The main Baptist minister was seeking help from the owner of the Avondale Mill to build a new church; he doubted that those mill people would organize. The Methodist and Baptist ministers in poorer mill-village churches were equally disappointing to Mason. The Methodist was "very narrow," and the Baptist was on the "mill side," against the CIO, perhaps because he was a member of the AFL Brotherhood of Electrical Workers.[26] In all these cases, however, it is important to note that the visits came at the outset of an organizing campaign that often preceded the worst of employer resistance and whatever conflict might arise, factors that inevitably affected ministers' opinions and actions.

Mason and Gettinger often made snap decisions regarding preachers based on their perceptions of characteristics they believed would make clergy helpful to the CIO. Mason was particularly cryptic, with such assessments as "individualist and non-cooperative" or "innocent concerning unions," and even in one case, "stupid man." Community Relations staff members were attuned to the career or church-building aspirations of ministers, certain that if a preacher was "ambitious," he would find it in his interest to be anti-union.[27]

In their face-to-face meetings with ministers, Mason, Gettinger, and Ramsay worked to convince them that they should see the moral benefits of unionism for workers. The CIO proselytizers emphasized the dignity and self-respect that working people gained from having "a voice in their own economic destiny." They cited not only the pronouncements of the major denominational bodies, but also testimonials from ministers in communities where CIO unions had successfully negotiated contracts. One of Mason's favorite examples was Rock Hill, South Carolina, which she claimed was "one of the most organized cities in the South." She collected statements from local ministers who claimed that the CIO's success complemented "the active interest union people take in church matters." Another benefit was that increased union wages circulated through the local economy and "helped the income of the churches." One Rock Hill minister asserted that "almost 95 per cent" of his congregation's members were working people who tithed; thus "a wage raise affects our church," he said. Another pointed to the training and development that working people gained through union membership, leading to better citizens. Most important, one Rock Hill minister believed that people "cannot develop spiritually if they live on a low economic standard, with too little to have a decent life." The union thus had a broad effect on the churches, the businesses, and the civic life of Rock Hill.[28]

The Community Relations Department staff routinely emphasized their own religious backgrounds as evidence of the CIO's respect for the sacred. In correspondence and meetings, Mason reminded ministers that her "father and grandfather were Episcopal ministers and many of my uncles and cousins are in the ministry, so you see I know the church." In fact, she said, "[It was because] I love God and love my fellow men [that] I came into the CIO," which "has done more to lift the standard of living for millions of American men and women and their families than any other organization." Gettinger had the advantage of being a Southern Baptist and active in the North Carolina Council of Churches. She was a frequent speaker at YMCA and YWCA events as well as religious colleges, particularly in the Carolinas.[29] Ramsay had numerous religious affiliations, although some, such as his participation in the Federal Council of Churches, were not helpful. Still, the religious face of the CIO in the South could demonstrate that labor was not antireligion and, in fact, that many union leaders were committed church leaders.[30]

The Realities of Ministering

Southern preachers did not hear the CIO's message in a vacuum. Denominational meetings and resolutions and religious newspapers reacted to the efforts of labor's proselytizers to sanctify the union crusade. At the same time, ministers had to listen to their congregations, which might include employers, small businessmen, and other citizens, as well as community voices that commanded attention—city officials, law enforcement officers, newspaper editors, and civic associations. Then, there was the booming voice of the mill owners and the resources they had at their disposal. Whatever the inclinations of local ministers were at the moment that Mason, Gettinger, or Ramsay met with them near the onset of an organizing drive, there was bound to be need for them to adjust.

Of the major Protestant denominations, only Methodist and Episcopal ministers were likely to find strong support for union organizing in denominational statements. Many southern Presbyterians were too fearful of amalgamation into the northern denomination of their faith to wholeheartedly back anything that northerners advocated. When northern Presbyterians John Ramsay or Cameron Hall, who frequently invoked the Federal Council's approval of the CIO, addressed audiences in the South, they inevitably rankled southern Presbyterians.[31] Many of the Pentecostal and Holiness churches felt so strongly about their members avoiding the snares of membership in worldly organizations that few of their pronouncements encouraged union participation. In fact, they advised union membership only as a condition of employment.[32] The structure of the Southern

Baptist Convention also made it unlikely that the CIO could convince Baptist sources to endorse unionism. Although the Convention had issued a resolution in support of collective bargaining in 1938, its Social Service Commission in the postwar years only issued reports; it did not initiate policies or resolutions. Its reports offered only vague and tepid statements about unions, afraid that a strong policy on any issue might alienate its constituency of local churches, which cooperated on a purely voluntary basis.[33] One important counter to this trend emerged from the Southern Baptist Theological Seminary in Louisville, Kentucky. Ministers trained there came under the influence of such important Baptist voices for social Christianity as Charles Gardiner and Hugh Brimm. Some, like Acker C. Miller, became advocates for social action in the Baptists' Social Service Commission.[34]

In general, southern churches worried about the disruption in their communities that often accompanied union campaigns. People had to choose sides, which threatened congregational harmony. Denominations included workers and management alike. In recognition of that fact, the 1948 Southern Baptist Convention reported that the guiding principle of labor-capital relations should be Christian love, "never the selfish greedy interests of the few." Both labor and capital had the right to organize, but the church should not take sides; rather, it should mediate between the two parties and encourage mutual understanding "in an atmosphere of Christian ideals."[35] Southern Presbyterians also recognized that "labor unions are coming with industry into the South. They are welcomed in some communities, but bitterly opposed in others." There were "likely to be periods of labor unrest," Presbyterian Ernest Trice Thompson acknowledged, and the church should strive for balance between these forces so "that it may be strong to apprehend with all the saints (Ephesians 3:18)."[36] Concrete guidance on how Baptists or Presbyterians were to achieve these goals was, however, absent.

Like their working-class members, some churches worried that industrialization was also encouraging too much attention to materialism and consumerism, which appeared to lead to greater uniformity and bureaucratization. Pentecostals, especially, agonized that Christians were in danger of losing a "religion of the Spirit" by focusing on material gain. Southern Baptists also were alarmed. At its 1946 and 1947 conventions, the Social Service Commission issued reports that contained warnings about the social problems connected with prosperity. Materialism polarized public opinion, divided the country into a "society of groups," and contradicted "the most central tenet of the Baptist faith—the individual's free agency." This commitment to individual agency encouraged many Baptists to favor right-to-work laws, which spread through the South and proved particularly damaging for the CIO. For example, the normally liberal *Alabama Baptist* balked in 1946 when striking laundry workers tried to keep some ex-workers from crossing their picket line. At a time when many were agitating for full-employment policies, the paper "did not wish to invite a problem that could be even more vexatious, the problem of jobs without men willing or able to fill them."[37]

Strikes were another problem for clergy because they divided church fellowships and strained the resources of congregations. In Spartanburg, South Carolina, a textile strike completely disrupted the church life of the mill community. Strikers harassed strikebreakers and supervisory personnel on their way to church, and confrontations typically degenerated into name calling. One female unionist confronted the wife of a supervisory family that was a mainstay of the Methodist Church, asking her why she had stopped doing her mission work on Sunday afternoons. She continued: "I know the reason—you were afraid to, you old freckle face hussey, you ain't nothing." Sunday services at the Second Baptist Church during the strike resembled armed camps. In those circumstances when preachers asked a brother to lead a prayer, members from the other side of the sanctuary might be thinking, "Well, that fellow, he might have called me a S.O.B. on Friday afternoon."[38] While churches counseled mediation and coming together in an atmosphere of Christian ideals for peaceful change, they provided few examples of how ministers could achieve such accord in communities so bitterly split.

Some Methodist publications and pronouncements fought this trend. The *Alabama Christian Advocate*, for example, generally carried positive editorials and articles about the social activism of the church. In August 1947, Rev. A. S. Turnipseed defended Methodism against charges that it "over-emphasizes doing good at the expense of a dynamic Christian theology of sin and salvation by faith," or that it "seems to be a super social service program, tinted by Christian thinking, rather than a Christian orthodoxy that eventuates in service." Turnipseed praised the Holiness preachers, many of whom made their living in the mills and who now "are often leaders in the unions." "By this strange turn of history," he said, "some identification is being made between religion and daily toil."[39]

One message white southern church groups and denominations increasingly emphasized was the fear of Communism, building on a long obsession with identifying the Antichrist and finding him in socialist or communist movements. Although very powerful among Pentecostals and Fundamentalists, such trepidation pervaded even more liberal denominations like the Methodists. The *Wesleyan Christian Advocate*, published in Macon, Georgia, was fairly typical in its concerns about "atheistic Communism." The remedy was Christian democracy, which "dignifies the individual, replaces totalitarian rule with self-discipline, and offers Christian brotherhood."[40] Even in the Methodists' ultraliberal *Social Questions Bulletin*, which was sympathetic to the Southern Organizing Campaign, there was disquiet. In 1947 Congress passed the Taft-Hartley Act, which stipulated that officers of unions hoping to use the National Labor Relations process must sign affidavits stipulating that they were not members of the Communist Party. Then, in 1949, the CIO expelled unions it believed were Communist dominated, feeding anxieties fanned by anti-union forces in the South for years that CIO unions were communistic. UAW official Victor G. Reuther defended the expulsions, claiming that the CIO was a safeguard against the red menace and the "noisy distraction" that had hampered its efforts, but it also cast a pall over all union organizing in the South. Within a year, growing fears about Communism spilled into the Methodist Federation for Social Service in a campaign to remove its dynamic leader, Jack McMichael.[41] Despite working hard to distance its Southern Organizing Campaign from Communism, the mix of rumor, innuendo, and outright lies conservatives hurled against labor made most church groups and denominations reluctant to endorse the CIO.

Ministers in particular communities, on the other hand, had to weigh denominational messages against their own situations. Many, perhaps even the majority, tried to maintain a neutral position, whether because of personal beliefs, past experiences, or congregations that mixed people of different social classes. Texas-born Baptist minister B. Locke Davis was unusually sympathetic toward labor organizing and collective bargaining "for that time in the South," but he came to realize as a young minister during the 1930s and 1940s that "the application of the teachings of Christianity to the economic order would recognize the fact that there are basic rights on both sides—labor and management." Although Davis preached "a great deal" about social and economic justice, he felt that "seeking to win individuals to a right relation with God through Christ" was more effective in advancing social justice than trying to legislate controls over the economy.[42] Louisville Baptist preacher Roy C. McClung "didn't delve into it deeply enough to get a philosophical" position, but he "saw suffering and privation because of strikes. I saw families lose ground," he said, "even though at the end of the strike they got a raise in income." McClung never became anti-union. To him, "there needs to be an organization of the working man to protect him and to help him express his rights." But as for his preaching, he felt that his congregation responded most enthusiastically to "a ministry to the individual that came as a result of Christianity's focus on human need." "So," he said, "comfort, courage, the demand for integrity, the necessity for penitence and confession, the rejoicing in the divine forgiveness—these things I found to be very relevant."[43]

For many ministers, it was simply a question of where to put their emphasis. When author Herman C. Nixon wrote in 1946 about the lower Piedmont country, he focused on evangelist Samuel Porter Jones as the archetypal religious spokesman of the South. Jones was best known for his militant fight against alcohol, which Nixon noted "was about the whole content of his social gospel." Aside from the anti-liquor crusade, Nixon continued, most orthodox ministers like Jones "viewed the social scene with relative unconcern. Personal soul-salvation for the other world takes precedence over working for community salvation and social justice in this one."[44]

Ministers disliked being put in the middle of labor disputes. In Buffalo, South Carolina, the elderly and well-liked Baptist minister George H. Johnson noted that both the company and the CIO had tried to "use him." Johnson admitted to being in favor of unions, but he preferred that "it could be some other than the CIO" due to the "communist label" attached to it. Yet when mill managers questioned him about who in his congregation belonged to the union, he defended their rights to belong, adding that management "would find out that they were good people, even if they did belong to the union." Rev. Samuel H. Hay of Morristown, Tennessee, similarly asked to be left out of labor-management issues. "Please know that I have nothing against labor unions any more than against bankers and manufacturers' associations," he wrote. Labor unions had achieved a great deal for workers, and, Hay asserted, "it takes no particular piety or patriotism or philanthropy for me [to] say these things." However, he "could not see [the] relevance of ministers' association tangling also in the matter."[45] Still others tried to be somewhat more helpful. Rev. Charles R. Bell was a pointedly atypical Southern Baptist clergyman in Anniston, Alabama. He voted for Socialist Party candidate Norman Thomas in 1932, 1936, and 1940 and was interested in cooperatives, such as the one run by his friend Clarence Jordan of Koinonia Farm. Still, Bell recalled, "I didn't, for instance, in my pulpit, preach socialism as such to people. I tried to preach the Christian gospel." When labor conflict erupted at Utica Mills in Anniston, Bell "simply went to these people and asked them if they would come to church one Sunday." He thus "undertook to serve as conciliator."[46] Many preachers felt a powerful sacred duty to ameliorate conflict, even when they held strong personal opinions.

Many ministers with managers in their congregations felt it their duty to remain neutral. A Greensboro, North Carolina, clergyman told John Ramsay that he would attend a Labor-Religion Fellowship lunch "if he could pay for his own meal." He confided to another minister about being "faced with a prosperous congregation, some of whom think that there is danger to them from the CIO." Ruth Gettinger inferred that similar motives influenced Lutheran minister Hugh Dressler in Hickory, North Carolina. Although Dressler was familiar with Ramsay's successful work in New York, in Hickory he was "well entrenched" in an upper-crust church with many wealthy members. Gettinger doubted Dressler would do "anything helpful."[47]

Worry about remaining balanced and fair to all was a concern for many local ministerial associations, which tried to unite communities and bring together all Christians. The Macon, Georgia, clergy, for instance, were "unanimously of the opinion that to have [Ramsay] appear before the Ministerial Association as such would do more harm than good." This was not an outright rejection of the CIO. The vice president of the association "stated that he would not be averse to having such a meeting as a private individual, but would be entirely averse to having such a meeting in the name of the Association." In Brevard, North Carolina, the local ministerial association, as well as some individual churches, went on record in favor of unions, saying, however, "We believe that our duty as ministers of the gospel is not to jeopardize our position as counselors and guides both to labor and to management. This is particularly true so long as the present [organizing] campaign is in full swing."[48]

Some clergy were hesitant because they were ignorant about the CIO. One Methodist minister in Cleveland, Tennessee, seemed anxious to learn about the CIO because he was concerned about the large number of destitute people in his county. He asked Ramsay if the CIO organized Cleveland, would it "be able to help to raise their standards." He followed that question by asking whether "it was true that a plasterer would stop work if a nail had been left in the wall until a union carpenter could be found to remove it." Another minister was opposed to the CIO because he believed that John L. Lewis was still the CIO president.[49] Thus, there was confusion in the minds of many clergymen regarding the jurisdictional disputes of AFL unions as well as a lingering association of Lewis and the United Mine Workers' wartime strikes with the CIO.

In some cases, preachers refused to assist the CIO because of personal beliefs. Rev. John McMullen of the First Presbyterian Church in Milledgeville, Georgia, felt that he could not support the CIO until it addressed two overriding issues. First, McMullen saw too little evidence of "genuine democracy" within unions, which made him suspicious of union-shop agreements. He also agonized over the nation's economic future. He wrote, "[I do not] hold capitalism and 'free enterprise' as the sacred cows of my loyalties," unable as he was to reconcile them "with the attitudes [found] in the New Testament." However, McMullen wondered if the CIO's alternative of strikes or "some form of collective or socialistic society" was an improvement, especially since, in his mind, "the labor movement has come up without any real leaven of Christian ideals and convictions, at least in an organized way."[50] Similarly, Asheville, North Carolina, Baptist minister Rev. George Floyd Rogers believed that the CIO was a bit disingenuous in asking for help in attaining collective bargaining rights without mentioning the "question of strikes" as they affect the public. In his mind, the idea of refusing to provide vital services "in order to put pressure on others for the purpose of ameliorating a bad economic situation is unthinkable." Rogers "would rather die of poverty than live at the expense of such brutality." Lucy Mason replied to Rogers that most ministers did not have even a "rudimentary concept of why labor must organize, for its own protection . . . hence they are quickly irate with labor, but slow to see the guilt of management in labor disputes."[51]

Mason's presumptuous reply also hints at a problem that probably turned many preachers against the CIO. Emory Via, who in 1950 was teaching a class on the role of the church in small industrial communities at Emory University's School of Theology, found that the CIO was correct in thinking that many rural ministers

Lucy Randolph Mason with members of the Arkansas Industrial Union Council at Highlander Folk School, 1948. Courtesy of David M. Rubenstein Rare Book and Manuscript Library, Duke University, Durham, North Carolina.

had prejudices against organized labor. Via blamed labor for some of this. In his classes, he discovered that ministers were beginning to think more objectively about unions, but many "complained about representatives of labor that have talked with them [the ministers] in a 'you are all wrong' tone," he explained. "Most of them express no open hostilities towards unions, but most of the subtleties are there."[52] Newspapers and radio bombarded southern preachers with messages about CIO "outsiders" coming into the South to tell them what their religious beliefs should compel them to do. The fact that CIO people clearly did not comprehend the animosity many southern Protestants felt toward the Federal Council of Churches, the Catholic Church, and modernist trends in religion only exacerbated a normal defensiveness that arose against such lecturing. One minister responded to a visit from John Ramsay with the question "Since when did the C.I.O. get religion?" When Ramsay stated that the CIO had the backing of the Federal Council of Churches, the minister replied: "If he represented such things as they stand for it would be a distinct hindrance to his success in the South."[53]

Perhaps the worst offender on the CIO staff was David Burgess, who continued to write about southern ministers for a number of religious and secular publications even after joining the CIO staff in South Carolina. In the spring 1950 issue of *Prophetic Religion*, Burgess called Holiness preachers "company-paid hucksters" and lumped together the mill-town preachers, uptown-educated clergymen, and radio gospelers as "Sir Galahads, defending the innocent South against the wiles of Northern organizers." In an issue of *The Student World*, Burgess charged that "the churches of the South and their present-day teachings are becoming increasingly irrelevant to the everyday problems of the industrial workers of this region." In another manuscript, Burgess demonstrated that he had learned the value of citing Scripture to a southern audience, but did so in an almost mocking fashion that would have won few converts to the CIO cause.[54] In one case, Rev. G. H. Montgomery of the Pentecostal Holiness Church Publishing House took umbrage at a newspaper clipping "quoting [Burgess] as having allied [himself] with the C.I.O. in order to help us overcome ignorance and oppression in the South and establish true Christian churches." Montgomery then asked Burgess questions about his religious views on such issues as the authority of the Bible, the Resurrection, the Second Coming, and the existence of Heaven and Hell. Burgess ignored the request, justifying it by writing to Ramsay, saying, "When in Union Seminary I made a thorough study of the Pentecostal Holiness Church, and I found that it was viciously anti-labor in doctrine."[55] Whatever Burgess hoped to achieve with his condescending writings, he primarily succeeded in inflaming the hostility of many preachers.

For some ministers, personal experience with the results of CIO organizing and strikes made them question the value of unions. South Carolina Methodist pastor Walter Y. Cooley recounted his experiences in Ware Shoals, Lyman, and Tucapau. In Ware Shoals, newly unionized workers went on strike "under the spell of rosy promises." When the picket lines grew thinner, the union spent less on strike support, leaving supporters "to whatever shelter they could find." "Weeks later," he said, "a telegram was received telling these poor folks that the strike was over" and that "they were deserted." In Lyman, organizers arrived to find workers who "had good jobs, one of the cleanest towns in the state, and wages which never failed for a week, even during the dark days of the Depression." After convincing the workers that a union could get them better conditions, the workers walked out. Shortly thereafter, the union was gone, leaving the workers "to root hog or die." Tucapau was headed toward a similar scenario when Cooley advised his congregation not to strike. "They turned against me. I lived to see the horror of my prophecies enacted before my very eyes: People turned out of their homes, families divided and five months of agony—awful agony." Some turned to theft; others took jobs where they received only a few days' work each week. "One poor negro was murdered by two men who held CIO cards." Cooley concluded: "I will appreciate it very much if you will have your organizers skip my house when they arrive." It did not seem to matter to Cooley that the incidents he cited were AFL, not CIO, organizing drives; to him, all unions were reflections of the CIO bogeyman.[56]

The voices of ministers such as Cooley's commanded attention because employers magnified them. Rev. C. V. Martin, pastor of the Baptist church in Orrville, South Carolina, objected to a letter that the National Religion and Labor Foundation sent to employees of the Fiberglass Corporation of Anderson. The letter claimed, "Any Christian Church will teach you that you should work with your fellowman. Every Church will tell you that workers should be organized." Martin responded with a letter duplicated and distributed by the Anderson Citizen's Committee, a group funded and controlled by local employers, asserting that such claims were "misleading" and full of half-truths. "Christian churches," he wrote, "should be organized to witness for the Lord Jesus Christ and not to disturb the peace regarding labor and capitol [sic]." Martin admonished workers to "be careful lest you become part of an organization that has proven to be un-Christian many times," led by those "who have communistic tendencies."[57]

Even if many preachers tried to remain neutral concerning labor organizing, neither unions nor employers were content to let them decide for themselves. Employers, however, had far more tools at their disposal to cajole, convince, or intimidate ministers to back the companies that supplied jobs to their congregations and, in many cases, financial assistance to their churches. Very early in the Southern Organizing Campaign, Lucy Mason met a Baptist editor in Greenville, South Carolina. She found him to be "a sensible, liberal old gentleman with whom [she] had a good talk. But he can't tackle these mill village men."[58] The implication was that regardless of his inclinations about the relative benefits of union versus nonunion status for the workers of Greenville, he was unlikely to side with the CIO.

Employers could expect assistance from local law enforcement in reminding preachers who their friends were. In Cuthbert, Georgia, police told a Methodist minister to stop allowing unions to meet in his church. When he replied that people had a right to join unions, the police warned that "he was liable to wake up one morning to find everything burnt up around here." Other places were no less menacing. In Trinity, Texas, the state's CIO director and John Ramsay were scheduled to address a union meeting at the local Baptist Church. When they arrived, the church was locked because a deacon had received a "mysterious message" warning him to take the keys and not let the CIO meet in his church. In Nacogdoches, the local ministerial association invited Ramsay to address the group, but at the last minute canceled. A local black minister then invited Ramsay to address the sawmill workers at his church, but a local policeman, "who was feared by the Negroes because he had killed one recently, went to the home of a church deacon," demanding that the invitation to Ramsay be withdrawn, which it was.[59]

More typical were the financial enticements that won over preachers. In 1947, the CIO began a drive to organize the Clarke Thread Company in Clarksdale,

Georgia. Just as the CIO came to town, both the Baptists and Methodists kicked off campaigns to build new churches, and both pastors admitted receiving promises from the company to make substantial contributions to the building efforts. After the union lost its election, the congregations had two new brick buildings, although only the Baptist minister, Rev. J. A. Landers, had preached sermons against the union. Landers became a true convert to anti-unionism. In May 1949, he traveled to Marietta, Georgia, to deliver a radio address in which he quoted from Philippians 4:11 and Hebrews 13:5 about being content with what one has. He then added that "some people could not be cont[ent]ed with Jesus Christ, and the old Devil has never satisfied and never will, so leave him alone."[60]

The companies in mill towns could also play on the ethnic and religious prejudices of Protestant ministers. In Lyman, South Carolina, the Pacific Mills Company distributed a leaflet attacking the Textile Workers Union of America. The leaflet read in part: "Who are the men who are running this union, anyway? I will name some of its main leaders to you: Baldanzi, Rieve, Chukka, Genis, Jabor, Knapik, Rosenberg. Where do you think these men come from? Are their background, their upbringing, their beliefs, their faiths and their principles anything like yours and mine?" Days later, a local Baptist minister challenged his congregation: "It's either Christ or the CIO," he shouted. "You can either be a Christian or a CIO man, but you can't be both!" Complementing such leaflets were the religious hate sheets: *Gospel Trumpet*, *Militant Truth*, *The Shuttle* of Spartanburg, and *The Observer* of Greenville, South Carolina.[61]

Some companies were very systematic in approaching preachers. In March 1950, the CIO initiated an organizing drive in Great Falls, South Carolina, following earlier work with ministers by Ramsay. Franz Daniel learned to his dismay that the J. P. Stevens Company called all the ministers in town to the company office for a meeting and that a Rev. Sargent of the Nazarene church "stayed an hour after the others left and the report is that he made a special recording." Daniel noted that Sargent was a second hand in the mill but was rumored to be in line for an overseer's job. Meanwhile, Rev. A. C. Madden of the Church of God told his congregation that his denomination's General Assembly prohibited membership in unions.[62] Ruth Gettinger arrived in April to try and counteract these ministers but discovered that some of those who had met Ramsay had changed their minds. J. P. Stevens had reproduced the letter from Rev. Cooley, mentioned above, and distributed it to clergy. Presbyterian minister John S. Steele, who Ramsay had believed would be most friendly, told Ruth Gettinger that he wanted "no further visits from representatives" of the CIO. "I am not going to be put in the position of being used as an informer, telling what has transpired at ministers' meetings, etc." He objected, "The union comes to me to find what the company is doing . . . then the company wants me to tell them what the union is doing." His wife was more emphatic, saying, "The mill is our bread and butter . . . we want nothing to do with the union!" Gettinger found other ministers no more welcoming. Madden stood by his opinion that the Church of God opposed unions despite Gettinger's evidence to the contrary. Baptist ministers Luther T. Knight and J. M. Pickler refused to answer their doorbells, although their cars were in their driveways. Phone calls and visits were fruitless; Gettinger believed that the company had locked up access to Great Falls's clergy.[63]

Probably no campaign better captures the tools that companies were prepared to use to keep ministers on their side than the CIO drive in Hazelhurst, Georgia. The organizing drive began when voters ousted the town's political dynasty, directed by Colonel John Rogers at the behest of the Cook Lumber Company, Hazelhurst's largest employer. For years the machine had "held undisputed sway in matters of politics and religion." In retaliation, the Cook Company fired employees who supported the anti-Cook forces. Cook's workers then decided to organize and contacted John Scott of the CIO. Scott called on John Ramsay to visit local merchants, professionals, ministers, and town officials to explain the purposes of the CIO. The Baptist minister was "most friendly"; the Methodist minister "listened attentively"; a minister in nearby Lumber City was a member of the AFL Boilermakers Union and wished Ramsay success; and Rev. Harold G. Johnson, pastor of the Gospel Tabernacle, had once been a CIO member. When the company became aware of the CIO union, it began by demoting one of its leaders, Marcus Trowell, to the "back-breaking rock-pile." Trowell then filed a complaint with the National Labor Relations Board. To fend off an investigation, the company found a job for Trowell as a clerk and put pressure on his family and his pastor to convince Trowell to take the job, thus robbing the union of "its most able Christian leader." Meanwhile, the company called a meeting of local ministers, pointing out that the CIO pretended to be Christian, but plied the "rougher element" with liquor. Company officials also reminded the preachers that they had "given generously to the Lord's houses." Colonel Rogers turned his attention to the local merchants and businessmen, publishing the names of CIO supporters in the *Jeff Davis County Ledger* and organizing a citizen's committee to fight the CIO in Hazelhurst.[64]

The Cook Lumber Company and the citizen's committee were not finished. On July 31 organizer Scott arrived at the company to distribute CIO literature as workers came through the gate. As he finished, a man attacked Scott from behind, striking him on the head and neck and biting the bridge of his nose. Scott staggered away, received medical treatment, and headed to the train station. Local citizens believed he had understood the message. Instead, Scott met two other CIO representatives, John Ramsay and Bill Strength, who arrived to address a union meeting the next day. The three went back to the plant gate to distribute flyers. Seven men, led by a local attorney, then assaulted the three CIO men, who did not resist, "other than to protect their faces with their arms." The men shouted as Scott, Ramsay, and Strength drove away: "If you come back, bring your caskets with you." Although the CIO men could identify their attackers, none of the town officials were in their office or available to talk by phone. A physician bandaged the bloodied CIO representatives, who then retired to their hotel. The local union decided to postpone its meeting until Saturday, but when the day arrived, a mob of fifty men, armed and led by the burly Philip Truitt, gathered across the street from the hotel. Ramsay phoned the local sheriff, who made it clear that he would help only if the CIO men left town, which they did under the sheriff's escort. Rev. Johnson—the Gospel Tabernacle pastor and former CIO member—delivered a coda to the episode. He preached a sermon on "Unionism under the Searchlight of God's Word," in which he relied on Daniel 11 and Revelation 13 to imply that the CIO "was paving the way for the Antichrist."[65]

Yea, Though I Walk . . .

Confronted with such examples as Great Falls and Hazelhurst, it is tempting to dismiss any hope that preachers might side with the CIO against daunting odds. In so many towns, once the stakes rose, Community Relations Department staff members were stunned at how decisively clergy opinion turned against them. Given the messages ministers heard from denominational sources and local newspapers, their own desires for community harmony, their sense of duty to win people to Christ, and their disappointments with labor's inability to deliver what it promised or to stand by defeated workers, the CIO faced a demoralizing task, made even harder by racism and anticommunism. Still, we should not be too quick to write off preachers as timid or unsympathetic or too wrapped up in their own aspirations to lend support to the Southern Organizing Campaign. It is necessary to examine some of the ministers who defied their denominations, the businessmen who contributed to their churches, and, at times, even their own congregations because they believed that the message of social and economic justice preached by the CIO was more in keeping with their notions of Christianity.

What characterized southern ministers who supported organized labor? Denominational affiliations might offer some clues. When the CIO drive began in South Carolina, Ruth Gettinger asked Nelle Morton of the Fellowship of Southern Churchmen for a list of clergy favorable to labor. Morton supplied twenty-six names of fellowship members in South Carolina who she believed might be willing to help the CIO. Two were black (one Methodist and one Baptist). Of the twenty-four white ministers, there were twelve Methodists, six Baptists, three Presbyterians, two Episcopalians, and one Unitarian.[66] Although Baptists accounted for more than half of the Protestant population in the state, they produced only a quarter of the prolabor clergymen. Methodists were just the opposite. While hardly scientific, the list is suggestive and appears to confirm the predilections expressed in denominational publications. Certainly Methodist and Episcopalian ministers represented denominations that were more hierarchical and provided more support for clergy against local forces. Baptist ministers were much more vulnerable to pressure from their congregations and thus less likely to be able to follow their own consciences in defiance of the local culture. It is telling that of the ministers who founded the liberal, pro-union, Baptist magazine, *Christian Frontiers*, in 1946, three left the Southern Baptists for the Episcopal Church, complaining that the lack of centralized authority in Baptist ecclesiology inhibited an effective Baptist voice for social action.[67]

Holiness and Pentecostal preachers represented a special case for the CIO. David Burgess expected little from them. He harbored prejudices against them from his time in migrant labor camps. His published writings during his years in the CIO vilified Holiness preachers.[68] But Lucy Mason had a different opinion. In 1947 she visited several industrial cities in eastern Tennessee and was favorably impressed with the Church of God minister in Johnson City. In Elizabethton, the Church of God minister was secretary of the Ministers' Association and "really the best informed man on unions in general and why they are necessary for the people in Elizabethton." At one time the Church of God had banned membership in labor unions, but the ban was lifted in the 1930s, even if some Pentecostal preachers continued to cite it (as was the case in Great Falls). Even when it was in effect, Pentecostal churches in the coalfields often incorporated union membership into their theology. Moreover, Holiness and Pentecostal preachers were more likely to be part time and to earn most of their livelihoods through another occupation. This gave them greater independence and might also have given them more empathy for members who responded to tough employers or harsh conditions at work by forming a union.[69]

The working-class composition of congregations often was a factor influencing pro-union sympathies, and not just for Holiness and Pentecostal ministers. A Baptist minister in Concord, North Carolina, preached to "an entire congregation" of millworkers. As a result, the CIO found that "he preaches a good sermon and is a very likable, human person" who was "greatly in favor of our organization." In Macon, Georgia, a Disciples of Christ minister testified to a local Religion-Labor Fellowship dinner that it takes "more intestinal fortitude to go on a picket line than many people realize." His working-class congregation appreciated that he would go to them on a picket line and say: "As a disciple of Jesus Christ, I am concerned about you as a brother—I am concerned about your family and hunger and shelter" for them.[70] But Episcopal ministers in the South developed a good reputation for supporting labor even though their congregations tended to be the most affluent. Baptist minister Charles R. Bell of Anniston, Alabama, recalled that the minister most "sympathetic to all liberal causes" in the area was Charles Hamilton, an Episcopal pastor. Lucy Mason, an Episcopalian, found the "real progressive fighting spirit" of the church exemplified in Rev. Robert Cook in Tennessee, Rev. William H. Marmion in Birmingham, and the church's Missouri Bishop, William Scarlett. Marmion, in particular, worked closely with the labor members of the Committee for Alabama (the state branch of the Southern

Conference on Human Welfare) on issues of interest to both the AFL and the CIO. His church in Birmingham was also the only place in the city that would host interracial meetings of Ramsay's Religion and Labor Fellowships.[71]

CIO staff also discovered many labor-friendly clergy among those who were part-time ministers or who came from working-class families. Rev. Larry Rankin of Dallas, Texas, had formerly worked at a power plant in Radford, Virginia; he volunteered to help the CIO in his new home. In Elizabethton, Tennessee, state CIO director Paul Christopher relied on a "Missionary Baptist preacher" who had a little church there. The preacher was also "a good union member" at North American Rayon. In Ruston, Louisiana, Rev. G. Avery Lee arranged a luncheon meeting for Ramsay because he had worked with CIO unions in Baton Rouge.[72] But a labor or working-class background did not guarantee that a preacher would support the CIO, as Lucy Mason discovered in Anniston, Alabama. There she met three ministers who had some union experience in their past; not one of them believed that the CIO would be successful in organizing Avondale Mills, nor did any of them offer to help.[73]

Clergy who supported the CIO at times did so despite risk to their careers. CIO organizer Don McKee had a great deal of admiration for Kenneth Phifer, a young Presbyterian minister in Rock Hill, South Carolina, whose congregation included many textile company executives. McKee and David Burgess, who visited the church, found themselves "shaking hands between the pews with the 'Bosses' who greeted us warmly on a Sunday—but argued with us Monday through Saturday!" Nevertheless, Phifer "had a way of saying what he believed, regardless of the opposite opinions that he knew prevailed in the congregation." On one occasion, after McKee had lunch with Phifer at a local hotel, the "leading church officials" told him, "We think you're seeing too much of that CIO union organizer, McKee." Phifer did not shrink from the accusation. "Well, if you think McKee is as evil as you say, that's where I should be spending my time. Our task is to save the sinners, not the righteous," he replied. When Burgess applied for membership in Phifer's church, the governing body rejected his application. Again, Phifer defied his flock. He gathered the church leaders and gave them an ultimatum: "Either you admit the Rev. Burgess to membership—or you start looking for another minister." A few days later, Burgess and his family became members.[74]

Others suffered when they lacked the backing of their congregations. Rev. Joseph A. Rabun, an ex-Marine chaplain who had experienced some of the fiercest fighting in the Pacific theater during World War II, grew increasingly disturbed by the anti-union and racial violence in postwar Georgia, much of which appeared to flourish in the undemocratic political structure of the state. Efforts to change the system endorsed by the CIO and other liberal organizations had elicited a backlash of Ku Klux Klan activity and a proposal in the state legislature to reinstate the whites-only Democratic primary. Rabun, who was pastor of the Baptist church in McRae, which was the home church of Governor Eugene Talmadge, decided to act. He testified against the white-primary bill at a public hearing at the Georgia state capitol. He defended his testimony to a reporter, declaring that if he stood by as his black neighbors were victims of violence and intimidation, "I would immediately forfeit all I have of virtue." He was under no illusions about what his testimony might mean: "My stand might place my position in the community where I live in jeopardy," but for him there was a sacred commitment to democracy that he first felt at the time of his religious conversion. Cost him it did. His congregation asked for and received his resignation, but Georgians had not defeated Rabun's spirit. With the backing of many CIO rank-and-file activists, Rabun ran for governor in the Georgia Democratic Party primary in 1948 on a program that denounced racial hatred and sought to protect labor's rights to organize and bargain collectively. Unfortunately for the courageous Rabun, CIO political forces in the state could not unite over whether to support the insurgent Rabun or the moderate Melvin Thompson, who many felt had the best chance of defeating the reactionary Herman Talmadge. In the end, the CIO not only lost the election, the organization also lost the voice of a man that the liberal magazine *The Nation* believed was "one of the South's new leaders" in a moral crusade for social justice.[75]

Even where unions had made headway in northern Georgia, pro-CIO clergy were not safe. In May 1950 John Ramsay advised Textile Workers Union representative Joe Pedigo to look for help in Rome, Georgia, from an "outstanding local minister who has a sincere interest in labor," Rev. Arthur A. Hyde. The minister had recently moved to the First Christian Church in Rome, and Ramsay and Pedigo needed help to set up a Religion and Labor Fellowship there. In April 1951 Ramsay visited Rome and met with Hyde and Rev. Delmar Hagood about meeting with the local Ministerial Alliance. Then in May, the Alliance extended an invitation to Ramsay to speak. But the climate that led Hyde to feel he had support for cooperation with the CIO had begun to change. A long and unsuccessful strike by the Textile Workers local union and a CIO-inspired congressional investigation of labor-management relations in the southern textile industry invigorated anti-union forces around Rome. Ramsay's scheduled meeting with the Ministerial Association failed to materialize because the owner of the restaurant where the meeting was slated to take place refused to allow black ministers to attend. Meanwhile, Hyde lost favor with his congregation. On October 2 he wrote to Ramsay: "[Interest in the CIO] proved my undoing in Rome. We will not be here much longer it seems." Although Hyde did not reveal who was behind the First Christian Church's decision to relieve him of his position, or whether the decision resulted from his transgressions of the racial or class norms of the local community, he was looking for a new job.[76]

Another minister whose support for both the CIO and black civil rights endangered his career was Sam Howie of Memphis. Howie, born in Mecklenburg

County, North Carolina, in 1901 spent most of his youth in an orphanage. Never-theless, he managed to work his way through college and graduated from Union Theological Seminary in Richmond in 1928. After stops in several small Presby-terian churches in Mississippi, Howie was pastor of the Westminster Presbyterian Church in Memphis when the CIO became active in the city. During World War II, Lucy Mason praised Howie—"Glory be for a Christian like Dr. Sam Howie"—for his willingness to open his church to unions and his work in starting the Memphis Interracial Commission, which united segments of the black and white ministerial associations. Howie worked closely with Mason, believing "that the place to begin to change adverse public opinion about labor unions is through the churches." Mason knew there would be costs. She wrote to CIO leaders in Memphis: "If Dr. Howie opens his church to unions, as he wishes to do, organized labor should surely support him. He will have attacks from industrialists and business men and will find it hard to keep his church going unless unions stand solidly with him." Another labor activist praised Howie for standing "up to the big-wigs of the community" and "showing the spirit of the Southern clergyman as that of fighters for their right to advise and bring the benefits of religion to their parishioners, whether they clip coupons or belong to the Tenant Farmers Union."[77]

The unions in Memphis either could not or did not provide enough support to protect Howie; by 1945, his congregation in Memphis had forced him to leave. Intimidation did not weaken Howie's commitment to social and economic jus-tice. At his next church in Fayetteville, North Carolina, Howie continued to be a progressive voice on race and class issues. For the graduation ceremonies at the all-black Fayetteville State University, he provided a baccalaureate sermon that honored Dr. Benjamin Mays, and he worked with David Burgess and the CIO's Political Action Committee on the liberal Frank Porter Graham's senato-rial campaign in 1950. After spending twelve years in Fayetteville, Howie was called in 1957 to be pastor of the one-thousand-member Presbyterian church in Oak Ridge, Tennessee, a community with a strong union presence due to the successful organizing of the nuclear facility workers. Although a more conducive atmosphere for Howie, he continued to be a controversial figure who refused to compromise his principles. He led his congregation in the area of social concerns and civil rights. The Oak Ridge Church history recalled his nine years there as "an activist ministry."[78]

Pastoring in an active union community did not always shield ministers from reprisals. In Danville, Virginia, the CIO made a breakthrough at the huge Dan River Mills during World War II. The city's clothing workers, letter carriers, print-ers, and construction workers also were organized, making it one of the most unionized locales in the state. In the summer of 1946 the Textile Workers Union organized a broad-based community effort to help working people deal with skyrocketing rents and prices resulting from the breakdown of the wartime price controls, which had curbed inflation. Director of the Southern School for Workers, Brownie Lee Jones, went to Danville to head up a campaign "involving the whole community." One of her first contacts was "a liberal minister who offered to call a group of representative citizens together for an exploratory meeting." The minister, Cleveland J. Bradner of the West End Christian Church, was a twenty-nine-year old native South Carolinian who had been in Danville only a short time. Nevertheless, forty people from seventeen organizations, including unions, the Junior Chamber of Commerce, the Business and Professional Women's Club, the Ministerial Association, and the Veterans of Foreign Wars, attended. The meeting organized a Citizens' Committee to gather information, organize mass meetings, and boycott merchants who charged unreasonable prices. The committee set up booths around the city and distributed cards with the pledge "I will buy only what I need—I will buy wisely and cooperate with the Citizens' Committee." The first mass meeting, held in Bradner's church, attracted three hundred people "in spite of rain and a local bus strike." Attendees were black and white, representing churches, clubs, schools, veterans, and unions. The gathering appointed Bradner as temporary chairman of the Citizens' Committee.[79]

Bradner's church, as well as the YWCA, became a center of activity for the Committee. The group collected facts, helped people register complaints against merchants and landlords, and sent volunteer workers into the various communities to solicit cooperation from business people. Although the committee sought to "be entirely representative of all interests," CIO unions provided a good deal of the energy. Before July was over, opponents began voicing charges that the committee "had been started by labor unions with 'Communistic leanings.'" Bradner denied the charges, pointing to the diverse "community-wide cooperation" that characterized the "protest campaign." Brownie Lee Jones even used her work in Danville as a model for other communities to follow when she testified at hearings of the Decontrol Board of the Office of Price Administration.[80] When Lucy Mason visited Danville in March 1947, she was astounded at the transformation of Danville brought on by union growth and stability, which had stimulated community campaigns for social services and a new interest in politics. Textile workers, she reported, had not only made gains in wages and working conditions, but also had "become active and informed citizens, taking part in political elections, civic enterprises and social welfare programs." Textile Workers Union local director Lewis Conn had even convinced local ministers to make a statement for use by the CIO Organizing Committee.[81]

Bradner's story was less uplifting. He quickly rose to prominence in Danville and in CIO circles generally. In January 1947, Bradner was one of the featured religious leaders who called on ministers to attend a Religion and Labor Conference in Atlanta and take advantage of the "unprecedented opportunity to put into practice their respective faiths, by interpreting labor's struggle in accord with the will of God for a social order of divine justice and an abundant life for all."

In his church, however, things did not go so well. In July Bradner resigned from his church because a "conservative element" was "exerting all sorts of pressure, particularly economic pressure. He finally came to a conviction that the pattern of things would not change sufficiently." CIO people tried to come to the rescue, suggesting that they build a new "people's" church "which could really respond to Bradner's type of ministry." Lewis Conn was "desperately anxious not to lose Bradner," he said, adding, "but as you know, even ministers have to eat." Lucy Mason, John Ramsay, and even Van Bittner all became involved in the effort to help establish a community church for Bradner in Danville, but in the end Bradner decided to return for additional education at Columbia and the University of Chicago. In 1952 Bradner joined the faculty of Denison University in Ohio and directed its Christian Emphasis Program.[82]

Ultimately, Bradner's story may have had a chilling effect in Danville. In 1951 the Textile Workers Union was deeply divided and pushed into a strike against an intransigent new regime at Dan River Mills. Lucy Mason's visit in 1951 was far less upbeat. She found a "citizens committee set up to fight the union," led by the president of the bank. She also found that most ministers were either neutral or "against the union." She did find one young promising Baptist pastor, Raymond Bryan Brown, who had studied at Yale under Liston Pope and graduated from the Baptist seminary in Louisville. Brown, Mason learned, "intends to preach a prophetic religion when he is firmly established." However, the banker who led the citizens committee was a member of Brown's congregation, which was "the largest, wealthiest and most conservative in town." Mason admitted that she could expect little during the current crisis: "He has to be careful for the present." Unfortunately, the strike at Dan River Mills was a disaster, perhaps preventing Brown from ever having an opportunity to revive the broad alliance presided over by Bradner.[83]

Through these vignettes of Phifer, Rabun, Howie, Hyde, and Bradner, it is possible to see the strength of commitment that some ministers gave to labor and social justice. They defied the pressures that led many less courageous preachers to capitulate or attempt to remain neutral even as class conflict threatened the harmony of their congregations and communities. But it is difficult to pinpoint exactly what separated a Howie or a Phifer from someone like J. A. Landers, the Clarksdale, Georgia, Baptist preacher who gave radio sermons against the CIO, or Harold Johnson, the former union member who became Hazelhurst Gospel Tabernacle pastor and later warned that the CIO was helping lay the groundwork for the Antichrist.

One minister whose path to a prophetic prolabor ministry might be broadly suggestive is Rev. John B. Isom. Born in 1909 in rural Cullman County in north-central Alabama, Isom was the son of a farmer who purchased sixty acres from his father-in-law. Isom's mother died when he was eight, and when his father married for the third time, the family moved to New Hope. Isom had fond memories of his mother and a great deal of respect for his father, who modeled a "life of simple honesty and fairness, by which he judged himself, others and human institutions" and set "an example of human decency." Neither his parents nor grandparents were overly religious, but when the family moved to New Hope, he began attending the Baptist Church, which was one of the hubs of social life in the small community. Little of the ideas and beliefs which young Isom encountered in church had much effect on him until he was in high school, but he recalled a local Sunday school teacher and two sayings from the Bible: "Love your neighbor as you do yourself" and "Do unto others as you would have others do unto you."[84]

At age seventeen, Isom's road turned decisively. He became involved in the Baptist Young People's Union, which had recently organized at New Hope Baptist Church. He learned the things that Baptists believed and studied materials compiled by the Sunday School Board of the Southern Baptist Convention. The Bible verses that had guided his early instincts he now recognized "as being what The Triune God expected of me." Even more important, he began believing "that God would never expect better of me than what the ethics of love and equality expected of me, as those ethics are defined by those two verses of scripture." Later, Isom began teaching Sunday School and was eventually recruited as an "expert" to work with the Sunday School Enlargement Campaign in rural northern Alabama. Also during those years, Isom had his first encounter with racism. In the rural Alabama where he grew up, there were no blacks: "The people there, from the beginning, had only equals by whom to measure themselves," he wrote. "All had been poor whites and their descendants." On a visit to Prattville he was introduced to "Uncle Bill," an elderly black man, with whom he entered into a conversation. Out of respect to Uncle Bill's age, Isom fell into the habit of saying "yes sir" and "no sir" in response to questions. Eventually, one of the white adults pulled Isom aside and chastised the teenager, "You don't say 'yes sir,' 'no sir' to a nigger." Although Isom did not protest, he felt "no guilt or shame for having spoken to Uncle Bill in a manner consistent with the love and equality principles as taught in the Bible."[85]

At age twenty-three Isom enrolled at Howard College (later Samford University) and graduated in 1936. He then attended the Southern Baptist Theological Seminary in Louisville, from which he received a Master of Divinity degree in 1939. His first position was with a small church in Courtland, Virginia, where he gradually stirred up controversy. In February 1942, Isom preached a sermon he titled "A Religion of Loyalty." In it, he recounted the glaring poverty of Southampton County's black population and suggested that it was a result of exploitation at the hands of the white farm owners. Isom was trying "to plant in their minds the suggestion that loyalty to Jesus should be expressed by helping to do what Jesus said he came to do." He reminded his congregation that Jesus came to preach "the Good News" to the poor, and then he asked the question, "What would be good news to poor families with incomes less than six hundred dollars a year?"

"Good news," he continued, "would be a solution to their problem of poverty; a way of life, a social order, an economic system that would make it possible for them to earn a decent living by the work of their hands and minds." Later, one of his church members pulled Isom aside and said, "Some of 'the boys' were in my store last night. They were upset by your sermon last Sunday." Nevertheless, the congregation continued to treat Isom with respect, in part because the minister had done so much in the community, such as organize a Boy Scout troop. Still, the "horrors of race prejudice" were etched into Isom's consciousness.[86]

From 1942 to 1945 Isom served as a chaplain in the U.S. Army, stationed at Camp Sibert near Gadsden, Alabama, and then at Camp Croft near Spartanburg, South Carolina. As his time was coming to a close, the Saxon Baptist Church minister invited Isom to preach a sermon. When the congregation liked him, the minister, who was ready for retirement, asked Isom if he would be interested in replacing him. Isom hesitated and honestly shared some of his "non-Baptist notions." The minister not only had no problem with Isom's theology, he replied that he had "been working thirteen years here just to lay a foundation for a guy like you." When the Army discharged Isom, he took over at Saxon, a very atypical mill-village church. Although the mill owner, John A. Law, had donated the land for the church and provided it with gas, electricity, and insurance, Saxon Baptist Church had a contentious relationship with the dictatorial attitude of "Old Man Law." Saxon was one of the few churches in the area where the preacher could not be fired as easily as a millhand. The vast majority of those in the congregation were former millworkers who "had been fired, laid off or quit." They gained employment at one of the other local mills so that they could remain at Saxon.

Isom recalled that he knew little about unions when he took over at Saxon, but he quickly learned that "organized labor was the greatest fear of owners and managers." The relationship between John Law and Saxon had its origins in the 1920s, when Spartanburg millworkers protested the "stretch out" and Saxon Baptist Church had supported them. One of Saxon's congregation was Jud Brooks, a World War I veteran fired by Law in the 1920s. When Isom arrived in 1946, Brooks had moved to the neighboring community of Una and published a little six-to-eight-page newspaper that carried stories about labor in Spartanburg. Another member was Clarence Guthrie, who worked for the post office and helped Jud Brooks. As a result of such a congregation, Isom had a level of support shared by few ministers in southern mill towns. He felt emboldened to speak out, "ever so softly" as he recalled, about three issues that were dear to him—the plights of poor workers, the sin of race prejudice, and the nuclear arms race. In his first years in Spartanburg, he wrote a letter to the left-leaning newspaper, *PM*, advocating a picket line around Congress until they agreed to stop filibustering and pass the legislation desired by President Truman. As well, he gave a speech at the state Baptist Convention denouncing segregation, and he published a letter in the *Spartanburg Herald* condemning the lynching of Willie Earl near Pickens, South Carolina.[87]

Isom also began working with unions. At a meeting in 1946 he was happy to speak because he felt that "the attitude of the church toward organized labor has been wrongly represented by a few people who call themselves preachers of the gospel." He singled out Sherman Patterson, who published *Militant Truth*, and Parson Jack Johnston, who published *The Trumpet*. Isom rejected the ideas expressed in these papers—"that organized labor is atheistic and Communistic, and that organized labor's attitude towards Negroes is unchristian." He pointed to the Southern Baptist Convention's adoption of a resolution approving of collective bargaining and the Methodist Church's appointment of a minister to labor, noting that like the churches, organized labor was "dedicated to the task of raising the spiritual and physical well being of all people." Isom charged his audience, "When you hear of someone being called a communist, look him up. Ninety-nine times out of every one hundred you will find him to be a real American who believes in real Democracy for everyone, including workers." Similarly, those who try to turn you against the CIO because it stands "for democracy for the Negro citizens of the country" were the "old exploiters" who "know that as long as the enemies of labor can appeal to the race prejudice of [the] white worker and get his vote for their political and religious stooges," there was no chance that the CIO could "really help the workers."[88]

As he worked in Spartanburg, Isom became ever more hopeful for organized labor. In 1947 he wrote to J. B. Weatherspoon of the Southern Baptist Theological Seminary, who was collecting information for his report to the Southern Baptist Convention on race relations, "that the position taken by the C.I.O. and the A.F.L. is one of the greatest forces in the South for better race relations." He believed that unions could have taken advantage of traditional race prejudice and "been more successful in organizing the white workers than they have," but chose not to. Meanwhile, the mill owners, many of them northerners, "have not hesitated to take advantage of race prejudice to fight the drive to organize the southern workers." Isom invited John Ramsay to speak at Saxon Baptist Church, even though the local ministerial association had refused Ramsay a meeting. They even exchanged lists of preferred readings. On behalf of the CIO, Isom also visited other ministers, such as "young minister Shands" of the Spartanburg First Baptist Church. He found Shands "to be a fair prospect for what Clarence Darrow called the 'Fools Club'—made up of those who had little enough sense to agitate for justice for the poor. If the church will let him," Isom believed, "there is hope" for Shands.[89]

Hope was diminishing for Isom, however. Although he was safe in his church, he began to feel a crisis of conscience about continuing as a Baptist minister. His own theology was changing drastically from what most Baptists believed, and although the Baptists allowed for a great deal of leeway, Isom's 1950 Easter Sunday sermon, taken from the writings of George Bernard Shaw's play "Back to Methuselah," challenged even his most diehard supporters. Just the week before, newspapers carried stories of Shaw's recent death, equating his views with "communism and atheism." Equally vexing to Isom were the visits from members of his congregation. One came asking for the church letters of his wife and mother to take to another church because Isom was not preaching "the red hot gospel" but rather Communism and racial equality. Others "seemed to be enslaved" by their fears of Russia or empowered by their support of the Dixiecrats. One even informed Isom that the minister was a target of FBI investigators. In July 1951 Isom wrote to Ramsay informing him of his resignation from Saxon Baptist Church. He was not only leaving for Louisville, he was also leaving the Baptists for a Unitarian Church. Isom wanted to do more for workers, but he felt that he could not do that in a church. To him, "one of the great problems in the South is the quality of religion that is being fostered and fed to the working people. They would be better off without any religion at all."[90] And yet Isom's life story was a testament to the ways that even an uninspiring religious upbringing might etch certain principles of Christian morality into a person's outlook. He lived his life guided by two biblical sayings that placed him outside the cultural norms of southern society and involved him in the struggle for social justice.

It is tempting to dismiss Isom as an aberration. He adopted unconventional views even as he tried to square them with traditional Baptist theology. He admired mostly mavericks in his youth and during his career as a Baptist minister, and he found his greatest opportunity pastoring one of the most unorthodox mill-village churches in the South. But perhaps Isom represents a type of southern Protestant minister who, given the right opportunities, could have developed into a robust advocate for social and economic justice. What if many of those attentive or kind ministers whom Lucy Mason and Ruth Gettinger met at the outset of CIO campaigns truly were concerned about the wages and conditions of the working class but refused to act because they had to worry about their own families? Would there have been enough of them to offset those opposed to unions for personal or theological reasons? What would that say about southern Protestantism? While it is impossible to answer these questions, we can see that more ministers stood with the companies than with the unions during the Southern Organizing Campaign. Nevertheless, John Isom, Cleveland Bradner, Sam Howie, and others remind us how complicated and contingent are the interactions between religious beliefs and actions on behalf of social movements.

CHAPTER 7

Red Scares and Black Scares

On the evening of May 18, 1946, a crowd of more than 250 people gathered at the Bible Baptist Tabernacle in Knoxville, Tennessee. Most were past middle age, "bald and grey," and, to one observer, distinctly rural in origin. At 8:15, the Fundamentalist minister Rev. A. A. Haggard of nearby Maryville opened the meeting by thanking his host, Rev. T. Wesley Hill, a man always willing to "help a worthy cause." After singing evangelical hymns and saluting the "Christian Flag," Haggard launched into a tirade against Communism, which he said had made "definite plans to take over America this year, using 'organized labor and the Negroes.'" Haggard claimed that "God had called the meeting together," concerned that the Southern Baptist Convention had recently passed a resolution denouncing the Ku Klux Klan. He told the audience that he and "all fundamentalist preachers are first on the communist death list." Haggard spoke for an hour, although his main responsibility was to introduce the main speaker, Rev. Clarence E. Garrett of Harding, Kentucky. Garrett also spoke about fighting Communism and defending white supremacy. The Klan, he explained, "far from provoking race riots, is instrumental in warding them off and putting them down after they are 'stirred up by communists preaching social equality.'" Garrett claimed that there were one thousand Communists in Knoxville, and they had been responsible for forcing WNOX to cancel the radio preaching of conservative evangelist J. Harold Smith. Like Smith, Garrett asserted that religious freedom was at risk, and that the Klan was one group that could withstand Communism, racial equality, the CIO, and the Federal Council of Churches.[1]

That Communism, racial advancement, the CIO, and modernist religion could be so easily linked in the minds of many evangelicals was a problem that the Southern Organizing Campaign had to confront. Knoxville rallies could attract ten thousand people and convince hundreds of them to write to the Federal Communications Commission on behalf of the radio evangelism of J. Harold Smith.[2] The mix of racism, anticommunism, and evangelicalism offers an easy explanation for the failure of the CIO's Operation Dixie. Historians exploring some of the campaign's most promising moments have attributed its failures to the CIO's unwillingness to tackle head on the racism that divided the region's working class, in large part because of its own internalized anti-Communism. Starting with the brash statement of Van Bittner that the CIO had no desire for help from radicals (arguably some of the best and most successful organizers of black workers) combined with a decision to focus on the predominately white textile industry, through the aversion to Henry Wallace's Progressive Party campaign in 1948, the CIO's actions have seemed to historians as anti-red, anti-black, and anti-success. The expulsion of the left-led unions from the house of labor beginning in 1949 only cemented the fate of a deeply flawed CIO strategy that sought to present the southern drive as a respectable, moderate crusade, shorn of its most progressive elements.[3]

What difference did it make that the CIO launched Operation Dixie in a region so overwhelmingly populated by evangelical Protestants? As the example of the Knoxville meeting shows, there were resonating chords of anticommunism sung by southern evangelicals. In addition, many southern Protestants were reading their Bibles for evidence in support of racial segregation. However, as the biographies of John Isom, Sam Howie, and Cleveland Bradner from the previous chapter make clear, the ministers most likely to risk everything for the CIO were also among the boldest opponents of racial injustice. Would they also have supported the CIO if the Southern Organizing Campaign had cooperated with Communists? That is a more difficult proposition to defend. Even a minister as unconventional as the Chapel Hill, North Carolina, Presbyterian Charles M. Jones, president of the Fellowship of Southern Churchmen and a man who protected early freedom riders in 1947 from a mob, felt that friends who supported Communism had gone down "the wrong road." Pentecostal miners in Kentucky and Baptist textile workers in north Georgia similarly abandoned established unions once they discovered the organizations were led by Communists.[4]

The religious people whom the CIO put in charge of building relationships with southern preachers were even less sympathetic to Communism. Not only had many of them fought against Communists earlier in their career, but also their personal faiths spurned Communist ideology. That does not mean that the CIO's religious activists played it safe. On numerous occasions, anti-union organizations and even congressmen targeted them for investigations of their political beliefs. They went into some of the most dangerous situations: several of them suffered beatings and even a shooting that came perilously close to ending the life of Franz Daniel.[5] With respect to a commitment to an interracial labor movement, the CIO's religious liaisons had strong, but not unblemished, records of standing on principle against Jim Crow, even when it meant harming an organizing drive. Moreover, they took this principled position at a time when many southerners labeled anyone who stood for desegregation as a Communist, and Communist was a dirty word in the era of McCarthyism.

This chapter explores the intertwined story of racism and anticommunism that hampered the CIO's Southern Organizing Campaign and the part that religion played in the expectations and disappointments the CIO experienced. While religious beliefs made it more difficult for some in the campaign to work with Communists, it provided a righteous idealism that sought to make the organizing drive live up to its pronouncements on interracialism.

Days of Hope?

African Americans viewed the CIO's southern drive with a mix of hope and trepidation. Many recognized that the elements of southern society that most persistently fought unions were often the same people who viciously attacked blacks. The tense wartime and postwar race relations that gripped the South had given organized labor opportunities to demonstrate its commitment to defending black civil rights and helping blacks advance economically. There were significant gains. By the end of World War II, 1.25 million blacks had industrial jobs, an increase of 150 percent over 1940. AFL and CIO unions had 750,000 African American members, triple the number of black union members at the start of the war. Blacks made up roughly 7 percent of all union members in 1945, up from under 4 percent five years earlier. The CIO took particular pride in these changes. Lucy Mason, who certainly had more reason to boast about civil rights activities than most, made a case for the CIO's efforts. In the *Journal of Negro Education* in 1945 she pointed to the CIO's Committee to Abolish Discrimination and member unions' efforts "to promote full employment opportunities for Negroes." She also noted the large black membership of several CIO unions in the South, despite the loss of the United Mine Workers. Looking to the future, Mason claimed that CIO unions were helping blacks "obtain full suffrage" and claim their civil liberties. Moral concerns, she added, were key to the CIO outlook on race: CIO members were also church members. By bringing their Christianity into the union hall, the CIO enabled blacks and whites to share a "natural expression of religion [which was] another means by which prejudice and misunderstanding are replaced by appreciation and good-will."[6]

There was a good deal of truth in Mason's article. The CIO had made breakthroughs in several key southern industries such as iron and steel, tobacco, woodworking, and maritime trades that employed large numbers of black workers. Where successful, the new black union members frequently turned to politics. For instance, when the International Woodworkers of America won collective bargaining agreements in the Mississippi Valley or in eastern North Carolina, organizers found that new black union members often wanted to register to vote. Court decisions undermining the all-white primary and continued efforts to abolish the poll tax—two strategies that whites had used to deny blacks political voice—only increased that urge. Meanwhile, the CIO's Political Action Committee recognized this as a critical opportunity to change the political landscape and thus funded organizers to work with the NAACP on voter registration drives for black workers. The CIO's chief political strategist in the South, Palmer Weber, even convinced the organization to assign an African American to work on black voting full time.[7]

Churches actually played a major role in a growing voting-rights movement. In cities throughout the South—Memphis, Savannah, Atlanta, New Orleans, Jacksonville—a labor-church coalition emerged. In Atlanta, Rev. Williams Holmes Borders invited the Hotel and Restaurant Employees Union to meet at his Wheat Street Baptist Church, while Rev. A. L. Davis of Mount Zion Baptist Church in New Orleans worked with labor to create the People's Defense League to protect black voter registration. Alabama witnessed a statewide contest in June and July 1944, when the AFL, the CIO, the United Mine Workers, and the NAACP all competed to register voters in what one labor leader termed was a campaign for the "liberation of the ballot." Leading black ministers cooperated with CIO and some AFL representatives to register more than twenty-three thousand black voters in Alabama and more than thirty-five thousand in Florida. In some cities, registration drives showed remarkable results—more than ten thousand new black voters in Macon and more than five thousand in Savannah, Georgia.[8] Consequently, Mason could point to signs of hope for a bright future of black economic and political progress arising from interracial unionism.

Others were less sanguine about the long-term significance of the CIO's efforts. William Y. Bell Jr., the southern field director of the National Urban League, noted that black workers had made most of their gains in industries that were "subject to cut-backs in peacetime." He also claimed that despite the increased number of blacks in skilled and semi-skilled jobs, "the proportion of colored skilled workers to other skilled workers remained the same as in 1940."[9] African-American organizers like Elijah Jackson, who organized for the CIO's shipbuilding union in Mobile, Alabama, witnessed firsthand the resistance of some local unions to equalizing opportunities for blacks. When the union and the Fair Employment Practices Committee ordered the Alabama Dry Dock and Shipbuilding Company to promote twelve black men to skilled welder jobs, a mob of four thousand whites rioted against the promotions, driving black workers from the shipyards with pipes, wrenches, and other weapons.[10]

In some ways, the Mobile riot marked a turning point during the war. The hopes and actions of blacks began to elicit a reaction from whites. As the war and the defense industries it spawned began to wind down, competition for jobs became more combative. At the same time, industrial centers had to deal with the combustible mix of returning veterans, high inflation, and cutbacks in overtime hours. The ensuing turmoil reenergized groups like the Ku Klux Klan and caused some CIO leaders to shrink back from their commitment to a civil-rights-oriented biracial unionism. This was what worried Osceola McKaine, field secretary of the Southern Conference for Human Welfare, as he visited every southern state in

1946. He recognized the promise that flowed from union membership and CIO help in voter registration drives, and he also knew that blacks had come to a new realization that politics and job opportunities were linked. But McKaine was also alarmed at the retrenchment he witnessed among CIO leaders, particularly as some unions began to organize in the South without a commitment to the CIO's policy barring racial discrimination. In a private letter to CIO vice president Allan S. Haywood, McKaine asked the CIO to insist that organizers live up to what the organization professes. It was this letter that elicited Van Bittner's public statement rejecting help from the Left in the Southern Organizing Campaign.[11]

Despite Bittner's declaration, the African American press expressed cautious optimism at the outset of Operation Dixie. Journalist Harry Keelan advocated that the National Urban League make a formal alliance with the CIO. He believed that the CIO's "basic philosophy—that you cannot win a strike unless you can call out every man in the plant" meant that it had to include black workers. He added that the CIO includes "many Afro-Americans in executive positions, whose race one never recognizes until their pictures appear in the newspaper." Luther P. Jackson put the CIO in the same category as the Southern Regional Council, the Southern Conference for Human Welfare, and the Fellowship of Southern Churchmen for their refusal "to give support to the spurious doctrine of white supremacy." He felt that the labor organization would be instrumental in "the cracking of the Solid South." The *Baltimore Afro-American* picked up on the CIO's effort to give a sacred character to the southern drive, approving of CIO president Philip Murray's claim that Operation Dixie was "a holy crusade," and that "the CIO would carry political and economic salvation to the South, just as church workers spread the word of spiritual salvation."[12]

In many cases, the African American press supported the CIO because of who opposed the organizing campaign. The *Atlanta Daily World* warmed to unionism in August 1946 when Klan members attacked Mike Ross, a white CIO organizer in Macon, Georgia; if the Klan opposed the CIO, then the unions must be doing something right. Blacks also welcomed CIO agitation against Klan intimidation. The *Daily World* applauded when Florida CIO director Charles Smolikoff demanded a federal investigation of the Klan and claimed that "the campaign against the klan in Florida is growing faster than the klan itself." Although one black journalist argued that, for selfish reasons, labor rose to the defense of black workers beaten or intimidated by the KKK, black newspapers in general expected that the Southern Organizing Campaign would help offset the "forces of hate" in Dixie.[13]

Other black journalists felt that blacks should join the CIO despite skepticism. In the *Atlanta Daily World*, William A. Fowlkes wrote that even "with all their human faults," labor unions had "done more in the past twenty years to advance the cause of the common man and of the minorities than any other single group." Earl Conrad, who reported on Operation Dixie from Georgia, noted that the

campaign there was "very sensitive to the Negro question. It surrounds the organization process very much like the Negro issue permeates every phase of life in
the South." Still, he found it "significant that in plant after plant Negro and white
have been united at least on the economic level. If the CIO continues to hold
to that policy, if it does not yield to supremacist threats, if it does not enter into
political deals with the Old Guard for the sake of staying in existence, progress
will continue."[14] Recognizing the growing backlash against interracial unionism,
blacks realized it was necessary to keep pressure on the CIO. The *Chicago Defender*
warned, "It is not enough for the CIO leadership to reiterate their determination
to organize" both black and white workers; if "not implemented to the full," it
"would be merely to give lip-service to the ideals and aims of the CIO."[15]

Some black journalists worried that the simultaneous campaign by the AFL
could be an impediment to black advancement. George McCray pointed to George
Googe, director of the AFL's drive, who "has always held that the responsibility
for making things better for Negroes in the south is not the AFL's responsibility."
He worried that the CIO was too concerned about matching the AFL in avoiding
"offense to the sensibilities of southern white gentlemen" rather than adhering
to CIO principles. Likewise, the *Chicago Defender* reported that "on the matter
of Negro-white relations, it is hardly debatable that the CIO has maintained a
high standard of equality," but that challenges from the AFL threatened to make
Operation Dixie fall "flat for want of a little boldness in coping with the region's
traditional bigotry and oppressive institutions."[16] Of particular concern was the
fear that the AFL's red-baiting would encourage employers to avoid the CIO.
One columnist reporting on the AFL's 1946 southern regional convention in
Asheville, North Carolina, reminded blacks that AFL president William Green
warned southern employers "to sign up with the AFL before the godless CIO got
a chance to upset the applecart by preaching equal treatment and opportunity
for all workers." He then noted that the CIO and AFL campaigns were wasting
efforts "battling each other for votes in dozens of small plants all over the South."
George McCray gave yet another, more ominous version of Green's speech: "You
people of the south, both labor and industry, have got to sign up with us, the
AFL, pure and clean, or have your religion, your patriotism, your traditions,
and sacred beliefs destroyed by the Communist dominated CIO. Yes, folks, it's
America or Russia."[17] At a time when Christian free-enterprise advocates were
saying much the same thing, black reporters wondered if the CIO would buckle
under such charges, particularly when the AFL's southern campaign was winning
more collective-bargaining agreements than the CIO.

Skeptics found evidence of a lackluster CIO commitment to blacks. One of the
first signs for reporters was the American Newspaper Guild's "compromise with
racial prejudice." When black reporters in Richmond, Virginia, tried to gain membership in the guild in October 1946, the guild assigned them to a "northern city
guild some several hundred miles away." Another report pointed to the resurgence

of the Ku Klux Klan and wondered what the CIO was prepared "to do about those Klansmen who are themselves members of CIO or AFL unions." In fact, the *Atlanta Daily World* reported a rumor that the Alabama CIO's support for a state resolution condemning the Klan "hit a snag among leaders of a powerful section of labor where the KKK is said to have strong influence."[18] P. L. Prattis called attention to the fact that "neither the Organizing Campaign nor the Advisory Committee for the CIO campaign" included the name of a single black leader. Another report found it "significant that the CIO took no official part in the [1946 Georgia] primary campaign either on the side of Talmadge or Carmichael, although this would have certainly been the time" to fight a man known to be hostile to both labor and African Americans. Meanwhile, Osceola McKaine reported from South Carolina that the CIO's tobacco workers union had to force local unions in the state to abolish segregation in its meetings and then compel a white business agent "to permit Negroes to meet in his union's hall."[19]

Consequently, the CIO's Community Relations Department and the CIO's religious activists had an uphill battle to demonstrate their commitment to black workers. Charles Webber began laying the groundwork for the CIO even before the Southern Organizing Campaign began. In the spring of 1945, the United Packinghouse Workers confronted a hostile company and community in its effort to organize the P. D. Gwaltney Jr. Company of Smithfield, Virginia. The union asked Webber to investigate. Although Webber was a Methodist minister, the Smithfield Methodist Church denied him access, so he began holding meetings with the largely black workforce at two black Baptist churches. When the union lost the NLRB election, Webber had the results overturned by charging that "a company and community conspiracy" against the union violated the National Labor Relations Act. Webber documented the company's and community's "abridgement of freedom of speech within church institutions, social institutions, and industrial institutions." In fact, it was Webber's actions in Smithfield, not his position in the Virginia CIO, that so rankled white Virginia Methodists. Meanwhile, the black Methodist bishop, Alexander P. Shaw, became one of Webber's most vocal defenders.[20]

Webber quickly developed a reputation as one of the best Virginia CIO leaders on race issues. When future civil rights movement activist Marvin Caplan arrived in Richmond in 1946, veterans of the local racial justice movement insisted that Caplan meet two labor people—Brownie Lee Jones of the Southern School for Workers and Charles Webber. For the next five years, Caplan recognized Webber and Jones as two of the attendees at many of the important meetings called to work on racial justice in the city.[21] Webber's positions on civil rights as president of the Virginia CIO and director of the state CIO's Political Action Committee made a strong impression. The African American press appreciated his work in the political campaign against Harry F. Byrd, Virginia's conservative Democratic senator. In addition, black newspapers praised Webber for his role in featuring important African American speakers at state CIO conventions and at gatherings to discuss political strategy in the state.[22]

Even when Webber disagreed with their politics, he defended the rights of African Americans. One of the "inside agitators" of the civil rights movement, the liberal activist Virginia Durr, praised Webber for his actions at a meeting addressed by Henry Wallace during Wallace's Progressive Party presidential campaign. The meeting attracted a large interracial crowd to a huge municipal hall in Norfolk, Virginia. Although organizers thought they had police approval for nonsegregated seating, when the meeting opened, more than one hundred police arrived and sent notice to Durr that the races would have to separate. Instead, Durr started the meeting by having the audience sing the Star Spangled Banner (all four verses) and then called on Webber to offer an opening prayer. Webber did not support Wallace's candidacy, but he was at the meeting. Not only did he respond, but Durr recalled that "Charlie prayed and prayed, for the brotherhood of man, and especially for the police" until his breath gave out. By that time, Wallace had started down the middle aisle and the police gave up the notion of trying to segregate the crowd.[23]

Until he left to work on political action with the UAW in 1953, Webber continually promoted civil rights in the Virginia labor movement. He personally solicited money for the Virginia State Conference of the NAACP, and he pushed the state CIO to "call upon President Truman to set up a Fair Employment Practice Commission by Executive Order." In 1950 Webber sent a cavalcade of private cars and buses that carried Virginians to the National Emergency Civil Rights Mobilization in Washington, D.C. Under his leadership the Virginia CIO worked closely with African American labor and political leaders like Philip Weightman of the National CIO-PAC and Luther P. Jackson of the Virginia Voters' League on building black political participation in Portsmouth, Norfolk, Danville, Richmond, and other Virginia cities. Webber was also a frequent speaker at black political, fraternal, and educational institutions, and in the Methodists' *Social Questions Bulletin* he praised the "fight in Virginia for first-class citizenship."[24] Thus, as president of a southern state's Industrial Union Council and as a Methodist minister, Webber was a visible, vocal, and active leader in putting the CIO on record in support of black workers and civil rights. In the later 1950s Webber took over as the religious-relations representative of the AFL-CIO and continued to earn praise from the black press for his work with civil rights organizations.[25]

Like Webber, Lucy Mason's involvement with the civil rights of black workers predated the Southern Organizing Campaign. She had been on the scene numerous times in Memphis in the years before World War II, soliciting help from the U.S. Justice Department as well as Eleanor Roosevelt in protecting the rights of blacks during one of the bleakest periods for the local African American community. She was also at the Alabama Dry Dock and Shipbuilding Company in Mobile when racial tensions exploded during the war, working with the War Manpower Commission to effect a compromise that helped quell the violence and provide black workers with more opportunities for advancement. Wherever race and civil rights were at issue in the South, Mason was likely there representing the CIO.[26] Black newspapers appreciated Mason's work. They recognized her contributions in support of lobbying for full and fair employment legislation as well as her role as a charter member of the new Southern Regional Council in 1944. The council was a merger of the older Commission on Interracial Cooperation with advocates of a new agency devoted to "the improvement of economic, civic, and racial conditions in the South." Mason's support of blacks also included participation in the Georgia branch of the Southern Conference for Human Welfare's fight against the white primary and the poll tax.[27]

The backlash against black advancement that coincided with the end of World War II and onset of Operation Dixie meant that the need for Mason's investigations of civil rights was greater than ever. CIO efforts to organize black workers often brought violations of civil rights. In Cuthbert, Georgia, the sheriff, solicitor, and city clerk attended a meeting of black workers to intimidate them into leaving a union and forced a black pastor to stop allowing the union to meet there. In Buena Vista, Georgia, local police threw black strikers in jail and released some "upon their promise to return to work." After a visit from a particularly intimidating local policeman, the black Antioch Baptist Church of Nacogdoches, Texas, refused to allow union meetings there, and sheriffs and police in Tifton, Georgia, took an African American striker for a ride in a sheriff's car and "mauled [him] about the face and head," leaving his face "badly swollen from jaw to forehead, his left eye completely closed and the right eye in bad shape." Mason routinely took charge of gathering facts and testimony as well as contacting Turner L. Smith, chief of the Justice Department's Civil Rights Section.[28]

For Mason, one of the most inspiring aspects of black participation in CIO unions was the religious spirit they brought to organized labor. In many cases where law enforcement officials violated black rights, black churches were the scene of the action. While organizing black workers in Arkansas and Mississippi, Mason "was especially impressed with the enthusiasm of the Negroes. They have carried over the church technique to their union meetings—prayers, singing, both hymns and union songs—spontaneous remarks—all had the more primitive church pattern. Ministers opened the meetings with prayer and led in the singing." In Vicksburg, Mississippi, Mason recalled the almost martyr-like bravery that enabled black timber workers to confront a sheriff who threatened to shoot a bunch of "burr-headed Negroes." In defiance, the workers "filled to overflowing" a black church, and the pastor introduced Mason as "this white lady from heaven, who is here to help us." Mason appreciated the potential of an expressive Protestantism for building a black-white alliance based on evangelical religion, but she believed that the CIO had done more "to increase understanding and good will between the two races than has any other institution, including the Church."[29]

As a veteran of nearly a decade of organizing for the CIO in the South, Mason knew about the racism of white CIO members. Her familiarity with the issue was critical to the Community Relations Department, since John Ramsay openly admitted he was unprepared to deal with the particular forms of white supremacy he found among union members in the South.[30] Employers often played on the racial fears of workers, to the dismay of CIO organizers. At the Bibb Manufacturing Company in Macon, Georgia, the company distributed a mimeographed letter with forged signatures of the Textile Workers local leaders addressed "To Our Colored Brothers," even though the textile firm had few black employees. Included was a photograph of the black vice president of the Tobacco Workers International Union and the emblazoned question, "Do you want the CIO after seeing this?" Bibb also distributed copies of *The Trumpet*, the right-wing weekly that made similar charges about the CIO's position on racial equality. The tactic worked: workers voted against the union. Appealing the unfair labor practices to the NLRB took eighteen months, limiting the union's ability to achieve new results.[31]

Both Ramsay and Mason encountered the divisive effect of race in CIO locals even where employers were not stoking those sentiments. Mississippi organizer R. W. Starnes told Ramsay that he should not attempt to have a meeting of clergy and black workers in Laurel because white union members there were "of the definite opinion that such a dinner . . . would have a tremendously adverse effect on the present organizations and organizational work." In Tennessee, members of a United Steelworkers local made up a leaflet to support their strike that "used the Johnny Reb [Confederate] flag and theme." As Operation Dixie was winding down, Mason expressed her frustration with racial sentiments in Alabama. She wrote state CIO director Carey Haigler that she had received two invitations to speak in Birmingham, one from a CIO education conference and the other from the local branch of the NAACP. Unfortunately, Mason mixed up the dates. When she realized her mistake, she contacted the organizations to see if she could speak to both groups simultaneously, but they refused. Dispirited, Mason cryptically wrote in the margins of her letter to Haigler: "Could not carry through because of anti-Negro bias of many Steel-Workers in Birmingham."[32] Mason similarly expressed disappointment in the caution of one of her protégés, Paul Christopher, president of the Tennessee CIO. She prodded Christopher to make the state CIO convention a truly interracial affair, including the dinners and social gatherings. Christopher, a close ally of numerous progressive groups, including Highlander Folk School, broached the subject with the executive board. However, he demurred to their judgment that the time was not yet right to integrate the social agenda of the convention. Thus white delegates dined at the fashionable Hermitage Hotel; blacks ate at the Elks Club.[33] It was difficult for even some of the better labor leaders to defy the South's racial traditions.

In one activity, the Religion and Labor Fellowships, Ramsay consistently disregarded those traditions. In the gatherings that Ramsay organized for ministers
and union leaders, the CIO helped close at least a bit of the distance between
blacks and whites. Jerome Cooper, who became a United Steelworkers attorney in
Birmingham, Alabama, recalled the Fellowship luncheons in that city. They met at
the Redmont Hotel, where a sympathetic manager allowed the integrated meals,
"even though they were illegal" in Alabama. To emphasize the religious nature of
the meetings, the group decided that they should meet at a religious institution.
When it came to selecting a place, however, most said: "Gosh, I would like to do
it at my church, but I have to be honest about it. I think it would cause all kinds
of commotion." Finally, Rev. William H. Marmion opened Highland Episcopal
Church, a church attended by many prominent people in Birmingham. Cooper
remembered that first luncheon as "revolutionary. . . . The air was electric." The
white ladies of the church who served the interracial gathering of unionists and
clergy "were polite but they never said a word." Marmion carried that courage with
him in his subsequent career. As the Episcopal Church bishop for southwestern
Virginia in the late 1950s, he challenged the church at large by holding interracial
youth conferences in the region.[34]

Rev. William Holmes Borders addressing a Labor-Religion Fellowship luncheon in
Atlanta, ca. 1950. Courtesy of the Southern Labor Archives, Georgia State University,
Atlanta.

It is difficult to measure the influence of Religion and Labor Fellowships in building a better racial climate. On the one hand, they appear to have been rather naïve, gathering together union members and ministers who were already willing to break down racial barriers. However, they also represented a visible challenge to the status quo, as that first luncheon in Birmingham should remind us. It included United Steelworkers District 36 director Reuben E. Farr, who was a former member of the Ku Klux Klan, as well as Rev. J. L. Ware, "a young black man" who was a militant on race issues but later served on the Community Affairs Committee of the Steelworkers. In Atlanta, the first meetings of the Religion and Labor Fellowship had to be held at the black YWCA building because the group could not find a hotel that would serve a meal to an interracial group. Eventually, the fellowship met in a variety of settings, including the theological seminary at Emory University. Ramsay recalled that the "first Negro to get on the School Board [in Atlanta] said he could never have made it without the Religion and Labor Fellowship." In Augusta, Georgia, the Chamber of Commerce tried to prevent the formation of a new fellowship by claiming that "labor was a bunch of Communists." Ramsay went to Augusta to meet with the mayor, who then actually helped arrange the meetings there. "We broke the barrier" in Augusta, Ramsay recalled. This is not to suggest that Ramsay's Religion and Labor Fellowships broke down racial barriers or that they attracted a representative cross section of ministers in any particular city, but at a time when many groups dared not disturb Jim Crow, Ramsay set up an example of interracial brotherhood that challenged whites.[35]

Religious activists who held organizing positions tried to balance a more delicate scale. Franz Daniel was the state director of Operation Dixie, first in South Carolina and later in North Carolina. Like Paul Christopher, he was charged with organizing and maintaining unions of predominately white workers who did not share his ideas about racial equality. Although Daniel supported the civil rights actions of such groups as the Fellowship of Southern Churchmen, he was inclined to tiptoe around issues that might inflame the sensibilities of white textile mill workers in the Carolina Piedmont region. For instance, although the Textile Workers Union had made a breakthrough in organizing a bleachery in Rock Hill, South Carolina, Daniel advised the education director to have separate training sessions for the black stewards. When told that "it would be of greater value to everyone if the stewards attended a session all together," Daniel insisted that some other arrangement be made. Daniel also warned David Burgess against attending "a proposed inter-racial Labor-Management affair to be held by the Fellowship of Southern Churchmen" unless he had prior approval. He reminded Burgess that "any such conference as proposed will have a direct bearing on organizing work."[36]

Daniel was well aware that race could thwart union hopes in an NLRB election. In organizing lumber workers at the Moss Mill in North Carolina, Daniel advised the CIO legal department to define the bargaining unit to exclude cabinetmakers and carpenters. He explained: "There are about ten (10) white cabinet makers and carpenters employed by Moss, who are anti-union and anti-Negro. They are definitely against us." Daniel felt the largely African American workforce at Moss might have a better chance of winning if white workers were excluded. At the same time, Daniel studiously avoided helping Nelle Morton of the Fellowship of Southern Churchmen rally support to protest a Klan march in Denmark, South Carolina, in 1949. "I think it is a big mistake for labor groups in a state like South Carolina to get out in front of a fight against a vicious thing like the Klan," Daniel wrote. He felt that he might be able to achieve more working quietly behind the scenes rather than exposing the CIO to the wrath of white workers whom they were trying to organize.[37]

David Burgess, although a protégé of Daniel, was far less timid about stepping outside the racial conventions of the South and much of the CIO staff. In 1948, Burgess wrote a blistering letter to the editor of the *Industrial Leader*, a labor weekly published in Winston-Salem, North Carolina. On March 19, the editor had reprinted an editorial from the city's newspaper telling blacks that they should "count their many southern blessings." Earlier, on March 5, the paper ran an editorial "which more or less praised the revolting Southern governors for their stand against President Truman on civil rights," which concluded, "We have got to avoid the racial boobytrap, now disguised as civil rights proposals." Burgess chastised the editor for "appealing to the latent prejudices trumpeted by the most reactionary newspapers of the South" instead of the official policies of the CIO and the Textile Workers Union.[38]

Burgess carried this same uncompromising spirit with him into work with the CIO Political Action Committee. While working on liberal North Carolina Senator Frank Porter Graham's reelection effort in 1950, Burgess recruited blacks to the campaign—even hiring black precinct workers with union funds—by emphasizing Graham's record on racial issues even as CIO spokespersons were denying that the senator was a supporter of fair employment practices. For his effort, many white workers cursed Burgess for supporting "that nigger lover," Graham.[39] Burgess also objected to PAC southern director Daniel Powell's refusal to cooperate with the black community except when he saw some advantage. Burgess wrote to the CIO's political director Tilford Dudley that he could no longer work for Powell, who appealed to the basest instincts of workers and used any means to obtain results, including lies and deceit. Apparently, Powell told Burgess that his "religious scruples" reduced his effectiveness. Burgess countered that his political work served a higher purpose, which was to help each worker be "a free man—responsible, respected, his own master. Negroes, more than whites, know the meaning of this sense of freedom." Moreover, he wrote, "Those of us in political action work would be much more effective if we grasped the full meaning of this human desire for freedom."[40]

The reality was far more complicated. As executive secretary of the Georgia CIO in 1952, Burgess experienced frustration when union members in northern Georgia supported candidates who voted against liberal Democrats in Washington. It was a "disgrace," he complained, to have representatives from a region with considerable CIO strength vote "against the interest of organized labor and against the National Democratic Party in favor of the Dixiecrats."[41] For a man of strong religious principles like Burgess, the rough and tumble world of southern politics near the end of the Jim Crow era was frequently disappointing.

The CIO's religious activists also played at least a small part in influencing a prominent national religious figure on racial segregation. In October 1950 Rev. Billy Graham planned a major revival crusade in Atlanta, the home base of Ramsay and Mason. Ramsay, upon returning from working in Texas, learned that the CIO had endorsed Graham's crusade. Ramsay immediately asked Graham's crusade team about the racial policy of the crusade and learned that the plan was for segregated meetings and seating. He then met with Methodist bishop Arthur Moore and explained that the CIO could not endorse such a policy. Moore took the issue to the committee sponsoring Graham's crusade, but the committee voted not to change the policy. Ramsay, in turn, canceled the CIO endorsement, telling CIO members "to work through their churches to go in and support this crusade." "We're all for the crusade," he said, "but we're not going to be separated children of God. When we go to a meeting, we're all God's children."[42]

Opponents of the CIO, however, were quick to take advantage. *Militant Truth* endorsed the crusade and began publishing Graham's crusade sermons in the paper alongside its typical antilabor and antiblack items. Both Mason and Ramsay tried to set up meetings with Graham during the campaign to alert him to the situation, but the staff rebuffed them. Mason recognized the quandary. Some in the CIO wanted to criticize Graham's connection to *Militant Truth*, but Mason objected, saying that nothing in the sermons was anti-CIO and that she did not want a controversy with Graham. "This seems to me a situation in which any attack by us would be very foolish," she wrote, "for they have the press and radio, and we don't. Also we would seem to be attacking a religious revival," not a good idea in the South.[43] Instead, Ramsay wrote a letter to Graham, asserting, "[If you] allow your name to be used in such a publication, it would seem to me that you are also in the mesh of materialism which you have been preaching against in our Atlanta Crusade." Ramsay reminded Graham that many CIO people supported the crusade, but the CIO itself could not. "The reason, you see, is that the C.I.O. is overcoming the unchristian attitudes that bring about bigotry and segregation in the south because of color. Many of us have prayed and hoped that you would challenge Atlanta on this issue." Two months later, Ramsay had a personal meeting with Graham arranged by Bishop Moore. When Ramsay showed Graham a picture taken from *Militant Truth*, Graham told him, "That will never happen again." In 1953, Graham's crusade in Chattanooga, Tennessee, made headlines when Graham personally removed the ropes that segregated blacks.[44]

Termites in the Temple

Evangelical opponents of desegregation (such as the Rev. Haggard introduced at the start of this chapter) typically associated racial reform with Communism. It was an idea that had deep roots in the South; some southerners, in fact, blamed foreign radicals for agitating among blacks even before the Civil War. World War I and the Bolshevik Revolution fertilized those roots, leading to open assaults on organizations that sought to give economic and political voice to blacks. In one of the most vicious of these, a vigilante group in Elaine, Arkansas, with white recruits from Mississippi and Tennessee and troops of the Arkansas National Guard, waged a bloody battle with the Progressive Farmers and Household Union of America, leaving five whites and twenty-five blacks dead. The interwar years witnessed a number of episodes that confirmed in the minds of many southerners the connections between struggles for black advancement and Communism. The Share Croppers Union in Alabama, the United Cannery, Agricultural, and Packing Workers in the Mississippi Delta region, the Scottsboro Boys' defense effort, and the Angelo Herndon case in Atlanta all demonstrated what nervous southerners perceived as a nefarious strategy that international Communists had for fomenting a revolution of disaffected blacks. There was ample evidence of Communists associated with these episodes to make the idea of a conspiracy seem plausible.[45]

World War II raised the stakes of Communist influence. Building upon the new evangelicalism's prophecies of doom as well as the spread of anti-totalitarian realism, religion contributed both an apocalyptic dynamic and a sober calculation to the fear of Communism. A business community distraught by the growing power of unionism and government regulations found anticommunism a convenient tool to roll back the New Deal. Even the labor movement contributed. In the AFL, some leaders despised the challenge raised by the CIO and its willingness to incorporate leftists in its drive to build an industrial union movement; it was these leaders who cooperated with the Federal Bureau of Investigation and the House Un-American Activities Committee to shine a bright light on Communist influence in the CIO. In fact, the Red Scare within the labor movement preceded the phenomenon known as McCarthyism by a number of years.[46] By the war's end, the nation—and the South—was ready for an all-out crusade against Communism.

To many historians of the CIO's Southern Organizing Campaign, postwar anticommunism doomed any chance that a civil-rights-oriented unionism would thrive. They argue that Communists were African American workers' best friends in the labor movement. Left-led unions such as the International Union of Mine, Mill, and Smelter Workers (Mine, Mill) and the Food, Tobacco, Agricultural, and Allied Workers (FTA) were pioneers of strategies linking industrial unionism and civil rights. The red scare within labor eliminated these unions as well as the United Electrical Workers (UE), the United Farm Equipment and Metal

March of members of the left-led and interracial Mine, Mill, and Smelter Workers Union in East Tennessee, 1940s, from the M. H. Ross Papers. Courtesy of the Southern Labor Archives, Georgia State University, Atlanta.

Workers (FE), and others that were helping to build the CIO in the South. When combined with the loss of the United Mine Workers, which left the CIO at the start of the war, these losses were blows to interracial unionism and to the energy and principles of the CIO's Southern Organizing Campaign.[47]

What part did the religious activists play in the interaction of Communism and Operation Dixie? Several of them had flirted with Communists prior to World War II. Charles Webber, for instance, had been a close associate of fellow traveler Harry F. Ward during their years in the Methodist Federation for Social Services. David Burgess had found a great deal to admire in the activism of Claude Williams and Owen Whitfield during his time with the Southern Tenant Farmers Union. Even John Ramsay had cooperated with Communists when he was building the Steelworkers Union in Bethlehem, Pennsylvania.[48] But as we have noted, American religion had taken a sharp turn away from the Left, and particularly Communism, and the CIO's religious activists in the South followed suit. During the Southern Organizing Campaign, these activists worked doggedly to distance the CIO from Communism, both for strategic reasons and on principle. Still, the ability of the CIO's opponents to link the southern drive to Communism negatively affected the campaign, something that none of them was ever able to completely counter. While the logic of the CIO's anticommunism will continue to be debated by historians, we believe that the CIO could not have been successful with Protestant white workers unless it professed zero tolerance for Communism. A CIO that refused to denounce the Left and pay at least some heed to racial norms may have been more heroic in the saga of the long civil rights movement, but it would not have made its goal of increasing union density in the South attainable.[49]

A Communist-anticommunist split ran deeply through those prophetic Christians allied with organized labor. The antagonism that occurred between Harry Ward and Reinhold Niebuhr at Union Seminary during World War II had a major influence on Burgess, Webber, and Daniel, who had all spent time there. For Daniel, it reconfirmed his opposition to Communism, a result of his early experiences as a Socialist Party organizer in Philadelphia. He never forgot or forgave Communist opponents, even breaking with friends at Highlander Folk School because the school followed "a consistent line that is helpful to the C. P. [Communist Party] in the South." Webber had his own run-ins with the party. In 1934 Communists threw Webber down the stairs of the Textile Workers hall in Allentown, Pennsylvania, because he opposed their "dual union policy." In 1939 he incurred the party's wrath for persuading the Methodists to condemn the Soviet Union for invading Finland, and just two years later for advocating lend-lease aid to Britain during the period of the Nazi-Soviet pact.[50] By the end of the war, Burgess was likewise disillusioned with the Communists he knew personally, such as Claude Williams.

For the religious activists who were part of the southern drive, disavowal of Communism was less a strategy than a sincere belief that it distorted the type of moral labor movement they hoped to build. The enthusiasm and idealism of the CIO's religious cadre came from this vision. Mason maintained optimism in some of the most difficult situations. Burgess and Webber chose to leave safer positions within the Congregational and Methodist Churches to pursue careers organizing workers because they felt a calling. Even Daniel, perhaps the most pragmatic of the group, wrote to Bruce Bliven during the war that he believed a new type of labor leader was emerging, one who was "young, progressive, and intellectual." This new leader, Daniel said, would still need "to put guts and hope into the lives of oppressed workers." "[But] without an idealistic philosophy by which each union experience is interpreted as a step toward a more decent and equitable society," Daniel added, "most present-day union leaders would find themselves hopelessly lost in a dreary world." Daniel knew that Communism provided that idealism for some, but not for him.[51] The same was true for Ramsay. In the 1940s, the *Christian Herald* was about to run an article about John Ramsay's career in the CIO when someone reported to the magazine's staff that Ramsay was a Communist. When the writers called Ramsay for a statement, he reminisced about his days at Bethlehem Steel and similar queries from his foreman about whether or not he was a radical. Ramsay admitted, "[From management's] point of view I probably would be considered radical." Not satisfied, the foreman stated that management wanted to know if Ramsay was a Communist, to which Ramsay answered: "You tell them I'm more radical than a Communist ever thought of being; I'm endeavoring to be a Christian!" This story must have satisfied the *Christian Herald*, which ran its article on Ramsay.[52]

In the postwar South, however, the nuances that Ramsay might use to separate his progressive activities from Communism were lost. Opponents of change in the South scoured for evidence that Communists were behind the demands for labor and civil rights. Winston-Salem newspaper editor J. Sanford Martin contemplated in 1946 how he might use John L. Lewis's testimony to the Dies Committee "concerning how the Communists were taken into the CIO." North Carolina governor Melville Broughton claimed: "The Democratic party has been taken over and is now in the hands of the Northern Negroes plus the left wing labor element and the C.I.O., headed by the Lithuanian immigrant, Sidney Hillman."[53] With such charges bandied about and featured in the right-wing publications like *Militant Truth* and *The Trumpet*, it became difficult for many southern workers to know where the truth lay.

The AFL, which was launching its own southern drive, realized that charges of Communism in the CIO could help them woo workers away from their rivals. AFL leaders frequently offered employers the lesser evil of signing contracts with their affiliates in order to avoid CIO campaigns. "Grow and cooperate with us," AFL president William Green reportedly told southern industrialists, "or fight for your life against Communist forces." In addition, the AFL accused the CIO of seeking social equality for Negroes and claimed that blacks who joined the CIO were Communists. Such assertions did not do the same damage to the CIO's chances with black workers who, at times, felt that if unions earned the label "Communist," they might be more willing to stand up for African Americans. But in industries that employed mostly whites, especially those that hired large numbers of women, such as textiles and clothing, organizers found that rumors of "social equality" with blacks were an impediment. In fact, even leftist leaders of mixed-race unions had to rethink their approach if they hoped to keep their unions strong. Historian Judith Stein cites the example of Mine, Mill, which realized too late that its adoption of the Communist Party's crusade against "white chauvinism" had harmed its standing with white members.[54]

Inevitably, the red-scare atmosphere took its toll on the time and energies of many who had no need to defend their commitment to civil rights. Lucy Mason felt obliged to emphatically deny following the party line. She proudly claimed that the CIO organized blacks even when doing so worked to its disadvantage in places like Georgia and Mississippi, and she asserted that "the Negro has had more opportunity to get into unions since the CIO was born than ever before— including those [unions] in the South." Moreover, she concluded, just because "the Communists also happened to believe in some of these measures, the rest of us democrats cannot reject our beliefs." She worried about the confusion, however.

In a letter to the deputy attorney general of the United States, she complained: "It sometimes happens that a southerner on the FBI staff has considerable racial prejudice—and *in his mind confuses communism and race relations*." As a result, she said, "my fellow southerners by the dozens have labeled perfectly good Democrats 'communist' because they had liberal attitudes in regard to race."[55]

Mason may have had in mind her good friend, Brownie Lee Jones, director of the Southern School for Workers. Jones and the school established a number of voter registration programs for blacks in Virginia, which earned her a reputation as a radical. AFL unions in particular, Jones recalled, "would make cracks about my working with both blacks and whites in the same place." But even some CIO union leaders "weren't going to have anything to do with 'Brownie Lee Jones, she was a Communist.'" In 1948 Earl Crowder of the United Steelworkers resigned from the school's board, intimating that it was "Communist." Around the same time, the Memphis director of the CIO, W. A. Copeland, reported a rumor that Jones was cooperating with Communists and the Progressive Party in Virginia. Mason and Textile Workers organizer Boyd Payton worked feverishly to head off the rumors, taking the matter up directly with William Crawford, the Southern director of the Steelworkers. Within days the rumors came to a halt, leaving Mason to wonder if Crowder "ate any crow on this calumny."[56]

Consequently, the CIO's religious cadre tried to delicately navigate when fighting against Communism and for the rights of black workers. One of the first challenges they faced was in Winston-Salem, North Carolina. At the R. J. Reynolds plant there, the Communist-led FTA had built a successful union, Local 22, during the war, relying principally on the support of black tobacco workers. When Operation Dixie began in 1946, Local 22 was in the midst of a campaign to spread the union and its benefits to the tobacco leaf house workers in the eastern part of the state, emphasizing the same community-oriented, social-justice approach to unionism. While ultimately successful, CIO organizing staff worried that trumpeting the gains and demands of the largely black FTA membership would harm the efforts to attract workers in the dominant industry in the state—textiles—with its overwhelmingly white workforce. Operation Dixie thus supplied little support to FTA and insisted that it pursue its organizing drive without raising "a negro nationalistic approach, which could easily be dangerous to us."[57]

Local 22 defied the Southern Organizing Campaign directors, running a black candidate, Rev. Kenneth R. Williams, for alderman in the 1947 city elections. The community political mobilization eventually gained the support of the CIO (and, ironically, the AFL) because the elections came amid the push for the Taft-Hartley Act in the U.S. Congress and right-to-work legislation in North Carolina. But no sooner had the pioneering election of Williams ended than the Reynolds Company forced Local 22 into another showdown in contract negotiations. This time the results were less satisfying. The company and the local middle class emphasized the Communist domination of Local 22, which found it more difficult to appeal to white workers, some of whom resented the union's ultraradical positions and constant charges of "white chauvinism" against opponents.[58] Other whites felt uneasy with what they perceived to be the local's persuasion of black workers to demand full equality. Furthermore, Reynolds began employing white strikebreakers, some of whom were rural workers who had absorbed the religious emphasis on self-reliance. Luther Ranson, one of the strikebreakers, asked, "Why have a union? . . . I don't need nobody to speak for me."[59]

The union needed help, and it sought assistance from the Fellowship of Southern Churchmen and other liberal organizations. Nelle Morton of the fellowship went to Winston-Salem with three Chapel Hill ministers to investigate, and then she contacted Franz Daniel and David Burgess for advice.[60] Despite the importance of the strike and the admirable racial advancements made under the aegis of Local 22, both Daniel and Burgess had reservations about helping the Communist-led union. Daniel urged the fellowship to issue an appeal for support but to remain open about the issue of Communism. Nothing "would be gained by ignoring or denying the charge—but so what?" Daniel continued: "You are not asking for relief for the leaders or the union. You are asking for relief of strikers whose cause is a just one. If the strike is won, there is a chance to clean up the union. If it is lost, there will be no chance to eliminate the C.P."[61] Burgess had weightier concerns. He suspected that the Communists were using the strike to raise money and attention for the party's purposes, not those of the strikers. Also, Burgess objected to how Communist union officials handled meetings with the fellowship's representatives, not letting local strikers speak. "The Commies, in my opinion, have no fundamental faith in the democratic process," Burgess wrote.[62]

The CIO's religious activists were not done with Winston-Salem. As leaders tried to revive the union's strength in the wake of the mixed strike results and the ongoing attack on the union for its Communist ties, the FTA realized that it needed to win the loyalties of white workers, most of whom had failed to join the strike. They called on John Ramsay for assistance. Ramsay, certainly no sympathizer with the Communists, nevertheless went to Winston-Salem and tried to drum up support for Local 22 among the clergy. Ramsay also addressed the rally that climaxed the organizing campaign: "There is one God, one Father, and one creation, and we're all part of it." He added, "Men and women who have a vision of great unity . . . are those who built the union," imploring workers to rebuild the organization that had transformed R. J. Reynolds. Local 22 also brought in Claude Williams to revive the union with his prophetic, radical Christianity, but by 1948 his message found little support among Reynolds's white church-going workers. Instead, the year brought the further decline of labor's influence in Winston-Salem during the divisive fighting over the Progressive Party candidacy of Henry Wallace. A year later, the CIO had expelled FTA and Ramsay was trying to help form a new union at Reynolds.[63]

The all-too-brief life of Local 22 certainly seemed to be an opportunity lost, but it is not clear that CIO opposition to the Left leadership of Local 22 was the critical reason. In fact, FTA organizer Jack Frye believed that more important than the "Red issue" were the weaknesses of the local among white workers, the technological changes that enabled Reynolds to restructure the workplace, the factional fighting between Local 22 and the FTA, and the withdrawal of support from the national union. Frye claimed: "I felt like I was being used, that they [the FTA] had to put up a façade that they were going all out to organize these people, but they didn't really believe that it could be done."[64] Frye's reminiscences do not suggest that the FTA represented what might have been achieved with a more courageous CIO.

The CIO's religious activists battled another Communist-led union in Louisville, Kentucky. At the end of World War II, International Harvester purchased a factory to begin production of small "cub" tractors. Louisville, in fact, experienced a burst of industrial activity in the 1940s, as General Electric Company also opened a huge new plant in the city. International Harvester's plant quickly attracted organizers from the United Farm Equipment and Metal Workers Union (FE), which successfully organized the plant in 1947. The company also hired significant numbers of black workers, creating an opportunity for FE Local 236 to practice its commitment to racial equality. The environment in Local 236 spilled over to interracial politics in the city, making the local unique in Louisville. In the memory of one black activist, Local 236, despite including some of the worst white racists, was "the closest to the most perfect union" he had ever experienced. Future civil-rights activist Anne Braden first became radicalized when her husband Carl took her to meetings of what were known as the "Seventh Street Unions"—Local 236, the Transport Workers Union, the United Public Workers, and the United Furniture Workers. All were Left-led unions of "vigorous human beings who were changing their own world," according to Braden.[65]

In 1948 Local 236 took the lead of the local Progressive Party movement and Henry Wallace's campaign for the presidency. The founding meeting of the Progressive Party in Louisville actually took place in the offices that Local 236 shared with the other Seventh Street Unions. Much of the energy for the Wallace campaign, however, came from the local's black members. White members increasingly resisted the Progressive Party as a result of charges in the Louisville media that Wallace was associated with Communists. In the recollections of black members of Local 236, that campaign was a turning point in civil-rights agitation, awakening blacks to their political power. Many went on to challenge local laws enforcing segregation in the city's parks, hotels, housing, and hospitals, as well as demanding fair hiring practices at General Electric. Gradually, the ethos of the union affected the rural-born whites, Braden argued. To her, the transformation of worker attitudes "was amazing, the kind of turnaround that people's minds had simply because they were in a different setting."[66] The Wallace campaign, however, signaled another important change for Local 236, hastening the expulsion of FE along with the other left-led unions from the CIO. Once excluded from the CIO, Local 236 became fair game for the United Auto Workers, which hoped to bring the local's three thousand members under its umbrella. In December 1949 CIO headquarters sent John Ramsay to work with local ministers in Louisville to convince them that International Harvester would be better off with a UAW contract. Ramsay won the support of Protestant ministers in the city, denouncing Local 236 as "representative of Godless Communism." Ramsay emphasized that ministers give a "personal interest" to the CIO's campaign to "maintain our nation of free people with freedom of Religion."[67]

Louisville was not the Deep South, however. It had a large Catholic population, causing the anticommunist Association of Catholic Trade Unionists to send Fr. Charles Owen Rice to persuade the city's priests to oppose the FE. In an ironic twist, the leaders of Local 236 accentuated the Catholic opposition and spread rumors that CIO President Philip Murray was an emissary of the Pope. On December 21, 1949, International Harvester workers voted for FE by nearly a two-to-one margin in an NLRB election. In the days following, Rev. Hugh A. Brimm, a professor at the Southern Baptist Theological Seminary in Louisville who was sympathetic to the CIO, surveyed the large number of Baptist workers at the plant and found that many of them voted for FE Local 236, "fearing Rome more than Moscow." Brimm wrote that men who had been convinced to vote for the UAW voted against it after the newspaper ran an article emphasizing Catholic support.[68] As was the case in Winston-Salem, the religious activists of the CIO faced difficult decisions when the options were fighting Communism or supporting a strong, interracial union.

There were a variety of factors shaping the choices of the CIO's religious activists. For Franz Daniel, Charles Webber, David Burgess, and Lucy Mason these imperatives came mostly from a career of dealing with a Communist Party they saw as deceitful and willing to approach any situation with a philosophy that the ends justified the means. This included the party's abrupt changes of position at the onset of World War II. Webber and Burgess were also involved in political work in the South, which was made far more difficult as a result of the fact that the CIO included left-led unions that followed the party line on many issues. Furthermore, they all felt that when Communist-led unions did not get their way, they would use rumor and innuendo to advance their cause. Daniel, for instance, discovered in 1948 that left-led unions in Charleston, South Carolina, were circulating rumors that the CIO's policy was to "organize segregated locals." And the FE gladly spread rumors about Philip Murray being an emissary of the Pope to win in Louisville. Lucy Mason, likewise, deplored the "Party tactics" that made special promises to blacks and led them "to expect a new world," despite the fact that she had consistently defended black civil rights. She admitted to being "a bit gun-shy of the Communists": "[It is] because I have suffered several times from the unconscionable tactics such persons can follow in the pursuit of their own ends."[69] Such use of lies did not make the left-led unions any worse than the AFL or CIO, which also spread rumors and innuendo, but it did not make them any better either.

For John Ramsay, an important factor in opposing the Communists was his participation in religious organizations that harbored strong anticommunist sentiments, but some of Ramsay's thinking stemmed from his personal connections to CIO president Philip Murray. The first time Ramsay met Murray at the Steelworkers headquarters, he saw him in his office "on his knees in prayer," wrestling with some union problem. When introduced, Ramsay said, "I'm glad to know you're a man of prayer." From that moment on, they had a special bond. Although they did not share the same faith, they developed a mutual respect for the importance of religion in each man's life.[70] During the time they knew each other, Murray had gradually come to embrace the cause of racial equality as a "holy and a noble work," not unlike Ramsay's view. Murray, in the early 1940s, joined the NAACP advisory board and tried to make the CIO an organization committed to fair hiring practices and civil rights. Still, Murray felt that the first step toward solving racial inequalities was to improve the material conditions of all workers, to push for full employment and a "bigger pie, enough for all."[71]

While the United Steelworkers was hardly a model organization dedicated to full racial equality, Ramsay absorbed Murray's outlook. He admitted that he had little understanding of the depth of racial feelings in the South when he joined the Southern Organizing Committee in 1946. The one example he knew, in steel, shaped what he thought was possible. In the Birmingham district of Alabama, many black workers loved the United Steelworkers and greatly admired Philip Murray. Ramsay recalled that when Murray came to speak at a union gathering in Alabama, "they had a rope between the white section and the black section and he insisted that rope be taken down." When Murray died in 1952, an African American gospel group sang:

> He was the CIO's loss, but he's Heaven's gain.
> In the day of Resurrection we'll see him again.
> Good God Almighty our best friend is gone.
> I want you boys to help me, just sing this song.

It was an unusual confluence of factors that earned Murray such loyalty from black steelworkers: the union's ability to win improved wages, better working conditions, and even some promotion opportunities for blacks—these things and a booming economy, too, made all steelworkers feel secure. Such factors enabled blacks in the United Steelworkers to attain protection, respect, and, on occasion, defense of their job rights against the hostile claims of white workers. The loyalty that resulted was a powerful sign for Ramsay.[72]

This personal relationship with Murray shaped Ramsay's involvement in another battle with a left-led union, the International Union of Mine, Mill, and Smelter Workers (Mine, Mill). Mine, Mill represented the iron ore miners and smelterers who often lived in communities that included steelworkers, but the black ore miners were steadfast in their devotion to Mine, Mill. They appreciated the union leadership's commitment to black equality, which included flouting southern cultural traditions by as shaking hands with African Americans. Many of the white members of Mine, Mill seethed at what they perceived as deliberate attempts to undermine their way of life and promote "social equality," buzzwords that typically roused hatred among white supremacists. However, there were other white Mine, Mill leaders in Alabama such as Leo Kendrick who had fought hard for black workers but resented the Communist Party's intrusion into union affairs that included replacing local leaders with party members and adopting an "ultramilitant" line. When the CIO expelled Mine, Mill, the two dissatisfied union groups in Alabama moved to secede from the union. Although there were Klan members among those who preferred secession, the leadership did not share those sympathies. A bitter struggle ensued, with both sides spreading rumors about each other and using violence to intimidate their opponents.[73]

Ramsay and Mason went to Birmingham and Bessemer to help build the CIO and United Steelworker presence there. They established a successful Religion and Labor Fellowship in Birmingham, and Ramsay sought to break down barriers with black ministers in Bessemer, trying to pave the way for their cooperation with the CIO. Neither Ramsay nor Mason was reluctant to emphasize that Mine, Mill was Communist dominated. Ramsay even made a radio broadcast in which he charged, "We have proof of a real communist threat" in Birmingham; "United Steelworkers of America-CIO is a strong and sound democratic union and a bulwark against communism."[74] Meanwhile, Mine, Mill began a campaign with its own slurs, one of which, Ramsay recalled bitterly, was that "they portrayed Phil Murray as a Klansman." Unfortunately for the future of race relations among Birmingham area steelworkers and ore miners, the Klan staged a rally supporting the secessionists who wanted to leave Mine, Mill, which the radical union used to advantage. Furthermore, the president of the Negro Voters League in Birmingham, Asbury Howard, was an organizer for Mine, Mill. Consequently, the local NAACP supported Mine, Mill in the election.[75]

In the end, the United Steelworkers won a very close election, but the union needed significant effort to repair the damages to race relations. Birmingham District 36 made plans to win over the black workers who had supported Mine, Mill by holding a Civil Rights Conference in July of 1950. One of the purposes of the conference was to develop political support in Alabama for a fair-employment-practices measure. White workers in the steel plants, however, rebelled against the notion. In May, District 36 director Reuben Farr wrote Murray that his initiative elicited "a very unfavorable reaction," and that some members circulated a de-certification petition at Fairfield Steel. A month later, the presidents of six United Steelworkers locals wrote Murray that their members resented the representatives the union had sent to the South: "[They] act as if we were backwoods people who only recently were run down and shod." They claimed, "Our people will not be moved by 'moralist' and 'idealists' such as these northern people believe themselves to be," and they doubted that they "could win a Union shop election if it were held today."[76] The Steelworkers recovered a bit with the appointment of Howard Strevel, a white Tennesseean, to the District 36 staff in 1951. Strevel was both an excellent grievance officer and someone sensitive to the concerns of black workers.[77] But as late as 1953 the Steelworkers and the NAACP in Birmingham had little to do with each other. Although both groups invited Lucy Mason to address their meetings, they would not attend a joint meeting. The local branch of the NAACP was led by two Mine, Mill activists, causing a number of black CIO members to refuse to join the NAACP in Bessemer. When the two organizations met in May 1953, Rev. J. L. Ware of the NAACP "expressed many strong criticisms of the Steelworkers Union and specific persons in the leadership of the CIO in Birmingham." Ware balanced his remarks with praise for others in the Alabama State CIO Council, although he was disappointed that the CIO did not take a strong position on segregation in the school system. Others felt that progress was being made, including the recruitment of blacks into Steelworker staff and local union leadership positions.[78]

The religious activists in the CIO made small gains against such powerful emotions. Ramsay remembered visiting Bessemer after the Steelworkers had defeated Mine, Mill. He insisted that the entire white staff of the union have dinner with the black ministers while he was there. At the end, he called for everyone to form "a friendship circle" and take the hand of the next person as they repeated, "May the Lord watch between me and thee while we're absent one from the other." After the meeting, one of the white staff members told Ramsay: "I never took hands with a nigger in my life. I saw what you were doing and I tried to get between two white fellows and I couldn't. I took hands [with a Negro] and I couldn't tell the difference!" A few years later, however, when Police Chief T. Eugene "Bull" Connor began arresting black civil-rights demonstrators in Birmingham in the early 1960s, Steelworkers' attorney Jerome "Buddy" Cooper got a call from the Washington headquarters telling him that President Kennedy had asked unions to post bail for the demonstrators. Cooper then called Reuben Farr and Howard Strevel of District 36, who agreed. The Steelworkers put up $250,000.[79] Equally important, the gains black workers had made through their struggles in the labor movement in Birmingham created a corps of trained, assertive, and educated local activists who were the "foot soldiers" of the later struggle for racial equality.[80]

Southern Traditions and Progressive Challenges

It is easy to say that the CIO's religious activists could have done better. On their moral principles alone, we might have expected that they would have grasped those opportunities when a left-led, community-based activism successfully united workers in biracial unionism that improved the lives of all. Of course, this disregards the beliefs of Webber, Mason, Daniel, Burgess, and Ramsay, to say nothing of many other CIO leaders whose strong religious faith and experiences caused them to view left-led unions with supposed Communist ties as suspect. Such leaders as William Mitch of the United Mine Workers and William Crawford, president of the Steelworkers District 35 in Georgia, were men of "genuinely Christian spirit" who earned plaudits from black civil rights activists but harbored profound suspicions of Communists. For both, their anticommunism dovetailed with their religious beliefs.[81] Many of the labor activists charged with building a bridge to the religious communities throughout the South felt that there could be no compromise with Communism. The religious press in the South spoke almost as one against Communism, even tarring the Federal Council of Churches and later the National Council of Churches with charges that they were abetting "termites in the temple." Moreover, it was a rare minister in the South who would express any sympathy with the Communist Left.[82] It was difficult enough to sit down with southern preachers and try to extoll the benefits that unions could bring to black and white working people without having to answer the accusation about the CIO's inclusion of "Godless Communists." Consequently, if the principle CIO goal was to organize the South's workers, it had to reject left-led unions and downplay its commitment to racial radicalism. Mason capsulized the problem; she was likely to ignore red-baiting herself, but she knew that "innocent workers" too often believed such charges. This was equally true of the "preachers, especially the Baptists," who gave their flock "the choice between the church and the union."[83]

It is certainly true that some working people, especially blacks, understood that red baiting was a long and trustworthy tactic used by employers to dampen enthusiasm for organized labor or any social movement. That some black workers were even drawn to organizations with reputations as Communist because they might expect greater assistance from them made sense. But the record is not completely one sided. In the woodworking industry, for example, the ousting of the Left-led United Furniture Workers was coupled with a turn toward "racial liberalism," according to historian William P. Jones. The director of Operation Dixie in North Carolina, William Smith, asserted that the Furniture Workers were "torn with dissention" and that "the type of organizers [the union] had were more interested in spouting the 'commie line' than they were in doing organizing." Smith believed that the CIO's International Woodworkers of America union was doing more than an adequate job, and where they were successful the Woodworkers organizers reported that black workers were getting politically organized. In Edenton, North Carolina, the local was working with ministers and civic groups to register union-protected black workers in a place where some blacks had lived for forty or fifty years and "this was their first time ever registering."[84]

Other Communist-led organizations in the South also failed to hold the loyalties of black clergy and black workers. Black longshoremen in New Orleans and Mobile preferred the AFL union to the left-led CIO version; two black preacher-organizers who led the Southern Tenant Farmers Union—E. B. McKinney and Owen Whitfield—worked with the Communists when the party shared their perspectives, but they also found Communists inconsistent and not completely committed to black equality. Even in Memphis and Winston-Salem, where left-led unions used a civil-rights strategy to build vibrant, interracial local labor movements, factionalism and the Communists' insistence on supporting Henry Wallace's Progressive Party campaign in 1948 cost them the support of some African American clergy and split the black community.[85] In fact, in Winston-Salem, when FTA Local 22 turned against the black alderman its members had helped elect, he turned to the CIO. In his reelection campaign in 1949, Kenneth R. Williams praised CIO members for the "untiring" efforts on his behalf as well as increasing the numbers of blacks registered to vote, "which definitely influenced the outcome." Williams was "very much interested in the work being done in our city" by the CIO and claimed that he would "be more than glad to support [the CIO's] cause." "My interests," he said, "are definitely on the side of labor."[86]

We can fault the CIO for its strategy to go after white workers first, but that was not the decision of the religious activists who signed onto the campaign, and it did not diminish their efforts to organize blacks. Nor did they ever promote segregation within local unions; Ramsay and Mason both asserted that they "lost elections rather than compromise" those principles.[87] Racial customs and Communism were two major problems that affected how deeply religious white workers viewed the CIO's Southern Organizing Campaign, and they inhibited its chances for success. Would a more open defiance of red-baiting and race-baiting have produced greater success? That is impossible to answer definitively. There is, however, ample evidence to support the assertion that for some labor activists religious faith supplied an idealism that pushed them to try and build a movement toward a more decent and equitable society for working people, whether white or black. If they failed, it was not for a lack of courage.

Conclusion

In early February 1953, during the last gasp of Operation Dixie, the Textile Workers Union believed that it had a good chance of winning an NLRB election at the Rhyne-Houser Mills in Cherryville, North Carolina. Three days before the scheduled election, seven Cherryville ministers—two Baptists, two Methodists, a Lutheran, a Presbyterian, and a Church of God—addressed a letter to the workers at Rhyne-Houser. The ministers asserted that the arrival of the union "threatens to disturb the good spirit and fellowship of our Community." While professing deep concern over the welfare of the workers, they said, "[We are] thoroughly convinced that it would be greatly to your disadvantage to have the Union to represent you." The ministers added, "Many of the benefits and special favors that you have had would no longer be yours under the Union." Concluding, they advised: "Consider this matter prayerfully before voting and May God guide you in your decision."[1] Three days later, the Textile Workers Union lost the election. The episode in Cherryville is pertinent because it appears to confirm widespread popular perceptions about the influence of Protestantism on the CIO in the South. At the end of the CIO's most ambitious campaign, southern unions still had only about half the union density rate of the North. Equally devastating for the CIO, the AFL had more than three times the number of CIO southern members. Where the CIO had concentrated its muscle—in the textile towns of the Carolinas—fewer than ten percent of the workers were in unions.[2]

There is another side to the Cherryville incident, however. The ministers' letter stirred a surprising amount of controversy. Textile Workers president Emil Rieve wrote a long rebuttal letter in which he contrasted their fears for the "good spirit and fellowship" with the "right to dissent," which he assumed that "most of us in this country agreed . . . outweighed the advantages of autocratic unanimity." Rieve asserted that the labor movement and the church "should not be enemies, but allies." Trade unionism's "whole effort is on behalf of the weak, the poor, the oppressed." "Our goal," he wrote, "is to provide men with an instrument through which they can help themselves by helping each other. And when we succeed our greatest reward, like yours, is of the spirit."[3] Rieve's letter touched a chord with many in the South. Many southern newspapers ran the story and excerpts from Rieve's response.[4] For all of the deflating numbers that reflected the CIO's inability to crack the southern wall of resistance, there were bright spots. In Tennessee,

Alabama, and Kentucky, where manufacturing was less reliant on textiles, nearly one-quarter of the workers were in unions. In Georgia, Louisiana, and Mississippi, union density rates had doubled between 1939 and 1953.[5]

In many respects, the Cherryville episode also underscores the differences within southern Protestantism. A number of ministers and laypeople in the South met with labor people to express their dismay at the stand taken by the local clergy. The Lutheran Church censured its Cherryville minister, and the Methodist Church denied that its Cherryville ministers reflected Church policy.[6] Officials of the Presbyterian Church and the Church of God, however, defended the "consciences and discretions of the ministers," and acknowledged that there was no official church policy on this matter. Evidence of a Baptist response is lacking, which was in keeping with church polity.[7] Thus, the two national churches with headquarters in the North and hierarchical church governance tried to distance their denominations from such blatantly anti-union sentiments. Those more distinctly southern churches—the Church of God, the Presbyterian Church in the United States, and the Southern Baptists—fell back on the individual consciences and beliefs of their ministers. They would not dictate either to clergy or to congregations on social issues, but they also would not protect their ministers against the powerful forces in their communities that sought influence over local clergy. In most southern communities, the most powerful forces were the employers. The religious autonomy of local communities nevertheless left considerable latitude for workers who wanted to join unions. There are plenty of stories of individuals who defied their ministers and chose the CIO. Recall, for example, Wilt Browning, whom we introduced at the beginning of chapter 6. Browning and his parents were in church when their Pentecostal minister condemned followers of the union as bearing the mark of the Beast and doomed to eternal damnation. Yet forty years later, Browning discovered that his mother had snubbed the minister and her husband and voted for the union. When he asked her if she had listened to the minister, she replied: "Certainly, I heard the sermon . . . but I was and still am fully capable of thinking for myself and making my own decisions."[8] This is one of the conundrums of southern evangelical Protestantism.

Were southern workers different? In a crucial way at a particularly important turning point, we believe that they were. Our study concentrated on a particular time when unions had perhaps their best opportunity to make the South a more "laboristic" society. In 1946 the combination of labor resources, a friendly federal government, a population that had left behind some of its parochialism in a time of Depression and world war, and an expanding manufacturing base made the region ripe for unionization. Indeed, even so astute an observer as V. O. Key Jr. expected that to occur.[9] But the majority of southern workers chose to vote against unions when the campaigns arrived in town. Obviously, there were many factors that contributed to Operation Dixie's failure, not the least of which was the power that employers and politicians brought to bear against labor and liberalism. But we would argue that evangelical Protestantism was a critical factor in the equation, one that intersected with all of the others and one that distinguished the southern white working class from the northern industrial workers who built the CIO.

This is not to argue that religion, per se, was opposed to unionism. Even in the South, as we have noted, there were many places where the mix of local factors made evangelical faith an ally of organized labor. The coalfields are the most obvious example. And the International Union of Electrical Workers successfully combatted employer attempts to use religion and the blandishments of Rev. George Heaton to thwart union organizing campaigns in the mid-1950s by cultivating religious support in southern towns like Rome, Georgia, and Greeneville, Tennessee.[10] Still, the values that most southern workers attached to their evangelical beliefs had a tendency to conflict with the principles, the organizational hierarchy, and the culture that the CIO offered as a model for unionism. When combined with a history of defeats, a pervasive anti-unionism in the media, and the potential costs of more failures, few workers found the CIO an attractive option for improving their lives.[11]

We have also attempted to acknowledge the problems created by the strategies of the CIO. Its concentration on organizing white workers and the companies that were committed to making the strongest fight against unionization proved to be a serious miscalculation. The idea that a few quick victories in the largest textile mills would change the anti-union culture of the region—and, indeed, an entire industry—ignored the mighty opposition they would face, the legacy of paternalism, and the perceptions among the workers that their lives were never better. The CIO also did not demonstrate much staying power; its Southern Organizing Campaign began to fizzle within its first year and then limped weakly into 1950, having closed up shop in Texas, Louisiana, Mississippi, and Alabama. A disastrous internal warfare within the Textile Workers Union was a final nail in the coffin, even undoing some of the gains made in textiles. In the end, the CIO had about ninety thousand southern textile workers under contract in 1952—but that actually represented a shrinking portion of the South's textile workforce.[12]

The South's repulsion of the CIO campaign changed the national landscape for labor and liberalism. It accelerated the relocation of industry that was so important to capitalist restructuring. Companies headquartered in the union-heavy rust belt recognized the opportunities for cheaper labor. This included not only the traditionally low-wage industries, like textiles and garments, but also such expanding high-wage industries as electrical manufacturing. It also gave employers a weapon that they could effectively use to discipline unionized northern workers, shifting production from union plants to nonunion sites. Ultimately, such strategies eroded prolabor sentiments in the North as well as the South.[13] If southern workers were the exception when Operation Dixie began, they were the norm by the time of Ronald Reagan's presidency.

Operation Dixie's failure also reinforced the anti-union politics in the South and enabled conservatives in Congress to overturn with confidence a presidential veto of the Taft-Hartley Act in 1947. The next decades witnessed a growing number of southern states pass right-to-work legislation and nullify whatever gains unions had made in the South during the New Deal and war years.[14] Southern liberalism also diminished. Southern liberal politicians who won election during the 1940s—Claude Pepper, Frank Porter Graham, Sidney McMath—were gone by the early 1950s. Defeat also made it difficult for organized labor to throw its weight behind the civil rights movement. The merged AFL and CIO took on more of the characteristics of the former, not the latter union federation. Moderates, such as Lister Hill and Orville Faubus, joined the chorus of politicians who threw their support to the "Southern Manifesto," decrying the Supreme Court's *Brown* decision. This is not to suggest that the path of the civil rights movement would have been smooth if more workers had been members of unions, as the complicated situation in Birmingham, Alabama, makes clear. But a stronger labor movement with a clearer commitment to racial equality in the South would have provided a counternarrative against segregation that might have better protected the job rights of black and sympathetic white workers. It would also have amplified an important institutional voice for social justice in the region.[15] Equally important, when the civil rights movement gained its important achievements in politics and citizenship rights, there was no powerful union movement to advance the economic interests of working people, black and white. In the end, the nation has retained a political map that shows roughly the same regional divisions that existed in the nineteenth century.

Given these outcomes, it is tempting to draw a line between the failure of Operation Dixie and the New Right, imagining that the southern white working class was the seedbed for evangelically inspired conservatism. Here, however, the connection is inconclusive. While white evangelical ministers from the South contributed mightily to the triumph of Christian free-enterprise ideas, there is less evidence that the white, Christian workers who lived through the Depression turned their backs on the New Deal policies that had done so much for them. In fact, recent work by political scientists demonstrates that those who were in the bottom third of the income brackets were the least likely to abandon either the Democratic Party or the social-welfare policies and ideas ushered in by the New Deal. Think back to southern millhands like Hoy Deal, whom we introduced in chapter 3. Deal was one of those premillennialists who remained a Democrat into the 1970s and kept pictures of John F. Kennedy and Martin Luther King Jr. on his wall.[16] Many other oral histories suggest the same commitment to a party and policies that had helped them through the Depression. Historians seeking the social roots of the New Right in the South, by contrast, are finding them in the emerging suburban middle-class enclaves, not in the mill towns or in working-class neighborhoods.[17] Evangelicalism was a key building block of the New Right, but the popular religiosity of the white working class joined that movement later. It was more likely a new generation of white, working-class evangelicals who became the adherents of Jerry Falwell and Pat Robertson, not those who remembered Franklin Roosevelt's New Deal with fondness and gratitude.

Ultimately, we hope that we have restored some of the contingency and complexity to the part played by religious faith in the actions of southern white workers. During the hard times of the Depression, they turned to a "religion for the blues," historian Wayne Flynt tells us. But their belief in God's grace and the hope of salvation were not solely fatalistic or escapist. Instead, their practices and faith were reassuring, they allowed the emotional release of "resentments and fears" and brought calm as well as excitement.[18] In different settings, this same faith might foster either a deep commitment to collective action or give meaning to a life of toil without much in the way of earthly reward. When the terms and conditions of work improved and new opportunities and anxieties filled the postwar years, that same faith bolstered a worldview that prized self-reliance, personal independence, and duty as spelled out in the Scriptures. For southern white working people in the postwar era, building communities of the faithful meant avoiding the sorts of conflict that divided believers and shunning those who were not part of the fellowship. Many also believed that the Bible taught them to reject worldly things and be thankful for the gifts they had received, the most vital of which was their faith in God and His grace. Finally, evangelical workers felt that their conversion experience compelled them to lead a new life doing God's work. These were not necessarily anti-union values, but anti-union forces better understood them and exploited them in combatting the CIO.

In the decades since Operation Dixie, there have been other moments when these same evangelical values promised a new day. The most obvious is the civil rights movement, which tapped into a rich alternative theology of the sort that prophetic figures like Alva Taylor, Claude Williams, or Witherspoon Dodge had fostered. Later, flashes of prophetic religion have lit up struggles of catfish workers in Mississippi, in the Justice for Smithfield Workers campaign in North Carolina, in the unionization of J. P. Stevens Company, and in recent struggles against the horrible labor and environmental devastation wrought by the coal industry. The possibilities of continuing the struggle for the soul of the South, as well as the soul of the nation, are still present. To do better than the CIO did between 1946 and 1953 requires that we understand the cultural and religious values to which working people cling most fervently and then construct movements that give meaning to that faith while encouraging them to welcome new opportunities to achieve social justice for everyone.

NOTES

SQB	*Social Questions Bulletin* (of the United Methodist Church)
SSICR	Southern States Industrial Council Records, Tennessee State Archives, Nashville
Taylor Papers	Alva W. Taylor Papers, Disciples of Christ Historical Society, Nashville, Tennessee
TWUA	Textile Workers Union of America
UEA	*United Evangelical Advocate*
USWAOHP	United Steelworkers of America Oral History Project, HCLA-PSU
Williams Papers	Claude C. Williams Papers, ALUA-WSU
ZH	*Zion's Herald*

Preface

1. Heyrman, *Southern Cross*; Wyatt-Brown, *Shaping of Southern Culture*; Wilson, *Flashes of a Southern Spirit*.

2. This argument is made most passionately in Goldfield, *Color of Politics*, 249–60; and Honey, "Operation Dixie," 216–44.

3. Eighmy, *Churches in Cultural Captivity*.

4. Lippy, *Being Religious*, 2–3.

Introduction

1. Bageant, *Deer Hunting with Jesus*, 185.

2. Bageant, *Deer Hunting with Jesus*, 161–93.

3. Thompson, *Making*. See the revealing discussion of one historian's journey through the assumptions guiding working-class historiography in Barrett, "Blessed Virgin," 117–47.

4. Gutman, "Protestantism and the American Labor Movement," 74–101. For an important critique of Gutman's influence, see Salvatore, "Herbert Gutman's Narrative," 64–66.

5. Griffith, *Crisis of American Labor*, chap. 7; Honey, "Operation Dixie," 224; Brattain, *Politics of Whiteness*, 126–27; Kennedy, *Southern Exposure*, 233–35.

6. Some of the best are: Hall et al., *Like a Family*, 277–88; Tullos, *Habits of Industry*, 88–92, 178–80; Flamming, *Creating the Modern South*, chap. 6.

7. Dochuk, *From Bible Belt to Sunbelt*; Moreton, *To Serve God*; Grem, *Corporate Revivals*; Kruse, "Beyond the Southern Cross," 286–307; Hammond, "God's Business Men."

8. Joe Creech, *Righteous Indignation*; Callahan, *Work and Faith*. The quote comes from Orsi, "Everyday Miracles," 7.

9. Hayes, "Hard, Hard Religion"; Greene, "Revival or Revolt?"; Pehl, "'Apostles of Fascism,'" 440–65. An excellent forthcoming sample of this work is included in *Between the Pew and the Picket Line: Christianity and the Working Classes in Industrial America*, by Christopher D. Cantwell, Heath W. Carter, and Janine Giordano Drake, from the University of Illinois Press.

10. See, especially, Flynt, "Religion for the Blues," 6–7; and Fones-Wolf, "Embedding Class."

11. Carpenter, *Revive Us Again*; Glass, *Strangers in Zion*, Wacker, *Heaven Below*; Alvis, *Religion and Race*. For the spiritual turmoil that many southerners felt in the postwar years, see Daniel, *Lost Revolutions*, 7–38; and Flynt, *Poor but Proud*, 338–43.

12. Flynt, *Dixie's Forgotten People*, 100–101.

13. Daniel, *Lost Revolutions*, 7.

14. See, for example, Fuller, *Naming the Antichrist*; and Martin, *With God on Our Side*.

15. Minchin, *What Do We Need*.

16. Korstad, *Civil Rights Unionism*, 290–300; Korstad and Lichtenstein, "Opportunities Found and Lost," 786–811; Honey, "Operation Dixie," 216–44.

17. See, especially, Sullivan, *Days of Hope*, 220–47.

18. Fones-Wolf and Fones-Wolf, "Sanctifying the Southern Organizing Campaign," 8–15.

19. Simon, "Rethinking," 465–84.

20. Simon, 465–84. See also Burton, "The South as 'Other,'" 7–50.

21. Carter, "More than Race," 129–55.

22. Hill's quotes are from his epilogue to Eighmy, *Churches in Cultural Captivity*, 200–201.

23. For a critique of the cultural captivity argument, but one which we feel slights the dynamism and contingency implied in Hill's use of the concept, see Dupont, *Mississippi Praying*, 6–7.

Chapter 1. The Wages of the "Problem South"

1. Alice Grogan Hardin interview with Allen Tullos, May 2, 1980, SOHP.

2. "From the Mountains Faring," in Terrill, ed., *Such As Us*, 121–27.

3. Wright, *Old South, New South*, chap. 7.

4. For an insightful analysis of the strengths and weaknesses of the *Report*, see Carlton and Coclanis, *Confronting Southern Poverty* (quote is from p. 47). See also, Schulman, *From Cotton Belt to Sunbelt*, 50–52.

5. Mims is quoted in Ring, *Problem South*, 216.

6. "Autobiography," typescript (ca. 1928), Taylor Papers, box 1.

7. "Autobiography," Taylor Papers; Alva W. Taylor to W. H. Hoover, October 3, 1928, Taylor Papers, box 2; Taylor to Mr. Douglas, October 28, 1932, Taylor Papers, box 2; Dunbar, *Against the Grain*, 28–29.

8. Taylor to Jerome Davis, January 28, 1933, and October 5, 1933, Taylor Papers, box 2; Taylor, "Obstacles to Progress," in King, *Social Progress*, 191.

9. Church Emergency Relief Committee to Dear Friend, November 3, 1932; Taylor to Myles Horton, December 6, 1932; Taylor to Nevin, December 26, 1932; Taylor to John L. Lewis, May 6, 1933, all in Taylor Papers, box 2.

10. Dunbar, *Against the Grain*, 28–33. For books dealing with Taylor's students, see Martin, *Howard Kester*; Lorence, *Hard Journey*; Gellman and Roll, *Gospel of the Working Class*.

11. This paragraph reflects information contained in the correspondence in the Taylor Papers, box 2. See, in particular, Taylor to "Dear Friends," February 28, 1934; Taylor to Jerome Davis, March 3, 1934; Taylor to Dear Paul, November 9, 1934; Taylor to Sherwood Eddy, December 14, 1935; Taylor to Ted Shultz, June 4, 1936; and Taylor to W. J. Lhaman, November 27, 1936.

12. Daniel, *Breaking the Land*, 73–90; Flynt, *Poor but Proud*, 286.

13. Alva W. Taylor, "Happy Days Are Here in Dixie," *CC*, December 27, 1933, p. 1654; Alva W. Taylor, "South's Farms in the Money," *CC*, October 3, 1934. For an economic analysis of federal farm programs in the South, see Wright, *Old South, New South*, 226–38.

14. Alva W. Taylor, "Tenancy Report Scores System," *CC*, December 23, 1936, p. 1730.

15. Alva W. Taylor, "Assert Croppers Robbed of Funds," *CC*, September 20, 1939, p. 1150; Taylor, "Tenancy Report Scores System," 1730. For excellent studies of the role of religion in the struggles of the rural working class in the region see Roll, *Spirit of Rebellion*; and Gellman and Roll, *Gospel of the Working Class*.

16. Alva W. Taylor, "Celery Farm Slums Worst in America," *CC*, February 12, 1941, p. 232.

17. Alva W. Taylor, "South Will Profit by New Industry," *CC*, September 12, 1934, p. 1152; Wright, *Old South, New South*, 238, 263–64; George B. Tindall, *Emergence*, 470–71.

18. Taylor, "South Will Profit," 1152; Alva W. Taylor, "Hosts Visit TVA Projects," *CC*, November 14, 1934, pp. 1464–65; Alva W. Taylor, "TVA Progress Still Threatened," *CC*, September 9, 1936, p. 1203.

19. Wright, *Old South, New South*, 259; Key, *Southern Politics*, 345–68.

20. Frederickson, *Dixiecrat Revolt*, 17–18.

21. Alva W. Taylor, "Courts Thwart TVA Extension," *CC*, January 20, 1937, pp. 94–95; Alva W. Taylor, "TVA Dams Show Their Importance," *CC*, March 10, 1937, p. 331.

22. Tindall, *Emergence*, 444–45, 451–57. For a sober estimate of TVA's impact on the economic development of the region, see Schulman, *From Cotton Belt to Sunbelt*, 36–37.

23. Among the best studies of the strike in textiles and the defeat of southern textile unionism are: Irons, *Testing the New Deal*; and Hall, et al., *Like a Family*.

24. Douty, "Development," 572–74; Fredrickson, *Dixiecrat Revolt*, 18; Tindall, *Emergence*, 513–17; Schulman, *From Cotton Belt to Sunbelt*, 34–35.

25. Carlton and Coclanis, *Confronting Southern Poverty*, 7–31; Schulman, *From Cotton Belt to Sunbelt*, 49–62.

26. Egerton, *Speak Now*, 188.

27. Alva W. Taylor, "South Registers Political Changes," *CC*, October 12, 1938, p. 1238; Taylor, "South's Liberals Affirm New Deal," *CC*, May 3, 1940, p. 584; Taylor, "Pastors Support Lynching Bill," *CC*, August 11, 1937, p. 1003; Taylor, "Call to Righteousness Enlists Support for Labor," *CC*, April 27, 1938, p. 535.

28. Taylor, "Industry Resists C.I.O. in South," *CC*, October 20, 1937, p. 1300; Taylor, "Stops Meeting of Tenant Farmers," *CC*, March 30, 1938, p. 413; Taylor, "Labor Organizers Terrorized by Anti-Union Gangsters," *CC*, June 16, 1943, p. 726.

29. Taylor, "A.F. of L. Bans Discrimination," *CC*, June 16, 1943, p. 726; Taylor, "Repercussions from Human Welfare Conference," *CC*, January 4, 1939, p. 31; Taylor, "Growing Support for Federal Anti-Lynching Law," *CC*, December 22, 1937, p. 1603; Taylor, "Whites Riot for Right to Lynch," *CC*, November 30, 1938, p. 1472; Taylor, "Klan Again Active," *CC*, January 17, 1940, p. 91.

30. Tyler, "Blood on Your Hands," 100–101. Our observation about the white working class comes from reading scores of oral histories, especially those in the SOHP. See also Simon, *Fabric of Defeat*, 90–108.

31. Alva W. Taylor, "South's Liberals Affirm New Deal," *CC*, April 20, 1940, p. 584. For the history of the links between segregation and anticommunism, see Woods, *Black Struggle, Red Scare*. See also, Egerton, *Speak Now*, 289–302.

32. Bailey address in the Minutes, March 2, 1938, of the Records of the SSICR, box 1. For the economic impact of the New Deal in the South, see Wright, *Old South, New South*, 236–38.

33. "Report of Proceedings of the Seventh Annual Meeting of the Southern States Industrial Council, Held at the Ansley Hotel in the City of Atlanta, Georgia, on Tuesday, January 23rd 1940," in SSICR, box 1.

34. Hammond, "'God's Business Men,'" 59–61 (quote on p. 61).

35. *Dr. George D. Heaton II, November 8, 1908–July 4, 1996*, pamphlet in Heaton Papers, box 1; Oral Memoir of Warren Tyree Carr, BUIOH.

36. Heaton, "Christian Principles in Industrial Relations," 6.

37. "Address of Dr. George D. Heaton," 4.

38. Brooks, *Defining the Peace*, 37–40; Sokol, *There Goes My Everything*, 21. Unfortunately for labor, most veterans had their pro-union sympathies challenged by business groups that controlled access to veterans' benefits. See Brooks, *Defining the Peace*, chap. 4.

39. Schulman, *From Cotton Belt to Sunbelt*, 82; Sennett, *Bound for the Promised Land*, 232; Daniel, *Lost Revolutions*, chap. 1.

40. Wright, *Old South, New South*, 241–49 (quote on p. 245); Chamberlain, *Victory at Home*, 20–23, 75–77; Woodruff, "Mississippi Delta Planters," 263–84; Grantham, "South and Congressional Politics," 23–24.

41. Schulman, *From Cotton Belt to Sunbelt*, 84, 102–5. While the South did not benefit as much as the rest of the nation from war industries, they did help spawn the later economic diversification. Traditional southern industries saw their share of regional employment shrink, while transportation equipment, iron and steel products, chemicals, and machinery expanded. There is some debate on this topic. In a recent article, Robert Lewis suggests that "wartime manufacturing investments either reinforced the South's existing economic structure or built an extremely fragile and unevenly developed economic base that did not last beyond the end of the war." See Lewis, "World War II Manufacturing," 840.

42. Zieger, *For Jobs and Freedom*, 123–24; Chamberlain, *Victory at Home*, 69–96.

43. Marshall, *Labor in the South*, 225; Schulman, *From Cotton Belt to Sunbelt*, has a table on p. 105 charting the diversity of manufacturing encouraged by war production. For the examples of the "second wave" of southern industrialization, see Combes, "Aircraft Manufacturing in Georgia"; and Colton, "Texas v. the Petrochemical Industry."

44. Chamberlain, *Victory at Home*, 17–20.

45. Moore, "Dismantling," 114–45.

46. Chamberlain, *Victory at Home*, 30–39; Minutes of the Board of Directors meeting, December 8, 1941, SSICR, box 2.

47. Minutes, Board of Directors meeting, February 1, 1943, SSICR, box 2; Schulman, *From Cotton Belt to Sunbelt*, 72–73.

48. Halpern, "Interracial Unionism in the Southwest"; Stein, "Southern Workers"; Ingalls, "Antiradical Violence in Birmingham."

49. Marshall, *Labor in the South*, 268; Douty, "Development," 576–80; Korstad, *Civil Rights Unionism*.

50. Martin, "Southern Labor Relations," 545–68; *The Story of Gadsden, Alabama, and the C.I.O.*, pamphlet, undated, Ramsay Papers, box 1569.

51. Lucy R. Mason to Mrs. Roosevelt, May 28, 1940, in ODR, reel 63; Honey, *Southern Labor*. The membership figures are on p. 213.

52. Chamberlain, *Victory at Home*, 42–43.

53. Reed, *Seedtime*; Chamberlain, *Victory at Home*, 4–6; Sitkoff, "African American Militancy," 81.

54. Sitkoff, "African American Militancy," 87.

55. *Afro-American* (Baltimore), June 10, 1944; *Norfolk (Va.) New Journal and Guide*, June 17, 1944, September 30, 1944; Zieger, *For Jobs and Freedom*, 124–25; Taft, *A.F. of L.*, 439–48.

56. Minutes, Board of Directors meeting, April 11, 1945, and January 28–29, 1946, bound in single volume, SSICR, box 2. See also Honey, *Southern Labor* 191–212, Chamberlain, *Victory at Home*, 173–80. Among the harshest criticisms of the CIO are Nelson, *Divided We Stand*; and Goldfield, *Color of Politics*, 240–49. A somewhat more favorable perspective can be found in Draper, *Conflict of Interests*; and Zieger, *For Jobs and Freedom*.

57. Frank T. de Vyver cited in Tindall, *Emergence*, 521–22; Douty, "Development," 576–80; Schulman, *From Cotton Belt to Sunbelt*, 105.

58. Grantham, "South and Congressional Politics," 26–27; Perman, *Pursuit of Unity*, 255–57; Sokol, *There Goes My Everything*, 21; Brooks, *Defining the Peace*, 6–7; Brattain, *Politics of Whiteness*, 122–26.

59. Perman, *Pursuit of Unity*, 259–60; Grantham, "South and Congressional Politics," 28–31; Gall, "Southern Industrial Workers," 223–49.

60. Lucy R. Mason, "Labor on Religion," typescript of a radio address over WBLJ, Dalton, Georgia, February 15, 1942, ODR, reel 64; Minutes of the Board of Directors meeting, November 19–20, 1945, SSICR, box 2.

61. Scott Hoyman interview with Bill Finger, July 16, 1974, SOHP; Simon, *Fabric of Defeat*, chap. 12.

62. Jesse Grace interviewed by Melonie Gardner, October 24, 1982, SamOHC; Springer quoted in Chamberlain, *Victory at Home*, 183. For the uneasy race relations in the Birmingham-Bessemer labor movement, see Nelson, *Divided We Stand*, 212–17.

63. Heaton, "Challenge to Management," 135.

64. Alva W. Taylor, "Labor and the Social Ideals," newsletter of the Labor Commission of the Fellowship of Southern Churchmen, no. 3 (undated), in Taylor Papers, box 2.

Chapter 2. Unrest in Zion

1. Anne Queen interview with Joseph Herzenberg, April 30, 1976, SOHP.

2. Carl and Mary Thompson interview with Jim Leloudis, July 19, 1979, SOHP.

3. Carl and Mary Thompson interview.

4. Green, "Believers for Bush," 13–15. See also, Wilson, "Preachin', Prayin'," 15–16.

5. Lorence, *Hard Journey*; Flynt, *Alabama Baptists*, 375; Wilson, *Flashes*.

6. See the overview of southern religion in Hill and Lippy, *Encyclopedia*, 26–28; and U.S. Bureau of the Census, *Religious Bodies: 1936*, vol. 1.

7. Hill, "Religion," 1269; Keith, *Country People*; Jones, *Faith and Meaning*; Ownby, "Struggling," 122–24.

8. Handy, "American Religious Depression," 3–16 (quote from Niebuhr is on p. 6).

9. U.S. Bureau of the Census, *Religious Bodies: 1936*, vol. 1, 376–415.

10. On the perceived crisis in African-American rural churches, see Sennett, *Bound for the Promised Land*, 210–40.

11. U.S. Bureau of the Census, *Religious Bodies: 1936*, vol.1, 376–415; Harvey, *Through the Storm*, 87–94.

12. Synan, *Holiness-Pentecostal Tradition*, 129; Wacker, *Heaven Below*, 87, 91. See also Crews, *Church of God*; Anderson, *Vision of the Disinherited*; and Harrell, "South" 45–57. The idea of the "solid South," at least with regard to white Protestantism, comes from Hill, *Religion*.

13. Data on the Church of God comes from Bush, "Faith, Power, and Conflict"; Interview with Granny Hager by Mike Mullins, Lothair, Kentucky, January 31, 1973, AppOHP;

Pope, *Millhands and Preachers*, 98–103; Harrell, "South," 45–57. See also, Hall et al., *Like a Family*, 220–21. For an excellent discussion of Holiness and Pentecostal religion in the coalfields of Kentucky, see Callahan, *Work and Faith*.

14. Anderson, *Vision of the Disinherited*, 6–8; Hooker, *Religion in the Highlands*, 160–63; Interview with Luther F. Addington, Wise, Virginia, January 14, 1974, AppOHP; Harrell, "South," 48–49; Flynt, "One in the Spirit," 23–44.

15. *Southern Baptist Convention Handbook 1923* (Nashville: Sunday School Board, 1923), cited in Hayes, "Hard, Hard Religion," 78–79.

16. Flynt, *Alabama Baptists*, 361–63.

17. Glass, *Strangers in Zion*, 195–97; Hankins, *God's Rascal*, 41–43; Flynt, *Alabama Baptists*, 373–76; Oral History Memoir of Acker C. Miller, August 5, 1971, BUIOH.

18. Oral History Memoir of Sara Lowrey, August 2, 1972, BUIOH; Greene, "Revival or Revolt"; Flynt, *Alabama Baptists*, 384–87.

19. Marsden, "From Fundamentalism," 147. For the best survey of the resurgence of Fundamentalism, see Carpenter, *Revive Us Again*.

20. Glass, *Strangers in Zion*, chapters 2 and 3.

21. Glass, *Strangers in Zion*, 134–38.

22. Balmer, *Making of Evangelicalism*, 33–35. For dispensationalism's divisive effects in the PCUS, see Glass, *Strangers in Zion*, 146–52.

23. Sutton, "Was FDR the Antichrist?" 1052–74.

24. Henry "Yodeling" Wade interview with Douglas Flamming, July 12, 1985, CrownOHP; Martin Lowe interview with Allen Tullos, October 21, 1979, SOHP; Ila Hendrix interview with Ben Hendrix, May 1, 1976, SamOHC.

25. Martha J. Atha interview with Jeremy Carney, March 25, 1998, OHA.

26. For the animosity toward Eleanor Roosevelt, see Simon, "Fearing Eleanor," 83–101. For the ability of Christian working-class whites to welcome class-based relief but reject parts of the New Deal aimed and racial issues, see Simon, *Fabric of Defeat*; Feldman, "Home and Hearth," 57–99; Mathews, "Lynching," 153–94.

27. Carpenter, "Fundamentalist Institutions," 62–75. Glass, *Strangers in Zion*, argues that these elements were actually the fastest growing parts of American Protestantism, and that their vitality undermines Robert Handy's thesis of a religious depression (27).

28. Oral Memoirs of Warren Tyree Carr, April 18, 1985, BUIOH; Hangen, *Redeeming the Dial*, 28–29; *Decisions and Orders of the National Labor Relations Board, May 29–June 30, 1940*, vol. 24 (Washington: Government Printing Office, 1940), 18—19.

29. Bucke, *History of American Methodism*, vol. 3, 403–6, 452–72; Manis, "City Mothers," 125–56; Hall, *Revolt against Chivalry*.

30. Taylor cited in Greene, "Christian Left."

31. Taylor's influence is covered in Dunbar, *Against the Grain*; Harvey, *Freedom's Coming*, 77–106.

32. Church Emergency Relief Committee to Dear Friend, November 3, 1932; Alva Taylor to Myles [Horton], December 6, 1932; and Alva Taylor to Jerome [Davis], January 28, 1933, and March 18, 1933, Taylor Papers, box 2; Roll, "Prophetic Front"; Lorence, *Hard Journey*, 37–40.

33. Lorence, *Hard Journey*, 52; "Findings, Conference of Younger Churchmen of the South," Monteagle, Tennessee, May 27–29, 1934, Kester cited in Greene, "The Christian Left," 7; Roll, "Prophetic Front."

34. Williams, in Gellman and Roll, *Gospel*, 70–71; Greene, "Christian Left," 9.

35. Moore, "When a Man Believes," 185.

36. Dodge, *Southern Rebel*, 121.

37. Kelley, *Hammer and Hoe*, 148–51; Gellman and Roll, *Gospel*, 73–110; Callahan, *Work and Faith*, 187; Sennett, *Bound*, 230–32; Savage, *Your Spirits*, 68–71.

38. This is beautifully described in Egerton, *Speak Now*, 185–97 (Graham quote on p. 188; Durr quote on p. 189).

39. Sutton, "Was FDR the Antichrist?" 1071–72; Carpenter, *Revive Us Again*, chap. 11.

40. Hangen, *Redeeming the Dial*, 112–22.

41. Smith, *Time of My Life*.

42. McArthur, "Liberal Concessions to Fundamentalism"; Boisen, "What War Does to Religion"; Braden, "What Can We Learn From the Cults?"

43. Hangen, *Redeeming the Dial*, 127; Fones-Wolf, *Selling Free Enterprise*, 218–31.

44. "Federal Council," *SPJ*, June 1943, 6–7; "Comments on the Federal Council of Churches," *SPJ*, December 1943, 3; Robert L. Vining, "Is the Federal Council Evangelical?" *SPJ*, May 1945, 22–25; letter from Charles Dickinson, *SPJ*, December 1942, 12; *Minutes of the Eighty-Eighth General Assembly of the Presbyterian Church in the United States, Atlanta, Georgia, May 27—June 2, 1948* (Austin, Tex.: PCUS, 1948), 62–63.

45. Wills, "Southern Baptists," 11; Flynt, *Alabama Baptists*, 407–8; Broadus E. Jones, "N.C. Council of Churches and Fear," *Biblical Recorder*, March 29, 1944, 7–8; W. E. Goode, "Fundamental Questions," *Biblical Recorder*, February 23, 1944, 8–10; Bartlett A. Bowers, "Baptists and the New World Order," *Biblical Recorder*, February 9, 1944, 6–7.

46. "Johnston, Parson Jack, 1946–47" file, Stetson Kennedy Papers, New York Public Library, New York, N.Y., reel 2; *Trumpet*, January 10, 1947; J. Frank Norris to Whom It May Concern, September 1, 1948, Norris to Parson Jack Johnston, September 24, 1948 and September 25, 1948, J. Frank Norris Papers, Billy Graham Center, Wheaton College, Wheaton, Ill., reel 13. On the Columbians, see Weisenburger, "Columbians, Inc.," 821–60.

47. Kennedy, *Southern Exposure*, 232–38; Lucy R. Mason to Rev. Billy Graham, n.d. [ca. 1950], ODR, reel 64; Minutes of the Board of Directors, November 10–11, 1944, and April 11, 1945, SSICR box 2; *Militant Truth*, January 1945, February 1945.

48. Martin, *Howard Kester*, 119–25; Alva W. Taylor to J. M. Allen, March 28, 1942, and Taylor to Henry Smith Leiper, December 13, 1943, Taylor Papers, box 2; Gellman and Roll, *Gospel*, chap. 4; Myles Horton to Franz Daniel, May 4, 1942, Daniel Papers, box 5; Kersten, *Labor's Home Front*, 68–99.

49. Hulsether, *Building a Protestant Left*, 11–14, 44–45; "Theology and the Economic Order," *Christianity and Crisis*, May 1, 1944, 1–2.

50. Hulsether, *Building a Protestant Left*, 24–25; Alva Taylor to J. M. Allen, March 28, 1943, box 2, Taylor Papers.

51. Biographical sketch of Charles C. Webber, ca. 1953, in box 14, United Auto Workers Public Relations Department Records, ALUA-WSU.

52. "Partial List of Clergymen who have Urged President Roosevelt to Exercise Executive Clemency for the Release of Earl Browder," ca. 1942, in Webber Correspondence, 2134-6-7:01, MFSSR; Charles Webber to Wade Crawford Barclay, April 23, 1944, Webber Correspondence, 2314-7-1:03, MFSSR; Charles C. Webber, "Chaplain to Organized Labor," *Michigan Christian Advocate*, October 24, 1946.

53. Computed from statistics in USBC, *Religious Bodies: 1936*, vol.1, 376–415; and reports of *Churches and Church Membership*, series C, nos. 32–51.

54. Minchin, *What Do We Need*, 48–68.

55. Simon, "Race Reactions," 239–59; Brattain, *Politics of Whiteness*, 132–62; Dailey, "Theology of Massive Resistance," 151–80. On the Baptists, see Eighmy, *Churches in Cultural Captivity*, 189–93; and Flynt, *Alabama Baptists*, 449–54.

56. Lucy R. Mason to Rev. Cameron Hall, August 30, 1946, ODR, reel 63; McMichael, "New Social Climate"; Brooks, *Defining the Peace*, 37–38.

Chapter 3. "If You Read Your Bible"

1. This biographical sketch of Simmons and all of the quotes come from two extraordinary oral history interviews, Ralph Simmons's interviews with Patty Dilley, summer 1977, SOHP.

2. A useful guide here are the essays in Wilson, *Flashes*.

3. Lippy, *Being Religious*, 2–3, 10.

4. On the persistent and in many respects revitalized strength of the primary denominations in the South, see Flynt, "One in the Spirit," 23.

5. Eva Hopkins interview with Lu Ann Jones, March 5, 1980, SOHP; Ethel Marshall Faucette interview with Allen Tullos, November 16, 1978, and January 4, 1979, SOHP.

6. Worley Johnson interview with Myrl Hall, no date, AppOHP; Kathleen Knight interview with Daniel Knight, January 27, 1975, SamOHC.

7. Hopkins interview, SOHP; Margaret Dorsett interview with Lonette Lamb, February 26, 1979, SamOHC.

8. Flake and Nellie Mae Meyers interview with Pat Dilley, August 11, 1979, SOHP.

9. Pope, *Millhands and Preachers*; Flynt, "Religion for the Blues," 17.

10. Ethel Hilliard interview with Allen Tullos, March 29, July 21, and August 10, 1979, SOHP; Portelli, *Death of Luigi Trastulli*, 226–27; James Pharis interview with Cliff Kuhn, July 24, 1977, SOHP.

11. Portelli, *They Say*, 92.

12. Earle, Knudsen, and Shriver, *Spindles and Spires*, 100–109; Suggs, *"My World Is Gone,"* 119–31.

13. Albert Shock interview with Norman D. Munsey, February 24, 1980, OHA; Pope, *Millhands and Preachers*, 104–5.

14. U. S. Bureau of the Census, *Religious Bodies: 1936*; *Churches and Church Membership*, Series A.

15. Morland, *Millways of Kent*, 105–8.

16. Martin Lowe interview with Allen Tullos, October 21, 1979, SOHP; Anna Mae Cook interview with Cora Lee Hairston, October 5, 1973, AOHP.

17. Lowe interview; Hoy Deal interview with Pat Dilley, June 17, 1974, SOHP.

18. Ila Hartsell Dodson interview with Allen Tullos, May 23, 1980, SOHP; Alice P. Evitt interview with Jim Leloudis, July 18, 1979, SOHP.

19. Morland, *Millways of Kent*, 110–17.

20. Morland, *Millways of Kent*, 118–29.

21. Morland, *Millways of Kent*, 121–35.

22. Suggs, *"My World Is Gone,"* 119–20; Morland, *Millways of Kent*, 143–44.

23. Sam Johnson, in Shackelford and Weinberg, *Our Appalachia*, 288–95; Carroll Lupton interview with Mary Murphy, May 18, 1979; Versa Vernon Haithcock interview with Mary Murphy, April 4, 1979; and Ina Lee Wrenn interview with Allen Tullos, March 23, 1979, all in SOHP.

24. Luther F. Addington interview with Laurel and Don Anderson, January 14, 1974, AOHP; Robert Eugene Latta interview with Mary Murphy, April 17, 1984, SOHP.

25. Morland, *Millways of Kent*, 131; Suggs, *"My World Is Gone,"* 119–31; Hoy Deal interview, SOHP.

26. Edward Harrington and Mary Terry interview with Mary Murphy, February 28, 1979, SOHP.

27. Morland, *Millways of Kent*, 131–49.

28. Ethel Hilliard interview with Allen Tullos, March 29, July 21, August 10, 1979, SOHP; Mary Gattis interview with Douglas DeNatale, August 13, 1979, SOHP.

29. Martha Atha interview with Jeremy Carney, March 25, 1998, OHA; Willie Mae Defore interview with Douglas Flamming, July 19, 1985, CrownOHP; Earl Hardin interview with Douglas Flamming, June 25, 1985, CrownOHP; Paul and Pauline Griffiths interview with Allen Tullos, May 30, 1980, SOHP; Suggs, *Washing*, 59–60. For the pervasive presence of religious music in southern culture, see Wilson, *Flashes of a Southern Spirit*, 178–92.

30. Flynt, *Poor but Proud*, 230–33; Malone, *Don't Get*, 98–101.

31. Lawrence Baldridge interview with Ron Daley, November 16, 1975, AOHP.

32. Bass quoted in Flynt, *Poor but Proud*, 219–20.

33. Martha J. Atha interview; Suggs, *Washing*, 12–13.

34. Coles, *Children of the Crisis*, 584–5.

35. Suggs, *"My World Is Gone,"* 65–67; Harrington and Terry interview, SOHP.

36. James Pharis interview with Cliff Kuhn, July 24, 1977, SOHP.

37. Francis M. Curnutte interview with Francis M. Curnutte Jr., May 1, 1974, OHA; Raymond J. Adkins interview with Guy Sutphin, August 11, 1974, OHA.

38. An excellent example from the World War II period is found in Morland, *Millways of Kent*, 110–17. The best example from today is Bageant, *Deer Hunting with Jesus*.

39. Flynt, "Religion for the Blues," 11–12.

40. Louise Jones interview with Mary Frederickson, October 13, 1976, SOHP.

41. Morland, *Millways of Kent*, 148–49.

42. Morland, *Millways of Kent*, 150–51.

43. Portelli, *The Death of Luigi Trastulli*, 226–7.

44. Fannin, *Labor's Promised Land*, 293; Naison, "Claude and Joyce Williams," 44–48; Gellman and Roll, *Gospel*, 41–70.

45. Alva Taylor to Claude Williams, March 25, 1944, box 3, Williams Papers. See also the similar points made in Grammich, *Local Baptists*, chap. 3.

46. Harry Koger to Williams, January 7, 1945, box 14, Williams Papers; Craig, *Religion and Radical Politics*, 164.

47. Lilly interview in La Lone, *Appalachian*, 237; Portelli, *They Say*, 90.

48. Hager interview; Debbie Spicer interview quoted in Bush, "Faith, Power, and Conflict," 205. See also, Callahan, *Work and Faith*, chapters 4 and 5.

49. Callahan, *Work and Faith*, 187.

50. Frank Bonds interview with Patty McDonald, March 21, 1979, SamOHC; Christine Cochran interview with Jerry Tapley, May 24, 1979, SamOHC; Eula McGill interview with Jacquelyn Hall, February 3, 1976, SOHP; Jack Durden interview with Alex Ruffner, October 8, 1982, SamOHC.

51. Hiram Hutto interview with Bill Teem, February 2, 1980, SamOHC; Frank Bonds interview; Erskine Bonds interview with Bob Baggott, April 2, 1979, SamOHC.

52. Nancy Letitia Inman interview with Barry Anderson, April 1, 1979, SamOHC; Allen Buster interview with Debra Ann Burks, November 29, 1974, SamOHC; Samuel A. Un-

derwood interview with Tricia Agee, October 23, 1982, SamOHC; Jesse Grace interview with Melonie Gardner, October 24, 1982, SamOHC.

53. Wade interview; Earl Hardin interview with Douglas Flamming, June 25, 1985, CrownOHP; Flamming, *Creating the Modern South*, chapter 10.

54. Thelma Parker interview with Douglas Flamming, June 11, 1985, CrownOHP; Sibyl Queen interview with Flamming, June 26, 1985, CrownOHP.

55. Quoted in Flamming, *Creating the Modern South*, 214.

56. John Bramblett interview with Flamming, June 29, 1985, CrownOHP. See similar examples for a later period in Grammich, *Local Baptists*, 123–26.

57. Alice P. Evitt interview with Jim Leloudis, July 18, 1979, SOHP; Geddes Elam Dodson interview with Allen Tullos, May 26, 1980, SOHP.

58. Flynt, *Poor but Proud*, 338–43; Frederickson, *Cold War Dixie*; Suggs, "*My World Is Gone*," 119–20.

59. Flynt, *Dixie's Forgotten People*, 93–102; Sparrow, "Nation in Motion," 169; Minchin, *What Do We Need*, 48–68.

60. Malone, *Don't Get*, 101–4.

61. Eula and Vernon Durham interview with Jim Leloudis, November 29, 1978; Pete and Mabel Summers interview with Mary Murphy and Patty Dilley, July 25, 1979, SOHP. Of course, this theme comes through strongly in Hall et al., *Like a Family*.

62. Murphy Yomen Sigmon interview with Patty Dilley, July 27, 1979, SOHP; S. L. Hardy interview with Doug Sawyer, November 18, 1974, SamOHC; Des Ellis interview with Douglas Flamming, CrownOHP.

63. Latta interview, SOHP.

64. Josephine Glenn interview with Cliff Kuhn, June 27, 1977, SOHP.

65. Flake and Nellie Meyers interview with Patty Dilley, August 11, 1979, SOHP.

66. Carl and Mary Thompson interview with Jim Leloudis, July 19, 1979, SOHP; Walter Scott Workman, notes of interview with Patty Dilley, summer 1977, SOHP.

67. Ina Lee Wrenn interview with Allen Tullos, March 23, 1979, SOHP.

68. Lora and Edward Wright interview with Allen Tullos, June 7, 1979, SOHP. Part of Psalm 91 reads as follows:

> [9] If you say, "The Lord is my refuge,"
> and you make the Most High your dwelling,
> [10] no harm will overtake you,
> no disaster will come near your tent.
> [11] For he will command his angels concerning you
> to guard you in all your ways;
> [12] they will lift you up in their hands,
> so that you will not strike your foot against a stone.

69. Sibyl Queen interview with Douglas Flamming, June 26, 1985, CrownOHP; Edward H. Ratcliff interview with Richard C. Smoot, May 4, 1980, OHA.

70. Wilson quoted in Conway, *Rise Gonna Rise*, 153–54; Thomas Snipes notes of interview with Tony Mace, December 2, 1978; SOHP.

71. Hilliard interview; Rhoda Napier interview with Sandra Richter, August 15, 1972, AOHP; Christine Cochran interview with Jerry Tapley, May 24, 1979, SamOHC.

72. Louise Rigsbee Jones interview with Mary Frederickson, September 20, 1976, SOHP; Fred Fox interview with Jacqueline Hall, December 15, 1979, SOHP.

73. Everett Faye and Mary Elizabeth Padgett interview with Allen Tullos, May 28, 1980, SOHP; Johnnie Jones interview with Brett Glass, August 27, 1976, SOHP.

74. Virgil Ivan Prewett interview with Michael Brownfield, January 8, 1977, SamOHC.

75. Willie Mae Defore interview; and Thelma Parker interview with Flamming, June 11, 1985, CrownOHP.

76. Mack Fetrell Duncan interview with Allen Tullos, June 7, 1979, SOHP; George and Mamie Shue interview with James Leloudis, June 20, 1979, SOHP.

77. Ethel Faucette interview with Allen Tullos, November 16, 1978 and January 4, 1979, SOHP; George R. Elmore interview with Brent Glass, March 11, 1976, SOHP.

78. Lucille Hall interview with Douglas Flamming, June 22, 1985, CrownOHP; Musker Semple Moore interview with Allen Tullos, May 17, 1979, SOHP.

79. Johnson quoted in *Our Appalachia*, 285–87; Smith quoted in Conway, *Rise Gonna Rise*, 171.

80. Annie Mae Perkins notes of interview with Susan Sink, October 26, 1978, SOHP; John Bramblett interview; J. W. Crow interview with Flamming, July 1, 1985, CrownOHP.

81. Loyd Winn notes of interview with Lanier Rand, July 1977, SOHP; James Pharis interview with Cliff Kuhn, July 24, 1977, SOHP; Ernest Carico interview with Ray Ringley, December 6, 1973, AOHP.

82. Bramblett interview; Carico interview; Winn interview.

83. Pharis interview; Clifford Simmons, notes of interview with Patty Dilley, Summer 1977, SOHP; Claude C. Thomas interview with LuAnn Jones, April 18, 1980, SOHP.

84. Hoy Deal interview; Eula Durham interview; Ila Hendrix interview; Martha Atha interview.

85. The classic statement about the cultural captivity idea is found in Eighmy, *Churches*.

86. Philip J. Clowes to John Ramsay, February 23, 1956, box 1565, Ramsay Papers. For the efforts of segregationists to develop a "theology" for their beliefs, see Dailey, "Theology of Massive Resistance," 151–80.

87. Glenn interview; Eunice Austin interview with Jacquelyn Hall, July 2, 1980, SOHP.

88. Mary Robertson interview with Jacquelyn Hall, August 13, 1979, SOHP; Jefferson Robinette interview with Cliff Kuhn, July 1977, SOHP.

89. Eunice Austin interview with Jacquelyn Hall, July 2, 1980, SOHP; Pauline Griffiths interview with Allen Tullos, May 30, 1980, SOHP; Emma Whitesell interview with Cliff Kuhn, July 27, 1977, SOHP.

90. Geddes Dodson interview with Allen Tullos, May 26, 1980, SOHP; Bill and Jean Morris interview with Kimberly Hultin, April 23, 1998, OHA; Beatrice M. Adkins interview with Mary Kay Plovanich, June 7, 1999, OHA.

91. George and Tessie Dyer interview with Lu Ann Jones, March 5, 1980, SOHP.

92. See the excellent discussion of this in Hayes, "Recovering."

Chapter 4. Constructing a Region of Christian Free Enterprise

1. Oral memoirs of Roger Norman Conger, October 28, 1975–April 21, 1977, BUIOH. On the lynching, see Carrigan, *Making*, 108–9.

2. Oral memoirs of Harry Mayo Provence, August 22, 1975–July 10, 1984, BUIOH.

3. Conger memoirs.

4. Fones-Wolf and Fones-Wolf, "Christianity with Its Sleeves Rolled Up."

5. Schulman, *From Cotton Belt to Sun Belt*, 102–5. While the South did not benefit as much as the rest of the nation from war industries, they did help spawn the later economic diversification. See also Lewis, "World War II Manufacturing," 840.

6. Friedman, "Exploiting," 323–48.

7. George M. MacNabb, "The South Bets on Industry," *American Mercury*, January 1957, 14–20; Julius Hirsch, "America's 3rd Migration," *Nation's Business*, March 1953, 39, 84–85.

8. Kersten, *Labor's Home Front*, 19.

9. Zieger, *CIO*, 212–27.

10. Haberland, "Seeking the Lowest Level"; Schulman, *From Cotton Belt to Sunbelt*, 105. On the difficulties in organizing the textile industry, see Daniel, *Culture of Misfortune*, chapter 5.

11. "Industry's Big Gains in South: Firm Foothold for New Factories," *U.S. News & World Report*, July 5, 1946, 28–29; Carlton and Coclanis, *South*, 172; Schulman, *From Cotton Belt to Sun Belt*, 105; Carrier and Schriver, "Plant Location Studies," 136–40.

12. Board of Directors minutes, April 11, 1945 and January 28–29, 1946, SSICR, box 2.

13. Schulman, *From Cotton Belt to Sunbelt*, 78–79.

14. Kennedy, *Southern Exposure*, 251–53; Pierce, "Orval Faubus," 98–113; Kersten, *Labor's Home Front*, 57–66.

15. Marshall, *Labor in the South*, 241–45; Kennedy, *Southern Exposure*, 254–55.

16. O'Brien, *Color of the Law*, 230–32. The AFL's wartime racial policies made it much less a threat to southern racial norms. See Kersten, *Labor's Home Front*, 68–99.

17. Friedman, "Exploiting the North-South Differential," 329–36. See also, Cobb, *Selling of the South*, 35–63.

18. Fuller, *Naming the Antichrist*, 152–56; Martin, *With God*, 29–33 (the first Graham quote is on p. 29, the second on p. 33). Luff, *Commonsense Anticommunism*, chapter 10, highlights the AFL's role in furthering the link between Communism and the CIO in the popular mind.

19. *Plant Community Relations Program* (n.p., General Electric, 1952), 10.

20. Frank F. Gilmore, "Thinking Ahead," *Harvard Business Review*, March 1951, 140.

21. *Polk's Rome City Directory 1952*, ix, xv; *Baldwin's Rome, Georgia, City Directory 1940*, 12–13. Although separated by twelve years, the language used to entice employers is the same.

22. Rosell, *Surprising Work of God*, 97–98.

23. *Evangelicals Move Forward for Christ* (Indianapolis, 1950), p. 12, pamphlet in NAER, box 99; *UEA*, March 15, 1946, 12.

24. Harold G. Taylor to Brother Pastor, October 13, 1949, NAER, box 66B; National Association of Evangelicals to Rev. Dan Plies, May 31, 1946, NAER, box 66B; J. Elwin Wright to Harold G. Taylor, June 23, 1944, NAER, box 65; Dochuk, "Moving Mountains," 83.

25. Dochuk, "Moving Mountains," 82–85.

26. Ernest L. Chase, "Pray for the Businessmen–They Need It," *UEA*, January 15, 1948, 3–4; Dochuk, "Moving Mountains," 82; "Scriptural Proof for the Free Enterprise System," undated typescript, NAER, box 40.

27. Alex to Dear Stet, August 20, 1947, and Stetson Kennedy, "Preachers of Disunity," unpublished typescript, ca. 1947, both in Stetson Kennedy Papers, New York Public Library, microfilm, reel 2, "Johnston, Parson Jack, 1946–47 file."

28. Board of Directors Minutes, November 10–11, 1944, April 11, 1945, in SSICR, box 2; *Militant Truth*, special labor edition (no date, ca. 1946).

29. See, for example, Gentry, "Christ Is Out," 15–24; Griffith, *Crisis of American Labor*, 108–16.

30. Carpenter, *Revive Us Again*, 212–14, 144–52; Wuthnow, *Restructuring of American Religion*, 16, 67; Allitt, *Religion in America*, 31.

31. National Association of Evangelicals to the Lutheran Laymen's League, March 15, 1946; and Leslie R. Marston to Dear Brethren, October 23, 1945, both in NAER, box 66B.

32. *Militant Truth*, February 1945, July–August, 1950.

33. Hangen, *Redeeming the Dial*, 112–20.

34. *Brethren Missionary Herald*, February 5, 1944; *Church Press*, June 7, 1945; *UEA*, September 15, 1945, 7; "Big Churches Learn Radio 'Savvy' to Counter Revivalist Air Racket," *Newsweek*, January 22, 1945, 74.

35. *Decisions and Orders of the National Labor Relations Board*, vol. 24 (Washington, Government Printing Office, 1940), 17–20; Memo re conversation between Mr. Brown, Harold Smith and Preachers, December 12, 1940, Federal Communications Commission Records, RG 173, box 3364, docket 8489, National Archives, College Park, Md.

36. Smith, *Termites*; *Knoxville Journal*, April 15, 1946. The letters are part of the docket files for the case, contained in RG 173, boxes 3367 to 3369.

37. Dochuk, *From Bible Belt to Sunbelt*, 53–66; Walter G. Courtenay, *Building a Better America* (Nashville, 1946), and "Let the South Beware," press release 55, August 12, 1945, both in SSICR, box 5.

38. Carpenter, *Revive Us Again*, 161–74 (Torrey quote on p. 171); Miller, *Billy Graham*, 16.

39. Fones-Wolf and Fones-Wolf, "Christianity with Its Sleeves Rolled Up."

40. Beverly Smith, "God's Chief Engineer," *American Magazine*, June 1946, 100, 102; Rufus Jarman, "LeTourneau: America's Most Spectacular Maker of Earth-Moving Machines is 'In Partnership With God,'" *Life*, October 16, 1944, 50, 52; Lorimer, *God Runs My Business*, 88–91, 143; Amy Porter, "God's Partner," *Collier's*, December 25, 1943, 36, 75–76.

41. Rodney Cain Brown, "Industrial Chaplaincy in America–A Profile for the National Institute of Business and Industrial Chaplains, (unpublished report), May 5, 1981, file 2620-5-2:34, Records of the United Methodist Church General Board of Higher Education and Ministry, Methodist Archives, Drew University; Madison, N.J.; "A Picture Story on Industrial Chaplaincy," March 14, 1945, 163; "LeTourneau Ruled Against," *ZH*, June 20, 1945, 90; Hammond, "'God's Business Men,'" 46–47, 61–63.

42. Brown, "Industrial Chaplaincy in America"; Thomas B. Foster to Cameron P. Hall, June 27, 1946, box 2, folder 1, RG 301.6, BNP; Notes on Informal Conference on Industrial Chaplaincy, May 16, 1946, Cameron P. Hall to Dear Chaplain, August 27, 1946, FCCR, box 46; Industrial Chaplains: A Memorandum, n.d., Ramsay Papers, box 1572.

43. The FCC's James Myers contended that there were "possibilities for good work in Industrial Chaplaincy *under the right conditions*, but extreme danger of a lot of harm under the wrong conditions, which I fear are most likely to prevail if corporations take the initiative." Myers to Seward Hiltner, 4, October 1945, FCCR, box 65; Notes on Informal Conference on Industrial Chaplaincy;" Cameron P. Hall to Dear Chaplain, August 27, 1946; "Are Evangelicals Being Taken for a Ride? *CC*, May 16, 1945, 597.

44. *UEA*, June 1944, 3; *UEA*, March 1945, 1; *UEA*, November 1945, 6; "Evangelicals Convene," *CC*, May 16, 1945, 612; "Are Evangelicals Being Taken for a Ride, *CC*, May 16, 1945, 597; A. H. Armerding, "A Need and Its Remedy," *Industrial Chaplain*, 1945, in NAER, box 53. Also see Hammond, "God's Business Men," 247–62.

45. Response of Charlie Martin to NAE Industrial Chaplain Counselor Questionnaires for Survey Materials, December 2, 1957, NAER, box 53; Thielo, "Industrial Chaplain"; *Chicago Daily News*, April 5, 1954; John S. Parks, "Counselor Service Program Helps Workers Do Better Job," *Petroleum Refiner*, June 1954, in Charlie Martin, *Shirtsleeve Religion*, n.p.,

n.d. Central Bible College Library, Springfield, Mo.; *Tulsa Daily World*, August 22, 1952; Charlie Martin, "Industrial Chaplain-Counselor Program," n.d., Ramsay Papers, box 1572.

46. Response of Charlie Martin to NAE Industrial Chaplain Counselor Questionnaires for Survey Materials; Charlie Martin, "Industrial Chaplain-Counselor Program," n.d., Ramsay Papers, box 1572; *Wall Street Journal*, March 3, 1959; Charlie Martin, "Winning Souls in Industry, Augugust 8, 1957, *Missions At Home*, in Irene Joliff, compiler, *Shirtsleeve Religion*, n.p., n.d., Cordas C. Brunett Library, Springfield, Mo.; Smith, "Industrial Chaplain," 21.

47. Clarence Woodbury, "Religion in Industry," *Nation's Business*, June 1954, 30; *Wall Street Journal*, March 3, 1959; Thielo, "Industrial Chaplain"; Smith, "Industrial Chaplain"; Burke, "Consideration."

48. Heaton, "Christian Principles in Industrial Relations," *Baptist Record*, November 1, 1944, 6; *Dr. George D. Heaton II, November 8, 1908–July 4, 1996*, pamphlet in Heaton Papers, box 1. The inventory for the Heaton Papers at Auburn University lists scores of companies for which he offered consulting services between the 1940s and the 1980s.

49. *Address of Dr. George D. Heaton*, 4; Heaton, copy of a speech given to Burlington Mills Corporation, October 16, 1954, Heaton Papers, box 6.

50. For types of class theologies, including social harmony, see McCloud, *Divine Hierarchies*, 118–23.

51. Heaton to C. C. Hartwig, June 29, 1949, but see also the series of letters between Hartwig and Heaton in 1949, Heaton Papers, box 6.

52. T. N. Barbour to Mr. R. V. Green, October 15, 1952, Heaton Papers, box 8.

53. J. Elwin Wright, "Two Conflicting Ideologies," *UEA*, August 1, 1947, 12.

54. *History of American Methodism*, vol. 3. The quote comes from p. 404.

55. Manis, "City Mothers," 125–56; *Alabama Christian Advocate*, June 20, 1946, 2, and January 17, 1946, 14; *Wesleyan Christian Advocate*, July 20, 1945, 11, and August 9, 1946, 6.

56. *Alabama Christian Advocate*, June 6, 1946, 7; *Wesleyan Christian Advocate*, August 31, 1945, 1, 8, and July 27, 1945, 6; Jack R. McMichael, "The New Social Climate in the South," *SQB*, May 1945, 4, 15; *SQB*, October 1946, 99.

57. Dorothy Dennison to Dr. James A. Moss, July 12, 1946, in MFSAR, 2134-7-1:09; "For Laymen Only," *ZH*, May 8, 1946.

58. *Wesleyan Christian Advocate*, August, 19, 1948, 7, November 8, 1946, 2, and December 20, 1946, 2.

59. "Asks Webber Surrender Credentials," *ZH*, June 19, 1946, 588; "Labor Chaplain," *ZH*, July 24, 1946, 712; "An Important Committee," *ZH*, October 2, 1946, 949; "Chaplain to Labor Causes Dispute," *ZH*, September 3, 1947, 848.

60. Leiffer, "United Methodism," 503, 551.

61. Alvis, *Religion and Race*, 51–52. Glass, *Strangers in Zion*, 154–58.

62. Robert L. Vining, "The Federal Council: Foe of Capitalism," *SPJ*, August 1943, 5–7; Vining, "Is the Federal Council Evangelical?" *SPJ*, May 1945, 22–25; "Protestants–Catholics and Communism," *SPJ*, July 15, 1946, 3–4.

63. L. E. Faulkner, "The Federal Council of Churches of Christ in America: Let's Look at the Record," *SPJ*, April 15, 1947, 12–14; J. E. Flow, "The Federal Council and Race Segregation," *SPJ*, May 15, 1946, 9–10.

64. Mrs. Walter P. Sprunt to Mrs. Coffin, March 22, 1942; and E. K. Reagin (President, Bethel College) to Samuel McCrea Cavert, April 6, 1942, both in FCCR, box 15.

65. See, among others, Aubrey N. Brown to Dr. Sam Cavert, June 19, 1947; Cavert to Brown, June 24, 1947; T. B. Jackson to Cavert, August 1, 1947; Alfonso Johnson to Cavert,

June 24, 1947; George Crosby to Federal Council of Churches, August 31, 1947; and Mary Byrd to Cavert, March 25, 1947, all in FCCR, box 20.

66. *Minutes of the Eighty-Sixth General Assembly of the Presbyterian Church in the United States*, 34; *Minutes of the Eighty-Seventh . . .*, 91–92; Glass, *Strangers in Zion*, 159–66.

67. Henry H. Sweets to Samuel McCrea Cavert, July 31, 1947, FCCR, box 20.

68. *Annual of the Southern Baptist Convention Nineteen Hundred and Forty-Seven, Ninetieth Session*, 300; Cavalcanti, "God and Labor," 650–56.

69. Cavalcanti, "God and Labor in the South," 655–57; Rosenberg, *Southern Baptists*, 133–62.

70. *RH*, August 15, 1946, 11.

71. *RH*, February 8, 1945, February 15, 1945, February 22, 1945, March 8, 1945; Rosenberg, *Southern Baptists*, 161–65; *Baptist and Reflector* (Nashville, Tennessee), January 25, 1945.

72. E. P. Alldredge to Dr. E. D. Head, August 2, 1948, and J. Frank Norris to E. P. Alldredge, August 31, 1948, both in Southern Baptist Convention, Executive Committee Files, box 3, AR 627-1, SBLA; Parson Jack Johnston to J. Frank Norris, August 23, 1948, and Norris to Whom It May Concern, September 1, 1948, both in J. Frank Norris Papers, (microfilm) reel 13, Billy Graham Center, Wheaton College, Wheaton, Illinois; Glass, *Strangers in Zion*, 185–90.

73. Szpak, "Removing" 46–61; Wacker, *Heaven Below*, 194–95; Synan, *Holiness-Pentecostal Tradition*, 45–46.

74. Lucy R. Mason to Rev. Cameron Hall, August 30, 1946, ODR, reel 63.

75. *Herald of Holiness*, July 14, 1947, 2; February 4, 1946, 3–4; Wacker, *Heaven Below*, 216–23.

76. Wacker, *Heaven Below*, 194–95; "The Hidden Antichrist," *Pentecostal Evangel*, March 9, 1946, 5.

77. Wacker, *Heaven Below*, 253–61; "The Labor War," *Pentecostal Evangel*, January 19, 1946, 8; D. Shelby Corlett, "The Church and Labor," *Herald of Holiness*, August 26, 1946.

78. Harrell, "Introduction," 4. See also, Flynt, "One in the Spirit," 23–44.

Chapter 5. *The Bible Speaks to Labor*

1. "Biographical Sketch," in Burgess Papers, box 2; Burgess, *Fighting*, 55–71. For the story of the Highway 61 protest, see Gellman and Roll, "Owen Whitfield," 303–48.

2. "Fellowship of Southern Churchmen Newsletter," June 1945, 1–2, FSCR, box 1; Burgess, *Fighting*, 93.

3. David S. Burgess to Jim [Dombrowski] and Paul [Christopher], May 22, 1945, AFL-CIO Region 8 Records, box 1893, SLA-GSU; Burgess, *Fighting*, 93.

4. "Welcome Labor Unions!" *Christian Frontiers*, November 1946, 277–78; Danville Citizens' Committee scrapbook, Boyd Payton Papers, RBMSC-Duke.

5. David Burgess, "The Fellowship of Southern Churchmen: Its History and Promise," *Prophetic Religion* (Spring 1953): 3–11; Dunbar, *Against the Grain*, 59–61, 74–75; Martin, *Howard Kester*, 115–22.

6. Martin, *Howard Kester*, 60, and generally.

7. Martin, *Howard Kester*, 106–7. Gellman and Roll, *Gospel*, chap. 3, covers this internecine warfare between Socialists and Communists from Williams's perspective.

8. Burgess, "Fellowship," 6. See also, Martin, *Howard Kester*, chap. 6.

9. Kester quoted in Burgess, *Fighting*, 92.

10. B. A. Thompson, "Nelle Morton: Journeying Home," *CC*, August 26–September 2, 1987, 711–12; Nelle Morton interview with Dallas A. Blanchard, June 29, 1983, SOHP. See also Burgess, *Fighting*, 93–95.

11. Morton interview, SOHP; F.S.C. Members—Ministers," FSCR, box 1.

12. Burgess, untitled typescript, April 1942, Burgess Papers, box 6. For an assessment of Niebuhr's changing theology, see Hulsether, *Building*, 11–18.

13. Burgess, *Fighting*, 49–50; David S. Burgess, "Final Report: 'Working with Migrants' under the Direction of the Home Missions Council of North America," May 7, 1943, Burgess Papers, box 5; David S. Burgess, "The Gospel to the Poor," *CC*, October 20, 1943, p. 1197.

14. Burgess to Jim and Paul, May 22, 1945, AFL-CIO Region 8 Records, box 1893.

15. "Fellowship of Southern Churchmen Newsletter," June 1945, 1–3.

16. Burgess to Dear Comrades, March 18, 1946, Burgess Papers, box 3.

17. Burgess to Dear Pop, October 16, 1946, Burgess Papers, box 2.

18. Brownie Lee Jones to Nelle Morton, February 19, 1946; Nelle Morton to Jack R. McMichael, February 22, 1946; David S. Burgess to Dear Friend, February 27, 1946, all in FSCR, box 2. Also see David S. Burgess, *Trade Unions and Preachers* (n.p., Labor Commission of the Fellowship of Southern Churchmen, n.d.), in the Pamphlet Collection, Duke University Library.

19. Burgess and T. B. Cowan to My dear fellow minister, August 26, 1946, ODR, reel 29.

20. Adams, *James A. Dombrowski*, 40–43. Ward, a British immigrant, was a founder of the Methodist Federation for Social Action and the author of the *Social Creed of the Churches* (1908), which greatly influenced the Federal Council of Churches.

21. Franz Emil Daniel, "Labor Experience," typescript, ca. 1944, in Daniel Papers, box 6; Adams, *James A. Dombrowski*, 40–43, 94.

22. Franz Daniel to Jim Dombrowski, May 31, 1935; Daniel to Myles Horton, March 2, 1939; Daniel to Dear Skipper, August 2, 1940; Daniel to Rose Bush, August 4, 1941; Dombrowski to Daniel, June 9, 1941, all in Highlander Research and Education Center Papers, box 10, SHSW; Myles Horton to Daniel, May 4, 1942, box 5, Daniel Papers. See also, Adams, *James A. Dombrowski*, 117, 128.

23. Daniel, "Labor Experience;" Harry Ward to Daniel, April 3, 1943; Gladys Dickason to Sidney Hillman, March 24, 1943; Hillman to John L. Lewis, March 23, 1943; Jim Loeb to Daniel, March 28, 1943, Daniel Papers, box 5. For an account of the LaFollette episode, see *PM Magazine*, March 26, 1943.

24. "CIO Trouble-Shooter Steals Show with Revivalist's Zeal," unidentified clipping, Daniel Papers, box 6; Father J. A. Drolet to Daniel, March 27, 1943, Daniel Papers, box 5.

25. Nelle Morton to Daniel, November 23, 1946, ODR, reel 20; Scott Hoyman interview with Carolyn Ashbaugh and Dan McCurry, fall 1973, SOHP; Joe Pedigo interview with Bill Finger, April 2, 1975, SOHP.

26. Burgess, *Fighting*, 81; Daniel to Burgess, November 22, 1946, Burgess Papers, box 3; David Burgess interview with Jacquelyn Hall and Bill Finger, September 25, 1974, SOHP.

27. "The Fellowship of Southern Churchmen, 1947 accomplishments," ODR, reel 18. For a treatment of Koinonia Farm and the threats the community faced, see K'meyer, *Interracialism*.

28. O'Brien, *Color of the Law*, 1; Woods, *Black Struggle*, 26–27.

29. Dodge, *Southern Rebel*, 13–70.

30. Dodge, *Southern Rebel*, 70–93.

31. Dodge, *Southern Rebel*, 121–22, 139.

32. Dodge, *Southern Rebel*, 139–54.

33. This summary of Dombrowski's career comes from Adams, *James A. Dombrowski*, 5–131.

34. "Equal Justice in Columbia," *Southern Patriot*, February 1946, 7; "The Negro Veteran Comes Home," *Southern Patriot*, March 1946, 6; Adams, *James A. Dombrowski*, 158–62.

35. "The Truth about *Militant Truth*," *Southern Patriot*, May 1946, 3–6; "Your Stake in Labor's Organizing Drive," *Southern Patriot*, June 1946, 1–2.

36. *New York Times*, April 19, 1946; Lucy R. Mason to Clark H. Foreman, December 8, 1946, and Paul R. Christopher to Foreman, December 17, 1946, ODR, reel 44.

37. Archer Torrey to Nelle Morton, January 1, 1946, FSCR, box 2; Lorence, *Hard Journey*.

38. Gellman and Roll, *Gospel*, 18–31.

39. Gellman and Roll, *Gospel*, 41–54.

40. Gellman and Roll, *Gospel*, 113–50. For the wartime religious scene in Detroit, see Pehl, "Apostles of Fascism," 440–65.

41. Alva Taylor to Claude Williams, March 25, 1944, Williams Papers, box 3.

42. Williams to Rev. William Sullivan, February. 10, 1944, Williams Papers, box 3; Harry Koger to Williams, November 16, 1943, and January 10, 1944, Williams Papers, box 3; Harry Koger to Williams, January 7, 1945, Williams Papers, box 14.

43. "Get Your Robes Laundered," Bulletin of the People's Institute of Applied Religion, July 1946, Williams Papers, box 6; Williams to William F. Cochran, June 24, 1947, Williams Papers, box 7; Don West to Williams, November 21, 1947, Williams Papers, box 15.

44. Myles Horton interview with Dallas Blanchard, SOHP.

45. David Burgess to Nelle Morton, October 1, 1946, FSCR, box 5.

46. Liston Pope to Myles Horton, December 19, 1944, Williams Papers, box 4; Nelle Morton to Rev. Eugene Smathers, January 7, 1947, FSCR, box 6. For examples of Williams charging others with being pro-fascist, see Williams to Rev. William Wallace Sullivan, September 13, 1944, Williams Papers, box 4, in which he writes that John Ramsay of the Steelworkers "significantly symbolizes the profascist two-thirds of organized religion."

47. Horton interview, SOHP.

48. Dunbar, *Against the Grain*, 41–45.

49. Horton interview, SOHP; Horton quoted in Harvey, *Freedom's Coming*, 104.

50. Myles Horton to J.D., December 20, 1944, Highlander Research and Education Center Papers, box 10; Catherine Winston to Carey E. Haigler, July 9, 1946, Highlander Papers, box 14; Minutes of Meeting of Executive Council of Highlander Folk School, January 31, 1947, ODR, reel 64; Cotham, *Toil*, 208–16, 252–59.

51. Mason, *To Win These Rights*, 3–4.

52. Mason, *To Win These Rights*, 12–17. See also, Salmond, *Miss Lucy of the CIO*, 1–74.

53. Mason, *To Win These Rights*, 179–82.

54. Mason, *To Win These Rights*, 33–125; Lucy R. Mason to Molly Dewson, September 6, 1937, ODR, reel 62. Mason's papers, held at Duke University, were included in the Operation Dixie Records when they were microfilmed. However, much of her correspondence predates the Southern Organizing Campaign.

55. Lucy R. Mason to Rev. F. M. McConnell, March 10, 1938, ODR, reel 62.

56. Henry G. Hart to Miss Lucy, January 26, 1943; Lucy R. Mason to Henry G. Hart, January 29, 1943; George N. Mayhew to Lucy Mason, February 1, 1943; and Alfred D. Moore to Mason, February 22, 1943, ODR, reel 62. For more on the episode, see Salmon, *Miss Lucy*, 113–15.

57. For Memphis, see Mason, *To Win These Rights*, 104–14; Honey, *Southern Labor*, 165–68, 177–78. For her work with the Presbyterian Church in the United States, see Lucy R. Mason to Allan S. Haywood, October 19, 1943, ODR, reel 62. For her efforts with Pentecostal churches, see Lucy Mason to Rev. J. H. Walker, January 13, 1942; A. J. Tomlinson to Lucy R. Mason, January 15, 1942, ODR, reel 62; Lucy R. Mason to Rev. R. L. Decker, July 5, 1950, ODR, reel 64. For her more favorable attitude about local Pentecostal churches, Lucy Mason to Cameron Hall, August 30, 1946, ODR, reel 63.

58. Mason, *To Win These Rights*, 162; William H. Marmion to Lucy R. Mason, July 7, 1950, ODR, reel 64.

59. S. E. Howie to Mason, March 1, 1943, and September 1, 1943, ODR, reel 62; Mason to William E. Henderson, undated but circa 1947, ODR, reel 38.

60. Mason, *To Win These Rights*, 7–8; Brownie Lee Jones interview with Mary Frederickson, April 20, 1976, SOHP.

61. The Southern School for Workers was an outgrowth of the Progressive Era Southern Summer School for Women Workers, which had opened at Sweet Briar College in 1927. It was affiliated with similar summer schools for women in industry at Bryn Mawr, Wisconsin, and New York.

62. Jones interview, 38–45; Brownie Lee Jones to Mason, November 8, 1948; Mason to B. L., November 6, 1948; Jones to Mason, November 11, 1948, ODR, reel 63.

63. Mason, *To Win These Rights*, 11–13, 162–63; Jones interview, 48–50, 73.

64. Jones oral history interview, 28–30, 55–57.

65. Charles C. Webber, "How I Became a Chaplain to Organized Labor," *SQB*, December 1946, 128, 138; Mason, *To Win These Rights*, 182–83; "Labor Chaplains," *Business Week*, June 29, 1946, 102, 104.

66. Charles C. Webber, "Chaplain to Organized Labor," *Michigan Christian Advocate*, October 24, 1946.

67. Webber quoted in Rev. Edgar M. Wahlberg, "The Industrial Chaplaincy," February 1, 1954, typescript in United Auto Workers Education Department Records, box 1, ALUA-WSU.

68. *Baltimore Afro-American*, November 30, 1946.

69. Charles C. Webber, "Chaplain to Organized Labor," *ZH*, October 23, 1946, p. 1025.

70. *UEA*, August 1, 1946, 17. See also the article from the New Orleans *Christian Advocate*, July 11, 1946, included in *ZH*, July 24, 1946, 712.

71. Webber, "How I Became a Chaplain," 138.

72. Zieger, *CIO*, 229–41; Marshall, *Labor in the South*, 225–45. For the importance of court and government rulings in the transportation industry, see Arnesen, *Brotherhoods of Color*, 181–229.

73. Marshall, *Labor in the South*, 246, 267–68.

74. Zieger, *CIO*, 227–31. For the earlier efforts in textiles, see Irons, *Testing the New Deal*; and summaries of the 1937 campaign in Daniel, *Culture of Misfortune*, 73–82. For the chilling effect of earlier defeats, see the telling comments by Scott Hoyman interview with Bill Finger, July 16, 1974, SOHP.

75. Zieger, *CIO*, 230–31.

76. Frederickson, *Dixiecrat Revolt*, 39–47; Bailey quoted in Zieger, *CIO*, 230.

77. CIO Executive Board minutes, March 15–16, 1946, *Minutes of the Executive Board of the Congress of Industrial Organizations, 1935–1955, Microfilm edition* (Bethesda, Md.: University Publications of America, 1994), reel 9; Zieger, *CIO*, 231.

78. Griffith, *Crisis*, 22–24; *Gastonia (N.C.) Daily Gazette*, May 4, 1946.

79. Joe Pedigo interview with Bill Finger, April 2, 1975, SOHP.

80. Griffith, *Crisis*, 24–25.

81. Alva Taylor to Claude Williams, April 19, 1946, and Claude Williams to Edwin L. Clark, December 3, 1946, Williams Papers, box 6; Carey Haigler to Mary Lawrence, April 24, 1946, Highlander Records, box 14; Lorence, *Hard Journey*, 130; Adams, *James A. Dombrowski*, 166–67. This episode features prominently in the excellent description of "the closing circle of Democratic politics" in Sullivan, *Days of Hope*, 209–10.

82. Minutes of Meeting of Executive Council of Highlander, January 31, 1947; Harry Koger to Claude Williams, September 5, 1946, Williams Papers, box 6; David Burgess to Nelle and Scotty, May 13, 1946, FSCR, box 3.

83. Burgess to Nelle and Scotty, May 13, 1946, FSCR, box 3. Foreman is quoted in Egerton, *Speak Now*, 444.

84. "Initial Report on the Kannapolis Situation," July 9, 1946, cited in the chapter describing the failure in Kannapolis in Griffith, *Crisis of American Labor*, 46–61 (quote page 53). Historian Timothy Minchin notes that the material conditions of millworkers were never better in the late 1940s due to the Fair Labor Standards Act and wartime wage regulations. Southern workers made less than northern ones, but the differential had narrowed. See Minchin, *What Do We Need*, 48–68.

85. Mason, *To Win These Rights*, 27; Jerome Cooper oral history memoir, March 27, 1968, USWAOHP. For a sampling of the importance of religion in the thinking of Piedmont millworkers, see Fones-Wolf and Fones-Wolf, "No Common Creed," 111–36.

86. Griffith, *Crisis*, 109–11; Sloan, "Misguided Quest," 14–15.

87. Mason, *To Win These Rights*, 26; Salmond, *Miss Lucy*, 128; Griffith, *Crisis*, 109–11.

88. Memo on Thomasville, Ga., by Lucy R. Mason, April 8, 1947, Ramsay Papers, box 1563.

89. "From C. E. to Organized Labor: The Story of John G. Ramsay," *Christian Endeavor World*, July 1945, 5; John Ramsay, interview with Leslie S. Hough, May 17, 1976, Ohio Labor History Project, Ohio Historical Society, Columbus, Ohio; Fones-Wolf and Fones-Wolf, "Conversion at Bethlehem," 381–95.

90. Fones-Wolf and Fones-Wolf, "Conversion at Bethlehem," 383–89.

91. Clark, *Oxford Group*, 75–82; Grogan, *John Riffe*, 140; Fones-Wolf and Fones-Wolf, "Conversion at Bethlehem," 388; John Ramsay interview with Alice M. Hoffman, December 16, 1976, 26–29, USWAOHP.

92. Fones-Wolf and Fones-Wolf, "Conversion at Bethlehem," 391–95; Ramsay interview with Hough; Ramsay interview with Hoffman.

93. Ramsay interview with Hoffman, 31.

94. Ramsay interview with Hoffman, 28–29.

95. Lucy Mason to Nelle and Dave, July 16, 1946; and Press Release, August 2, 1946, both in FSCR, box 4.

96. Mason, *To Win These Rights*, 185–90; Kenneth L. Wilson, "Portrait of a Labor Leader," *Christian Herald*, September 1949, 17, 38–40.

97. John G. Ramsay, "How Can the Church Win the Laboring Man?" *Michigan Christian Advocate*, February 28, 1946, 16–17; John G. Ramsay, "Church and Labor—Workers Together," *Motive*, April 1946, 35; John G. Ramsay, "Labor as a Christian Vocation," *CC*, May 27, 1953, 624–26; John G. Ramsay, "How to Bridge the Gap Between Religion and Economic Life," *ZH*, November 14, 1945, 732–33, 740; John G. Ramsay, "Labor and Religion Together," *Adult Student*, September 1946, 3–8; John G. Ramsay, "The Reconciliation of

Religion and Labor," in Pope, *Labor's Relation*, 105–16. The quotes are from "Labor as a Christian Vocation," 626.

98. Transcript of an interview with John Ramsay, held in Berea, Kentucky, in the summer of 1982, original copy in the Presbyterian Historical Society, Philadelphia, Pa., p. 10.

99. Ramsay to Christopher, July 2, 1946, ODR, reel 38.

100. Sokol, *There Goes My Everything*.

101. Lippy, "Popular Religiosity," 41–42, 47. See also Lippy, *Being Religious*. Our thanks to our student, Joseph Super, for pointing us to these sources.

102. One of the best examples of this is Don West's work with Rev. Charlie T. Pratt's Church of God of the Union Assembly in Dalton, Georgia, in the 1950s, covered in Flamming, *Creating*, 289–306.

Chapter 6. Ministering in Communities of Struggle

1. Browing, *Linthead*, 11–22.

2. Griffith, *Crisis*, 106–22; Gentry, "Christ is Out," 15–24; Patton, "The CIO," 1, 4; Minchin, *Fighting*, 41. There are, of course, some historians who are more appreciative of the complexity of religion. See Gellman and Roll, *Gospel*, and Waldrep, *Southern Workers*, as examples.

3. David Burgess, "The Role of the Churches in Relation to the C.I.O. Southern Organizing Drive," undated typescript [12 pages], Ramsay Papers, box 1556. See also, Burgess, "Ministers against Organized Labor," typescript, April 24, 1950, Burgess Papers, box 1; and Burgess, *Fighting*, 76–78.

4. Gunn, *Spiritual Weapons*, 107–30.

5. Lloyd Gosset, cited in Griffith, *Crisis*, 116.

6. Lucy Randolph Mason to Dave S. Burgess, April 6, 1950, ODR, reel 6.

7. Burgess and Cowan to My dear fellow minister, August 26, 1946, FSCR, box 4.

8. *Fellowship of Southern Churchman Newsletter*, November 1946, 4, FSCR, box 5.

9. R. W. Childress reply, written on the Burgess and Cowan circular, undated, FSCR, box 4; C. E. Derby reply, written on the circular, undated, FSCR, box 4.

10. Unsigned reply, written on the circular, undated, FSCR, box 4; unsigned letter to Dear Sir, August 26, 1946, FSCR, box 4.

11. Roy D. Coulter to Fellowship of Southern Churchmen, November 1, 1946, box 5, FSC Papers; Gaston Boyle to David S. Burgess, September 10, 1946, FSCR, box 4.

12. "Religion and Labor Fellowship," undated typescript, ODR, reel 65.

13. Press release, written for *Steel Labor*, undated, Ramsay Papers, box 1560; "Report of the Committee on Religion and Labor to the Texas C.I.O. 1950 Convention," Ramsay Papers, box 1556.

14. "Report of John V. Riffe, Director C.I.O. Organizing Committee on the Activity of the Community Relations Department," undated, box 1556, Ramsay Papers. Also, see newspaper clippings in Ramsay Papers, box 1575. For the minimal presence of AFL officials at the meetings, see the minutes and lists of the Knoxville meeting, December 7, 1951, ODR, reel 43; the Columbia, South Carolina, meeting, Spring 1949, Ramsay Papers, box 1560; and Clifford Zirkel (Baton Rouge) to Willard Uphaus, February 16, 1951, Ramsay Papers, box 1564.

15. Willard Uphaus's National Religion and Labor Foundation had supported connections between churches and unions since its founding in 1932. A creation of the Federal Council

of Churches, the Foundation worked primarily in the North, but it had lent support to the Southern Tenant Farmers Union. In the 1950s, Uphaus was red-baited and served time in jail for refusing to disclose names to the House Un-American Activities Committee.

16. "Report of John V. Riffe," Ramsay Papers, box 1556.

17. Report by Ruth A. Gettinger on Gaston County, N.C., October 17, 1946, ODR, reel 3; *CIO News*, May 5, 1952. Also, see Paul W. Norris (Station Manager, WTIK) to Ruth Gettinger, September 30, 1947, ODR, reel 3.

18. David S. Burgess to Franz Daniel, June 12, 1948, ODR, reel 6; "Testimony of Lucy Randolph Mason . . . re: Intimidation of union representatives by the Anderson Citizens Committee," April 10, 1950, ODR, reel 65; Lloyd P. Vaughan to John V. Riffe, September 16, 1950, and Vaughan to Federal Communications Commission, March 7, 1951, ODR, reel 16. For an overview of organized labor's struggle for access to broadcasting, see Fones-Wolf, *Waves of Opposition*.

19. Radio Program in Rome [Georgia] by TWUA, April 14, 1946, ODR, reel 63; Address by John G. Ramsay . . . over Station WDAK, Columbus, Georgia, July 6, 1947, Ramsay Papers, box 1560.

20. Script of Textile Workers Union of America-CIO Organizing Committee, Station WDOD, Chattanooga, Tennessee, November 27, [1949], Ramsay Papers, box 1559.

21. Script of Textile Workers Union of America, CIO Organizing Committee, Station WHIN, Gallatin, Tennessee, October 2, 1949, Ramsay Papers, box 1568.

22. Radio script used in Worship service, University of Oklahoma, February 25, 1948, ODR, reel 64; Radio Broadcast over Station WSJS, Winston-Salem, [N.C.], May 23, 1949, Ramsay Papers, box 1560.

23. Ruth Gettinger to William Smith, July 23, 1946, Ramsay Papers, box 1566.

24. Lucy Mason memo on Cuthbert, Georgia, summer 1947, ODR, reel 64.

25. Morristown Memo by Lucy R. Mason, visit 5 days, September 19–24, 1948, ODR, reel 64.

26. Lucy Mason, Memo visit to Pell City, July 19–20, inclusive, 1948, ODR, reel 64. For Anniston and the Dwight Mills, see English, *Common Thread*, 153–76.

27. See the reports and memos cited above, in notes 22 to 25.

28. "Rock Hill Citizens Say CIO Has Helped the Community," typescript, ca. 1950, attached to Lucy R. Mason to Franz E. Daniel, May 17, 1950, ODR, reel 20.

29. Lucy R. Mason to Rev. R. H. Daniell, February 12, 1945, ODR, reel 63; Ruth Gettinger to John G. Ramsay, September 9, 1951, Ramsay Papers, box 1566.

30. This tone comes through the many pamphlets on the subject circulated by the Community Relations Department. See, for example, *Church Answers Labor's Critics: Religious Leaders Endorse Organized Labor Movement* (Atlanta: CIO Organizing Committee, n.d.); *The Church and the CIO Must Co-Operate: A Vital Message to Southern Ministers* (Atlanta: CIO Organizing Committee, n.d.); *The Church and the CIO Together: A Vital Message to Southern Ministers* (Atlanta: CIO Organizing Committee, n.d.); John G. Ramsay, *Bridging the Gap* (New York: Laymen's Movement for a Christian World Inc., n.d.).

31. Aubrey N. Brown to Dr. Sam Cavert, June 19, 1947; Cavert to Brown, June 24, 1947; T. B. Jackson to Cavert, August 1, 1947; Alfonso Johnson to Cavert, June 24, 1947; George Crosby to Federal Council of Churches, August 31, 1947; and Mary Byrd to Cavert, March 25, 1947, all in FCCR, box 20.

32. Wacker, *Heaven Below*, 194–95.

33. Eighmy, *Churches*, 94–95.

34. Oral Memoir of Acker C. Miller, August 5, 13, 1971, January 3, February 23, 1972, BUIOH; Oral Memoir of Warren Tyree Carr, April 18, 1985, BUIOH.

35. *Annuals of the Southern Baptist Convention* (Nashville: Executive Committee, Southern Baptist Convention, 1948), 336, 53. See also the excellent overview of Baptist thought on unions, Cavalcanti, "God and Labor," 639–60.

36. Thompson, *Changing South*, 122, 138–39.

37. Anderson, *Vision*, 228–29; Cavalcanti, "God and Labor," 655–56; Charles F. Leek, "Watching the World," *Alabama Baptist*, February 21, 1946, 4. See also Wills, "Southern Baptists and Labor," 142–43.

38. Waldrep, *Southern Workers*, 166.

39. *Alabama Christian Advocate*, August 28, 1947, 5.

40. *Wesleyan Christian Advocate*, October 25, 1946, 2; December 20, 1946, 2; March 28, 1947, 6; February 13, 1948, 2. See also, Fuller, *Naming the Antichrist*, 148–60; and Hankins, *American Evangelicals*, 90–95.

41. *SQB*, October 1946, 99; "What is Behind the CIO Purge?" *SQB*, June 1949, 108; Edgar M. Wahlberg to Bishop F. J. McConnell, May 8, 1950, McConnell Correspondence, MFSS; Walter George Muelder, "What about the Methodist Federation? Should It Be Abolished?" *ZH*, April 1950, 315–17, 332.

42. B. Locke Davis interview with Wayne Flynt, January 22 and 22, 1976, SamOHC.

43. Oral History Memoir of Dr. Roy C. McClunt, May 5, 1976, BUIOH.

44. Nixon, *Lower Piedmont Country*, 84, 92.

45. Ruth Gettinger to Lloyd Vaughan, February 20, 1951, ODR, reel 19; Samuel H. Hay to Lucy R. Mason, October 8, 1948, ODR, reel 63.

46. Charles R. Bell interview with Wayne Flynt, January 28, 1972, SamOHC.

47. Wilson Woodcock to John Ramsay, April 29, 1947, Ramsay Papers, box 1566; Ruth Gettinger report on work in Hickory, North Carolina, September 1953, Ramsay Papers, box 1560.

48. Vernon A. Crawford to Ramsay, February 26, 1948; and R. H. Kindschir to Ramsay, February 16, 1954, both in Ramsay Papers, box 1561.

49. John Ramsay to Paul Christopher, January 18, 1952, ODR, reel 43; Ruth Gettinger to Lloyd Vaughan, April 3, 1951, ODR, reel 19.

50. John McMullen to Lucy R. Mason, December 4, 1945, ODR, reel 63.

51. George Floyd Rogers to Mason, June 24, 1946; and Mason to Rogers, July 19, 1946, ODR, reel 63.

52. Emory Via to Ramsay, July 11, 1950, Ramsay Papers, box 1561.

53. "Federal Council of Churches Fostering the C.I.O.," *Orthodox Baptist Searchlight*, October 25, 1946, clipping in Ramsay Papers, box 1575.

54. David S. Burgess, "Mill Charity and Church Freedom," *Prophetic Religion*, Spring 1950, 8–10; David S. Burgess, "The Gospel and the Workers of the South," manuscript for *The Student World*, ca. 1950, Burgess Papers, box 1; "The Bible and the Labor Union," manuscript, ca. 1950, Burgess Papers, box 1.

55. G. H. Montgomery to Rev. Dave Burgess, July 22, 1947; and Burgess to Ramsay, August 7, 1947, Ramsay Papers, box 1568.

56. Rev. Walter Y. Cooley to George Baldanzi, undated, but ca. 1950, and John Ramsay to Rev. Walter Y. Cooley, February 14, 1950, ODR, reel 64.

57. "This You Should Read," mimeo of a letter from Rev. C. V. Martin to All Employees, Fiberglass Corporation, August 20, 1952, Ramsay Papers, box 1568.

58. Lucy Mason to Franz Daniel, September 14, 1946, ODR, reel 63.

59. Lucy Mason to Turner L. Smith, August 1, 1947, ODR, reel 63; David S. Burgess to Robert Cahoon, March 26, 1950, Ramsay Papers, box 1568. The Burgess letter included summaries of incidents he was collecting for his testimony to a Congressional committee investigating the role of the clergy in anti-union activities.

60. Burgess to Cahoon, March 26, 1950, Ramsay Papers, box 1568.

61. Burgess, "The Role of the Churches in Relation to the C.I.O. Southern Organizing Drive." For a copy of a similar flyer see, "To the Employees of Dacotah Cotton Mills, Inc.," January 17, 1949, Burgess Papers, box 5.

62. Franz Daniel to John Ramsay, March 30, 1950, ODR, reel 18.

63. Ruth Gettinger, Memo on Great Falls, S.C., April 1950, ODR, reel 19; Burgess to Cahoon, March 26, 1950.

64. David S. Burgess, "Place: A Georgia Town. Time: 1952," *CC*, August 27, 1952. Reprint issued by the CIO Organizing Committee, Atlanta, Ga.

65. Burgess, "Place: A Georgia Town."

66. Ministers and laymen in South Carolina favorable to labor, November 10, 1947, typed list with notations of Ruth Gettinger, ODR, reel 3.

67. Eighmy, *Churches*, 155–56.

68. Burgess, *Fighting*, 48–50.

69. Lucy Mason to Paul Christopher, January 24, 1947, ODR, reel 38; Mason to Rev. Lawrence E. Brooks, April 23, 1949, ODR, reel 63. For evidence of Church of God ministers hiding behind the outdated ban, see footnote 60, above. For the union activity of Pentecostal ministers in the coalfields, see Callahan, *Work and Faith*, and Bush, "Faith, Power, and Conflict."

70. Ruth Gettinger to William Smith, July 23, 1946, box 1566, Ramsay Papers; Radio Script, undated typescript (ca. 1952), Ramsay Papers, box 1560.

71. Charles R. Bell Jr. interview with Wayne Flynt, January 28, 1972, SamOHC; Lucy Mason to Rev. Robert Cook, August 3, 1946, ODR, reel 38; William Scarlett to Miss Mason, March 22, 1949, ODR, reel 63; Mason to Rev. William H. Marmion, January 13, 1949, and Marmion to Mason, July 7, 1950, ODR, reel 64; Committee for Alabama flyer, October 31, 1946, and Rosalie Oakes to Malcolm C. Dobbs, March 18, 1947, series 2, box 8, William H. Marmion Papers, Special Collections, Virginia Polytechnic Institution, Blacksburg, Virginia.

72. John Ramsay to John Riffe, July 25, 1951, Ramsay Papers, box 1562; Paul Christopher to Ramsay, September 2, 1952, Ramsay Papers, box 1568. This is similar to what Clifford Grammich found in sectarian Baptist churches. See Grammich, *Local Baptists*, 118–26.

73. Lucy Mason, Memo visit to Pell City, July 19–20, 1948, ODR, reel 64.

74. Don McKee, "Organizing Southern Textile Workers: Early Days with the CIO," typed manuscript, box 8, Don McKee Papers, SLA-GSU.

75. Brooks, *Defining the Peace*, 37–47, 110–11; Typescript of campaign speech by Joe Rabun, 1948, Mss 396, Textile Workers Union of America Records, box 479, SHSW; *The Nation*, January 10, 1948.

76. John Ramsay to Joe Pedigo, May 19, 1950; Ramsay to U. W. Malcolm, April 16, 1951; U. W. Malcolm to Ramsay, May 12, 1951; Arthur Hyde to Ramsay, October 2, 1951; and Ramsay to Hyde, October 4, 1951, all in Ramsay Papers, box 1563. For the background on Rome, see Brattain, *Politics of Whiteness*, 205–09.

77. Lucy Mason to William R. Henderson, no date, ca. 1943, ODR, reel 38; S. E. Howie to Lucy Randolph Mason, March 5, 1943, and Howie to Mason, September 1, 1943, ODR, reel

62; Metropolitan Inter-Faith Association, "Diversity and Unity," available at http://www.mifa.org/diversityandunity (accessed May 25, 2013); Booton Herndon to Franz Daniel, undated, ca. 1945, in Daniel Papers, box 5.

78. David S. Burgess to Rev. Sam Howie, June 9, 1950, ODR, reel 1; *The Voice* (Fayetteville, N.C.), April 29, 1948; "An Activist Ministry: The Sam Howie Years," at www.fpcor.org/historychurch.html#samhowie (accessed May 25, 2013). On the success of Operation Dixie in Oak Ridge, see Olwell, *At Work*, chapter 7.

79. Press release, Danville, Va., August 6, 1946, in Danville Citizens' Committee scrapbook, Boyd Payton Papers, RBMSC-Duke; *Danville Register*, July 20, 1946.

80. *Danville Register*, July 21, 1946; *Danville Bee*, July 31, 1946; *Industrial Leader*, August 23, 1946, in Danville Citizens' Community scrapbook.

81. Lucy Mason, Danville memo, March 27–29, 1947; Lewis Conn to A. L. Swim, April 11, 1947, both on ODR, reel 64.

82. Lewis Conn to John Ramsay, July 14, 1947; Mason to Conn, July 26, 1947, ODR, reel 63; *The Denisonian*, September 19, 1952.

83. Report by Lucy R. Mason of trip [to Danville] January 16⁻23, 1951; Mason to Harriet Fitzgerald, July 28, 1951; Mason to Dear Adelaide, August 9, 1951, ODR, reel 64.

84. This sketch of John B. Isom's life comes from his online memoir written in 1984. See John B. Isom, "As I Remember Me," at http://www.johnbisom.com (accessed April 8, 2013).

85. Isom, "The Uncle Bill Story" (see n84).

86. Isom, "The Most Effective Sermon I Ever Preached," no date (see n84).

87. *PM*, January 29, 1946, 19; John B. Isom, "State Convention Speech," at http://johnbisom.com/StateConvention.html (accessed April 8, 2013); *Spartanburg Herald*, February 18, 1947. For more on the context of Saxon Baptist Church, see Waldrep, *Southern Workers*, 119, 122, 175.

88. John B. Isom, "Labor and the Church," speech given at a union meeting in 1946 (see n84).

89. John B. Isom to J. B. Weatherspoon, April 28, 1947, ODR, reel 20; John G. Ramsay to Isom, May 21, 1947, and Isom to Ramsay, May 23, 1947, ODR, reel 21.

90. Isom, "The Saxon Baptist Church, Part 5" (see n84); Isom to Ramsay, July 3, 1951, Ramsay Papers, box 1568.

Chapter 7. Red Scares and Black Scares

1. Memo about Klan Public Meeting, Knoxville, Tennessee, May 18, 1946 (nine-page typescript), Stetson Kennedy Papers, reel 1, New York Public Library, New York, N.Y.

2. See the letters, which are part of the docket files contained in Federal Communications Commission Records, RG 173, boxes 3367 to 3369, National Archives, College Park, Md.

3. Among the strongest arguments made along these lines can be found in Honey, "Operation Dixie," 216–44; Korstad and Lichtenstein, "Opportunities Found and Lost," 786–811; Goldfield, *Color of Politics*, 240–49; Karl Korstad, "Black and White Together," 69–94. A more recent overview is in Minchin, *Fighting*, 38–62.

4. Charles M. Jones, interview with Joseph A. Herzenberg, November 8, 1976, SOHP; Callahan, *Work and Faith*, 187; Flamming, *Creating*, 296–99.

5. Sidney Hillman to John L. Lewis, March 23, 1943, Daniel Papers, box 5.

6. Mason, "CIO and the Negro," 522–31. Statistics are from Zieger, *For Jobs*, 123–25.

7. Sullivan, *Days of Hope*, 206–10; Jones, *Tribe*, 161–67.

8. Chamberlain, *Victory at Home*, 182–86.

9. *Baltimore Afro-American*, July 28, 1945.

10. Jones, "'Simple Truths,'" 250–51.

11. Sullivan, *Days of Hope*, 202–10. The quote from Bittner, so frequently cited, is from *New York Times*, April 19, 1946.

12. Harry Keelan, "Voice in the Wilderness," *Afro-American*, February 16, 1946; Luther P. Jackson, "The Cracking of the Solid South," *Norfolk [Va.] New Journal and Guide*, April 6, 1946; *Afro-American*, April 20, 1946.

13. "Klan Faces Stiffer Worker Opposition," *Atlanta Daily World*, August 15, 1946; "Fiery KKK Crosses Warn South of New Terror," *Chicago Defender*, April 6, 1946; "KKK Battles on Operation Dixie," *New York Amsterdam News*, June 22, 1946; "CIO Races against Forces of Hate to Win Dixie Labor," *Chicago Defender*, August 3, 1946; "Negro, White Workers Join Fight against Klan," *Philadelphia Tribune*, August 20, 1946.

14. William A. Fowlkes, "Labor Saviour," *Atlanta Daily World*, April 27, 1947; Earl Conrad, "Equal Wage Policies Mark 'Operation Dixie,'" *Chicago Defender*, September 14, 1946.

15. "Organization of South Will Hasten Progress," *Chicago Defender*, June 1, 1946.

16. George McCray, "Rights Surrender," *Atlanta Daily World*, February 16, 1947; "The CIO and Southern Prejudice," *Chicago Defender*, June 29, 1946.

17. M. Moran Weston, "Labor Forum," *New York Amsterdam News*, September 14, 1946; George F. McCray, "AFL and CIO Shun Race Issue in South," *Philadelphia Tribune*, May 25, 1946.

18. *Norfolk [Va.] New Journal and Guide*, October 19, 1946; *Pittsburgh Courier*, June 22, 1946; *Atlanta Daily World*, July 3, 1948.

19. P. L. Prattis, "Labor Everywhere," *Pittsburgh Courier*, May 18, 1946; *Pittsburgh Courier*, February 1, 1947; O. E. McKaine, "Palmetto State," *Norfolk [Va.] New Journal and Guide*, July 20, 1946.

20. "Labor Chaplains," *Business Week*, June 29, 1946, 102, 106; Charles C. Webber, "Chaplain to Organized Labor," *Michigan Christian Advocate*, October 24, 1946.

21. Caplan, *Farther Along*, 29–36, 70–71, 90–91.

22. "Labor Pastor in Va. Aids Minority, Defies Bishop," *Afro-American*, November 30, 1946; "Text of Press Statement Issued on Virginia State CIO-PAC Meet," *Norfolk [Va.] New Journal and Guide*, September 20, 1947; "Virginia CIO Convention to Hear Ferdinand Smith," *Norfolk [Va.] New Journal and Guide*, April 26, 1947.

23. Durr, *Freedom Writer*, 52–53. For a survey of white southerners who worked in the civil rights movement, see Chappell, *Inside Agitators*.

24. Charles C. Webber to Officers of Local 511, TWUA, February 7, 1950, ODR, reel 74; "Richmond Delegation to Join March on Washington," *Norfolk [Va.] New Journal and Guide*, January 14, 1950; Charles C. Webber, "The Fight in Virginia for First-Class Citizenship," *SQB*, May 1949, 83. Also, see the reports of Webber as president of the Virginia CIO and director of the Virginia CIO-PAC in box 2 of the Philip Weightman Papers, Robert F. Wagner Labor Archives, Tamiment Institute, New York University, New York, N.Y.

25. See, for example, "150 Religious Leaders Play Important Role at NAACP Confab," *Philadelphia Tribune*, July 22, 1958; "Picket Set for Another Round against Y Policy," *Afro-American*, March 28, 1959.

26. Honey, *Southern Labor*, 161–69; Salmond, *Miss Lucy*.

27. "Southern Regional Council Is Launched," *Norfolk [Va.] New Journal and Guide*, February 26, 1944; "South Represents Nation's Greatest Home Markets," *Atlanta Daily*

World, July 24, 1945; "Fisher Cites Evils in Georgia Politics," *Atlanta Daily World*, January 17, 1946; "Ga. Rights Foe Wins Fight at Labor Parley in Capital," *Afro-American*, December 11, 1948.

28. See, among many, Mason to Turner L. Smith, August 1, 1947; Mason to Smith, October 8, 1947; Mason to Smith, November 27, 1947; Mason to Abbot Rosen, May 3, 1948, all on ODR, reel 63.

29. Mason to Rev. E. T. Mollegen, May 11, 1945; and Mason to Kent Ruth, October 19, 1948, ODR, reel 63; Mason, *To Win These Rights*, 77–78.

30. John Ramsay interview with Alice M. Hoffman, December 16, 1976, USWAOHP.

31. "Racism Serves Reaction," *Pittsburgh Courier*, October 25, 1947; "Anti-Union Weekly Outlawed by NLRB," *New York Times*, March 27, 1949.

32. R. W. Starnes to John Ramsay, November 7, 1947, Ramsay Papers, box 1565; Ray Warwick to Paul [Christopher?], April 16, 1952, ODR, reel 3; Lucy Mason to Carey Haigler, January 26, 1953, and February 3, 1953, ODR, reel 64.

33. Minutes of the Tennessee CIO staff meeting, April 30, 1951, and June 11, 1952, box 1907, AFL-CIO Region 8 Records, SLA-GSU.

34. Cooper's memories are included in Huntley and Montgomery, *Black Workers' Struggle*, 141–42; Mason to Rev. William H. Marmion, April 24, 1950, ODR, reel 64; and the files dealing with Hemlock Haven in the Marmion Papers, box 39. Marmion, it should be noted, went on to become a major force for black equality as the Episcopal Church bishop of southwestern Virginia in the late 1950s and 1960s. For a letter discussing the influence of Ramsay's interracial insistence in Louisville (Ky.), Birmingham, Gainesville (Fla.), Atlanta, Chattanooga (Tenn.), and Knoxville (Tenn.), see Ramsay to Vincent Sweeney, May 6, 1946, Ramsay Papers, box 1558.

35. "Religion-Labor" press release for *Steel Labor*, undated, Ramsay Papers, box 1560; Ramsay interview with Hoffman; Huntley and Montgomery, *Black Workers' Struggle*, 141. See also, Sloan, "Misguided Quest," 63–78.

36. Pat Knight to Franz Daniel, October 14, 1947, ODR, reel 20; Franz Daniel to David S. Burgess, August 28, 1948, ODR, reel 16.

37. Daniel to John Brownlee, August 18, 1950, ODR, reel 1; Nelle Morton to Daniel, February 8, 1949, and Daniel to Morton, Feburary 16, 1949, ODR, reel 18.

38. Burgess to Wm. Bradford, March 21, 1948, ODR, reel 16.

39. Burgess, *Fighting*, 86–88;

40. Burgess to Ted Tilford, July 30, 1951, Burgess Papers, box 3.

41. Burgess quoted in Brattain, *Politics of Whiteness*, 224.

42. Ramsay to Rev. Paul S. James, chair of Billy Graham Crusade in Atlanta, October 19, 1950; James to Ramsay, October 20, 1950, Ramsay Papers, box 1559; Ramsay interview with Hoffman.

43. Mason to Ramsay, November 1, 1950, and Mason to Paul E. Harding, November 1, 1950, Ramsay Papers, box 1559.

44. Ramsay to Dr. Billy Graham, December 8, 1950, and Mason to Bishop Arthur Moore, February 14, 1951, Ramsay Papers, box 1559; Ramsay interview with Hoffman; Miller, *Billy Graham*, 28. The issue of *Militant Truth* that carried the picture and sermon of Graham was September 1950.

45. Woods, *Black Struggle, Red Scare*, 17–25. Among the best books emphasizing the importance of Communists to these episodes of southern uprising are Honey, *Southern Labor*; Korstad, *Civil Rights Unionism*; Kelley, *Hammer and Hoe*; Gellman and Roll, *Gospel*; Lorence, *Hard Journey*; and Gilmore, *Defying Dixie*.

46. On the long buildup of a red scare in the labor movement, see the excellent book by Luff, *Commonsense Anticommunism.*

47. Zieger, *CIO,* 226; Goldfield, *Color of Politics,* 245. For a different assessment of Mine, Mill and FTA, see Stein, "Ins and Outs," 59–62.

48. See Fones-Wolf and Fones-Wolf, "Sanctifying," 23–30; Fones-Wolf and Fones-Wolf, "Conversion at Bethlehem," 381–95.

49. Such an argument is made most forcefully in Goldfield, *Color of Politics,* 249–60, and in Honey, "Operation Dixie," 235–39, but it is also implied in Korstad and Lichtenstein, "Opportunities Found and Lost," 801–6. Honey writes of the reticent CIO strategy: "Yet there is an important difference between fighting the good fight and losing, and fighting a bad fight and losing" (238).

50. Franz Daniel to Rose Bush, August 4, 1941, box 6, Daniel Papers; "Statement by Charles Webber" in response to HUAC charges, undated, in UAW Public Relations Department Records, box 14, ALUA-WSU.

51. Daniel to Bruce Bliven, September 15, 1942, Daniel Papers, box 6.

52. Ramsay interview with Hoffman.

53. Chester Davis to Gordon Gray, July 16, 1946, J. Sanford Martin Papers, box 10, RBMSC-Duke; and Constitutional Democrats to Josephus Daniels, undated, Martin Papers box 9.

54. Green quote from Korstad, *Civil Rights Unionism,* 292. See also, Honey, "Operation Dixie," 223; Stein, "Ins and Outs," 61.

55. Mason to William G. Watkins, November 5, 1946, ODR, reel 63; and Mason to Hon. Peyton Ford, April 18, 1951, ODR, reel 64 (italics in the original).

56. Brownie Lee Jones interview with Mary Frederickson, April 20, 1976, SOHP; Brownie [Jones] to Dear Lucy, November 2, 1948; Mason to B. L. [Jones], November 6, 1948; Boyd Payton to Mason, December 21, 1948, ODR, reel 63.

57. Korstad, *Civil Rights Unionism,* 289–300.

58. Jack Frye interview with Karl Korstad, October 16, 1981, SOHP; Junius Scales interview with Robert Korstad, May 2, 1987, SOHP.

59. Luther Ranson interview with Robert Korstad, July 17, 1990, SOHP. On the objections to black equality, see Blanche Fishel interview with Robert Korstad, no date, SOHP.

60. Korstad, *Civil Rights Unionism,* 301–33; Nelle Morton to David Burgess, June 1947; Morton to C. E. Matheson, July 3, 1947, FSCR, box 8.

61. Daniel to Nelle Morton, June 5, 1947, ODR, reel 18.

62. Burgess to Nelle Morton, June 5, 1947, and Morton to Burgess, May 30, 1947, FSCR, box 8.

63. Ruth Gettinger to Ramsay, July 13, 1949; and George Baldanzi to Organizers, March 27, 1950, Ramsay Papers, box 1566; Frye interview; Korstad and Lichtenstein, "Opportunities Found," 786–811.

64. Frye interview; Korstad and Lichtenstein, "Opportunities Found," 801–6.

65. Gilpin, "Left by Themselves," 420; Braden, *Wall Between,* 32–33. See also, Adams, *Way Up North,* 109–10.

66. Gilpin, "Left by Themselves," 508–35 (Braden quote from 534); Adams, *Way Up North,* 109–12.

67. Ramsay to "The Clergymen of Louisville and Vicinity," December 16, 1949, Ramsay Papers, box 1564.

68. Gilpin, "Left by Themselves," 536–39; Hugh A. Brimm to John Ramsay, January 16, 1950, Ramsay Papers, box 1564; Wills, "Southern Baptists and Labor," 170.

69. Tilford E. Dudley to Charles Webber, May 3, 1951, with clipping attached, CIO Political Action Committee Records, box 10, ALUA-WSU; Burgess, *Fighting*, 82; Franz Daniel to Van A. Bittner, January 21, 1948, ODR, reel 16; Lucy Mason to Eleanor Roosevelt, August 19, 1950, and Mason to Bruce Hunt, March 5, 1950, ODR, reel 64.

70. John Ramsay, interview with Leslie S. Hough, May 18, 1976, Ohio Labor History Project, Ohio Historical Society, Columbus, Ohio.

71. Nelson, *Divided We Stand*, 201.

72. Nelson, *Divided We Stand*, 212–15; Ramsay interview with Hoffman.

73. For competing versions of this struggle, see Nelson, *Divided We Stand*, 213–15; Goldfield, *Color of Politics*, 223–24; and Stein, "Ins and Outs," 59–61.

74. Huntley and Montgomery, 141–2; Salmond, *Miss Lucy*, 133; Ramsay to George Baldanzi, May 1, 1950, box 1556, and "Radio Script #4, Station WAPI, Birmingham, Ala., Ramsay Papers, box 1562.

75. Ramsay interview with Hoffman; Herbert Hill memo to Walter White, reporting on a conference in Birmingham, May 8—17, 1953, USWA Civil Rights Department Records, box 5, HCLA-PSU.

76. R. E. Farr to Philip Murray, May 19, 1950; and E. T. Earp et al., to Murray, June 13, 1950, USWA Civil Rights Department Records, box 3.

77. Nelson, *Divided We Stand*, 214–15.

78. Herbert Hill memo to Walter White; Lucy Mason to Carey Haigler, January 26, 1953 and February 3, 1953, ODR, reel 64.

79. Ramsay interview with Hoffman; Cooper interview reproduced in Huntley and Montgomery, 145. The oral histories reproduced in that book offer no easy answer about the effect of the Steelworkers' struggle against Communism or for black civil rights.

80. See the excellent article by Krochmal, "An Unmistakably Working-Class Vision," 923–60.

81. For Mitch, see Huntley and, 9; and Jack McMichael, "The New Social Climate in the South," *SQB*, May 1945, 4–5. For Crawford, see Nelson, *Divided We Stand*, 215–16.

82. The phrase comes from the wildly popular radio evangelist, J. Harold Smith. See his pamphlet, *Termites*.

83. Lucy Mason to Nelle Morton, September 21, 1946, FSCR, box 4.

84. Jones, *Tribe*, 159–80; William Smith to Lorne H. Nelles, June 23, 1949, ODR, reel 1; Hudson to Carl Winn, May 28, 1952, box 192, International Woodworkers of America Records, SLA-GSU.

85. Nelson, "Class and Race," 19–45; Naison, "Black Agrarian Radicalism," 47–65; Gellman and Roll, *Gospel*, 123–24; Korstad, *Civil Rights Unionism*, 402–12; Honey, *Southern Labor*, 241, 248–51.

86. Kenneth R. Williams to William Smith, May 18, 1949, ODR, reel 3.

87. Ramsay interview with Hoffman.

Conclusion

1. E. S. Elliott, Walter R. Kelly, Waldo Mullen, J. W. Kiser, Leroy Trexler, Henry Liles, and George L. Riddle to Dear Friends, February 7, 1953, in TWUA records, mss. 396, box 38, SHSW.

2. Marshall, *Labor in the South*, 268, 298.

3. Emil Rieve to Elliott, Kelly, Mullen, Kiser, Trexler, Liles, and Riddle, February 19, 1953, TWUA records, mss. 396, box 38.

4. TWUA Southern Staff meeting minutes, March 3, 1953, TWUA Records, mss. 396, box 610.

5. Marshall, *Labor in the South*, 299.

6. See letters from Rev. Robert Carl Griffith (Methodist), March 7, 1953, from C. Franklin Koch (Lutheran), February 24, 1953, and G. Bromley Oxnam, May 23, 1953, in TWUA records, mss. 396, box 38.

7. Rev. Vernon S. Broyles Jr. to Rieve, March 4, 1953; and Homer A. Tomlinson to Rieve, February 21, 1953, in TWUA records, mss. 396, box 38.

8. Browning, *Linthead*, 22.

9. Key, *Southern Politics*, 315.

10. Fones-Wolf and Fones-Wolf, "Religion, Human Relations, and Union Avoidance," 154–85.

11. For the pervasive anti-unionism in American culture, see Richards, *Union-Free America*, 38–88. For the effect of previous defeats, see Fones-Wolf and Fones-Wolf, "No Common Creed," 126.

12. Griffith, *Crisis of American Labor*, 22–26, 161–62; Minchin, *What Do We Need*, 154–76; Frederickson, *Looking South*, 152.

13. See Schatz, *Electrical Workers*, 233–36; Cowie, *Capital Moves*, 73–99.

14. Minchin, *What Do We Need*, 69–98.

15. For Birmingham, see Huntley and Montgomery, *Black Workers*. For the difficulty that labor had in convincing white workers to follow official CIO policies on desegregation, see Draper, *Conflict of Interests*. For the prosegregationist character of southern white churches in the absence of a counternarrative, see Dupont, *Mississippi Praying*.

16. Hoy Deal interview with Pat Dilley, June 17, 1974, SOHP.

17. Shafer and Johnston, *End of Southern Exceptionalism*, 22–50; Lassiter, *Silent Majority*; Kruse, *White Flight*. A somewhat different opinion is available in Elisabeth Jacobs, "Understanding America's White Working Class: Their Politics, Voting Habits, and Policy Priorities," available at: http://www.brookings.edu/~/media/research/files/papers/2012/11/05%20white%20working%20class%20jacobs/jacobs%20wwc%20full%20text.pdf (accessed February 22, 2014).

18. Flynt, "Religion for the Blues," 11–12.

BIBLIOGRAPHY

Primary Sources

MANUSCRIPT COLLECTIONS

Archives of Labor and Urban Affairs, Walter Reuther Library, Wayne State University, Detroit, Michigan
    Claude C. Williams Papers
    CIO Executive Board Minutes (microfilm edition)
    David S. Burgess Papers
    Franz Daniel Papers
    United Auto Workers Education Department Records
    United Auto Workers Public Relations Department Records
Auburn University Library Special Collections, Auburn, Alabama
    George D. Heaton Papers
Billy Graham Center, Wheaton College, Wheaton, Illinois
    J. Frank Norris Papers (microfilm edition)
    National Association of Evangelicals Records
Disciples of Christ Historical Society, Nashville, Tennessee
    Alva W. Taylor Papers
Historical Collections and Labor Archives, Pattee Library, Pennsylvania State University, University Park, Pennsylvania
    United Steelworkers of America Records
    United Steelworkers of America Civil Rights Department Records
    William Mitch Papers
National Archives, College Park Maryland
    RG 173, Federal Communications Commission Records
New York Public Library, New York, New York
    Stetson Kennedy Papers (microfilm edition)
Presbyterian Historical Society, Philadelphia, Pennsylvania
    Federal Council of Churches of Christ in America Records
    National Council of Churches of Christ in America Records
Rare Book, Manuscript, and Special Collections Library, Duke University, Durham, North Carolina
    Boyd E. Payton Papers
    J. Sanford Martin Papers
    North Carolina Council of Churches Records
    Operation Dixie Records (microfilm edition, including Lucy Randolph Mason Papers)

Robert F. Wagner Labor Archives, Tamiment Library, New York University, New York, New York
  Philip Weightman Papers
Southern Baptist Historical Library and Archives, Nashville, Tennessee
  Southern Baptist Convention, Executive Committee Files
Southern Historical Collection, Wilson Library, University of North Carolina, Chapel Hill, North Carolina
  Fellowship of Southern Churchmen Records
Southern Labor Archives, Georgia State University Library, Atlanta, Georgia
  AFL-CIO Region 8 Records
  Don McKee Papers
  International Woodworkers of America Records
  John G. Ramsay Papers
Special Collections, Virginia Polytechnic Institution, Blacksburg, Virginia
  William H. Marmion Papers
State Historical Society of Wisconsin, Madison, Wisconsin
  Highlander Research and Education Center Papers
  Textile Workers Union of America Records
Tennessee State Archives, Nashville, Tennessee
  Southern States Industrial Council Records
United Methodist Archives, Drew University, Madison, New Jersey
  Methodist Federation for Social Action Records
  Methodist Federation for Social Service Records, Charles Webber Correspondence
  United Methodist Church General Board of Higher Education and Ministry Records

ORAL HISTORY COLLECTIONS

Appalachian Oral History Project, Microfiche Collection
Crown Company Oral History Collection, Special Collections, Virginia Polytechnic Institute and State University, Blacksburg, Virginia
Institute for Oral History, Baylor University, Waco, Texas
Labor Oral History Collection, Historical Collections and Labor Archives, The Pennsylvania State University, State College, Pennsylvania
Oral History of Appalachia, Marshall University, Huntington, West Virginia
Samford University Oral History Collection, Samford University, Birmingham, Alabama
Southern Oral History Program, Southern Historical Collections, University of North Carolina, Chapel Hill, North Carolina
Voices of Labor Oral History Project, Southern Labor Archives, Atlanta, Georgia

NEWSPAPERS, PERIODICALS, AND SERIALS

Afro-American (Baltimore, Maryland)
Alabama Baptist (Baptist)
Alabama Christian Advocate (Methodist)
Annuals of the Southern Baptist Convention
Atlanta Daily World
Baptist and Reflector (Baptist)
Biblical Recorder (Baptist)
Chicago Defender

Christian Century
Christian Evangelist (Disciples of Christ)
Christian Frontiers (Baptist)
Christian Herald
Christianity and Crisis
Fellowship of Southern Churchmen Newsletter
Herald of Holiness (Church of the Nazarene)
Militant Truth
Minutes of the General Assembly of the Presbyterian Church in the United States
Motive (Methodist)
New Journal and Guide (Norfolk, Virginia)
Pentecostal Evangel (Assembly of God)
Philadelphia Tribune
Pittsburgh Courier
Prophetic Religion
Religion in Life
Religious Herald (Baptist)
Social Action Magazine (Congregational Church)
Social Questions Bulletin (Methodist)
Southern Patriot
Southern Presbyterian Journal
Sword of the Lord (Independent)
The Trumpet (Columbus, Georgia)
United Evangelical Advocate
Wall Street Journal
Wesleyan Christian Advocate (Methodist)
Zion's Herald (Methodist)

Secondary Sources

BOOKS

Adams, Frank T. *James A. Dombrowski: American Heretic, 1897–1983*. Knoxville: University of Tennessee Press, 1992.

Adams, Luther. *Way Up North in Louisville: African American Migration and the Urban South, 1930–1970*. Chapel Hill: University of North Carolina Press, 2010.

Allitt, Patrick. *Religion in America Since 1945: A History*. New York: Columbia University Press, 2003.

Alvis, Joel L., Jr. *Religion and Race: Southern Presbyterians, 1946–1983*. Tuscaloosa: University of Alabama Press, 1994.

Anderson, Robert Mapes. *Vision of the Disinherited: The Making of American Pentecostalism*. New York: Oxford University Press, 1979.

Arnesen, Eric, ed. *The Black Worker: A Reader*. Urbana: University of Illinois Press, 2007.
———. *Brotherhoods of Color: Black Railroad Workers and the Struggle for Equality*. Cambridge, Mass.: Harvard University Press, 2001.

Bageant, Joe. *Deer Hunting with Jesus: Dispatches from America's Class War*. New York: Three Rivers, 2007.

Balmer, Randall. *The Making of Evangelicalism: From Revivalism to Politics and Beyond.* Waco, Tex.: Baylor University Press, 2010.

Boles, John B. *The South through Time: A History of an American Region.* Englewood Cliffs, N.J.: Prentice-Hall, 1995.

Botsch, Robert Emil. *We Shall Not Overcome: Populism and Southern Blue-Collar Workers.* Chapel Hill: University of North Carolina Press, 1980.

Braden, Anne. *The Wall Between.* New York: Monthly Review, 1958.

Brattain, Michelle. *The Politics of Whiteness: Race, Workers, and Culture in the Modern South.* Princeton, N.J.: Princeton University Press, 2001.

Brooks, Jennifer. *Defining the Peace: World War II Veterans, Race, and the Remaking of Southern Political Tradition.* Chapel Hill: University of North Carolina Press, 2004.

Browing, Wilt. *Come Quittin' Time.* With Marlene Burke and Doris Browning. Kernersville, N.C.: Alabaster, 2011.

———. *Linthead: Growing up in a Carolina Cotton Mill Village.* Asheboro, N.C.: Down Home, 1990.

Bucke, Emory Stevens, ed. *The History of American Methodism in Three Volumes.* New York: Abingdon, 1964.

Burgess, David S. *Fighting for Social Justice: The Life Story of David Burgess.* Detroit: Wayne State University Press, 2000.

Callahan, Richard, Jr., *Work and Faith in the Kentucky Coal Fields: Subject to Dust.* Bloomington: Indiana University Press, 2009.

Caplan, Marvin. *Farther Along: A Civil Rights Memoir.* Baton Rouge: Louisiana State University Press, 1999.

Carlton, David L., and Peter A. Coclanis, eds. *Confronting Southern Poverty in the Great Depression: The Report on Economic Conditions of the South with Related Documents.* Boston: Bedford/St. Martin's, 1996.

Carlton, David L., and Peter A. Coclanis. *The South, the Nation, and the World: Perspectives on Southern Economic Development.* Charlottesville: University of Virginia Press, 2003.

Carpenter, Joel A. *Revive Us Again: The Reawakening of American Fundamentalism.* New York: Oxford University Press, 1997.

Carrigan, William D. *The Making of a Lynching Culture: Violence and Vigilantism in Central Texas, 1836–1916.* Urbana: University of Illinois Press, 2004.

Chamberlain, Charles D. *Victory at Home: Manpower and Race in the American South during World War II.* Athens: University of Georgia Press, 2003.

Chappell, David L. *Inside Agitators: White Southerners in the Civil Rights Movement.* Baltimore, Md.: Johns Hopkins University Press, 1994.

Cherny, Robert, William Issel, and Kieran Walsh Taylor, eds. *American Labor and the Cold War: Grassroots Politics and Postwar Political Culture.* New Brunswick, N.J.: Rutgers University Press, 2004.

Churches and Church Membership in the United States: An Enumeration and Analysis by Counties, States and Regions. New York: National Council of the Churches of Christ in the U.S.A., 1951.

Clark, Walter Huston. *The Oxford Group: Its History and Significance.* New York: Bookman, 1951.

Cobb, James C. *The Selling of the South: The Southern Crusade for Industrial Development, 1936–1980.* Baton Rouge: Louisiana State University Press, 1982.

Coles, Robert. *Children of the Crisis, Volume II: Migrants, Sharecroppers, Mountaineers.* Boston: Little, Brown, 1971.

Conway, Mimi. *Rise Gonna Rise: A Portrait of Southern Textile Workers*. Garden City, N.Y.: Anchor, 1979.

Cotham, Perry C. *Toil, Turmoil, and Triumph: A Portrait of the Tennessee Labor Movement*. Franklin, Tenn.: Hillsboro, 1995.

Cowie, Jefferson. *Capital Moves: RCA's Seventy-Year Quest for Cheap Labor*. New York: New Press, 2001.

Craig, Robert H. *Religion and Radical Politics: An Alternative Christian Tradition in the United States*. Philadelphia: Temple University Press, 1995.

Creech, Joe. *Righteous Indignation: Religion and the Populist Revolution*. Urbana: University of Illinois Press, 2006.

Crespino, Joseph. *Strom Thurmond's America*. New York: Hill and Wang, 2012.

Crews, Mickey. *The Church of God: A Social History*. Knoxville: University of Tennessee Press, 1990.

Dailey, Jane, Glenda Elizabeth Gilmore, and Bryant Simon, eds. *Jumpin' Jim Crow: Southern Politics from Civil War to Civil Rights*. Princeton: Princeton University Press, 2000.

Daniel, Clete. *Culture of Misfortune: An Interpretive History of Textile Unionism in the United States*. Ithaca, N.Y.: ILR, 2001.

Daniel, Pete. *Breaking the Land: The Transformation of Cotton, Tobacco, and Rice Cultures since 1880*. Urbana: University of Illinois Press, 1985.

———. *Lost Revolutions: The South in the 1950s*. Chapel Hill: University of North Carolina Press, 2000.

Dochuk, Darren. *From Bible Belt to Sunbelt: Plain-Folk Religion, Grassroots Politics, and the Rise of Evangelical Conservatism*. New York: Norton, 2011.

Dodge, D. Witherspoon. *Southern Rebel in Reverse: The Autobiography of an Idol-Shaker*. New York: American Press, 1961.

Draper, Alan. *Conflict of Interests: Organized Labor and the Civil Rights Movement in the South, 1954–1968*. Ithaca, N.Y.: ILR, 1994.

Dunbar, Anthony P. *Against the Grain: Southern Radicals and Prophets, 1929–1959*. Charlottesville: University Press of Virginia, 1981.

Dupont, Carolyn Renee. *Mississippi Praying: Southern White Evangelicals and the Civil Rights Movement, 1945–1975*. New York: New York University Press, 2013.

Durr, Virginia Foster. *Freedom Writer: Letters from the Civil Rights Years*. Edited by Patricia Sullivan. Athens: University of Georgia Press, 2006.

Earle, John R., Dean D. Knudsen, and Donald W. Shriver Jr. *Spindles and Spires: A Re-Study of Religion and Social Change in Gastonia*. Atlanta: John Knox, 1976.

Egerton, John. *Speak Now against the Day: The Generation before the Civil Rights Movement in the South*. Chapel Hill: University of North Carolina Press, 1994.

Eighmy, John Lee. *Churches in Cultural Captivity: A History of the Social Attitudes of Southern Baptists*. Knoxville: University of Tennessee Press, 1972.

English, Beth. *A Common Thread: Labor, Politics, and Capital Mobility in the Textile Industry*. Athens: University of Georgia Press, 2006.

Eskew, Glenn T., ed. *Labor in the Modern South*. Athens: University of Georgia Press, 2001.

Fannin, Mark. *Labor's Promised Land: Radical Visions of Gender, Race, and Religion in the South*. Knoxville: University of Tennessee Press, 2003.

Feldman, Glenn. *Before Brown: Civil Rights and White Backlash in the Modern South*. Tuscaloosa: University of Alabama Press, 2004.

———, ed. *Politics and Religion in the White South*. Lexington: University Press of Kentucky, 2005.

Fink, Gary M., and Merle E. Reed. *Race, Class, and Community in Southern Labor History.* Tuscaloosa: University of Alabama Press, 1994.

Flamming, Douglas. *Creating the Modern South: Millhands and Managers in Dalton, Georgia, 1884–1984.* Chapel Hill: University of North Carolina Press, 1992.

Flynt, Wayne. *Alabama Baptists: Southern Baptists in the Heart of Dixie.* Tuscaloosa: University of Alabama Press, 1998.

——. *Dixie's Forgotten People: The South's Poor Whites.* New edition. Bloomington: Indiana University Press, 2004.

——. *Poor but Proud: Alabama's Poor Whites.* Tuscaloosa: University of Alabama Press, 1989.

Fones-Wolf, Elizabeth A. *Selling Free Enterprise: The Business Assault on Labor and Liberalism, 1945–1960.* Urbana: University of Illinois Press, 1994.

——. *Waves of Opposition: Labor and the Struggle for Democratic Radio.* Urbana: University of Illinois Press, 2006.

Frederickson, Kari. *Cold War Dixie: Militarization and Modernization in the American South.* Athens: University of Georgia Press, 2013.

——. *The Dixiecrat Revolt and the End of the Solid South, 1932–1968.* Chapel Hill: University of North Carolina Press, 2001.

Frederickson, Mary E. *Looking South: Race, Gender, and the Transformation of Labor from Reconstruction to Globalization.* Gainesville: University Press of Florida, 2011.

Fuller, Robert. *Naming the Antichrist: The History of an American Obsession.* New York: Oxford University Press, 1995.

Gellman, Erik, and Jarod Roll, *Gospel of the Working Class: Labor's Southern Prophets in New Deal America.* Urbana: University of Illinois Press, 2011.

Gilmore, Glenda Elizabeth. *Defying Dixie: The Radical Roots of Civil Rights, 1919–1950.* New York: Norton, 2008.

Glass, William R. *Strangers in Zion: Fundamentalists in the South, 1900–1950.* Macon, Ga.: Mercer University Press, 2001.

Goldfield, Michael. *The Color of Politics: Race and the Mainsprings of American Politics.* New York: New Press, 1997.

Grammich, Clifford A., Jr. *Local Baptists, Local Politics: Churches and Communities in the Middle and Uplands South.* Knoxville: University of Tennessee Press, 1999.

Grantham, Dewey W. *The South in Modern America: A Region at Odds.* New York: Harper Collins, 1994.

Gregory, James N. *The Southern Diaspora: How the Great Migrations of Black and White Southerners Transformed America.* Chapel Hill: University of North Carolina Press, 2007.

Grem, Darren E. *Corporate Revivals: A Business History of Born-Again America.* New York: Oxford University Press, forthcoming.

Griffith, Barbara S. *The Crisis of American Labor: Operation Dixie and the Defeat of the CIO.* Philadelphia: Temple University Press, 1988.

Grogan, William. *John Riffe of the Steelworkers: American Labor Statesman.* New York: Coward, McCann, 1959.

Gunn, T. Jeremy. *Spiritual Weapons: The Cold War and the Forging of an American National Religion.* Westport, Conn.: Praeger, 2009.

Hall, David D. ed. *Lived Religion in America: Toward a History Practice.* Princeton, N.J.: Princeton University Press, 1997.

Hall, Jacquelyn Dowd. *Revolt against Chivalry: Jesse Daniel Ames and the Women's Campaign against Lynching*. New York: Columbia University Press, 1979.

Hall, Jacquelyn Dowd, et al. *Like a Family: The Making of a Southern Cotton Mill World*. Chapel Hill: University of North Carolina Press, 1987.

Hangen, Tona J. *Redeeming the Dial: Radio, Religion, and Popular Culture in America*. Chapel Hill: University of North Carolina Press, 2002.

Hankins, Barry. *American Evangelicals: A Contemporary History of a Mainstream Religious Movement*. Lanham, Md.: Rowman and Littlefield, 2008.

———. *God's Rascal: J. Frank Norris and the Beginnings of Southern Fundamentalism*. Lexington: University Press of Kentucky, 1996.

Harrell, David Edwin, Jr., ed., *Varieties of Southern Evangelicalism*. Macon, Ga.: Mercer University Press, 1981.

Harvey, Paul. *Freedom's Coming: Religious Culture and the Shaping of the South from the Civil War through the Civil Rights Era*. Chapel Hill: University of North Carolina Press, 2005.

———. *Through the Storm, Through the Night: A History of African American Christianity*. Lanham, Md.: Rowman and Littlefield, 2011.

Haverty-Stacke, Donna T., and Daniel J. Walkowitz, eds. *Rethinking U.S. Labor History: Essays on the Working-Class Experience, 1756–2009*. New York: Continuum, 2010.

Heaton, George S. *Address of Dr. George D. Heaton Before the Thirty-Eighth Annual Meeting of the North Carolina Cotton Manufacturers Association, Inc.* North Carolina Cotton Manufacturers Association, 1944.

Heyrman, Christine Leigh. *Southern Cross: The Origins of the Bible Belt*. Chapel Hill: University of North Carolina Press, 1992.

Hill, Samuel S., Jr., ed. *Religion and the Solid South*. Nashville, Tenn.: Abingdon, 1972.

Hill, Samuel S., and Charles H. Lippy, eds. *Encyclopedia of Religion in the South*. Macon, Ga.: Mercer University Press, 2005.

Honey, Michael K. *Southern Labor and Black Civil Rights: Organizing Memphis Workers*. Urbana: University of Illinois Press, 1993.

Hooker, Elizabeth R. *Religion in the Highlands: Native Churches and Missionary Enterprises in the Southern Appalachian Area*. New York: Home Missions Council, 1933.

Hulsether, Mark. *Building a Protestant Left: Christianity and Crisis Magazine, 1941–1993*. Knoxville: University of Tennessee Press, 1999.

Huntley, Horace, and David Montgomery. *Black Workers' Struggle for Equality in Birmingham*. Urbana: University of Illinois Press, 2004.

Hurt, R. Douglas, ed., *The Rural South since World War II*. Baton Rouge: Louisiana State University Press, 1998.

Irons, Janet. *Testing the New Deal: The General Textile Strike of 1934 in the American South*. Urbana: University of Illinois Press, 2000.

Jones, Loyal. *Faith and Meaning in the Southern Uplands*. Urbana: University of Illinois Press, 1999.

Jones, William P. *The Tribe of Black Ulysses: African American Lumber Workers in the Jim Crow South*. Urbana: University of Illinois Press, 2005.

Keith, Jeannette. *Country People in the New South: Tennessee's Upper Cumberland*. Chapel Hill: University of North Carolina Press, 1995.

Kelley, Robin G. *Hammer and Hoe: Alabama Communists during the Great Depression*. Chapel Hill: University of North Carolina Press, 1990.

Kennedy, Stetson. *Southern Exposure*. New York: Doubleday, 1946.

Kersten, Andrew E. *Labor's Home Front: The American Federation of Labor during World War II*. New York: New York University Press, 2006.

Key, V. O. *Southern Politics*. New York: Knopf, 1950.

King, William P., ed. *Social Progress and Christian Ideals*. Nashville: Cokesbury, 1931.

Kirby, Jack Temple. *Rural Worlds Lost: The American South, 1920–1960*. Baton Rouge: Louisiana State University Press, 1987.

K'meyer, Tracy Elaine. *Interracialism and Christian Community in the Postwar South: The Story of Koinonia Farm*. Charlottesville: University of Virginia Press, 1997.

Korstad, Robert Rodgers, *Civil Rights Unionism: Tobacco Workers and the Struggle for Democracy in the Mid-Twentieth Century South*. Chapel Hill: University of North Carolina Press, 2003.

Kruse, Kevin. *White Flight: Atlanta and the Making of Modern Conservatism*. Princeton, N.J.: Princeton University Press, 2007.

La Lone, Mary B. *Appalachian Coal Mining Memories: Life in the Coal Fields of Virginia's New River Valley*. Blacksburg, Va.: Pocahontas, 1997.

Lassiter, Matthew D. *The Silent Majority: Suburban Politics in the Sunbelt South*. Princeton, N.J.: Princeton University Press, 2006.

Lassiter, Matthew D., and Joseph Crespino, eds. *The Myth of Southern Exceptionalism*. New York: Oxford University Press, 2010.

Leonard, Bill, ed. *Christianity in Appalachia: Profiles in Religious Pluralism*. Knoxville: University of Tennessee Press, 1999.

Lichtenstein, Nelson, and Elizabeth Shermer, eds. *The Right and Labor in America: Politics, Ideology, and Imagination*. Philadelphia: University of Pennsylvania Press, 2012.

Lippy, Charles H. *Being Religious, American Style: A History of Popular Religiosity in the United States*. Westport, Conn.: Praeger, 1994.

Lorence, James J. *A Hard Journey: The Life of Don West*. Urbana: University of Illinois Press, 2007.

Lorimer, Albert W. *God Runs My Business: The Story of R. G. LeTourneau*. New York: Revell, 1941.

Luff, Jennifer. *Commonsense Anticommunism: Labor and Civil Liberties between the World Wars*. Chapel Hill: University of North Carolina Press, 2012.

Malone, Bill C. *Don't Get above Your Raisin': Country Music and the Southern Working Class*. Urbana: University of Illinois Press, 2002.

Marshall, F. Ray. *Labor in the South*. Cambridge, Mass.: Harvard University Press, 1967.

Marsh, Charles. *God's Long Summer: Stories of Faith and Civil Rights*. Princeton, N.J.: Princeton University Press, 1997.

Martin, Robert Francis. *Howard Kester and the Struggle for Social Justice in the South, 1904–1977*. Charlottesville: University Press of Virginia, 1991.

Martin, William. *With God on Our Side: The Rise of the Religious Right in America*. New York: Broadway, 1996.

Mason, Lucy Randolph. *To Win These Rights: A Personal Story of the CIO in the South*. New York: Harper, 1952.

Maxwell, Angie, and Todd G. Shields, eds. *Unlocking V. O. Key, Jr.: "Southern Politics" for the Twenty-first Century*. Fayetteville: University of Arkansas Press, 2011.

McCloud, Sean. *Divine Hierarchies: Class in American Religion and Religious Studies*. Chapel Hill: University of North Carolina Press, 2007.

McMillen, Neil R., ed. *Remaking Dixie: The Impact of World War II on the American South*. Jackson: University Press of Mississippi, 1997.

Miller, Steven P. *Billy Graham and the Rise of the Republican South*. Philadelphia: University of Pennsylvania Press, 2009.

Minchin, Timothy J. *Fighting against the Odds: A History of Southern Labor Since World War II*. Gainesville: University Press of Florida, 2005.

————. *What Do We Need a Union For? The TWUA in the South, 1945–1955*. Chapel Hill: University of North Carolina Press, 1997.

Moreton, Bethany. *To Serve God and Wal-Mart: The Making of Christian Free Enterprise*. Cambridge, Mass.: Harvard University Press, 2010.

Morland, John Kenneth. *Millways of Kent*. Chapel Hill: University of North Carolina Press, 1958.

Nelson, Bruce. *Divided We Stand: American Workers and the Struggle for Black Equality*. Princeton, N.J.: Princeton University Press, 2001.

Nixon, Herman C. *Lower Piedmont Country*. 1946. Freeport, N.Y.: Books for Libraries, 1971.

O'Brien, Gail Williams. *The Color of the Law: Race, Violence, and Justice in the Post–World War II South*. Chapel Hill: University of North Carolina Press, 1999.

Olwell, Russell B. *At Work in the Atomic City: A Labor and Social History of Oak Ridge, Tennessee*. Knoxville: University of Tennessee Press, 2004.

Pascoe, Craig S., Karen Trahan Leathem, and Andy Ambrose. *The American South in the Twentieth Century*. Athens: University of Georgia Press, 2005.

Perman, Michael. *Pursuit of Unity: A Political History of the American South*. Chapel Hill: University of North Carolina Press, 2009.

Phillips-Fein, Kim, and Julian E. Zelizer, eds. *What's Good for Business: Business and American Politics since World War II*. New York: Oxford University Press, 2012.

Pope, Liston, ed. *Labor's Relation to Church and Community: A Series of Addresses*. New York: Institute for Religious and Social Studies, 1947.

————. *Millhands and Preachers: A Study of Gastonia*. New Haven, Conn.: Yale University Press, 1942.

Portelli, Alessandro. *The Death of Luigi Trastulli and Other Stories: Form and Meaning in Oral History*. Albany, N.Y.: State University of New York Press, 1991.

————. *They Say in Harlan County: An Oral History*. New York: Oxford University Press, 2012.

Reed, Merl E. *Seedtime for the Modern Civil Rights Movement: The President's Committee on Fair Employment Practice, 1941–1946*. Baton Rouge: Louisiana State University Press, 1991.

Richards, Lawrence. *Union-Free America: Workers and Antiunion Culture*. Urbana: University of Illinois Press, 2008.

Ring, Natalie J. *The Problem South: Region, Empire, and the New Liberal State, 1880–1930*. Athens: University of Georgia Press, 2012

Roll, Jarod. *Spirit of Rebellion: Labor and Religion in the New Cotton South*. Urbana: University of Illinois Press, 2010.

Rosell, Garth. *The Surprising Work of God: Harold Ockenga, Billy Graham, and the Rebirth of Evangelicalism*. Grand Rapids, Mich.: Baker Academic, 2008.

Rosswurm, Steven, ed. *The CIO's Left-Led Unions*. New Brunswick, N.J.: Rutgers University Press, 1992.

Rosenberg, Ellen M. *The Southern Baptists: A Subculture in Transition*. Knoxville: University of Tennessee Press, 1989.

Salmond, John A. *Miss Lucy of the CIO: The Life and Times of Lucy Randolph Mason, 1882–1959*. Athens: University of Georgia Press, 1988.

Salvatore, Nick, ed. *Faith and the Historian: Catholic Perspectives.* Urbana: University of Illinois Press, 2007.

Savage, Barbara Dianne. *Your Spirits Walk Beside Us: The Politics of Black Religion.* Cambridge, Mass.: Harvard University Press, 2008.

Schatz, Ronald W. *The Electrical Workers: A History of Labor at General Electric and Westinghouse, 1923–60.* Urbana: University of Illinois Press, 1983.

Schulman, Bruce J. *From Cotton Belt to Sunbelt: Federal Policy, Economic Development, and the Transformation of the South, 1938–1980.* New York: Oxford University Press, 1991.

Schweiger, Beth Barton, and Donald G. Mathews, eds. *Religion in the American South: Protestants and Others in History and Culture.* Chapel Hill: University of North Carolina Press, 2003.

Scranton, Philip, ed. *The Second Wave: Southern Industrialization from the 1940s to the 1970s.* Athens: University of Georgia Press, 2001.

Sennett, Milton. *Bound for the Promised Land: African American Religion and the Great Migration.* Durham, N.C.: Duke University Press, 1997.

Shackelford, Laurel, and Bill Weinberg, eds. *Our Appalachia: An Oral History.* Lexington: University Press of Kentucky, 1977.

Shafer, Byron E., and Richard Johnston. *The End of Southern Exceptionalism: Class, Race, and Partisan Change in the Postwar South.* Cambridge, Mass.: Harvard University Press, 2006.

Simon, Bryant. *A Fabric of Defeat: The Politics of South Carolina Millhands, 1910–1948.* Chapel Hill: University of North Carolina Press, 1998.

Smith, J. Harold. *Termites in the Temple.* Knoxville, Tenn.: Radio Bible Hour, 1946.

———. *The Time of My Life: The Autobiography of J. Harold Smith.* Orlando, Fla.: Daniels, 1981.

Sokol, Jason. *There Goes My Everything: White Southerners in the Age of Civil Rights, 1945–1975.* New York: Knopf, 2006.

Steed, Robert P., and Lawrence W. Morland, eds. *The 2000 Election in the South: Partisanship and Southern Party Systems in the 21st Century.* Westport, Conn.: Praeger, 2001.

Suggs, George G., Jr. *"My World Is Gone": Memories of Life in a Southern Cotton Mill Town.* Detroit: Wayne State University Press, 2002.

———. *Washing the Disciples' Feet: Vignettes of White Oak Original Free Will Baptist Church of Bladenboro, North Carolina.* Bloomington, Ind.: iUniverse, 2011.

Sullivan, Patricia. *Days of Hope: Race and Democracy in the New Deal Era.* Chapel Hill: University of North Carolina Press, 1996.

Synan, Vinson. *The Holiness-Pentecostal Tradition: Charismatic Movement in the Twentieth Century.* Grand Rapids, Mich.: Eerdmans, 1997.

Taft, Philip. *The A.F. of L. from the Death of Gompers to the Merger.* New York: Harper, 1959.

Terrill, Tom E., and Jerrold Hirsch, eds. *Such As Us: Southern Voices of the Thirties.* Chapel Hill: University of North Carolina Press, 1978.

Thompson, E. P. *The Making of the English Working Class.* New York: Vintage, 1966.

Thompson, Ernest Trice. *The Changing South and the Presbyterian Church in the United States.* Richmond, Va.: Knox, 1950.

Tindall, George B. *The Emergence of the New South, 1913–1945.* Baton Rouge: Louisiana State University Press, 1967.

Tullos, Allen. *Habits of Industry: White Culture and the Transformation of the Carolina Piedmont.* Chapel Hill: University of North Carolina Press, 1989.

U.S. Bureau of the Census, *Religious Bodies: 1936.* Washington, D.C.: GPO, 1941.

Wacker, Grant. *Heaven Below: Early Pentecostals and American Culture.* Cambridge, Mass.: Harvard University Press, 2001.

Waldrep, G. C. *Southern Workers and the Search for Community: Spartanburg County, South Carolina.* Urbana: University of Illinois Press, 2000.

Webb, Clive, ed., *Massive Resistance: Southern Opposition to the Second Reconstruction.* New York: Oxford University Press, 2005.

Wells, David F., and John D. Woodbridge, eds. *The Evangelicals: What They Believe, Who They Are, Where They Are Changing.* Grand Rapids, Mich.: Baker, 1977.

Wilson, Charles Reagan. *Flashes of a Southern Spirit: Meanings of the Spirit in the U.S. South.* Athens: University of Georgia Press, 2011.

Wilson, Charles Reagan, and William Ferris, eds. *The Encyclopedia of Southern Culture.* Chapel Hill: University of North Carolina Press, 1989.

Wilson, Charles Reagan, and Mark Silk, eds. *Religion and Public Life in the South: In the Evangelical Mode.* Walnut Creek, Calif.: AltaMira, 2005.

Woods, Jeff. *Black Struggle, Red Scare: Segregation and Anti-Communism in the South, 1948–1968.* Baton Rouge: Louisiana State University Press, 2004.

Wright, Gavin. *Old South, New South: Revolutions in the Southern Economy since the Civil War.* New York: Basic, 1986.

Wuthnow, Robert. *The Restructuring of American Religion: Society and Faith Since World War II.* Princeton, N.J.: Princeton University Press, 1998.

Wyatt-Brown, Bertram. *The Shaping of Southern Culture: Honor, Grace, and War, 1760s–1890s.* Chapel Hill: University of North Carolina Press, 2000.

Zieger, Robert H. *The CIO, 1935–1955.* Chapel Hill: University of North Carolina Press, 1997.

———. *For Jobs and Freedom: Race and Labor in America since 1865.* Lexington: University Press of Kentucky, 2007.

———, ed. *Organized Labor in the Twentieth-Century South.* Knoxville: University of Tennessee Press, 1991.

———, ed. *Southern Labor in Transition, 1940–1995.* Knoxville: University of Tennessee Press, 1997.

ARTICLES AND CHAPTERS

Barrett, James R. "The Blessed Virgin Made Me a Socialist: An Experiment in Catholic Autobiography and the Historical Understanding of Race and Class." In Salvatore, *Faith and the Historian,* 117–47.

Biles, Roger. "The Urban South in the Great Depression." *Journal of Southern History* 56, no.1 (February 1990): 71–100.

Boisen, Anton T. "What War Does to Religion." *Religion in Life* 14, no. 3 (Summer 1945): 389–400.

Braden, Charles S. "What Can We Learn from the Cults?" *Religion in Life* 14, no. 1 (Winter 1944): 52–64.

Brattain, Michelle. "Making Friends and Enemies: Textile Workers and Political Action in Post–World War II Georgia." *Journal of Southern History* 63, no. 1 (February 1997): 91–138.

———. "'A Town as Small as That': Tallapoosa, Georgia, and Operation Dixie, 1945–1950." *Georgia Historical Quarterly* 81, no. 2 (Summer 1997): 395–425.

Burton, Orville Vernon. "The South as 'Other,' the Southerner as 'Stranger.'" *Journal of Southern History* 79, no. 1 (February 2013): 7–50.

Carpenter, Joel. "Fundamentalist Institutions and the Rise of Evangelical Protestantism, 1929–1942," *Church History* 49, no. 1 (March 1980): 62–75.

Carrier, Ronald E., and William Shriver. "Plant Location Studies: An Appraisal," *Southwestern Social Science* Quarterly 47 (September 1966): 136–40.

Carter, Dan T. "More than Race: Conservatism in the White South since V. O. Key, Jr." In Maxwell and Shields, *Unlocking V. O. Key, Jr.*, 129–55.

Cavalcanti, H. B. "God and Labor in the South: Southern Baptists and the Right to Unionize, 1930–1950." *Journal of Church and State* 40, no. 3 (Summer 1998): 639–60.

Colton, Craig E. "Texas v. the Petrochemical Industry: Contesting Pollution in an Era of Industrial Growth," in Scranton, *Second Wave*, 146–67.

Combes, Richard S. "Aircraft Manufacturing in Georgia: A Case Study of Federal Industrial Development," in Scranton, *Second Wave*, 24–42.

Dailey, Jane. "The Theology of Massive Resistance: Sex, Segregation, and the Sacred after *Brown*." In Webb, *Massive Resistance*, 151–80.

Dochuk, Darren. "Moving Mountains: The Business of Evangelicalism and Extraction in a Liberal Age." In Phillips-Fein and Zelizer, *What's Good for Business*, 72–90.

Douty, H. M. "Development of Trade-Unionism in the South." *Monthly Labor Review* (October 1946): 555–82.

Draper, Alan. "The New Southern Labor History Revisited: The Success of the Mine, Mill, and Smelter Workers Union in Birmingham, 1934–1938." *Journal of Southern History* 62, no. 1, (February 1996): 87–108.

Feldman, Glenn. "Home and Hearth: Women, the Klan, Conservative Religion, and Traditional Family Values." In Feldman, *Politics and Religion*, 57–100.

Flynt, Wayne. "One in the Spirit, Many in the Flesh: Southern Evangelicals," in Harrell, *Varieties*, 23–44.

———. "Religion for the Blues: Evangelicalism, Poor Whites, and the Great Depression." *Journal of Southern History* 71, no. 1 (February 2005): 3–38.

Fones-Wolf, Elizabeth, and Ken Fones-Wolf, "Christianity with Its Sleeves Rolled Up: Business and the Postwar Industrial Chaplain Movement," *Business History Review*, forthcoming.

———. "Conversion at Bethlehem: Religion and Union Building in Steel, 1930–42," *Labor History* 39, no. 4 (1998): 381–95.

———. "No Common Creed: White Working-Class Protestants and the CIO's Operation Dixie." In Haverty-Stacke and Walkowitz, *Rethinking U.S. Labor History*, 111–36.

———. "Religion, Human Relations, and Union Avoidance in the 1950s: The Electrical Industry's Southern Strategy and Its Limits." *Enterprise and Society* 13, no. 1 (March 2012): 154–85.

———. "Sanctifying the Southern Organizing Campaign: Protestant Activists in the CIO's Operation Dixie." *Labor: Studies in Working-Class History of the Americas* 6, no. 1 (Spring 2009): 5–31.

Fones-Wolf, Ken. "Embedding Class among the Troops Who Study Southern Religion." *Journal of Southern Religion* 13 (2011). Available at http://jsr.fsu.edu/issues/vol13/fones-wolf.html (accessed May 9, 2014).

Friedman, Tami J. "Exploiting the North-South Differential: Corporate Power, Southern Politics, and the Decline of Organized Labor after World War II." *Journal of American History* 95, no. 2 (September 2008): 323–48.

Gall, Gilbert J. "Southern Industrial Workers and Anti-Union Sentiment: Arkansas and Florida in 1944." In Zieger, *Organized Labor*, 223–49.

Gellman, Erik S., and Jarod H. Roll. "Owen Whitfield and the Gospel of the Working Class in New Deal America, 1936–1946." *Journal of Southern History* 72, no. 2 (May 2006): 303–48.

Gentry, Jonathan. "'Christ Is Out, Communism Is On': Opposition to the Congress of Industrial Organizations' 'Operation Dixie' in South Carolina, 1946–1951." *Proceedings of the South Carolina Historical Association, 2003* (Columbia, 2003), 15–24.

Goldfield, Michael. "The Failure of Operation Dixie: A Critical Turning Point in American Political Development?" In Fink and Reed, *Race, Class, and Community*, 166–89.

Grantham, Dewey W. "The South and Congressional Politics." In McMillen, ed., *Remaking Dixie*, 21–32.

Green, John C. "Believers for Bush, Godly for Gore: Religion and the 2000 Election in the South." In Steed and Morland, *2000 Election*, 11–22.

Grem, Darren E. "*Christianity Today*, J. Howard Pew, and the Business of Conservative Evangelicalism." *Enterprise and Society* 15, no. 2 (2014): 337–79.

Gutman, Herbert G. "Protestantism and the American Labor Movement: The Christian Spirit in the Gilded Age." *American Historical Review* 72, no. 1 (October 1966): 74–101.

Halpern, Rick. "Interracial Unionism in the Southwest: Fort Worth's Packinghouse Workers, 1937–1954." In Zieger, *Organized Labor*, 158–82.

Handy, Robert T. "The American Religious Depression, 1925–1935." *Church History* 29, no. 1 (March 1960): 3–16.

Harrell, David Edwin, Jr., "Introduction." In Harrell, *Varieties*, 1–6.

———. "The South: Seedbed of Sectarianism." In Harrell, *Varieties*, 45–57.

Hayes, John. "Recovering the Class-Conscious New South." *Journal of Southern Religion* 13. Available at http://jsr.fsu.edu/issues/vol13/hayes.html (accessed May 9, 2014).

Heaton, George S. "Christian Principles in Industrial Relations." *Baptist Record*, November 1944, 6.

———. "The Challenge to Management." In *Industrial Relations: The Road Ahead! A Summary of the Twenty-Eighth Annual Conference on Human Relations in Industry, Blue Ridge, N.C., July 16–19, 1947* (n.p.: Southern Conference on Human Relations in Industry, [1947]), 135.

Hill, Samuel S. "Religion." In Wilson and Ferris, *Encyclopedia of Southern Culture*, 1–20.

Honey, Michael K. "Operation Dixie, the Red Scare, and the Defeat of Southern Labor Organizing." In Cherny, Issel, and Taylor, *American Labor*, 216–44.

Ingalls, Robert P. "Antiradical Violence in Birmingham during the 1930s." *Journal of Southern History* 47, no. 4 (November 1981): 521–44.

Jones, William Powell. "'Simple Truths of Democracy': African Americans and Organized Labor in the Post–World War II South." In Arnesen, *Black Worker*, 250–70.

Klibaner, Irwin. "The Travail of Southern Radicals: The Southern Conference Educational Fund, 1946–1976." *Journal of Southern History* 49, no. 2 (May 1983): 179–202.

Korstad, Karl. "Black and White Together: Organizing in the South with the Food, Tobacco, Agricultural & Allied Workers (FTA-CIO), 1946–1952." In Rosswurm, *CIO's Left-Led Unions*, 69–94.

Korstad, Robert, and Nelson Lichtenstein. "Opportunities Found and Lost: Labor, Radicals, and the Early Civil Rights Movement." *Journal of American History* 75, no. 3 (Fall 1988): 786–811.

Krochmal, Max. "An Unmistakably Working-Class Vision: Birmingham's Foot Soldiers and Their Civil Rights Movement." *Journal of Southern History* 76, no. 4 (November 2010): 923–60.

Kruse, Kevin. "Beyond the Southern Cross: The National Origins of the Religious Right." In Lassiter and Crespino, *Myth*, 286–307.

Lewis, Robert. "World War II Manufacturing and the Postwar Southern Economy." *Journal of Southern History* 73, no. 4 (November 2007): 837–66.

Lippy, Charles H. "Popular Religiosity in Central Appalachia." In Leonard, *Christianity in Appalachia*.

Manis, Andrew M. "'City Mothers': Dorothy Tilly, Georgia Methodist Women, and Black Civil Rights." In Feldman, *Politics and Religion*, 125–56.

Marsden, George. "From Fundamentalism to Evangelicalism: A Historical Analysis." In Wells and Woodbridge, *Evangelicals*.

Martin, Charles H. "Southern Labor Relations in Transition: Gadsden, Alabama, 1930–1943." *Journal of Southern History* 47, no. 4 (November 1981): 545–68.

Martin, Robert F. "A Prophet's Pilgrimage: The Religious Radicalism of Howard Anderson Kester, 1921–1941." *Journal of Southern History* 48, no. 4 (November 1982): 511–30.

Mason, Lucy Randolph. "The CIO and the Negro in the South." *Journal of Negro Education* 14 (1945): 522–31.

Mathews, Donald G. "Lynching Is Part of the Religion of Our People: Faith in the Christian South." In Schweiger and Mathews, *Religion*, 153–94.

McArthur, Harvey. "Liberal Concessions to Fundamentalism." *Religion in Life* 14, no. 4 (Autumn 1945): 535–44.

McMichael, Jack R. "The New Social Climate in the South." *Social Questions Bulletin*, May 1945, 4–5.

Moore, Ida L. "When a Man Believes." In Terrill and Hirsch, *Such As Us*, 170–87.

Moore, Toby. "Dismantling the South's Cotton Mill Village System." In Scranton, *Second Wave*, 114–45.

Naison, Mark. "Black Agrarian Radicalism in the Great Depression: The Threads of a Lost Tradition." *Journal of Ethnic Studies* 1 (Fall 1973): 47–65.

———. "Claude and Joyce Williams: Pilgrims of Justice." *Southern Exposure* 1 (1974): 44–48.

Nelson, Bruce. "Class and Race in the Crescent City: The ILWU, from San Francisco to New Orleans." In Rosswurm, *CIO's Left-Led Unions*, 19–45.

———. "'CIO Meant One Thing for the Whites and Another Thing for Us': Steelworkers and Civil Rights, 1936–1974." In Zieger, *Southern Labor*, 112–45.

Norrell, Robert J. "Labor at the Ballot Box: Alabama Politics from the New Deal to the Dixiecrat Movement." *Journal of Southern History* 67, no. 2 (May 1991): 201–34.

Orsi, Robert A. "Everyday Miracles: The Study of Lived Religion." In Hall, *Lived Religion*, 3–21.

Ownby, Ted. "Struggling to Be Old-Fashioned: Evangelical Religion in the Modern Rural South." In Hurt, *Rural South*, 122–48.

Patton, Randall L. "The CIO and the Search for a 'Silent South.'" *Maryland Historian* 19, no. 2 (Fall/Winter 1988): 1–16.

Pehl, Matthew. "'Apostles of Fascism,' 'Communist Clergy,' and the UAW: Political Ideology and Working-Class Religion in Detroit, 1919–1945." *Journal of American History* 99, no. 2 (September 2012): 440–65.

Pierce, Michael. "Orval Faubus and the Rise of Anti-Labor Populism in Northwestern Arkansas." In Lichtenstein and Shermer, *Right and Labor in America*, 98–113.

Salvatore, Nick. "Herbert Gutman's Narrative of the American Working Class: A Reevaluation." *International Journal of Politics, Culture, and Society* 12, no. 1 (Fall 1988): 43–80.

Simon, Bryant. "The Appeal of Cole Blease of South Carolina: Race, Class, and Sex in the New South." *Journal of Southern History* 62, no. 1 (February 1996): 57–86.

——. "Fearing Eleanor: Racial Anxieties and Wartime Rumors in the American South, 1940–1945." In Eskew, *Labor*, 83–101.

——. "Race Reactions: African American Organizing, Liberalism, and White Working-Class Politics in Postwar South Carolina." In Dailey, Gilmore, and Simon, *Jumpin' Jim Crow*, 239–59.

——. "Rethinking Why There Are So Few Unions in the South." *Georgia HistoricalQuarterly* 81, no. 2 (Summer 1997): 465–84.

Sitkoff, Harvard. "African American Militancy in the World War II South: Another Perspective." In McMillen, *Remaking Dixie*, 70–92.

Sparrow, James T. "A Nation in Motion: Norfolk, the Pentagon, and the Nationalization of the Metropolitan South, 1941–1953." In Lassiter and Crespino, *Myth*, 167–89.

Stein, Judith. "The Ins and Outs of the CIO." *International Labor and Working Class History* 44 (Fall 1993): 59–62.

——. "Southern Workers in National Unions: Birmingham Steelworkers, 1936–1951." In Zieger, *Organized Labor*, 183–222.

Sutton, Matthew Avery. "Was FDR the Antichrist? The Birth of Fundamentalist Antiliberalism in a Global Age." *Journal of American History* 98, no. 4 (March 2012): 1052–74.

Szpak, Michael. "Removing the 'Mark of the Beast': The Church of God (Cleveland, Tennessee) and Organized Labor, 1908–1934." *Labor's Heritage* 6, no. 1 (Summer 1994): 46–61.

Thrift, Bryan Hardin. "Jesse Helms's Politics of Pious Incitement: Race, Conservatism, and Southern Realignment in the 1950s." *Journal of Southern History* 74, no. 4 (November 2008): 887–926.

Tyler, Pamela. "'Blood on Your Hands': White Southerners' Criticism of Eleanor Roosevelt during World War II." In Feldman, *Before Brown*, 96–116.

Weisenburger, Steven. "The Columbians, Inc.: A Chapter of Racial Hatred from the Post–World War II South." *Journal of Southern History* 69, no. 4 (November 2003): 821–60.

Woodruff, Nan Elizabeth. "Mississippi Delta Planters and Debates over Mechanization, Labor, and Civil Rights in the 1940s." *Journal of Southern History* 60, no. 2 (May 1994): 263–84.

Wright, Annette C. "The Aftermath of the General Textile Strike: Managers and the Workplace at Burlington Mills." *Journal of Southern History* 60, no. 1 (February 1994): 81–112.

Zieger, Robert H. "From Primordial Folk to Redundant Workers: Southern Textile Workers and Social Observers, 1920–1990." In Zieger, ed., *Southern Labor in Transition*, 273–94.

——. "Is Southern Labor History Exceptional?" In Zieger, ed., *Southern Labor in Transition*, 1–14.

THESES, DISSERTATIONS, AND UNPUBLISHED PAPERS

Burke, Garwin Edison. "A Consideration of the Ordained Christian Minister Serving Within the Industrial Plant." Master's thesis, Southern Baptist Theological Seminary, 1955.

Bush, Carletta. "Faith, Power, and Conflict: Miner Preachers and the United Mine Workers of America in the Harlan County Mine Wars, 1931–1939." PhD diss.: West Virginia University, 2006.

Gilpin, Toni. "Left by Themselves: A History of the United Farm Equipment and Metal Workers Union, 1938–1955." PhD diss., Yale University, 1992.

Greene, Alison Collis. "The Christian Left, Agricultural Labor Unions, and the Sacralization of Rural Life in the 1930s." Unpublished paper delivered at the American Historical Association annual meeting, Boston, January 7, 2011.

————. "Revival or Revolt? Religious Foretelling at the Dawn of the Great Depression." Paper delivered at the Organization of American Historians annual meeting, Washington, D.C., April 8, 2010.

Grem, Darren. "The Blessings of Business: Corporate America and Conservative Evangelicalism in the Sunbelt Age, 1945–2000." PhD diss., University of Georgia, 2010.

Haberland, Michelle. "Seeking the Lowest Level: The Apparel Industry Heads South, 1937–1980," Unpublished paper delivered at North American Labor History Conference, Detroit, October 21, 2006.

Hammond, Sarah Ruth. "'God's Business Men': Entrepreneurial Evangelicals in Depression and War." PhD diss., Yale University, 2010.

Hayes, John Herbert. "Hard, Hard Religion: Faith and Class in the New South." PhD diss., University of Georgia, 2007.

Roll, Jarod. "Prophetic Front: The New Era School of Social Action and Prophetic Religion and the Fight against Jim Crow in the 1930s." Paper delivered at the Organization of American Historians annual meeting, Washington, D.C., April 8, 2010.

Sloan, Michael. "A Misguided Quest for Legitimacy: The Community Relations Department of the Southern Organizing Committee of the CIO during Operation Dixie, 1946–1953." Master's thesis, Georgia State University, 2006.

Thielo, F. Paul John. "The Industrial Chaplain," BD Thesis, Concordia Seminary, 1956.

Wills, Keith Cameron. "Southern Baptists and Labor, 1927–1956." PhD diss., Southwestern Baptist Theological Seminary, 1958.

INDEX

ELIZABETH FONES-WOLF is a professor of history at West Virginia University and the author of *Waves of Opposition: Labor, Business, and the Struggle for Democratic Radio, 1933–1958*.

KEN FONES-WOLF is the Stuart and Joyce Robbins Chair of history at West Virginia University and the author of *Glass Towns: Industry, Labor, and Political Economy in Central Appalachia, 1890–1930s*.

THE WORKING CLASS IN AMERICAN HISTORY

The University of Illinois Press
is a founding member of the
Association of American University Presses.

———————————————————————

Typeset in 10.5/13 Adobe Minion
Composed by Lisa Connery
at the University of Illinois Press
Manufactured by Sheridan Books, Inc.

University of Illinois Press
1325 South Oak Street
Champaign, IL 61820-6903
www.press.uillinois.edu